IN MEMORIAM
JORGE VILLA S.
VIRI CLARISSIMI
PATRIS MEI
INTELLEGENTIOR BENEVOLENTIOR
QUO NEMO GENEROSIOR

———

IN HONOUR ALSO
OF ALL THOSE CANADIANS
WHO SET SAIL ON 18 AUGUST 1942
FOR US

THE
ILLUSTRATIONS
APPEAR
BETWEEN
PAGES
122
AND
123

# Contents

# Acknowledgements

I gladly acknowledge first my two mentors at Harvard, the late William L. Langer, and Ernest R. May, whose influences should be visible in the following study. Langer was perhaps the most distinguished modern disciple of the Rankean tradition in diplomatic history. What attracted me to him from my first days as a student was his extraordinary ability to pull startling revelations out of the most mundane-appearing documents. At squeezing lemons he was the best I have ever seen, and I hope this study displays some of the resourcefulness he taught so well. Langer was always accessible, and even before I entered Graduate School I counted him as a friend. Professor May, who succeeded him as my adviser, has offered me that same friendship in generous measure. He set very different goals before his students. Whereas Langer asked us to be able to account for every last grain of historical sand that passed between one's fingers, May stressed thinking imaginatively and creatively—about ways of assembling fragments of analysis and about how each piece fitted into a larger conceptual whole. He was even then far ahead of his time in being open to the findings of political scientists. Some readers will see his influence in this book.

My tutors, who prepared me for Langer and May, also deserve acknowledgement: Charles Wood, for encouraging my love of history and for putting my feet on this path; Fritz Ringer and Mack Walker, who developed my tool-box; and finally Ronald Coons, who, with immense dedication, guided me through a successful Senior Honours Thesis—he will recognize similarities between that study and this book.

The late General George A. Lincoln, a distinguished military strategist and scholar as well as a friend, taught me much about grand strategy at the highest level. For insights into the art of diplomacy under difficult times, I had the benefit of the long diplomatic experience of another friend, Ambassador Marcello Mininni.

Professor William Dray, one of Canada's most accomplished philosophers of history, offered me unstinting encouragement. He poured over the political-science Appendix and contributed many helpful insights; though its length had to be drastically reduced, I hope it reflects my attention to his penetrating questions. Professor Dray believes historians should be very conscious of their own assumptions and *modus operandi*, and it is in part as a souvenir of our lively discussions that I have made a frank exposé of the way I came to this subject, and how I handled it, in the methodological Appendix.

Bearing more directly on Dieppe, and on the British War Government, numerous thorny questions were helpfully answered by Lord Lovat, who distinguished himself as a military leader at Dieppe; by Sir William Deakin, who assisted Churchill in his historical writings; and by Sir Ian Jacob, one of the chief staff officers working for Churchill while he was Minister of Defence.

A study of this kind is greatly facilitated by families who are willing to open papers, and by archivists who helpfully meet a deluge of requests and still find time to draw attention to promising piles. Over many years of research, my memory sadly dims a bit and new faces and names replace those whose assistance was indispensable in the first years. I remember their help, though not always their names. Such is the case with the archivist at Christ Church, Oxford—John Wing, if memory serves me right —who helped me greatly with the Portal Papers. In other instances it would be unfair to try to single out names, as in the case of the Public Record Office, London and Kew, where the number of staffers who assisted me over the years exceeds two dozen. They all deserve an accolade for being both helpful and very professional. Staffing and budgetary cuts have unfortunately taken their toll at Kew (as they have in virtually every British governmental archive), and the Public Record Office may no longer stand at the pinnacle of the world's historical archives for efficiency and speed; but the willingness to help and the professionalism of what is offered are still *non pareil*. When I began my work the Cabinet Historical Office in London (whose primary function is to serve the Cabinet and official historians) was able occasionally to help private scholars when recommended by official historians, and I was fortunate to profit from the kind assistance of, first, John Cheattle, and then Colin Smith. I also owe thanks to the Controller of Her Majesty's Stationery Office for permission to quote from Crown copyright material.

Invaluable assistance was received from King's College, London, where Patricia Methven and her staff helped me greatly in identifying key documents, and in the cumbersome process of securing the permission to quote from the Brooke and Ismay Papers, for which I thank the Estates of Lord Alanbrooke and Lord Ismay. Permission to quote from the speeches and writings of Sir Winston Churchill is gratefully acknowledged to Curtis

Brown on behalf of the Estate of Sir Winston Churchill. Copyright the Estate of Sir Winston Churchill. An immense debt is owed to Lord Brabourne and the Mountbatten Estate for permission to quote from Lord Mountbatten's writings, as well as to Richard Hughes-Hallett for permission to quote from his uncle's writings. My sense of obligation is all the greater as Lord Brabourne continued to offer me every assistance even after I wrote him to report that my study was likely to be critical. Richard Hughes-Hallet also divined that I would have few kind words to say about his uncle. In the light of this, their willingness to continue to offer help—trusting that I would try to be fair—is touching, and nothing would have given me more pleasure than to be able, in gratitude, to soften my portraits of Lord Louis Mountbatten and Admiral J. Hughes-Hallett, both of whom achieved great and well-earned distinction in the larger extent of their careers. Those who find my portrayal of Lord Mountbatten too harsh may at least turn to Philip Ziegler's official biography, where a strong defence is skilfully and reasonably presented. (I owe much to Ziegler's able work, and to his willingness to correspond and debate the central issues in a friendly spirit of scholarly exploration, as I do to Ronald Atkin, author of *Dieppe 1942: The Jubilee Disaster* (1980), for like reasons.) Hughes-Hallett unfortunately has no biographer, and his important memoirs remain unpublished. As yet there is nothing, save his own scattered articles and speeches, to set against my sometimes severe criticism—a gap that I hope will be filled in the not-too-distant future. History, like theology, progresses (as Abelard taught) by *sic et non*.

I owe thanks to Mrs M. Chalk, who first guided me through the Mountbatten papers at Broadlands, and to Dr Christian Woolgar, Archivist at the University of Southampton, where the Mountbatten papers are gradually finding their final resting-place. Without Dr Woolgar's ever-so-patient and immensely helpful assistance, and that of his very professional staff, I doubt that I could ever have completed this study. Dr Woolgar also helped me secure the final permission from the Mountbatten Estate to quote documents and reproduce photographs, for which I am most grateful. A similarly vital role was played by Dr Roger Morris, Archivist of the Royal Maritime Museum, Greenwich, who made available the Baillie-Grohman Papers which, though few in number, are vital. Similar thanks are due to the staff of the Imperial War Museum, the custodian of a portion of the Hughes-Hallett Papers, who courteously helped with the selection of photographs and gave permission to use them. A host of other archivists in Britain also deserve thanks, notably those at the Foreign Office Library, London; at the Churchill Centre, Churchill College, Cambridge; at the several service historical offices in Whitehall; at New College and Nuffield College, Oxford; and at the British Museum.

On this side of the Atlantic the staffs of both the Manuscripts and Government Documents Divisions of the National Archives of Canada,

Ottawa, have been extremely helpful. The National Archives arguably provides the best working environment of any archive in the world, and the excellent staff—including Barbara Wilson and George Bolotenko—contribute to this reputation. My special thanks are due to the staff of the Directorate of History, National Defence Headquarters, Ottawa, and particularly to four official historians, for this work is in a sense part of an extended dialogue with them. W.A.B. Douglas and Norman Hillmer provided wise counsel. If my ingrained recalcitrance prevented me from accepting it all, they are certainly not to be blamed. Brereton Greenhous, Canada's leading authority on Dieppe, not only tolerated my poaching on his field but at every turn helped me beyond the demands of mere courtesy. I owe much to his constructive criticism. Stephen Harris, one of Canada's most accomplished military historians, educated me on critical aspects of the Second World War. Similarly stimulating has been the assistance of John Campbell of McMaster University, whose knowledge of, and publications on, Dieppe are of the first order. All these scholars wield very sharp rapiers in argument, and fencing with them was, and is, great fun. In the United States I have profited from the advice and help of Bill Cunliffe and Ed Reese of the National Archives and Records Service, Washington. I appreciated also the help extended by the staffs of the Franklin D. Roosevelt Library, Hyde Park, and of the Dwight D. Eisenhower Library, Abilene, Kansas.

Thanks are also due to colleagues at the University of Ottawa who gave me moral support or showed enormous forbearance as this study consumed so many years of effort, particularly the various Chairmen—Michael Behiels, Cornelius Jaenen, Jacques Monet, Fernand Ouellet, Pierre Savard, and Susan Trofimenkoff—and my Dean, Marcel Hamelin, who found a niche for me and my work. Many of my immediate colleagues also helped, but special thanks must go to Jacques Barbier, whose mind moves with ease and insight from his own field of expertise, Bourbon Spain, to any other subject under the sun. He read a large portion of this study and made countless constructive suggestions. Thanks also go to the Graduate School Grants Committee, and particularly to the Social Sciences and Humanities Research Council of Canada, who generously provided aid for many related projects and will readily see in this study the fruit of their support. The constant encouragement over the years of Yves Mougeot has been much appreciated.

My thinking was influenced by ideas contributed by my seminar students, and my work by graduate students who dug up documents or double-checked files for me—particularly Peter Henshaw, Bill Rawling, and Brian Farrell. One brilliant, questioning student sparked this whole project—Peter Sammon, who, in a course many years ago, asked me questions about Dieppe that I could not immediately answer. His insistence on answers finally pushed me into writing this book. (We worked together on an article about Dieppe, which I hope will one day see the light of day.)

Of a different order was the challenge laid down by Barry Hunt and Donald Schurman, whose excellent article on Dieppe—modestly titled 'Prelude to Dieppe: Thoughts on Combined Operations Policy in the "Raiding Period", 1940-1942'—convinced me that there was a very real historical conundrum behind the raid. Though they did not themselves arrive at a resolution of the problem in that essay, the clear challenge they offered was a great incentive to me.

I am grateful to many people who kept up my spirit and encouraged me to persevere. For Lawrence and Margaret Perin, Colin and Kate Wells, Davison and Barbara White, and my immediate family, generosity, kindness, and friendship are bywords. Without them I might not have reached my goal.

Finally I wish to thank William Toye. No author could be more fortunate than I in having such an extraordinarily conscientious editor who was willing to contribute, over a long period, so much useful advice and attention to detail in guiding the manuscript to publication.

*Ottawa, Ont.*                                                    BRIAN LORING VILLA
*May 1989*

# Introduction

On 19 August 1942 a mainly Canadian force of some six thousand soldiers and marines, supported by nearly 4,000 men at sea and in the air, left England in an attempt to seize within a few hours the German-occupied port of Dieppe just across the Channel. Originally planned in April as Operation *Rutter*, the raid had been cancelled at the beginning of July only to be revived as *Jubilee* a few weeks later. It was described as the largest raid ever attempted in history, and so it was, but the resulting casualties were appalling. The losses suffered by the pilots were moderate, but they were heavy for the sailors, and were devastating for the soldiers and marines — among whom the casualty rate reached nearly 60 per cent. The overall casualty rate averaged more than 40 per cent, the highest in the war for any major offensive involving the three services. Many units were decimated beyond their ability to function as recognizable entities.[1]

This débâcle soured relations between Britain and her partners in the war — most noticeably with Canada, but also with America and the Soviet Union. It led to an ugly vendetta waged for decades by the Canadian-born Lord Beaverbrook against Lord Mountbatten, the Chief of Combined Operations, whose career would ever afterwards be tarnished by this episode. And it also spawned a seemingly endless historical controversy.

Had Dieppe been a success, not one-thousandth of what has been written about it would ever have crossed the minds of the many historians who have tackled the subject. Success does not prompt investigation. Indeed, many students of history will accept the most facile explanations for success — anything from sheer luck to intangibles, such as a nation's inherent genius. Disaster, on the other hand, elicits vigorous, searching questions, and even competent explanations seldom satisfy. The interrogator becomes skeptical about all answers. Job was reckoned blessed for having had the kind of searing experiences that prompted him to ask truly penetrating questions — questions that other men, with more ordinary experiences, could scarcely even conceive. Disasters bring us face to face with the limits of our abilities to offer explanations.

The historian must also realize that even the best answers will not easily lay a tragedy to rest, and that beyond a certain point — where what one cannot accept blurs into what one will not understand — all attempts at explanation are fruitless. The passage of time will do more to instil acceptance than all the efforts of the best historians. The great mystery that once surrounded Abraham Lincoln's death has almost evaporated, not necessarily because we know more, but because we can better accept it. Such is not yet the case, for example, with the Kennedy assassinations. The historian who thinks that research can allay uncertainties about these recent tragedies is sadly mistaken. Any investigator of a historical conundrum should therefore ask, at the start, whether it is really a problem of historical comprehension or one of psychological acceptance. If the former the historian's investigations, to be convincing, ought to make an impact; if the latter, the game may not be worth the candle. In dealing with disbelief that is born of a refusal to accept reality, philosophers or theologians are undoubtedly more helpful than historians.

Dieppe represents a problem of acceptance, particularly for Canadians. That some 5,000 soldiers and engineers from a nation that had willingly joined the fight against Hitler should wait over two-and-a-half years for combat and then be killed, maimed, or captured within a single morning is undeniably one of the great tragedies of the Second World War. The defeat was bitter, humiliating, and sad — fate had been too cruel. Many therefore concluded that more than bungling played a part, that some villain or villains caused it, or even set up the tragedy. Those who cannot accept an event find it all too easy to indulge in wild speculations and even to dally with manifest distortions behind the façade of history, producing what can only be called pseudo-history. The sophisticated historian may tend to dismiss such literature out of hand. But myths — for example, that the Germans had been tipped off, perhaps even by British Intelligence, to prove that a Second Front was impossible — die hard. After thirty-five years of continual repetition and seemingly authoritative refutation, this particular myth refuses to die. Even Eisenhower's grandson, in a recent book marked by thorough research and general soundness, is inclined to accept it. When a myth has such staying power, historians must recognize that they have to some degree failed and must reassess their approach to a historical conundrum. Certainly the professional historian is, and probably must be, suspicious of the questions, agenda, and suggestions put forward by those who refuse to accept a tragedy. But perhaps they should also be highly resourceful, even experimental, when they examine calamities that have previously defied all attempts at conventional explanation.[2]

In the case of Dieppe, the more immediate questions of course are: What kind of event was it? Is there some genuine mystery? Had it been successful, would it still puzzle us?

As the reader will learn in the pages that follow, there *is* a mystery about the decision to execute the raid on Dieppe, for it can easily be shown that the British Government, and the Chiefs of Staff in particular, had been convinced for more than a year that this sort of operation made little sense: it was extremely hazardous and was unlikely, even if it were to succeed, to be worth the cost. As Lord Lovat, who led the one completely successful commando group at Dieppe, later commented: '. . . only a foolhardy commander launches a frontal attack with untried troops, unsupported, in daylight against veterans, . . . dug in and prepared behind concrete, wired and mined approaches — an enemy with every psychological advantage . . . It was a bad plan and it had no chance of success.' This critique is not based solely on hindsight. Time and time again the notion of large raids had been rejected for sound reasons that were fully vindicated by the results of Dieppe. Ignoring all warnings, the Allies handed Germany a propaganda victory of major proportions. The *Deutsche Allgemeine Zeitung* could say, just a few days after the raid, with little fear of contradiction, that as executed 'the venture mocked all rules of military logic and strategy'. Lord Haw Haw's propaganda broadcasts from Berlin emphasized that the slaughter was the result of Winston Churchill's desire to appease the Soviet Union. Within days the Germans had produced a documentary film, showing the fresh carnage on the beach, that was widely distributed, in order to convince German soldiers that there was nothing to fear from the West.[3]

The evidence that British planners knew perfectly well that the operation had virtually no hope of success has been almost hidden from view in later efforts to justify the raid *ex post facto* as having produced a rich harvest of important lessons. From the first these efforts betrayed a certain strain. A 1943 official book describing Combined Operations argued that many lessons of great value were learned from Dieppe, though it avoided specifying them on the grounds that 'the details of these experiences must not be revealed.[4]

Though some lessons *were* learned, we can now see that none were unknown beforehand, or could not have been learned far more easily and at far less cost by other means. Major General Sir Leslie Hollis, who as principal assistant-secretary to the British Chiefs of Staff committee observed the planning and execution of military strategy and policy more closely than almost anyone else in the war, described the lessons as being that 'a frontal attack on a strongly defended position was of little use' and that 'Army units destined for amphibious operations must be trained.' Few readers of his book could be convinced that these well-known gems of military wisdom counterbalanced his judgement that tactically the operation was an 'almost complete failure', and that 'many lives were sacrificed for no tangible result.' The boast of *Jubilee*'s Naval Force Commander, Captain John Hughes-Hallett, that '. . . we proved once and for all that a frontal assault on a strongly defended port was not on' could scarcely impress anyone save complete neophytes in the art of war. T. Murray Hunter, the author of one of the most recent reviews of Dieppe, can come up with nothing more significant by way of lessons than the statement that the raid 'certainly contributed a heightened sense of urgency to technical and technological developments' and a 'renewed respect for the enemy's capability'. Others have been less charitable. Some reputable historians have suggested that Combined Operations' efforts in this period reflected a psychopath at work.[5]

General E.L.M. Burns, who was called in to take over the 2nd Canadian Division from the ground commander at Dieppe, General J.H. Roberts, spoke for many when he expressed dissatisfaction in 1970 with the existing literature: 'The final judgement on the Dieppe operation has yet to be delivered. More explicit statements of the decisions of the responsible authorities . . . will have to be published before final judgement can be made — if it ever will.[6]

Some eight years and as many books later, two of Canada's leading military historians, in a historiographical review of the literature published in 1978, concluded that 'In fact, no really adequate analysis of Dieppe has appeared from any pen.' In 1982, four years after that judgement, John Keegan, author of *Six Armies in Normandy*, found the situation little improved, noting that Dieppe, 'in retrospect, looks so recklessly hare-brained an enterprise that it is difficult to reconstruct the official state of mind which gave it birth and drove it forward'; Nigel Hamilton, Field Marshal Montgomery's biographer, regretfully added his voice to the chorus, complaining that 'The Story of the Dieppe raid . . . is still surrounded by prejudice, myth and inadequate documentation'; and the leading Canadian authority, C.P. Stacey, complained that a 'fair amount of sensational nonsense' was being written about Dieppe. Hunter concluded that satisfactory answers would never be found. Any attempt at a full assessment would 'require a very large volume' and would only 'raise more questions than it answered.'[7]

The first mystery of Dieppe, about which the reader will learn more later, concerns the inability of the participants to determine with any clarity or logic why they had undertaken the operation. This has been compounded by the pre-raid documents' lack of precision in identifying the objectives of the operation, or its utility. In addition, the participants never succeeded in recalling when or how the decision was taken. Scores of authors have tried to uncover the decisive evidence that would explain such central questions.

Broadly speaking, there are only two ways of responding to these problems of historical understanding. One is to say that the participants knew perfectly well why they undertook the Dieppe raid but simply could not later admit the reason, for to do so would indicate their responsibility and their error. Better to feign ignorance than to admit responsibility. (Success, according to the old adage, has a thousand fathers, but defeat is an orphan.) If this was the case — that the reason was buried in a great cover-up — the historian must ignore protestations of ignorance, denials, and perhaps even the destruction of evidence, and ferret out the original motives. This involves searching exhaustively through contemporary records in order to produce a convincing reconstruction of the environment that may reveal the motives, or at least the main objectives, of the principal players. Establishing motive and opportunity, the historian may then, like a prosecuting attorney, build a circumstantial explanation of sufficient solidity to warrant acceptance by the profession.

The implied analogy with criminal cases is misleading, however, because the life of a government is composed not of one set of circumstances but of a great number of sometimes distinct, sometimes interrelated circumstances affecting different branches of government, and they are difficult to reconstruct. Myriads of threads are interwoven. The responsible historian must weigh all the potentially relevant circumstances and compare them, one against the other, before favouring the legitimacy of any one, or any combination. Fairness requires that the main lines of alternative explanations also be presented to the reader. This makes a straightforward chronological historical narrative impossible. Inherent in any analytical presentation is an inescapable amount of overlap, since a fact that is found to have particular significance in one context must also be examined for different significance in another.

A second broad approach to the mystery of Dieppe is to try to explain it in terms not of some hidden motive but rather of drift. If indeed there was no sharply defined purpose, either avowed or hidden, then one is probably examining a vague process often described as institutional momentum. In this conception a patently flawed idea that has been around for some time gradually acquires support simply because institutions and policy-makers adapt to it, and begin to calculate how they can use it to advantage — even though they do not believe in it totally. As each distinct bureaucratic unit sees the proposal differently, its utility acquires a particular definition that may not mesh at all well either with the original goals or with those of other agencies. In a polycentric bureaucracy, alliances are not always formed on the basis of logic. Indeed, bureaucratic alliances are forged *because* the life of a government is made of multiple conflicting interests; in this environment policy becomes the prisoner of momentum. (See Appendix I.)

In order to understand how a questionable policy develops momentum, it is vital to examine the complex of circumstantial situations within a government and to show how different bureaucratic units adapted themselves to the original proposal. A certain amount of repetition cannot be avoided in seeking to discover how a convergence of interests may have led to the acceptance of a half-baked policy by normally competing agencies. In the case of Dieppe, such a careful examination of the decision-making environment amounts to nothing less than a history of the first three years of the war.

This study, the result of more than eight years' research, includes both the above approaches. It originally totalled over 1,700 typescript pages and was clearly too long to impose on any reader or publisher. (A detailed examination of the Soviet dimension is in preparation.) The present volume focuses on the decision-making process, and may thus be regarded as a work of political science. But as it also seeks to assign responsibility and explain why the evidence surrounding the background to the Dieppe raid has become so hopelessly muddled, it is at the same time a historical study. I hope that it will reveal the truth that has lain hidden in the murky waters of doctored evidence.

This volume begins with a description of the event itself, the origin of the historical controversy, the political setting, and the strategic debate. Chapters 5 to 7 describe the situation in which the three British Chiefs of Staff found themselves in 1942, and outline the evolution of their service interests over the three preceding years. Chapters 8 and 9 describe Mountbatten's ascent into the high councils of war and his involvement in Dieppe. Chapter 10 explains the Canadian involvement and Chapter 11 gives historical conclusions. Appendix I uses concepts drawn from political science to shed further light on the Dieppe decision and suggests how the analysis of that event can contribute to the refinement of decision-making theory — a useful, though often neglected, tool for further analysis of historical events. The purpose in treating the evidence in this manner is to try to answer that most vexing question: Why do governments often do what they know they should not do? Some serious flaws in an apparently functional decision-making structure are revealed—exposing the real lesson to be gleaned from a wartime offensive that resulted in four thousand casualties.

# 1

# The Bare Facts of a Historical Tragedy

Just before dawn on 19 August 1942 a swarm of landing-craft approached the coast around the sleepy port town of Dieppe on the English Channel. The largest raid in history was on. A flotilla of 250 small naval craft were engaged, and overhead the largest single air-battle of the war was about to get underway. Over 50 squadrons, some 800 fighters — Spitfires, Hawker Typhoons and Hurricanes (more than had been engaged in the Battle of Britain) — would see action that day, many flying repeat missions, together with approximately 100 light and medium bombers — Blenheims and Bostons. Six thousand men would soon be trying to storm ashore from the landing-craft.

The coastline is generally straight, but at Dieppe it forms a small horse-shoe with high cliffs on either side. At the centre lies the town, through which the river Arques makes its way to the sea, forming in succession narrow inner and outer harbours. It was from this small town, huddled about the inner harbour, that in peacetime the ferry unloaded British tourists — most of them heading for Paris. Because the harbour and river were shunted to the east, it had been possible to develop the rest of the gap between the cliffs most attractively with a broad promenade. A strip of pebbled beach stretched almost from cliff to cliff between the esplanade and the sea. Fronting on this promenade at the western end was a large casino. In peacetime this ocean front was the scene of all the small pleasures of a minor resort. Now the two-storey casino was heavily fortified, the beach was covered by machine-gun points along the housefronts, and, at the ends, by pill-boxes and a tank that had been set in concrete. These strong-points, together with guns sited in caves on both headlands, permit-ted enfilade (raking fire) right across the beach — a most effective form of fire, since any advancing force must at some point intersect it. A defending force would not even have to calculate range. Meanwhile, at a distance of two to three miles inland, Dieppe was circled by a perimeter of field batteries, just beyond a cordon of barbed wire, that gave protection from airborne attack in the rear, while heavy coastal batteries set back on the cliffs, well off to each flank, defended against attack from the sea. Just inland was a small air-field near Arques-la-Bataille.

Dieppe's defences constituted a very considerable German investment. Though the town itself was of slight importance, the Germans saw in Dieppe an obvious point for a British attack: it was within the range of RAF support and it was familiar as the terminal of the Dieppe-Newhaven ferry. Furthermore, Hitler had reason to suspect action at the coastal towns. In February 1942, after German divisions had overrun much of European Russia, Stalin stunned the West by signalling, in an astonishingly public way, his willingness to negotiate with Germany and his unhappiness with his Western allies. He declared publicly that Hitlers may come and go but Germany as a great nation would always remain, and that the Soviet Union was fighting simply in self-defence. The Foreign Office analysis noted with alarm:

> The whole speech, in fact, ignores the [Anglo-Soviet] Alliance or the whole war other than the 'liberation of Soviet Territory'. It would be hard to devise anything more deliberately unfriendly. And at the same time it holds out an unmistakeable hand to the Germans to the extent of hinting that the ousting of Hitler, though it would be 'welcome', is not in Stalin's view an absolutely essential 'result' of the war for the 'liberation of our Soviet land'.[1]

There were three possible explanations, depending on how desperate the Soviet leader was and how convuluted were his calculations. Stalin might be genuinely seeking to arrange an immediate truce of sorts; or, by suggesting the possibility of a separate peace, he might be trying to force his Western allies to help him resist Germany; he might believe that galvanizing the West would force Germany to grant better terms. Indeed, he might be trying to keep all three irons in the fire. In any case, the Western powers were under intense pressure to reassure Stalin with some measure of military assistance.

For his part, Hitler drew a prescient conclusion from Stalin's speech. In a directive of 23 March he stated that the Western powers would be impelled by 'obligations to allies, and political considerations' to employ what capability they had to mount raids, possibly even committing airborne forces. Accordingly, he ordered that German troops along coastal regions susceptible to British attack were to be kept permanently in a high state of readiness.[2]

Hitler's erratic intuition was working at top form. Planners in Britain were indeed coming under the sort of pressures he predicted. At Combined Operations Headquarters (COHQ) — headed since October 1941 by the young Lord Louis Mountbatten, who was just beginning his meteoric rise in the British military establishment — staff planners were thinking out the implications of renewed pressures from the War Cabinet to help the Soviet Union. Anticipating that they would lead to further demands for raids, one of the principal Naval planners, Captain John Hughes-Hallett, was drawing up a list of possible targets for the raiding season that would begin late in May.[3]

Hughes-Hallett recognized that a lot of small raids would be necessary, but that they would scarcely satisfy the Soviet Union or Cabinet. Something big and impressive would therefore be needed. Thus the plan for a huge raid on Dieppe came into being. As Field Marshal Montgomery's biographer, Nigel Hamilton, noted in 1981: 'Every military consideration argued against this expensive form of exercise, and it is noticeable that the Germans declined utterly to indulge in such operations on the British coast.' But Hitler did not have to worry about public opinion and the press. Hughes-Hallett, knowing that from its inception the raiding program had been envisaged as a dimension of psychological warfare, also knew that Britain would be forced into doing something drastic. And indeed, before he and the staff could work up the full plans, pressures for action in Cabinet built up so quickly that Mountbatten was forced to lay the project prematurely before the approving authority, the Chiefs of Staff Committee. This body was composed of Mountbatten himself, initially sitting in only for commando operations, and each of the highest-ranking officers of the three services: the First Sea Lord, Admiral Sir Dudley Pound, for the Navy; General Sir Alan Brooke, who had just taken over the chair from Pound, for the Army; and Chief Air Marshal Sir Charles Portal, for the Air Force. They gave hasty, tentative approval to Mountbatten's project, and assigned it the code-name *Rutter* (it would later be changed to *Jubilee*), on the understanding that the plan would be refined by Combined Operations, as the co-ordinating and supplying agency, and by the three Force Commanders, who would be charged with carrying it out.[4]

The commanders nominated were, initially: the Canadian Major-General J.H. Roberts for the Army, who would command all Allied ground forces; Air Vice-Marshal Trafford Leigh-Mallory for the Air Force; and Rear-Admiral H.T. Baillie-Grohman (also later replaced by Captain John Hughes-Hallett) for the Navy. One of the most curious aspects of the raid was the employment of the 2nd Canadian Division to form the bulk of the attacking force, from which followed necessarily the appointment of its commander, Roberts, as the Army force leader for the Dieppe raid. Roberts was new to divisional command; even as a regimental commander sent to France after Dunkirk, he had not seen combat. Nor had the men under him. How, Montgomery's biographer, has asked, 'could anyone believe that a Combined Operation, using untried soldiers, could successfully smash its way into the heart of Dieppe and beyond — to the airfield of Arques — in a matter of hours and then be successfully re-embarked on the following tide?' Those chosen to lead the operation presumably thought they would find a way to do the impossible.[5]

In the succeeding months the plan was fleshed out by an exceptionally cumbersome process. The fundamental principle of the British military forces was that the commanding officer, charged with executing a plan, must give final approval. He could, in theory, refuse to accept it when first proposed, or subsequently could refuse to commit his troops to the engagement if he thought the plan was fundamentally unsound, or if he felt the necessary conditions on which it was predicated no longer existed —a reason that led to the cancellation of several raids. Given this right of negative veto, it was vital that force commanders be engaged from the beginning in the planning process, but since there were three commanders for *Rutter*, planning was a very difficult process. Added to this was the great imponderable of having assigned the lion's share of ground operations to Canadians. The overall Canadian Commander, General A.G.L. McNaughton, delegated responsibility to the Commander of the Canadian Corps, Lieutenant-General H.D.G. Crerar, who in turn delegated it to General Roberts, whose 2nd Canadian Division would be committed. This was consonant with the above-cited British military doctrine. But it was felt that the Canadians ought to be given a little more help than usual, perhaps because few had much confidence in either General Roberts (who had no experience of divisional combat command or amphibious operations) or his principal adviser for planning, Lieutenant-Colonel Churchill Mann. Therefore a significant modification was made in the procedures. Since Canadian troops were under Home Forces Command, their commanding officer, General Sir Bernard Paget, was asked to keep a watchful eye over the whole plan as it developed. He delegated this unusual advisory role to General Montgomery, who was then commanding the southeast sector.[6]

Principal responsibility for advising General Roberts and Colonel Mann went, of course, to the Combined Operations organization, which may be said to have existed for the purpose of giving advice. In recognition of this, Mountbatten's original title had been Adviser on Combined Operations. (COHQ, it should be noted, did not have the forces or the commanders for large operations, and had to request appropriate commands to participate on a temporary basis.) As soon as COHQ had blocked out the concept of the operation and received approval from the Chiefs of Staff, its role in the planning process was purely advisory, although it was weighty, because the staff at COHQ were still regarded as the experts in this sort of warfare and because they had first conceived the plan.

There were many hands in formulating the plan for Dieppe: COHQ, the Air Force Commander, the Ground Force Commander, and whatever advice was given him from Canadian Army and Corps staffs, the Naval Force Commander, the Home Forces staff, and particularly the South-East

Command. The reader will readily recognize in this multitude of planners a prescription for disaster. The Canadian commander naturally tended to rely on the British advisers at COHQ and Home Forces, whereas they, thoroughly imbued with the principle of a commander's veto, assumed that if Roberts was not complaining, he must be approving the plan. Though everyone paid lip-service to the principle that command, authority, and responsibility were undivided, these elements were in fact thinly spread all over the military establishment. This point was first made by the official Canadian historian, C.P. Stacey, and it is still a very telling one indeed.[7]

Those acquainted with organizational and bureaucratic models of decision-making, as first formulated by Professor Graham Allison, will recognize a further complicating factor. The advisers had to think of what was good for Roberts and his men, but they also had to think about what was good for their own institutional interests. Not surprisingly, they tended to compromise on differences, and as long as Roberts did not protest, they cheerfully assumed that everything was proceeding well. Roberts, knowing that this was his first opportunity to prove himself and that another might not be coming for a long time, made a point of never being difficult.

As different agencies made their suggestions, the plan underwent a number of significant changes. COHQ had itself originally favoured one that called for flanking attacks, which would converge on Dieppe from the rear. But it was feared, particularly by Montgomery, that the flanking attacks might never develop the steam to take the town, and without that achievement the raid would be seen by the public as a failure. Recognizing that much of the project's importance derived from the public perception of it, Montgomery supported the much riskier notion of making a frontal attack simultaneous with the flanking attacks, because this alone might give promise of capturing the town. Since it was becoming so clear that the raid's primary purpose was to grab headlines, one might have expected Combined Operations to make a powerful argument for the maximum amount of fire support from air and sea forces to ensure success. Strangely, when Mountbatten presented the rough outline to the Chiefs of Staff for their approval, he limited himself to remarking that there were many problematical aspects to the raid that would have to be worked out, but he did not then try to extract any substantial commitment of forces.[8]

A fundamental flaw in the whole conception was revealed when the planners sat down to figure out just when and where every landing vessel would be in the final approach. It was soon felt that there were too many simultaneous assaults in the Dieppe area, and that a traffic jam of sorts would occur if they all went in at the same time. Hence, to ensure clarity of command and control, it was decided that the flanking attacks would precede the frontal assault by half an hour (a frontal attack could not precede because, without taking the batteries on the flanks, any force approaching the centre would be destroyed by raking fire).[9]

This decision to let a half-hour elapse between the two major components of the assault constituted a major and, in the end, fatal change in plans. Everyone had recognized that while the flanking attacks always had some chance for limited success, the frontal assault in the centre, against the well-defended port itself, was a very doubtful proposition. Only with complete surprise could its capture be envisioned. This need for tactical surprise had been written into the outline plan, and the landing of tanks was to be employed for shock effect. But now the port was to be given a half-hour's warning by the start of the flanking attacks. Without surprise there might still have been some hope of succeeding if much heavier preliminary bombardment, and more extensive naval fire support, had been assigned. But the more preparatory fire support there was, the less would be the element of surprise. It was a vicious circle. This called for hard choices and crisp decision-making.

A clear decision should now have been taken, either to increase the air and naval support massively or to abandon the project. These options were never squarely confronted. No one could entertain any reasonable hope that without achieving tactical surprise in the centre, and with only minimal fire support, the frontal attack had any chance of succeeding. On 5 July, just six weeks before the raid, the German propaganda minister Goebbels, an amateur strategist at best, said that the enemy might be tempted to land on the French coast 'in a fit of military madness'. The day after the raid, with the beaches strewn with bodies amidst the wreckage of tanks and landing craft, that judgement did not seem far off the mark. One can easily understand why a German officer, interrogating the prisoners of war, wanted to hear their explanation for an operation that seemed to him to be clearly too big for a raid and just as clearly too small for a lodgement. For many, this has become the classic question about, if not the judgement on, the operation.[10]

Quite astonishingly, the planned amount of fire-power in support was actually reduced on 5 June, when — while Mountbatten was away in America — the preliminary heavy bombardment was cancelled. Montgomery and the Force Commanders obviously felt that restoring the prospects of surprise and facilitating the movement of the tanks they hoped to land were preferable to heavy preliminary bombardment, which their advisers apparently did not think could be made heavy enough.[11]

A number of other important events occurred between these crucial changes in June and the final modifications. A series of training exercises were carried out, as well as two full-scale dry-runs, *Yukon I* and *II*, in the Bridgport/West Bay area of the Dorset coast. In the course of *Yukon I* on June 11, it became apparent that the exact synchronization of so many simultaneous landings was difficult to achieve with the precision required as to both timing and location. This first trial was deemed a dismal failure; hence the raid on Dieppe was postponed to early July. An attempt to execute the plan — called *Rutter* — was made between 2 and 8 July, but after the men had boarded the craft that were to take them across the Channel, and been told what the objective was, the weather worsened. They were still confined to the vessels, awaiting better conditions, when five days later the Luftwaffe made an attack on the assembled craft. Because the weather forecast for the last possible day of favourable moon and tides was still poor, the force was disbanded. German intelligence was certainly good enough to draw the obvious conclusions. The following day a Führer order went out over Hitler's signature. Noting German victories on the Russian front, Hitler expressed his conviction that the Allies had the choice of 'immediately mounting a major landing in order to create a second front or of losing Soviet Russia as a political and military factor.' He concluded that it was 'highly probable that enemy landings will shortly take place in the area of C-in-C West.' 'The most probable area', he believed, would be 'the Channel coast, the area between Dieppe and Le Havre, and Normandy.' Additional defensive measures were ordered, and the key commanders were to report to Hitler on a daily basis on the measures taken. It is not clear whether this circular order was available to British intelligence.[12]

As some 6,000 men, with varying degrees of knowledge of the plan, returned to the barracks and pubs of Britain on 8 July, General Montgomery recommended to his superiors that the raid be cancelled for good. There is no record that this recommendation was discussed by the Chiefs of Staff Committee. It is recorded, however, that Mountbatten argued that the option of reviving plans for the the raid should be considered, because so much time and effort had been invested. The Chiefs agreed, which meant that the forces assigned to *Rutter* would continue to be held in reserve under Mountbatten's control until a decision was taken one way or another. Since Montgomery was not the least bit interested in any attempt to revive the project, it was undoubtedly by mutual accord that he was cut out of the chain of responsibility, even though the Canadian troops continued to be assigned to his command. The Naval Force Commander, Rear-Admiral H.T. Baillie-Grohman, was also reluctant to have anything more to do with the operation and was similarly cut out.[13]

Despite the negative opinion of such experienced commanders, COHQ was convinced that a revival of the operation was feasible and proceeded to try to make it so. A major problem would be attempting to maintain security. The troops must not be allowed to suspect that the raid might be mounted again. In a patent exercise in wishful thinking, it was assumed that both the troops and their morale were in such perfect condition that no further training — which might indicate another attempt — should be undertaken. This was a tragic mistake, for as Lord Lovat, the only commander who achieved his assigned objective, later observed, the plan required a 'split-second standard of excellence'. Hughes-Hallett decided to reduce dependence on large infantry landing ships; much of the attacking force would make the whole crossing in smaller landing-craft. They would leave from various points in southern England to avoid presenting a target or tipping off German intelligence. While these last two decisions improved the chances of concealing intent by dispersion, they added to the difficulty of navigating through the very narrow channel that would be cleared of German mines and also through the congestion of craft off Dieppe. This use of a multude of smaller craft also made it more likely that the necessary synchronization of the landings, always the critical problem, would prove difficult, particularly as the smaller unarmoured landing-craft were designed for short runs of five to ten miles, not the 70 miles to Dieppe — none of the training exercises had been based on so long a run by these craft. Finally, the employment of this unwieldy formation made it much more difficult to turn around should some last-minute danger, like the appearance of a German coastal convoy, appear. Somewhat more sound was the decision to substitute commandos for the airborne troops that were originally designated to take out the major flanking batteries. But the commandos had to be carried in by more naval craft, adding further to the congestion.[14]

The preliminary order for the operation, now called *Jubilee*, was issued by Combined Operations on 31 July. On the evening of 17 August the troops began their movement, leaving on the night of the 18th.[15]

Scores of books in prose, and even some in poetry, have been written solely about the military side of the engagement. The main events of that sad morning, beginning at 0450, can be told briefly. From east to west along the Channel front it was mostly a tale of disaster, punctuated by a few minor successes. At the extreme eastern end, where No.3 Commando was supposed to take out a major coastal battery, 23 landing-craft approached the beach and came under intense fire; only six actually reached shore. All the commandos aboard five of the remaining six vessels became casualties in the final run-in, or shortly after landing. Only men from the one remaining landing-craft came through the fire and managed to keep the heavy coastal battery out of action for most of two hours. A little to the west, the assault at Puys by the Royal Regiment and the Black Watch achieved nothing. They landed 15 minutes late — 8 minutes after the Germans had sounded the alert. Of the 500 who landed, only six soldiers returned unwounded. The rest were dispatched by a defending force numbering little more than 60 effectives.

The frontal attack on the centre by the Royal Hamilton Light Infantry and the Essex Scottish was a disaster, though it had started out promisingly. For the first minute or two after the fighter-bombers had shot up the harbour-front, the German defenders seemed dazed. But moments later German machine guns and mortars blazed into action as the first craft unloaded their men. 'High explosive bursting on shingle, the rattle of small-arms fire, the dull roar of distant naval guns and sharp report of high-velocity field pieces, the howling of aircraft engines, the screams of wounded men — these sounds in deafening combination numbed the minds of soldiers who had never before been under fire.' Though the first landings were perfectly timed, and two battalions were landed abreast, support from the destroyers offshore and the fighters overhead was insufficient. The tanks that were to provide some of the fire-support arrived fifteen minutes late, and by then momentum had been lost. Raked by withering fire, many of the infantrymen simply huddled beside the low sea-wall separating the beach from the promenade to await the end. A few units pushed ahead and managed to enter the town, but they could do little. Of the 27 tanks unloaded, about half managed to cross the sea-wall; but none penetrated the tank barriers protecting the town itself. Eventually all 27 had to be abandoned. A desperate attempt by General Roberts to reinforce the eastern half of the main assault by the Essex Scottish, by throwing in the Fusiliers de Mont-Royal, was of no avail because the former were largely still pinned against the sea-wall and the latter were unloaded at the wrong beach. Much more worthy of reinforcement was the action being carried out to the west by the South Saskatchewans and Cameron Highlanders, who were landed in reasonably good shape, the latter managing to penetrate some 2,000 yards inland in their attempt to enter the town from the flank; but before they could reach their objective, general evacuation had already been decided on (at 0900, nearly four hours after landing).[16]

The only real major success of the whole morning was at the extreme western end of the front. There Lord Lovat led No. 4 Commando in a successful assault on a German coastal battery, putting it entirely out of action. By 0830 he and his men had done their job and been successfully evacuated. Elsewhere, pulling the men off the beaches under vicious fire proved almost impossible. As Hughes-Hallett later recalled: 'I doubt whether a withdrawal has ever been attempted under such terrible conditions.' Heavy casualties attended the evacuation and the rear-guard was forced to surrender. By 1250, when a destroyer made a last cautious approach to the beaches to see who might be left to evacuate, there was little to be seen save the bodies of the dead and the burned-out hulks of abandoned tanks and landing-craft. There was nothing to do but limp back home.[17]

Perhaps the single most important factor in these tactical reverses was the delay in the landings — all scheduled to occur in the half-hour between 0450 and 0520 — even though none were off by more than 20 minutes. Mistimings, of course, affected vital elements of the plan. There had never been any chance of surprise at the centre because the flanking attacks were to commence half an hour earlier. Surprise for the enveloping attacks was nevertheless thought possible — though it would depend on the precisely timed arrival of units on the beaches. But any one of the many seemingly minor delays dashed this hope. It has been argued that some of the fateful delays were due to bad luck; particularly the unexpected collision with a small enemy convoy of the craft carrying the commandos for the easternmost attack. The resulting fire-fight certainly warned the Germans at two points east of the town, Puys and Berneval. Not surprisingly, after this collision some jittery landing-craft crews, aware both of the delay and of a possible alert, made for good reason their final approaches to the beach at a speed much greater than had been planned. The noise-level of the landing-craft engines was correspondingly loud, and many of the German defenders who had not heard the fire-fight were thus alerted.[18]

The collision, however, cannot be ascribed merely to bad luck for two reasons. First of all, the presence of enemy convoys was not the exception but the rule. They were constantly working the coasts because Dieppe was a frequently used terminus for the Germans. Moreover, two warnings of the convoy's likely route had been sent by the Commander-in-Chief Portsmouth to the *Jubilee* force shortly after their departure from England. Had this been a small commando operation, it would have been possible to make necessary adjustments by timing the final approach somewhat differently, or by making an end-run; but since it was a large operation in which exact synchronization of multiple parties was essential, these options were not available. The only feasible course was to cancel the operation. This was not done. It has been argued that there was a failure in signal transmission, which prevented the timely receipt of the warnings, but this has never been established. It seems more likely that the new Naval Force Commander, Hughes-Hallett, decided not to throw away the last chance to carry out this mission. He was nothing if not determined. He and Mountbatten later claimed that because bad-weather forecasts had been given, it had taken great courage to leave Portsmouth and commit the men to action. In fact the weather predictions were particularly good (as the weather in fact turned out to be). Such vaunted courage, or stubbornness, could more accurately be applied to the decision to proceed after two warnings about the German coastal convoy had been sent to Hughes-Hallett at 01:27 and 02:44. The collision with the convoy occurred one hour after the second warning.[19]

The cumulative effect of all these events — the clash with the convoy, the mistimings, the failure to neutralize all the key batteries, the loss of surprise for the frontal attack — translated into massive casualties. In some cases landing-craft returned without having attempted to disembark soldiers. Of the nearly 5,000 Canadians who embarked, nearly 1,000 were spared in this way. Of the remaining 4,000 who did attempt to land, only thirty per cent returned alive. In other words nearly 2,700 were killed or captured. Photographs of the gutted-out landing-craft, from which no survivors could possibly have emerged, and pictures of the carnage on the beaches, are still shocking today.[20]

About 1,300 of some 1,900 prisoners-of-war had managed to avoid being wounded, and a high proportion of these men, after enduring the misery of prisoner-of-war status for three long years, eventually returned home at war's end. By any standards this was a terrible balance-sheet. Dieppe may have been the biggest raid in history, and the largest air battle of the Second World War, but it also won the dubious distinction of being, as Nigel Hamilton has observed, 'the most tragic and, in ratio to participating forces, the most costly Allied offensive of the war'.[21]

The dreadful news was not reported immediately. British newspapers and radio stations were allowed to carry some word of the operation even as the raid was ending, but naturally the accent was on the positive. 'Morale of returning troops reported to be excellent,' was the message Mountbatten sent to Prime Minister Churchill in Cairo the next day. 'All I have seen are in great form.' To the War Cabinet he reported that the lessons learned would be 'invaluable' in planning the future cross-Channel invasion, and Churchill wired on the 21st: 'My general impression of "Jubilee" is that the results fully justified the heavy cost. The large scale air battle alone justified the raid.' When it had become evident that a disaster was in progress, the government moved to restrict coverage. In the meantime, however, inaccurate reporting had done some damage. The American press — seemingly unaware that the number of US rangers who participated in the raid was approximately fifty — headlined that the Yanks were storming Europe, an affront that left a lasting wound in Canadian-American relations. Canadian headlines were similarly sensational, though they at least managed to identify the main force correctly.[22]

Initial enthusiasm wore off in a matter of hours. On the evening of 19 August, CBC correspondent Rooney Pelletier, broadcasting to Canada, spoke of a 'noble occasion' and a 'day of of high honour', but he warned that the 'electric enthusiasm' was all a bit premature. 'It seems wise to exercise a bit of caution', Pelletier advised, 'before shouting full-throated hosannahs.' The next day the first detailed report by Ross Monroe was published in Canadian newspapers. Headlines announced a 'Blazing, Bloody Battle'. Underneath Monroe explained that 'Canadian shock troops had a rough time of it at several points and losses probably will not be small.' As the full dimensions began to sink in, a new phase commenced (not ended yet) in which commentators and analysts, and later historians, tried to see some good emerging from the operation. In a letter to Mountbatten at the time of the Normandy landing in July 1944, Eisenhower credited Dieppe with having provided many useful lessons. Since Eisenhower had long been a friend and booster of Mountbatten's, this confirmation of what had become a received opinion might well have been challenged when it was later invoked by Mountbatten to defend the operation.[23]

Within two weeks of the raid a report was released from the Canadian headquarters that tried to justify it as a vital learning experience. Its principal author, the Canadian military historian C.P. Stacey, admits now that this was something of a rationalization. Subsequent historians, offering points and counterpoints, have had no better success in presenting a convincing justification, though they have written so many studies that the literature on Dieppe is nearly as extensive as that on the Normandy invasion — completely out of proportion to Dieppe's military importance. Much bitterness has simmered under the surface of the long debate. Just a few months after the raid, Lord Beaverbrook confronted Mountbatten at a dinner party: 'You have murdered thousands of my countrymen. You took those unfortunate Canadian solders. . . . They have been mown down in their thousands and their blood is on your hands.' Beaverbrook was not alone in thinking this. For many Canadians, Dieppe has assumed the same importance Gallipoli has for Australians.[24]

How did such a disastrous undertaking come about when the odds against its success were well known? Why has there never been any clear designation of responsibility? Who, in the end, was finally responsible? These questions are answered in the pages that follow — in the course of which a large window is opened on the desperate first three years of the Second World War.

## 2

# Mountbatten and Myth:
# How the History of Dieppe
# Came To Be Written

The most promising attempt to unravel the mysteries of Dieppe was made in 1950 by Winston Churchill, who came to this task in a roundabout way. During the war years his physician, Sir Charles Wilson (later Lord Moran), had looked with anxiety and foreboding on the day when his most celebrated patient would leave political office, knowing that it was the pure delight in exercising power, far more than the coloured pills he prescribed, that kept his vital juices flowing. The months that followed Churchill's political defeat in 1945 seemed to prove that Wilson was right, as Churchill grew listless and morose — painting, bricklaying, or puttering around Chartwell — even if he occasionally displayed a certain craftsmanship in one of his many hobbies. But within a year Churchill began to spring back to life, having found a substitute for the exercise of political power in the writing of history. He had always enjoyed displaying his rhetorical and didactic skills. As Prime Minister he had often inflicted monologues and soliloquies on his guests long into the early hours of the morning. This inveterate need to verbalize now found expression, as it had in previous periods of political inactivity, in writing. He already had a very impressive bibliography of historical works to his credit. He would now give the world the history of the Second World War from *his* perspective, as only he knew it, and the result would be so authoritative that none would dare challenge it. The first volume of *The Second World War*, a six-volume work, was published in 1948; the last in 1954. In 1953 Churchill was awarded the Nobel Prize for Literature.

Seven-and-a-half years after the Dieppe raid, in January 1950, Churchill came to the point in his narrative where he had to describe it, and confront the sixty-per-cent casualty rate for some 5,000 Canadians who had set out on this venture. He did not like to dwell on defeats and disappointments, and so this episode presented difficulties. Though the details of how

Churchill composed the various chapters of his history are not generally known (most of the relevant papers are tightly controlled by his official biographer, Martin Gilbert, and the Estate), about his treatment of Dieppe there is some evidence.[1]

Like most retired public servants, Churchill had only modest secretarial assistance, but he did have at his disposal the drafting and editorial skills of three formidable assistants: Commodore G.R. Allen for naval questions, General Sir Henry Pownall for military questions, and the historian William Deakin for political and other matters. They faced a vast amount of files, which Churchill used as a point of departure for virtually every section of his work. He originally intended to build his history of Dieppe — for *The Hinge of Fate* — around a request he had made in December 1942, which Deakin had rummaged out of the cellar at Chartwell. In this eight-year-old document, addressed to his then representative on the Chiefs of Staff, General Sir Hastings Ismay, Churchill had asked for an explanation of the decision to execute the Dieppe raid and threatened an official inquiry — thus revealing that some four months after the raid, Churchill had been disturbed. Though he had asserted in speeches that it was necessary as a prelude to invasion, as a reconnaissance in force and a test of port defences, he privately admitted that this was just good morale talk. 'Although for many reasons everyone was concerned to make this business look as good as possible,' he wrote to Ismay, 'the time has now come when I must be informed more precisely about the military plans.'

> Who made them? Who approved them? What was General Montgomery's part in it? and General McNaughton's part? What is the opinion about the Canadian generals selected by General McNaughton? Did the General staff check the plans? At what point was V.C.I.G.S. informed in C.I.G.S.'s absence?

Commenting on these mysteries, Churchill noted:

> At first sight it would appear to a layman very much out of accord with the accepted principles of war to attack the strongly fortified town front without first securing the cliffs on either side, and to use our tanks in frontal assault off the beaches by the Casino, &c., instead of landing them a few miles up the coast and entering the town from the back.

Ismay had been instructed to make an investigation — after which, Churchill warned, 'I will then consider whether there should be a more formal inquiry and what form it should take.' This threat of a possible inquiry was strange, because it could only have followed Churchill's attempt to get answers from Mountbatten, who was an intimate friend and had been a frequent guest at Chequers. 'Dickie's' answers were presumably either unsatisfactory or insufficiently forthcoming. Ismay's immediate reaction on receiving Churchill's minute in December 1942 was to try to protect

Mountbatten by warning him of the impending storm and passing the list of incriminating questions to him. 'Treat this . . . as private, not to be shown even to your staff,' Ismay cautioned. A few days later Ismay took Mountbatten's evasive answers and reworked them into laconic replies to Churchill's questions, which were then given to Churchill. In forwarding the product of this collaboration, Ismay gave no hint that Mountbatten had been involved. Though his reply was sadly inadequate, Churchill let the matter drop. Rereading these documents in 1950, Churchill thought his exchange with Ismay would be a good point of departure for his section on Dieppe. He concluded that the questions were the same ones his readers would want answered more fully.[2]

Once most of the documentary record, and some of the key questions that flowed from it, were clear in his mind, Churchill usually consulted others for suggestions on how to elaborate it. For help with the Dieppe narrative he turned to General Sir Henry Pownall, who had served as Director of Military Operations and Intelligence at the War Office and was something of a wordsmith himself. In February 1950 Churchill exchanged letters with Pownall about where the Dieppe narrative should be placed. Pownall evidently thought it should be treated chronologically in the section dealing with Churchill's return to Cairo after his first meeting with Stalin in Moscow. Clearly nervous about how it should be handled, Churchill wrote Pownall on 20 March, saying that this was 'pretty big stuff', adding that there were 'some very large questions . . . involved. . . . It will be necessary for the whole story to be told. It cannot merely be a narrative of the actual military events. . . . [The reader must be told] How it happened. Why it was done. Who was responsible.' He noted that the military record alone was a 'great controversial issue and may conceivably need a chapter by itself.' He rejected Pownall's proposal that the story be inserted into the account of his two-week trip to Cairo and Moscow in the first half of August 1942. 'It could never come', Churchill wrote, 'in the middle of my picnic in the Desert as proposed. It is a very grave matter.'[3]

Since there had been little public criticism of Dieppe in Britain, Churchill was thinking here about his Canadian audience. But the question of who was responsible would also have repercussions in Britain. Churchill's assistants must have shuddered, for this was a game Churchill frequently played: he was notorious for denying anything but formal responsibility for disasters, which brought out in him a great awareness of the constitutional limitations of his office. When the fates stared coldly at him, he became only the head of the Cabinet, culling the best advice that was given to him, generously sharing responsiblity with those who had provided him with that advice. If, however, successes were involved, he was always ready to accept praise — stressing all the while the loneliness of his high office.

Where Dieppe was concerned, the two candidates for blame — for that was clearly what Churchill was trying to pinpoint in 1950 — were

Montgomery and Mountbatten, both of whom had large circles of followers and defenders. Montgomery had supervised the cancelled version of *Rutter*. On a higher level, Mountbatten had presided as Chief of Combined Operations over both *Rutter* and the project in its revised form, *Jubilee*. Gingerly, Churchill explored the problem with Pownall. 'Mountbatten', he noted, 'has taken a pretty strong line, claiming all the responsibility, which is scarcely more than he need bear.' One might add, it was also considerably more than Mountbatten had ever been willing to accept — it is hard to find any speech or private paper of Mountbatten's in which he even came close to assuming the responsibility Churchill attributed to him. Still, as the former Chief of Combined Operations, he was the obvious choice for a scapegoat, though there were other possibilities. Churchill reminded Pownall that Montgomery had expressed 'very strong views about this operation', and declared that 'he never accepted the slightest responsibility for the military side of the operation after the first attempt was cancelled.' With evident suspicion, Churchill concluded that 'His [Montgomery's] part in the affair requires careful elucidation. He has very strong views on the subject. All this must be carefully explored.' Here, then, was Churchill out on the prowl to find who among his favourites could be held up as a sacrificial lamb to satisfy Canadian public opinion.[4]

Left largely untouched in all this was the question of Churchill's own role. He approached that subject with great circumspection. He implicitly admitted to Pownall having approved the original project made by Montgomery. But then, 'Owing to weather or some misgivings, the operation was cancelled, after all the ten thousand men embarked had been told about it. I was not consulted about the resumption as I was away. I am sure I should have been most worried. . . . I think I had already started for Cairo and Moscow when the decision to renew the operation was taken. Certainly I heard about it and did not oppose it. There is no doubt Mountbatten pressed most strongly for it, and I expect you will find that the War Cabinet gave their assent in my absence.'[5]

Pownall could find no evidence that the Cabinet had done so. This absence of documentation clearly implicated Ismay, who after all had been Churchill's personal secretary to the Chiefs of Staff and was responsible for keeping Churchill fully informed of what the Chiefs were doing; he was therefore a regular member of the Chiefs of Staff. When Churchill left the country, Ismay, as Chief of Staff to the Minister of Defence, was in charge on the military side. By 1950 he had become Lord Ismay and had achieved great distinction as Mountbatten's Chief of Staff during the last vice-regency of India. In fact he was working, in Churchill's words, 'hand-in-glove and more' with him on his memoirs. Ismay, Mountbatten, and Montgomery were known as Churchill's men. All three had intimate ties, one to the other, in their own special network. And Pownall himself had served as Mountbatten's Chief of Staff in the South East Asia Supreme Command.[6]

Churchill's inquiry threatened to stir up old ghosts. Ismay had been a witness to a row shortly after Dieppe, when at a dinner party at Chequers, in the presence of the Prime Minister and his assembled guests, General Sir Alan Brooke — the Chief of the Imperial General Staff and Chairman of the Chiefs of Staff Committee — had openly attacked Mountbatten's competence, saying that the planning for Dieppe had been all wrong. Mountbatten, after a slow burn, exploded, threatening a full inquiry. Brooke backed down in the face of Mountbatten's defiance. But in December 1942, when Mountbatten finally produced a Report on the lessons learned from Dieppe, Brooke was scathing, telling Mountbatten that he was 'very disappointed with the paucity of ideas'.[7]

Well before that official Report, Mountbatten had been relaying to the press his own account of Dieppe, comprised of fuzzy explanations and excuses about the activity of Combined Operations. Indeed, from the very beginning of his tenure at Combined Operations he had been conscious of the public-relations angle and had even placed on his staff some prime Hollywood talent, including Jock Lawrence, one of Samuel Goldwyn's assistants, as well as Darryl Zanuck and Douglas Fairbanks Jr. Publicity in advance of the raid was so carefully arranged that one contemporary observer noted that the operation was virtually 'the best publicized military event of modern times . . . of all times.' Mountbatten saw to it that among the approximately twenty-five journalists carried by the command ship and the principal auxiliaries to the beaches off Dieppe, there were at least three journalists who were likely to turn out instant books. One was the Canadian correspondent of the *Montreal Standard*, Wallace Reyburn. Another was the American war-correspondent Quentin Reynolds, who was also on very familiar terms with Mountbatten's Hollywood crowd; the third was the well-known British correspondent A.B. Austin of the London *Daily Herald*.[8]

It is not surprising that the texts of their war books were subjected to censorship and tended to say only what Mountbatten was prepared to accept. He was not disappointed when Reyburn's *Glorious Chapter* (published simultaneously in Britain as *Rehearsal for Invasion*) and Reynolds' *Dress Rehearsal* appeared in 1943. The titles of both books, which quickly became best-sellers, embodied Mountbatten's defence of the raid as an essential learning experience from which the future invasion would be forged. A.B. Austin concurred, explaining in *We Landed at Dawn* (also published in 1943) that, '. . . it was a testing and rehearsing of all our combined military, naval and Air Force staff work, a detailed working out of plans on which once completed, weeks could be saved another time.'[9]

Accepting Mountbatten's assertion that the raid was a success, Austin gave him all the credit, since as Chief of Combined Operations Mountbatten was the principal officer responsible. The portrait of Mountbatten that emerged in these narratives was essentially how he wished to be seen — 'hard, cold, shrewd — the perfect war leader'. He was 'Public Hero No. 1'. He was shown as being upset that one commando group in a prior raid had landed at 8:31 instead of 8:30. Not surprisingly, Reynolds' book also contains the first evidence that Mountbatten might be seeking, if not to shift the blame, certainly to get the Canadians to take a fair part of it. Reynolds implied that the Canadians had insisted on undertaking the raid even though Mountbatten would have preferred more experienced troops. Also evident was the charge, largely erroneous, that Canadians had insisted on changing from a flanking to a frontal attack; this may be also regarded as an early salvo in the battle over who was to blame. Mountbatten's organization was portrayed as doing its work flawlessly. (Reynolds' book was excerpted and appeared in the May 1943 *Reader's Digest*.) In 1943 there were few sources and little opportunity to criticize these views. As conveyed by Reynolds, and presumably originating with Mountbatten, they were generally accepted. But this interpretation did not survive the end of the war, and was increasingly regarded as an extended press release from Combined Operations Headquarters, which to a large extent it was.[10]

Though Reyburn showed some resistance to the charisma of Mountbatten, his portrait was still that of a great commander. The rationalizations offered for the raid were the familiar ones put out by Combined Operations — that it was, in Reyburn's words, 'the prelude, the curtain-raiser, to the North African campaign which was to open three months later. It was the pivot in the Allies' switch-round from the defensive to the offensive in western Europe. . . . The raid produced valuable information to the allies about the enemy's defenses, the status of the Luftwaffe and the problems of landing tanks that they could never have understood without the sacrifice.' This was claiming a lot. As Mountbatten had done in his official Report, Reyburn pointed especially to the air battle and the 'terrific damage' inflicted on the limited German air strength. 'We were able to destroy definitely 170 enemy planes with the loss to ourselves of 106 aircraft.' A.B. Austin also liked this argument: 'The man who died at Dieppe, and who by the toughness of his fight not only gained us vital information, but forced the German Air Force to come out in defence of the German troops and be clawed down in scores, was doing as great a thing as if he had blown up an enemy battery or captured a general.' The mention of intelligence gained showed, however, that even Austin was not buying the argument that the air battle by itself was worth the effort. In fact the RAF loss was 106 aircraft; the Luftwaffe lost only 48.[11]

In a different class from the books by Reynolds, Reyburn, and Austin was the official White Paper produced by the Headquarters of the Canadian Commander in Britain, General Andrew McNaughton. At the time of Dieppe, McNaughton had on his staff a historian in uniform, Captain C.P.

Stacey. Shortly after the raid Stacey was involved in helping draft explanations of Dieppe for the Canadian press. In his first draft he showed some tendency to work the Mountbatten game in reverse, shifting the blame away from the Canadian staff officers and more towards Combined Operations Headquarters (COHQ) and the British. But after being subjected to a certain amount of pressure from those sources, Stacey produced a version that Mountbatten could live with. The raid, Stacey said, had a clear purpose, to prepare the way for a Second Front; it had largely succeeded in doing this and the costs had been reasonable. The *Daily Telegraph* printed it entirely; *The Times* gave an extensive summary; and the *New York Times* gave a front-page synopsis. In his recent memoirs Stacey has admitted that it must have seemed like a 'somewhat lame apologia'. This is too modest: it was a very able apologia.[12]

After the war Stacey went on to serve in the historical section of the Canadian Army, rising to become its chief. Over the next thirty years he would devote much of his career as a highly respected military historian to working and reworking his version of the original apologia. In the first postwar years Canadians did not have to toe the line quite so directly to British authorities as they had during the war, and when Stacey began to conduct interviews in preparation for the first official history of the Canadian Army in the war years he seemed to be on the point of writing a version of events that would differ greatly from his earlier White Paper and the accounts authorized by Combined Operations Headquarters. Stacey was an indefatigable researcher, determined to get all the facts. But he needed help from Mountbatten in explaining many fine points, and Mountbatten cooperated by offering the assistance of his very loyal Naval Force Commander at Dieppe, and one of the architects of the raid, John Hughes-Hallett, who was from several viewpoints an ideal source of information. Whereas many of the men involved with the planning had been rotated in and out of Combined Operations, Hughes-Hallett had been there from the first discussion of Dieppe down to the last after-action reports. Attentive to fine detail, possessed of a razor-sharp memory, he had kept a careful appointment diary. No one even remotely approached his extensive knowledge of the raid, save possibly Major Walter Skrine, the COHQ planner on the ground side. But strangely enough, the one event that Hughes-Hallett could not elucidate was the date of the decision to revive the Dieppe project after Montgomery had recommended that it be abandoned; nor could he say when, or if, the plans had been subsequently reviewed or approved. Writing to Stacey on 30 December 1952, the most Hughes-Hallett could offer was that 'I have no doubt that the whole plan must have been gone through yet again some time in July or early August, when *Jubilee* was decided upon, but I was not present and do not know exactly what happened.'[13]

Still, what Hughes-Hallett could document or remember about the evolution of the plan constituted an invaluable source. Stacey, who had to rely on those facts to a considerable extent, understandably produced an interpretation to match. It is hard to imagine how the balance between apologia and criticism could have been different, considering that however great the skills of the historian, he had become enmeshed in explanations — originating in the midst of war on behalf of military authorities — that are inevitably justifications.

Thus Stacey broke less new ground than he might have in the final version of his first book on the subject, *The Canadian Army, 1939-1945: An Official Historical Summary* (1948). His point of view was very much that of a veteran of Canadian Headquarters. Referring to the effect of the raid on the Canadian Army (of which he was a member at the time), Stacey wrote: 'There is no doubt whatever that in the Army it produced a new sense of pride' — though he admitted that at home 'the effects were different . . . public opinion continued to dwell upon it for months, and comment, frequently very ill-informed, continued in the press and elsewhere.' He left his readers in no doubt about where he stood: he was profoundly unsympathetic to critics, who, he implied, were facile and captious. His overall judgement did not differ significantly from Mountbatten's central contention that the raid paid handsome dividends. In a sentence that British historians would never tire of quoting, Stacey concluded: 'The casualties sustained in the Raid were part of the price paid for the knowledge that enabled the great [Normandy] operation of 1944 to be carried out at a cost in blood smaller than even the most optimistic had ventured to hope for.'[14]

Discussing the decision to remount the raid after its cancellation in July, Stacey remarked: 'For an early operation, such as was desirable for so many reasons [preparing the way for other cross-Channel assaults], the Dieppe scheme was the best possibility; it offered a ready-made plan and a force already trained.' Implying that adequate precautions had been taken against the possibility that the Germans might learn of the revived operation, he wrote categorically: 'Today, however, with all the enemy's records at our disposal we can say with complete certainty that he had no foreknowledge whatever of our operation.' On the decision to mount a frontal attack on a heavily fortified position, Stacey presented Combined Operations' version that no suitable alternative existed. He found reasonable the decision to continue with the raid even after the force had collided with a coastal convoy, and all hope of surprise — on which the whole plan depended — had vanished. He even supported the view expressed in an outline plan prepared for the Chiefs of Staff in May 1942 that Dieppe was 'not heavily defended', saying that 'This opinion was not seriously at fault', in spite of the fact that between the submission of the outline plan and the execution of the raid, the general area received so many reinforcements as to raise serious doubts about the validity of the raid. Stacey did not criticize the ambitious military objectives that supposedly justified the operation, including the capture of barges, German documents, and an air-field well beyond the town — all of which required time. (These goals were placed hopelessly out of reach when, to avoid having the landing-force destroyed by German reinforcements, now located within striking distance, Combined Operations decided to land and evacuate the force all on one tide, leaving only hours for tasks that could have taken days.) One would have thought that Stacey, a keen analyst of military operations, would have noted that once the raid was put on this compressed schedule, it lost most of its *raison d'être* as a test exercise for a sizeable cross-Channel attack.[15]

Recognizing that much went wrong with the Dieppe assault, Stacey attributed the shortcomings merely to bad luck. There was nothing in his account to match the probing questions that Churchill and Ismay had canvassed in 1942 and to which they returned in 1950. Stacey also had fulsome praise for the mother-country's armed forces. 'The conditions of evacuation were probably without parallel in the history of warfare; yet thanks to the boundless skill and courage of the Navy a considerable proportion of the force was successfully brought away.' He also spoke of the RAF's 'gallant and successful fight in support of the operation.' This was all justified, though the praise would have been more merited had the Admiralty allowed ships of greater firepower to support the raid, or had the RAF pushed, instead of discouraging, preliminary bombing.[16]

About the crucial question that was so to bother Churchill, how the decision had been reached, Stacey was uncritical. 'The perilous enterprise was not undertaken without deep consideration . . . Mr Churchill had, in fact, at an advanced stage of the planning after his return from the United States late in June, specifically sought the counsel of some of his most senior service advisers on the utility of the proposed raid in a private conference at Downing Street.' Stacey did not say that at that meeting of 30 June, Churchill expressed grave doubts about the whole project, and that none of his advisers had been able to reassure him. Nor did he attempt to explain one of the most bedevilling conundrums of Dieppe: Brooke's stepping in at this meeting to save the project by dismissing Churchill's questions about it. Stacey down-played Churchill's ambivalence and firmly placed responsiblity on the Prime Minister by quoting his September 1942 statement to Parliament on his return from the Middle East and Russia: 'I personally regarded the Dieppe assault, to which I gave my sanction, as an indispensable preliminary to full-scale operations.' Stacey seems not to have known of Churchill's statement of December 1942, accompanying the demand for an inquiry, in which he admitted that, 'Although for many reasons everyone was concerned to make this business look as good as possible . . . , the time has come to find out who was responsible,' for 'no matter what we say in public we must know ourselves what really happened' and 'who was responsible.'[17]

As for the difficult problem of when and how the Chiefs of Staff came to approve the decision to remount, Stacey merely asserted baldly in a footnote that this was done by the Chiefs of Staff Committee on 20 July — for which there was, and is, no adequate documentary evidence. The controversial question of Soviet pressure for action across the Channel was dismissed by Stacey in a few paragraphs, in which he stated: 'There is no evidence that the Russian situation was actually an important factor in the decision to revive the raid' — despite the fact, which Stacey knew, that Churchill scheduled a trip in the two weeks (2 to 17 August) before the raid was remounted, when he visited Moscow, using Cairo as his base of operations before and after. Stacey was apparently unaware, however, that Churchill cabled twice back to London, from Cairo and then Moscow, asking about the status of the project.[18]

Thus by 1950, when Churchill began to work on his Dieppe draft, there were many dogs asleep, thanks in no small measure to Stacey's ability to suppress troublesome doubts about Dieppe. The prospect of Churchill's publishing the searching questions he posed in December 1942 threatened to unravel all Mountbatten's patient efforts to control the historical conception of Dieppe that had found such broad acceptance in the journalistic accounts, as well as in the more scholarly, but still positive, interpretation provided by Stacey. The Cabinet office, and those responsible for writing the official British history of the Second World War, had also to be sensitive to the grave risk of reopening the wound in Canada, an increasingly important member of the Commonwealth.

This was indeed 'pretty big stuff', as Churchill had indicated. What he would say about Dieppe in his own account of the war would drown out what everyone else had said. It would inevitably reflect on Mountbatten's competence. Churchill's initial request for assistance in straightening out the account went not to Mountbatten but to Ismay, who had been Churchill's Chief of Staff and his principal channel to the Chiefs of Staff Committee on military operations. Ismay was remarkably astute in the delicate art of mediating between the military and Churchill, and making seemingly irreconcilable differences disappear. In his most soothing manner, he wrote to Churchill in March 1950 suggesting that many had shared responsibility — it could not be placed on any one person. He went on to thank him for sending a copy of the 'minute' that Churchill had given Pownall. 'I agree with every word of it,' Ismay wrote, though he immediately went on to try to dissuade Churchill from stirring the pot too vigorously. Churchill should not give the episode too much emphasis, he warned, inasmuch as 'it was not one of our most creditable ventures, because the underlying object was never sufficiently clearly defined nor, so far as I can remember was the chain of responsibility.' Throwing as much cold water as he could on Churchill's efforts, Ismay somberly observed: 'I do not . . . believe that we deserved success.' That was a dangerous admission, since Ismay was not yet quarrelling with Churchill's assertion that the final decision must have been taken sometime after he and his party had left for Cairo. Ismay had been left behind in London as Churchill's representative on the Chiefs of Staff Committee and should have exercised some supervision over any decision taken in Churchill's absence. The charter decreed by Churchill shortly after he became Prime Minister, under which Ismay operated, was very specific: 'Let it be very clearly understood that all directions emanating from me are made in writing, or should be immediately afterwards confirmed in writing, and that I do not accept any responsibility for matters relating to national defence, on which I am alleged to have given decision, unless they are recorded in writing.' Ismay thus failed in his duty if he had allowed a decision to be taken, in the Prime Minister's name, without committing it to paper. Sensing the implications, Ismay concluded by saying that he wanted to be kept abreast of the matter, writing separately to Pownall offering 'to co-operate' in producing material for Churchill's treatment of Dieppe.[19]

Meanwhile Pownall and Captain G.R. Allen, Churchill's two principal collaborators on this section of his book, were still drawing a blank, finding the official records of little help in answering their master's questions, and were hoping that Ismay would find the solution. Naturally Ismay was alarmed by gaps in the records, and suggested once again, on 21 July, that the incident should be given light treatment. He even told Churchill that the Dieppe section was 'redundant because the military story has been told so fully and accurately in other publications.' (The sole reference offered, however, was to Stacey.) If Churchill insisted on treating it, Ismay thought that Dieppe would be briefly disposed of in three paragraphs, the first of which might begin: 'Before I [Churchill] left England, I had approved an operation against Dieppe and I anxiously awaited news. . . .' This of course contradicted Churchill's recollection, that the final decision had not been taken at the time of his departure. But Ismay knew that Churchill wanted to be exonerated and therefore agreed that perhaps his request for an investigation in December 1942, in which Churchill distanced himself from all personal responsibility, could be reprinted along with Ismay's not very informative responses.[20]

None of these suggestions seemed to please Churchill, who on 2 August 1950 wrote a scathing letter to Ismay that began: 'I can see nothing in the papers I now have from you and Allen and my own record which explains who took the decision to *revive* the [plan for the] attack after it had been abandoned and Montgomery had cleared out. This is the crux of the story. Surely the decision could not have been taken without the Chiefs of Staff being informed. If so, why did they not bring it to my attention, observing I did not leave England till July 30 or 31[sic]? It was a major decision of policy. If the decision was taken after I left the country, was the Defence Committee or the War Cabinet informed? How did this all go?'[21]

At last, Churchill had struck the harpoon deeply into the Dieppe mystery. He now made some pretty strong allegations, insinuating that anyone could have seen that the mission was hopelessly compromised once the operation had been revealed to the 10,000 men originally scheduled to carry it out. But clearly the central question, much more important than the apportioning of blame, was what had gone wrong with the procedures by which decisions were taken and responsibility recorded. He wondered if perhaps the decision to remount had been 'pushed through by Dickie on his own without reference to higher authority?' But the more Churchill thought about that possibility, the less plausible it seemed: 'I cannot believe that he was allowed to do this without higher authority becoming responsible.' What particularly troubled Churchill was the fact that in all the drafts and reports before him the question of how the decision was reached was 'left blank'. The problem, he said, was, 'At what stage was this matter cut off from the supreme war direction [meaning the Chiefs of Staff and the War Cabinet], or how and when was it put up to them?' Churchill now told Ismay that he was no longer so much interested in what he would tell the world — that would be a matter for 'subsequent consideration' — but 'we must know ourselves exactly what the facts were.'[22]

A thoroughly alarmed Ismay now tried to distance himself from the mystery by shunting off Churchill's inquiries to Mountbatten, even though Mountbatten had failed to provide adequate answers in 1942. It was a delicate matter and Ismay tried to contact Mountbatten by telephone. But after a week of fruitless attempts to catch up with the First Sea Lord, he dispatched a carefully worded letter to him. It was as remarkable for what it did not say as for what it did. As Churchill's watchdog on the Chiefs of Staff Committee, Ismay should have been able to volunteer some recollections, but he was strangely enigmatic. He hoped Mountbatten might have some record that would clarify the decision to remount — recognizing, however, that this might not be the case. But 'anyway', he wrote to Mountbatten, '. . . you are in the best position to recall the sequence of events.' It was going to be a question, then, of Mountbatten's say-so. Cautiously Ismay coached the First Sea Lord about what he should say: 'I am absolutely clear that at least the Chiefs of Staff *must* [emphasis added] have been informed and given approval.' Though he said that a thorough search of every major military policy had failed to turn up any evidence of this approval, Ismay did report on one hopeful discovery for Mountbatten: he had found a cable from Churchill dated 17 August 1942, asking for news of *Jubilee*, which Ismay implied made it ' . . . pretty certain tht Winston himself must have given approval.'[23]

In replying to Churchill, Ismay began most apologetically. 'I am so sorry', he wrote, 'for being so inadequate about the Dieppe Raid', and then went on to make it quite clear that he was not convinced that Churchill's interest was academic. Ismay said, in so many words, that he would have nothing to do with shifting responsibility for the raid from Churchill to anyone else. Having made a search of the files, he reported that one of the questions Churchill had raised could be answered 'at once'. 'You yourself must have approved the operation in principle before you left England for the Middle East on the 2nd of August. Otherwise how could you have known of the operation's new code when you telegraphed to me [from Cairo] two days before it took place [ , ] on the 17th August, "Please report if and when Jubilee takes place." '[24]

For Churchill this was certainly a damning piece of evidence, particularly as he had been hinting that anyone could have known that the odds of success were very poor, going so far as to note that Clementine Churchill, who had been brought up in Dieppe, had warned against the cliffs, which could be filled with guns. If it was so obviously a doomed mission, why had he not killed it promptly?[25]

But looking for proof of Churchill's involvement, Ismay had in fact thrown out something of a red herring. He implied that the files showed Churchill to be *au courant* with the operation when he left London and was aware even of the new code-name. But he may have been practising a bit of deception on Churchill, for the files he consulted contained another telegraphic exchange that occurred two days earlier than the cable he cited. Churchill's cable from Moscow on the 15th was not about *Jubilee* but rather about *Rutter*; he was answered by Ismay, who corrected him saying, in an unpardonable breech of security, that the name had been changed to *Jubilee* and that it was now scheduled to take place on or about the 17th of August. So if the Prime Minister's knowledge of the new code-name (or lack of it) and of the approximate date was the test of whether it had been approved before Churchill's departure, the evidence confirmed Churchill's recollection that it had not.[26]

Why had Ismay argued the contrary? And why did he imply that the decision had been taken while Churchill was in London? Perhaps there was indeed something irregular about the way the decision was reached, which would be obscured if it could be asserted that the Prime Minister had made the decision prior to departure. Ismay actually raised that possibility himself when he admitted, in his first letter to Churchill, that the chain of responsibility ' . . . so far as I can remember . . . [had never been] sufficiently clearly defined.' Such definition is achieved through formal decisions and written orders. The two went hand-in-hand, and the absence of one implied the absence of the other. Writing in the comfort of Chartwell, but lacking the necessary papers to consult, Churchill did not contest Ismay's selective use of the files, nor did he deny having wanted such a raid. But he carefully distinguished between wanting it and authorizing it. With his enormous experience of government, Churchill was now more convinced than ever that something had gone wrong with the decision-making process. In his August letter to Ismay, it will be recalled, he said the central problem was 'at what stage was this matter cut off from the supreme war direction, or how and when was it put up to them?' He was now more suspicious than ever.[27]

Under Churchill's intense pressure, Ismay was forced to acknowledge that there might have been no approval: 'I have searched through all the records [presumably including the most confidential] and there is nothing therein which throws any light on the particular question posed in your minute of 2nd August.' The only thing he had managed to dig up was a brief minute in the Chiefs of Staff meeting for 23 December 1942, following Churchill's first request for an explanation of Dieppe, in which Mountbatten was reported to have brought up 'the withholding of information that the Dieppe raid was taking place', for which he claimed to have received 'special instructions from the Chiefs of Staff', and as a consequence 'had even been compelled . . . to mislead his own staff on this occasion.' No discussion of this point was recorded. Mountbatten was apparently referring to some instructions he supposedly received after the cancellation of *Rutter* when the Chiefs left open the possibility of reviving it. If he had indeed received instructions to keep the decision secret, that implied that there was a decision and that the Chiefs had approved it. But had that been the case, the minutes would simply have read: 'The Chiefs of Staff discussed the implementation of their directive to Mountbatten approving revival of the operation.'[28]

The minute in question clearly raised another possibility. If the Chiefs had not given formal authorization, had they asked Mountbatten to take the decision himself without notifying them, in effect washing their hands of the affair even before the fateful day? The fact that Churchill had been obliged to cable London from Moscow for information about *Rutter*, when he had with him Brooke, the Chief of the Imperial General Staff, perhaps suggests this. But if so, what is one to make of Mountbatten's assertions of December 1942 and the absence of a corresponding statement indicating that at least one of the other Chiefs recalled or agreed with what Mountbatten had said?

It would seem that at the meeting on 23 December the Chiefs were content to see Mountbatten twist in the breeze, trying to explain away one of the strangest anomalies of the raid: the fact that key officers on his staff were kept in ignorance. Indeed, this distancing from Mountbatten was part of a pattern indicating displeasure with the Chief of Combined Operations in the months after Dieppe. There had been Brooke's attack on Mountbatten's planning in front of Churchill's dinner guests, followed by Mountbatten's threat to demand an inquiry and Brooke's temporary retreat, to be followed in turn by Brooke's scathing criticism of the Dieppe report in December. There were signs that others were also displeased with Mountbatten. To his suggestions for administrative reform that same December, Ismay had replied with unaccustomed severity. 'My clear advice to you', he wrote, 'would be to leave the business alone for ... you are at present imperfectly informed both as to the present position, and as to the implications of the suggestions you put forward.' Mountbatten was undoubtedly under a cloud. Though he was allowed to justify his role to the committee — explaining why his staff had been kept in the dark and implying that the Chiefs of Staff had given approval to remount — corroboration was not forthcoming from those in a position to know. In later years Mountbatten would implicitly recognize that neither Churchill nor any of the Chiefs could recall having authorized the mission. He would also refer to this as the only 'unrecorded' operational decision of the war.[29]

Poking at any part of the Dieppe story invariably produced more surprises and incongruities than answers, and Ismay's attempt in August 1950 was no exception. Having supposedly settled matters by citing the December 1942 COS minute, Ismay went on in his letter to recall that he now remembered having been exposed to the 'fury of General Nye, then Vice Chief of the Imperial General Staff, who had no idea that the operation was on until reports started to flow in from the scene of the action.' Nye was no mere minor cog in the wheel: he was second-in-command after Brooke and replaced Brooke *ex officio* whenever the latter was out of the country (as Brooke was after 2 August). Surely it is astonishing that Mountbatten, for more than two weeks preceding the Dieppe raid, sat side-by-side in the Chiefs of Staff meetings with Nye, the principal military officer in England, and never mentioned the decision to remount the operation. Indeed, if the decision had not already been reached prior to Brooke's departure with Churchill for Cairo and Moscow, Nye's approval was required. Had the decision been reached by Mountbatten, Sir Dudley Pound (the First Sea Lord), and Sir Charles Portal (Chief of the Air Staff) — but not by Nye or Brooke — it could not have been considered a decision of the Chiefs of Staff, and indeed might not have been lawful. Nye's ignorance of the decision implied that, if it had been made, it must have been made earlier with Brooke's approval. But Churchill's cable from Moscow, employing the wrong code-name for the Dieppe raid, suggested that those in Churchill's party, which included Brooke, were not *au courant*. It implied that both Churchill *and* Brooke were ignorant of the decision.[30]

The fact that Nye was in the dark is just one anomaly. A careful search of the records reveals that the only high-level officers known to have been told by Mountbatten of the decision to carry out *Jubilee* were his intelligence chief, the Marquis of Casa Maury, the Force Commanders, and the overall Canadian Commander, General McNaughton. For comparable operations all the top staff were involved, supported by scores drawn from COHQ's lower levels.[31]

The most disconcerting problem in reconstructing the Dieppe decision has to do with Ismay himself. He was in London all during July and August 1942. Whether the decision had been taken before or after Churchill's departure, Ismay, by reason of his office, should have known if the Chiefs of Staff had approved of the Dieppe raid. The clear implication of Ismay's correspondence with Churchill in December 1942, and then in the spring and summer of 1950, was that he had *not* known; otherwise he would surely have informed Churchill of the decision. As there was no document with Ismay's signature noting a decision, he was able subsequently to exclude himself from any involvement. Indeed, recounting Nye's anger to Churchill seems to have been a way of preparing the ground should Churchill ask Ismay directly whether he knew. Ismay could then have replied that if Nye did not know, how was he supposed to have known? But as we have noted, the cabled exchanges between Churchill in Moscow and Cairo and Ismay in London proves that Ismay knew not only that some sort of a decision had been taken but the code-name as well (though he could have got this information from Mountbatten). Churchill in 1950 — on the trail of Mountbatten and Montgomery — seems never to have asked Ismay what he knew. Ismay, in glossing over his privileged knowledge of the plans for Dieppe, suggested that he realized there was something irregular about the way the decision had been taken; but the degree to which he had implicated himself escaped Churchill.

While awaiting Mountbatten's much-delayed reply, Ismay decided that he should discreetly warn Churchill's assistant, William Deakin, that satisfactory answers might never be forthcoming, and once more suggested that perhaps Churchill should not got into the Dieppe business too much. Deakin, perhaps not realizing the sensitivity of the matter, reported the conversation to Churchill. 'Ismay's frank opinion', Deakin told him, 'is that you will get little of value out of Lord Mountbatten who is at the moment playing polo and visiting Naval establishments.' Deakin went on to explain that Mountbatten had in any case taken responsibility for the operation in 1942. 'Six months later [i.e. December 1942] there is a minute of a Chiefs of Staff meeting at which Mountbatten stated that he had taken the responsibility himself.' Deakin, perhaps understanding that it might not be desirable to draw attention to this, concluded that the best thing would be for Churchill to settle for a 'bare summary' of the operation. He added that 'if anyone wishes to read the story of Dieppe there is a detailed account in the Canadian Official History.'[32]

Mountbatten, who had received the clear impression that there was trouble brewing over Dieppe, replied to Ismay's storm-warnings in characteristically breezy fashion: 'I have been flitting round the country like a firefly. . . . I can assure you that Whitehall appears more cuckoo to me in 1950 than it ever did in 1943.' But there was a glint of steel in this letter, for Mountbatten made clear that he would not sit still for Churchill's insinuations and was prepared to begin his own inquiry by writing to as many sources as possible to develop his own case, beginning with his former Chief of Staff in Combined Operations, General G.E.Wildman-

Lushington, and the Naval Force Commander at Dieppe, Captain John Hughes-Hallett.[33]

Hughes-Hallett came promptly to Mountbatten's defence, but somewhat nervously. He was 'bound to admit that I find Mr Churchill's questions difficult to answer.' The solution to the problem, he was sure, lay in simply telling Churchill that all that needed to be said had been written down by the official Canadian historian [C.P.Stacey], who had visited England and who 'spent a weekend with me . . . and cross examined me closely with the aid of voluminous records which he brought with him.' Stacey's account, Hughes-Hallett declared, was the 'best that has so far been published.' For Mountbatten's benefit, Hughes-Hallett now repeated the vague generalities he had given Stacey, adding a few details. After the cancellation of *Rutter*, he wrote, 'you and I had a private talk at which you told me the Prime Minister was bitterly disappointed and regarded the cancellation of two successive large operations as tantamount to defeat.' This was clearly quoting Mountbatten back to Mountbatten, but Hughes-Hallett also asserted that the 'Chiefs of Staff also agreed to the decision to remount the operation.' As there is no document that indicates this approval, and Hughes-Hallett did not sit on the Chiefs of Staff Committee, who could have been his source for this claim if not Mountbatten?[34]

For the historian, the difficulty with Hughes-Hallett's account, as with the many others that speak of Chiefs-of-Staff approval, is that they are all based on the same source: Mountbatten. There is no independent confirmation of them. When told of Churchill's questions in 1950, the Director of Combined Operations, Major General Wildman-Lushington, offered no recollection of final plans for a raid on Dieppe or their approval, even though he had been Mountbatten's Chief of Staff in 1942. After making a full search of all the official records, he had to admit to Mountbatten that 'we . . . have not really found entirely full and satisfactory answers' to Churchill's questions. He did find, however, in COHQ files a note saying that a full record regarding the operation was not being kept in the papers of the Chiefs of Staff for reasons of secrecy, but that detailed discussion was being recorded in the COS Secretariat's secret files (which were regularly retired to the control of the Cabinet office). But the note was misleading, for there were no documents in those files about the decision. The discrepancy is glaring. 'I do not understand', Lushington wrote, 'why the search through the Cabinet files has failed to reveal the record of the decision to remount.' The most probable explanation for the note Lushington had found was that it had been put in the files to reassure Mountbatten's staff that he was acting with authorization. When Wildman-Lushington checked in 1950 and was told that the Cabinet files did not contain the promised record, the spurious character of both the note and the assurances it was said to have contained was unmasked.[35]

Mountbatten was finding that all his correspondents, while unwilling to indict him, were increasingly uncovering more puzzling bits that prevented any definitive exoneration. By the end of August 1950 he had clearly had enough of this and wrote to Ismay, giving a summary of what his researchers had found and claiming that 'we all . . . agree on the enclosed answers.' These statements all neatly dodged the question of when or how the Chiefs of Staff had given their approval, but left the impression that they had done so. Realizing that his inability to state flatly that the Chiefs had approved the Dieppe raid on a given date was damaging his credibility, Mountbatten came back to what he saw as an incontrovertible fact: that Churchill had pressed strongly for such raids. Mountbatten explained to Ismay: 'I do hope that Winston will stress that what COHQ was really there for was to carry out his instructions given as long ago as October 1941, to prepare for the re-invasion of the continent; and if you would like some notes to help him on this I would be prepared to start work.' As Hughes Hallett had done, Mountbatten recommended that Churchill should study Stacey's account, 'as this gives the fairest report yet.'[36]

Churchill's first draft about the Dieppe raid, apparently forwarded to Mountbatten by Ismay, did not make any of the points Mountbatten wished to have made. So, having lined up his evidence as best he could, Mountbatten was now prepared to do battle with the formidable Winston, even if only indirectly through Ismay. Gone was the breezy tone when Mountbatten next wrote to Ismay. The suggestion that anyone should even contemplate publishing the Prime Minister's 1942 questions about the Dieppe disaster, and Ismay's reply of the time, angered him. He told Ismay that at least publication of the latter could be prevented: 'Legally you are the holder of copyright and he [Churchill] cannot publish it without your permission.' Ismay was advised to prevent publication of the document because it could only 'cause pain to the Canadians.' No mention was made of pain to Mountbatten.[37]

Mountbatten also took the opportunity to comment to Ismay on the latest draft of the Dieppe account that Churchill had sent him on 1 September. Angrily he denounced what he considered were Churchill's 'gratuitous' assertions. He particularly bristled at Churchill's statement, in the draft, that the Canadian Second Division lost 'nearly 70 per cent of the 5,000 men embarked.' Mountbatten angrily suggested that 'this figure can only be reached by adding in all the prisoners of war, all the wounded and all the killed.' Though casualty rates are routinely compiled in this fashion, Mountbatten objected to this as being 'a most pessimistic view to take and surely not one which our side should stress.' These remarks reveal Mountbatten's approach to history, which he viewed not as a dispassionate study of what happened but rather as a battlefield through which ran a line separating 'our side' from the other side. In closing, Mountbatten warned Ismay to keep Churchill in check. 'I am grateful', he wrote, 'that you intend to keep an eye on this Dieppe account because the people who know the true facts can certainly refute the statement he had originally contemplated publishing.'[38]

Since we have Mountbatten's comments on Churchill's draft, it is easy to see that he particularly objected to the statement that the Dieppe raid was revived 'on the initiative of Admiral Mountbatten'. This he crossed out. Churchill had also written:

> Before I left England for Cairo and Moscow on August 2, I knew that the operation was to be remounted. Though I took no part in the planning I was in principle favourable to an operation of this character at this time. I naturally supposed that it would be subjected to the final review of the Chiefs of Staff and Defence Committee [of the Cabinet] before whom I should certainly have the main issues brought prior to action had I not been abroad.

Beside this passage Mountbatten wrote, 'Please omit.' Crossed out was Churchill's factual statement that 'From the time when the enterprise was revived by Admiral Mountbatten, there is no written record of the revised plan being further examined, nor of any decision to launch it being taken by the Chiefs of Staff or by the Defence Committee or the War Cabinet.'[39]

Mountbatten's tone was much less abrupt when, on 4 September 1950, he wrote Churchill a letter full of glowing references to the great man. He explained the delay in answering 'Pug' Ismay's questions as being due to his determination 'to be quite certain that the replies should be thoroughly substantiated', which he asserted was now the case, as he had consulted very extensively with the people in a 'position to know'. On the question of responsibility, Mountbatten wrote: 'Following your great example I have never tried to evade responsibility, but it would have been improper for me to have claimed powers which were not mine.' On the question of initiative for the decision: 'You were (as ever) the moving spirit. . . .' As to who approved the plan, Mountbatten had by now decided to state firmly for the first time that 'You and the Chiefs of Staff went into the revived plans carefully', implying strongly, but still not quite saying, that they had given their approval. As to why so few knew, Mountbatten said that 'You decided to tell the Foreign Secretary but not the Defence Committee.' This completely ignored the fact that in July 1942 Mountbatten told, or rather strongly intimated to, General McNaughton, commanding the Canadian forces, that the War Cabinet had been consulted about *Jubilee* and had approved. As to why there were no records of decisions, the reason now advanced was that 'you [Churchill] and the Chiefs of Staff agreed to this.' A lawyer might pick through all these statements and note that Mountbatten did not actually say that the Chiefs of Staff had approved the decision to remount, or when. The main thrust of Mountbatten's reply was that it had been Churchill's decision, an explanation that would long continue to be the most popular, since the raid made so little sense militarily. As Lord Lovat later remarked, after reviewing how implausible the whole operation was, the raid must have gone forward for 'higher political considerations'. He added, 'I have little doubt that the Prime Minister's order to proceed was mandatory, and the reasons compelling.' Naturally Mountbatten preferred the version that said the raid was a military necessity; but if that argument would not fly, he was quite prepared to lay the responsibility at Churchill's feet. At least he was not claiming he, as Chief of Combined Operations, had the authority to launch on his own. As he admitted in later years: 'Of course we [Mountbatten and the three Force Commanders] had no authority to do more than put a proposal on these lines through me to the COS committee and then to the P.M.'[40]

Mountbatten took it upon himself to submit an account of Dieppe he had drafted for Churchill to consider including in his history of the war. It retained only Churchill's opening paragraph; the rest was entirely new. It did not say openly how and when he had received authorization (indeed, Mountbatten would never say). His draft implied, however, that Churchill and the Chiefs had ordered him to carry out the revived project (though neither Churchill nor Ismay could recall issuing such an order). Mountbatten was careful to leave Ismay an out. Perhaps in gratitude for Ismay's help, or perhaps because he feared contradiction, he told Churchill that 'I have read my letter and my redraft out to Pug Ismay on the telephone. He cannot remember the incidents but is clear that they must represent the facts.' This was a candid admission of Mountbatten's vulnerability in the absence of a single document that could substantiate the version that he pressed Churchill to publish. In later years, whenever the matter of approval by the Chiefs of Staff and the Prime Minister was raised, Mountbatten became less cautious, asserting with remarkable boldness, '. . . fortunately General Ismay remembered clearly what happened and confirmed my view that the P.M. and the COS approved the re-mounting of the Dieppe raid verbally only.'[41]

There is no evidence that Ismay ever said anything of the kind. This assertion, and indeed Mountbatten's history of the decision as submitted to Churchill, would seem to be another example of what Mountbatten's official biographer has called the Admiral's habitual determination to 'rewrite history with cavalier indifference to fact.' We have seen that not long after the event, in December 1942, when Churchill first suggested that an inquiry should be held, Ismay seemed to deny knowledge of how the decision had been reached. By 1950, however, after he had served as Mountbatten's Chief of Staff in India, Ismay was evidently willing to turn a deaf ear to Mountbatten's oral assertions. It is noteworthy that when Ismay came to write his own memoirs he passed over these difficult questions in silence. This did not help Mountbatten — but it did not hurt him either.[42]

Thus it came about that a truce of sorts settled over the history of Dieppe, with Mountbatten being allowed to propagate discreetly his version of events, while those in a position to know avoided either confirming or denying it. It was a truce that could be easily disturbed, and this undoubtedly helps to explain why Mountbatten always insisted Stacey's account was authoritative and avoided publishing his own memoirs or any detailed historical narrative of Dieppe, preferring to coach others from the sidelines or reminisce vaguely over a banquet table or in television interviews. In chatty gossip or private letters, Mountbatten could attribute almost anything he wanted to Ismay, so long as Ismay was not obliged to respond. Churchill's plan to publish the 1942 demand for an inquiry, and Ismay's embarrassed answers, would have shattered this truce. One can easily see why, from Mountbatten's perspective, it was vital that the documents of 1942 be suppressed. He soothingly suggested to Churchill that 'if you accept my redraft [of your chapter] the printing of your minute [of December 1942] to General Ismay and his reply is rendered unnecessary, the more so as Colonel Stacey's book deals with the important points very fully and with more recent knowledge.' Having said this, Mountbatten was prepared to be sychophantic, telling the old man how 'honoured and pleased I was to be called on to be of some service to you.'[43]

Churchill, now duly penitent for having beaten the bush for culprits, wrote Mountbatten on 12 September 1950 to thank him and to tell him that 'I have accepted practically verbatim your redraft.' This was literally true, for the published account differed from Mountbatten's version only in some minor details of punctuation and style. Churchill regretted that he could not remember all the details 'you mention', but he was willing to put this down to his poor memory. Evidently suspicious, however, that something was being slipped past him, Churchill noted again that 'I was abroad a fortnight before zero.' But, save for that one private qualification, Churchill fell into line with Mountbatten's version. 'Certainly I wanted a large raid in the summer of 1942,' he wrote, 'and of course the overall responsibility is mine.' Churchill also agreed not to publish his December 1942 minute asking why it had all happened.[44]

Perhaps the most extraordinary aspect of all this was that Churchill was willing to — and did — publish in his memoirs an account by someone else, the details of which he had no recollection, including the statement that 'I personally went through the plans' to remount the raid. Predictably the text Mountbatten offered was vague about times and places. Where there should have been specific details, or references to the files to substantiate Churchill's assertions, a footnote refers the reader to C.P. Stacey, who was credited with telling everything one needed to know 'most vividly'.[45]

Carrying all the authority of Churchill's great name, Mountbatten's account in *The Hinge of Fate* has served as bedrock for virtually every subsequent history of the Dieppe raid. The passages quoted most often are those in which Churchill shouldered responsibility for the decision to relaunch, together with the claim that the raid had been necessary and the results of great value:

> It was a costly but not unfruitful reconnaissance in force. Tactically it was a mine of experience. It shed revealing light on many shortcomings in our outlook. It taught us to build in good time various new types of craft and appliances for later use. We learnt again the value of powerful support by heavy naval guns in an opposed landing, and our bombardment technique, both marine and aerial, was thereafter improved. Above all it was shown that individual skill and gallantry without thorough organisation and combined training would not prevail, and that team work was the secret of success. This could only be provided by trained and organised amphibious formations. All these lessons were taken to heart. . . . Honour to the Brave. . . .

Quite naturally, no historian has thought to question whether these were in fact Churchill's conclusions. 'Sir Winston, above all, should know,' one author states after the ritual quotation about how necessary it all was. Some historians have followed such quotations with others from Mountbatten, to illustrate his complete 'agreement' with what Churchill had written. The way the two apparently independent accounts confirmed each other perfectly has been used to dispel doubts and uncertainty about why the raid was ever attempted.[46]

With this contribution to Churchill's history, Mountbatten had obliged Churchill to accept a very large measure of responsibility for the raid, even though no one could say when or how Churchill had given his approval. But even more important, he had managed to prevent Churchill from offering any new details, which would have been hard to square with the story Mountbatten had already told. Mountbatten had set a defensive moat around Stacey's account, to which Churchill's memoirs directed inquisitive readers, and which would remain the most authoritative for some time. Sadly, Churchill's promise that he would write some 'pretty big stuff' was never fulfilled. It would seem that Churchill the politician, who would have need of Mountbatten and Ismay were he to return to power, had triumphed over Churchill the historian. This possibility was foreshadowed when he wrote Ismay on 2 August: 'What we say about this is a matter for subsequent consideration, but we must at least know ourselves exactly what the facts were. . . .' In retrospect it was just as well that the Nobel Committee had no prize for history, only for literature.[47]

Still, Churchill's effort to write a history of the Dieppe raid had prompted a careful — indeed exhaustive — search of Combined Operations and Cabinet records by Mountbatten's supporters. None of the evidence needed to substantiate Mountbatten's version was found. Indeed, the inability to find any substantiation, after such exhaustive searches — in files still not yet vetted for release to the public, by officials with completely unrestricted access — speaks volumes about the plausibility of Mountbatten's account. Nevertheless, forewarned of Churchill's literary activity, Mountbatten had taken advantage of an opportunity to define and refine his version of events, an experience that would prove invaluable in the coming years when all the official British histories were being written and he was regularly consulted by their authors. Mountbatten had ready answers for them all. In positions that commanded respect — as Fourth Sea Lord, then as First Sea Lord, and finally as Chief of the Defence Staff — he was able to influence the way official history was written. After this bout with Churchill and his assistants Mountbatten, who the year before had been pressing the Government to honour a personal promise by Prime Minister Attlee to commission a full-scale official history of Combined Operations, changed his mind. Though he had demanded a study *in toto*, he now decided he preferred a narrow study confined to COHQ's 'contributions' to amphibious operations.[48]

Over the years Mountbatten retold his story with increasing confidence and panache. In a 1982 television interview thirty years after the event, he stated that the decision to remount Dieppe, after thousands had been briefed on the objectives, was based on his calculation 'that even if the Germans knew that an operation had been planned against Dieppe and then abandoned . . . the very last thing they'd ever imagine is that we would be so stupid as to lay on the same operation again. So I got the Prime Minister and Chiefs of Staff to agree to very special security measures — nothing about the remounting of the operation was put in writing anywhere.'[49]

Looking over this account, the historian must admit that it has a trace of plausibility. The operation had been severely compromised on several occasions, so that it was indeed imperative that the decision to remount be shared with the smallest possible number. All true enough. But this cannot explain why there was no record of it whatsoever. Modern government is based on the rigorous keeping of records. It is only with them that continuity of policy can be maintained and the experience necessary to redirect policy absorbed. Records are vital for fixing responsibility for decisions, rewarding the capable and weeding out the incompetent, as a government must do if it is to build a cadre of capable administrators. Without records a government is blind.[50]

Indeed, it is inconceivable that the Chiefs of Staff would have approved so tenuous and tricky an affair as this largest raid of the war without attaching condition or restrictions. On the two prior occasions when they had approved large operations, they had attached many qualifiers. Not recording a decision meant not recording conditions — issuing, in short, a blank cheque. Ordinarily the Chiefs were not inclined to give Mountbatten anything of the sort. Indeed, what Wildman-Lushington found in Combined Operations records was not that a record of the decision to remount Dieppe did not exist, but that it was allegedly being kept in the COS Secretariat's secret files.[51]

The implication of Mountbatten's claim that no record could be kept amounted to saying that the enemy, or unreliable personnel, could have had access to the most secret files of the COS secretariat — scarcely a credible supposition. If the Germans could have been privy to the most secret operational (O) series of COS papers, the war would have been as good as lost and the Chiefs of Staff might as well have gone out of the war-making business altogether.

It has been suggested that in stringently keeping secret the Dieppe raid, Mountbatten was acting like such great captains of the past as the American Stonewall Jackson, who was notorious for not informing his staff of his plans in order to guarantee surprise all round. But in the twentieth century, warfare in the Channel was a very different matter. British air and naval operations in the area, as well as intelligence-gathering missions, were constant. There had to be some way of preventing collisions in the dark (a point, incidentally, that even Stonewall Jackson should have observed, as he was shot by his own men, who did not know he was in their area). Elaborate precautions against such mishaps were regularly taken by the British government. The secretaries of the Chiefs of Staff Committee habitually routed the requisite information about planned operations in any given area to the appropriate agencies, particularly the Inter-Services Security Board, which was charged with maintaining security and co-ordinating with the deception planners. It was vital that the latter, in their attempt to confuse German intelligence, should not accidentally draw attention to areas where operations would actually take place. It is preposterous to suggest that the Chiefs would ever have countenanced Mountbatten's acting without the Board's co-operation and support, particularly as there had been so many security problems with *Rutter* that the Chiefs had even considered cancelling it for good. As the official history of British Intelligence during the Second World War has now revealed, none of the military intelligence service chiefs were warned of the decision to launch *Jubilee*, nor was the Inter-Services Intelligence Board or the Joint Intelligence Committee apprised. After Dieppe, rules were put in place so that the Board could never again be by-passed.[52]

One would like to know more about the entry Wildman-Lushington found in the Combined Operations files suggesting that a record was being kept *somewhere*, but this has not been detected by subsequent researchers. There are, however, scores of papers in the Combined Operations files clearly indicating that *Rutter* was being remounted, plans for the movements of troops, requests to keep landing-craft in the southern ports, and the like. But proof that the decision to launch had been approved is not to be found. When Hughes-Hallett was drafting his memoirs in 1971, Mountbatten reminded him that he should really write a bit on the 'only unrecorded decision of the war'. In a broadcast interview of 1972 he boasted: 'You can search the Cabinet offices — you'll find no records at all.' Thirty-five years of diligent searches by countless historians have indeed failed to produce a single assertion, oral or written, official or private by any participant, at the time or in later years, to substantiate Mountbatten's intimation that he had approval from the Chiefs. Pound died in 1943, but Brooke did not die until 1963, Ismay in 1965, and Portal in 1971. There was ample opportunity for all save Pound to offer corroboration.[53]

But was it really possible that Mountbatten had broken all the rules? There is much evidence that he was capable of doing so. A story he told on himself concerns naval exercises in the Mediterranean after the war in which he was being graded as a commander against his contemporaries. As he told it: 'I am afraid I pulled a fast one. I slipped my warrant telegraphist ashore at Gibraltar, on the pretext that he had a broken arm. Nobody paid much attention to him, and he was able to get right into the other ship's headquarters, and discover the movements of their ships. Then he relayed these to me on a portable transmitter. This was regarded in some circles as fearfully unfair. Well, possibly, I may still have had a lot to re-learn about handling ships, but I did know one thing about war: you can't always expect the enemy to play the game by Queensberry Rules.' When, in October 1943, Mountbatten was appointed Supreme Commander in South-East Asia, Brooke insisted that Mountbatten take as his Chief of Staff General Pownall, one of Brooke's most promising protégés. Pownall was instructed to report regularly to Brooke because Mountbatten was seen to be capable of acting without authority. Was Brooke thinking of Dieppe? When Beaverbrook later warned, 'Don't trust Mountbatten in any public capacity', was he too thinking of Dieppe? Could it be, as Mountbatten's official biographer suggests, that it was some memory of Dieppe that made Churchill reluctant to approve Mountbatten's promotion to First Sea Lord?[54]

The mystery of what kind of approval Mountbatten might have obtained for the Dieppe raid has been confronted unsuccessfully by numerous official British historians — and there is no better tradition of official history anywhere in the world than the British. An examination of their work reveals only confusion.

While Christopher Buckley, writing in a series of popular official histories, agrees with Stacey in supposing that the Chiefs of Staff gave their approval on 20 July, when they named Hughes-Hallett to be naval commander of the next large-scale raid, others have seen this as the first tentative step that was taken towards the creation of a permanent supporting force for amphibious operations and the designation of a standing commander for any appropriate contingency — what would after Dieppe be called J Force. Stephen Roskill, for one, saw that this was very different from approving the Dieppe operation. Writing while Mountbatten was First Sea Lord, he agreed with Mountbatten's claim that nothing was committed to paper; but on the subject of when and if the Chiefs had reached a decision, he neatly dodged the question by employing the passive voice and a vague qualifier in stating: 'The decision to remount the operation was taken by the Prime Minister in consultation only with Admiral Mountbatten, the Chief of Combined Operations; and the Chiefs of Staff.' What he meant by 'consultation' was never explained. A version of his book, intended as a reference source for internal British government use, called a 'confidential print', has no footnote for this sentence, though such prints normally have ample documentation. In 1964 Professor J.M.A. Gwyer, writing in the official volume on Grand Strategy, seemed to have another date. He prepared the groundwork by noting that 'On 27th July the Chiefs of Staff approved a broad policy directive to the Chief of Combined Operations, who was to be generally responsible for launching the operation.' On that day the Chiefs did indeed approve a general statement, defining the authority of the Chief of Combined Operations; but on careful reading it is quite clear that this did not give Mountbatten anything like final authority to remount *Rutter* as *Jubilee*. Indeed, there was no recorded discussion of any particular raid on the 27th, and therefore Gwyer's following statement that Mountbatten 'was to be generally responsible for launching *the* operation . . .' is both mistaken and misleading. As with Roskill, the confidential print of this book does not provide any reference for the supposed date of approval.[55]

More recently Professor F.H. Hinsley, in the 1981 second volume of the official history of British Intelligence in the Second World War, seems to have suspected something was wrong with the earlier accounts and proposes — indeed, asserts categorically — that 'The Chiefs of Staff gave their approval to *Jubilee* on 12 August, only a week before it was carried out', with a footnote indicating that this was a recorded decision, to be found in the minutes for that date. This at least indicates that Hinsley did not accept Mountbatten's story that the Chiefs had made a decision without recording it. But the minute speaks only of the approval of an 'outline plan' against an unidentified objective — this could mean Dieppe or any of a dozen other projects. The warning order that was used to launch the Dieppe raid speaks of the operation as taking place any time between 12 and 19 August. As Hinsley obliquely concedes, 12 August was therefore a very late date — indeed, ridiculously late — to approve an outline or preliminary plan. More importantly, no one on Mountbatten's staff ever claimed that Dieppe was the operation being referred to here. If it had been, the notice would surely have been placed in Combined Operations records, along with the other *Jubilee* papers — where, in fact, it does not appear. Finally, at the meeting of 12 August the Vice-Chief of the Imperial Staff, General Nye, was in attendance. But Nye, as we have noted, knew nothing at all about any decision.

With Brooke away in Cairo, Nye's agreement was required for any decision of the Chiefs of Staff.[56]

So after nearly twenty-five years of historical research by some of the best official historians in the western world — adding to the efforts of Churchill and the claims of Mountbatten — there is still this great enigma. But the matter of how much authorization was given for Dieppe can now be easily clarified. An operation requires orders, which generally state the authority under which they are issued; and even if they do not, the after-action report invariably does. When an operation is cancelled, as *Rutter* was, the authority to launch expires and the process of obtaining authority must begin again for any renewal. In the Combined (or after-action) Report issued in October 1942 for *Jubilee*, over Mountbatten's signature, beside paragraph 39 after a discussion of the cancellation of *Rutter*, there is the heading, 'New Directive to the Chief of Combined Operations'. At the conclusion of what seems like a quote from a Chiefs of Staff directive, the statement is made: 'It was under this Directive that the Chief of Combined Operations launched the operation.'[57]

This, then, is Mountbatten's original claim of authority, and is the one mentioned in Gwyer's history. But, as we have noted, the broad directive cited merely defines the authority of the Chief of Combined Operations and clearly did not give authorization to remount *Rutter*. It said that the Chiefs of Staff had to approve any outline plan, after which the Force Commanders would be appointed. It did not give authority — it merely spelled out the conditions under which Mountbatten could seek authority. In later interviews Mountbatten never again claimed that this or any other directive allowed him to launch a raid the size of Dieppe on his own. If confirmation is needed that this was not a directive to remount *Rutter*, the simple fact that it was not assigned an (O) operations classification would suffice.

The after-action report shows that, far from complying with that directive, Mountbatten acted the very next day as though he had authority. Annex 12 of the Combined Report on the raid indicates that on 28 July the Deputy Assistant Quartermaster General (for Raids) was informed that *Rutter* was being remounted under the code name *Jubilee*. The preliminary Operations orders were signed three days later, and the only authority cited was the same directive of 27 July. Though these orders were issued two days before Churchill left for the Middle East, he did not know of them. Had he known of them he would have been aware of the new code-name and would not have needed to cable from Moscow and Cairo to ask if the raid was on and when it might take place.[58]

Mountbatten's excuse for the absence of a record was the need to keep the operation secret. Even if this had been valid before the battle, he certainly could have cited the correct COS approval when the report was drafted in October, after the raid had taken place and the alleged need for maximum security had vanished. Here was *the* crucial flaw in Mountbatten's story, for though he had an alibi for why the approval had not been recorded before the raid, he had none for why it was not recorded after 19 August. Alive to the danger of being exposed, Mountbatten had tried to elevate the 27 July minute into something it was not. This was the clear indication of how the decision to mount *Jubilee* was taken: by Mountbatten, without authority — critical evidence overlooked by every subsequent historian. And it explains why Mountbatten's successors were so puzzled by the lack of records indicating approval. There was none.

What really happened can be pieced together from the well-scattered evidence. In Hughes-Hallett's papers there is a note from him to Mountbatten, dated 17 July, suggesting that he send to the 'Most Secret' distribution list — i.e. the top officers of COHQ — a 'draft information' chit informing them that an Operation *Jubilee* was to be mounted (without mentioning what the destination or objective would be). The explanation for the raid to be offered was that the 'Chiefs of Staff have directed that if possible an emergency operation is to be carried out during August to fill the gap caused by the cancellation of *Rutter*.' There is no evidence the Chiefs had ordered anything of the sort when Hughes-Hallett distributed his information chit. So Mountbatten had either already begun the deception, or he and Hughes-Hallett were anticipating they would get approval. In any case, the note implied that top staff were to be told that their services would not be required for *Jubilee* because everything would be left to the Force Commanders.[59]

This directive clearly indicates an attempt to restrict knowledge of *Jubilee* to the fewest people. But, intentionally or not, it also tipped off the staff to what was likely to happen, for it included the sentence: 'The locality and form of the new operation are being chosen so as to ensure that the training of individuals . . . will be as similar as possible to that which was given for *Rutter*.' It does not take much reading between the lines to see that if an 'emergency' substitute for *Rutter* was going to take place in the next month, with all the details being handled by the *Rutter* Force Commanders, and the operation was not going to require the services of the planners or any new training, then the only operation possible under these conditions was *Rutter* remounted.[60]

These tell-tale signs raise fundamental questions about Mountbatten's alibi: that the reason there was no record of COS approval was that the Chiefs had told him not to put anything on paper. It was not, in fact, possible to do an operation the size of Dieppe, involving so many participants, without creating a vast paper trail. Material had to be requisitioned, intelligence support requested, planes alerted, landing-crews prepared, the approval of the Canadian government had to be requested, etc. The notion that this could be done without touching pen to paper is preposterous. It is, *prima facie*, a figment of Mountbatten's imagination, and speaks volumes about his ignorance of military administration. Certainly it was not a concept that the three Service Chiefs could ever have entertained seriously. Given that *Jubilee* documents were going to be generated in the process of remounting (something the Chiefs fully understood), what harm to security could result from adding just a single sentence, viz., 'On such-and-such day the Chiefs of Staff approved the mounting of Operation *Jubilee*'? The answer is clearly none, and one must marvel at those historians who have accepted Mountbatten's claim that approval was not to be found because the Chiefs had ordered that it was not to be recorded. The internal COHQ notice that Hughes-Hallett asked Mountbatten to issue gives the lie to Mountbatten's version. Implicitly it recognized that the operation could not be remounted without something that looked like authorization, an admission that an official paper, or a reasonable facsimile, was required.[61]

Nevertheless the intention of the information chit was that most of Mountbatten's staff should be cut out of subsequent deliberations. Were Wildman-Lushington and Major-General Charles Haydon (Mountbatten's Chief of Staff and Deputy respectively) also to be cut out? In draft memoirs Hughes-Hallett later admitted that both Mountbatten's Chief of Staff and his Deputy were absent from a meeting on 11 July at which it was decided to make another attempt. Their names do not appear on a list given by Mountbatten to General McNaughton of COHQ officers in the know. Preposterous though this may sound, Hughes-Hallett seems to have intended to exclude them. These two key officers were also excluded from subsequent planning meetings for Dieppe, whereas for *Rutter* one or the other had always been present.[62]

Hughes-Hallett had also gone on to say in a note of 17 July to Mountbatten: 'In addition to the above local notice [the draft chit to senior COHQ officers], I think it essential that something should also be put out by the Chiefs of Staff, otherwise I shall certainly encounter difficulties in dealing with the Admiralty, and I dare say this will also arise with Bomber Command.' Accordingly he asked that a conclusion be circulated, i.e. an (O) series minute indicating that the Chiefs of Staff had directed the emergency operation, using so far as possible the same forces as had been designated for *Rutter*. The most amazing part of this document is that it reveals that Hughes-Hallett, Naval Force Commander, with the rank only of Captain, was setting out to do the liason work with Bomber Command and the Admiralty. Indeed, the record shows that Hughes-Hallett did go directly to the Chief of Bomber Command to arrange for the use of the very secret Gee navigation system as a navigational aid for the raiding force. This and subsequent activity clearly indicate that Mountbatten's Chief of Staff and Deputy were being cut out — for sensitive co-ordination was, by rights, the work of either of these two senior officers. Hughes-Hallett was just one of three Force Commanders, in fact the most junior. This paper trail also makes clear how much Hughes-Hallett later dissimulated, when, as we have seen, he wrote Stacey on 30 December 1952: 'I have no doubt that the whole plan must have been gone through yet again some time in July or early August, when *Jubilee* was decided upon, but I was not present and do not know exactly what happened.' Since he was doing all the high-level paper work, he knew better than anyone else exactly what was and what was not being reviewed.[63]

Still, it seems clear that Mountbatten would have preferred to proceed with approval. The records of the Secretariat of the Chiefs of Staff — which at war's end, if not sooner, were kept with the most secret Cabinet documents — show that, contrary to much of what Mountbatten later said, he did seek on 17 July to have the Chiefs of Staff Committee minutes record the decision to remount. Mountbatten submitted on that date a draft of the proposed COS minute that contains wording identical to that proposed by Hughes-Hallett, to the effect that the Chiefs of Staff had ordered him to mount a substitute for the cancelled *Rutter*, using the same troops. General Hollis, the Secretary to the Chiefs of Staff Committee, who received this draft proposal, was in the habit of noting on such requests the final disposition. If accepted, the number of the meeting would be written down in the margin. There is no such notation and no indication in the minutes that the Chiefs of Staff ever acted on Mountbatten's draft minute. In short, Mountbatten's suggestion had not been accepted, and he never got the directive in the minutes he had requested. Despite this, he went ahead and launched the raid. In the voluminous literature on Dieppe, no author has confronted this startling possibility. Churchill, however, briefly considered but rejected it: 'I cannot believe he [Mountbatten] was allowed to do this without higher authority becoming responsible.'[64]

Still we are left with many mysteries. Why did Mountbatten decide to go ahead without authority? Was Churchill really the major force, imposing the raid on Mountbatten despite the lack of approval by the Chiefs, as Mountbatten sometimes hinted and Roskill seems to have implied? Or did Mountbatten go ahead and launch the raid, without authority, for his own reasons? If it was the latter, two very difficult questions must be asked concerning the apparent passivity of the Chiefs of Staff. Why did none of them find out and stop him? Why did they not discipline him when they realized the full magnitude of what he had done?

These vital questions can be answered — but not easily. The official *Jubilee* records are among the most incomplete of any major operation of the war. The minutes of Force Commanders' meetings for the revived operation (with just a few exceptions) have disappeared from the official files. They were destroyed after the war, or so Mountbatten reported in confidence to Hughes-Hallett — a revelation he shared with no one else. Every new attempt to provide answers revealed more missing files. The explanations were sometimes more mystifying than the lacunae. According to one of Mountbatten's assistants, A.P.W. Maclellan, in 1962: ' . . . it is known that Mr. Churchill removed the odd paper from time to time, and I am informed that Field Marshal Montgomery . . . also removed some.' Files known to have existed in the post-war period in the originating departments, such as the Marine Records on Dieppe, mysteriously disappeared before being deposited at the Public Records Office. For historians the problem of a surprisingly incomplete dossier has been further aggravated by the endless commentary on what is left.[65]

As recently as 1978 one participant observed: 'For thirty years the truth has been wrapped in pink ribbons with saccharin added to sweeten the taste. . . . Time rolls on, but the buck passing is periodically renewed with explanations that draw still farther from the facts.' Thirty years of doctoring the records and manipulating the evidence prevent the truth from being established by anything save a very careful examination of the evidence and an equally painstaking analysis of the situation in which the principal decision-makers found themselves. As there are many parallel threads to follow, it is not a task for the faint-hearted. But careful analysis of the context does yield the answers, and they are interesting. They provide us with nothing less than a panorama of the war at a moment when it seemed to be well on its way to being lost by the Allies.[66]

3

# The Crisis at the Top:
# Churchill's Woes

How, Churchill asked Ismay in August 1950, had the Dieppe affair been related to the supreme direction of the war? By this he meant: What was the responsibility of the Chiefs of Staff and the ministers who had stayed behind in August 1942 while he, Sir Alan Brooke, and their party had travelled to Cairo and Moscow? It was a fair question that can best be answered only after we have examined the individual responsibility of each Chief of Staff, not just Mountbatten. But certainly Churchill was being disingenuous when he asked it. In his government virtually nothing of any significance happened without his having a hand in it, one way or another. In a very real sense the Prime Minister himself represented the supreme direction of the war. One can easily understand why Churchill placed Mountbatten and Montgomery at the top of his list of possible culprits behind Dieppe, but the historian who excludes the chief player upon the stage would be very remiss. Churchill's ability to deny responsibility was legendary. His physician, Sir Charles Wilson, recorded that Churchill 'had to school himself not to think about things when they had gone wrong, for he found that he could not live with his mistakes and keep his balance. This urge to obliterate had, in the course of time, grown into a cast of mind in which he seemed incapable of seeing tht he has been at fault.' Perhaps Mountbatten was thinking of this foible when he asked Ismay, in August 1950, to jog Churchill's memory into recalling that Combined Operations Headquarters was trying to carry out his own directive to unleash a vigorous raiding program.[1]

The relative merits of Churchill's and Mountbatten's attempts to implicate each other are central to the question of responsibility for Dieppe. It is highly probable that Mountbatten exaggerated, to cover himself, when he wrote to Churchill that 'You were (as ever) the moving spirit' and 'you and the Chiefs of Staff agreed to this'; but another possibility, that Churchill drove Mountbatten to do something questionable, is simply too plausible to be ignored. How much truth lay behind Mountbatten's suggestion that Dieppe played an important role in Churchill's hopes and plans ('to prepare for the re-invasion of the continent') can be determined only after first examining the general situation in which the Government and the Prime Minister found themselves when crucial decisions were being taken in 1941-2. This was a time when Churchill's mental and emotional balance was under considerable stress. That the Prime Minister was nearly at the end of his rope was evident not only to his physician but throughout Westminster, and in the capitals of Britain's principal allies. A complex concatenation of old memories and new disasters had combined to make Churchill vulnerable both to his political rivals and to his more un-scrupulous Tory colleagues. Following the harsh rules of nature, wolves circled round the old man, harrying him in what must have seemed like the eleventh hour of a cold winter's night. And this drama, which both Church-ill and his opponents later agreed should be covered up, undoubtedly helped shape the principal strategic decisions during that fateful spring and summer. It contributed to the decision not to attempt a Second Front in 1942 and to the substitution of a North African invasion (*Torch*) and the Dieppe raid, as well as to Churchill's decision to confront Stalin in the first summit meeting between a western leader and the master of the Kremlin.

The main lines of the drama can be easily reconstructed. There was first of all a long series of disasters associated with Churchill's name, which recalled to many the fact that in his earlier career he had been closely associated with calamities. The recent disasters in Norway, the Low Coun-tries, and France in 1940; in Greece, Crete, North Africa, and Hong Kong in 1941; in Singapore, the Indian Ocean, and Libya in 1942 — recalled earlier blows: Gallipoli in 1916, the India Bill of 1935, and the Abdication Crisis of 1936. To many Churchill in 1942 was beginning to look like a Jonah who might have to be cast overboard if Britain were to survive. His age (68), his idiosyncracies, his cast-iron values from a dusty past now seemed to be liabilities.

Disasters abroad, combined with secret back-stabbing at home, devas-tated Churchill. He was naturally prone to bouts of depression (perhaps accentuated by his massive consumption of alcohol), but the string of calamities that began in the late spring of 1941 provoked a year later a serious attack of what he himself called his 'black dog mood'. Although Churchill's desperate battle with severe depression was hotly denied when first made public in the memoirs of his physician, Churchill's official biographer, Martin Gilbert, has admitted that there was some truth in the report. Their severity, however, was much greater than he has acknowledged.[2]

Churchill's depression may have begun in a relatively minor way with the fall of Crete in May 1941 and the loss of Cyrenaica in Libya, which he admitted represented a 'sudden darkening of the landscape' and was particularly 'painful', coming after 'we had been cheered by a long succession of victories over the Italians. . . .' The press was harsh. Implicitly quoting Churchill against himself, *The Times* noted that the British people would not stand any more 'magnificent evacuations such as those in Norway, Dunkirk, Greece and now Crete'. Such criticism stung Churchill, who complained to Ismay that it was 'impossible to run a war efficiently if so much time has to be devoted to justifying one's actions in the House of Commons.'[3]

To restore British morale, Churchill pinned his hopes on a long-awaited counterattack in North Africa, Operation *Battleaxe*, to be launched by General Wavell on 15 June 1941 against the recently arrived Panzer force of General Rommel. Churchill — who had good reason to be hopeful, since Enigma intercepts provided decoded messages revealing the weaknesses of Rommel's position — telegraphed Wavell on 9 June, saying that 'The battle may well be the turning point of the whole campaign.' Air Marshal Sir Charles Portal, the Chief of the Air Staff, seconded this opinion when he said that 'The outcome of this battle must be of supreme and possibly decisive strategic importance to the Middle East and the whole war. Its political effect will be profound and world wide.' These expectations had stimulated the War Cabinet and Churchill to prod Wavell to an early attack, which resulted in a complete débâcle that not only failed to redeem the honour of British arms after Greece and Crete but helped to create the image of a most effective opponent in Rommel, the 'Desert Fox'. Churchill later admitted that this defeat was a 'most bitter blow', and that for some hours he was beside himself wandering 'about the valley disconsolately'. In the Foreign Office the Permanent Under-Secretary, Alex Cadogan, reacted in similar fashion. It was all, he noted, 'most depressing'. Churchill was soon given a respite when the long-anticipated engagement, *Crusader*, finally took place in mid-November and produced a brief victory over Rommel on the Libyan coast. But it soon became clear that the initial promise of a substantial victory would not be realized. Privately Churchill was 'very depressed' over the failure. To Auchinleck, the British Commander in the Libyan desert, Churchill wired a peremptory demand for an explanation 'from you about defeat of our armour by inferior numbers. The disappointment', Churchill admitted, 'cuts very deep.'[4]

He had not recovered from that disappointment before a new string of disasters took shape. Despite the specific warnings of his most senior naval advisers and General Smuts, Churchill had insisted on sending two of Britain's few capital ships — the *Prince of Wales* and the *Repulse* — to Singapore in November 1941 to bolster confidence among Britain's allies in the Far East. Hugh Dalton noted in his diary: 'The proposal to send them out without an aircraft carrier was minuted against right up through the Admiralty, including the first Sea Lord and the First Lord.' Subsequent research has confirmed those observations. As Russell Grenfell has observed:

> The principal cause [of so dangerously exposing capital ships to air attack without accompanying air cover] was the pressure in London of a Minister of Defence [Churchill] so convinced of his own individual competence as a master of naval strategy that he was prepared to ignore the advice of his professional naval experts and force upon them measures for the naval defence of Malaya which they clearly did not like.[5]

As soon as he had weakened Admiralty opposition, Churchill began to boast of the effect these ships would have, telling Roosevelt on 2 November that 'There is nothing like having something that can catch and kill anything.' On 7 December Japanese forces struck Pearl Harbor, and other American positions in Hawaii and the Philippines, and simultaneously British positions in Hong Kong and Malaya. Three days later the *Prince of Wales* and the *Repulse*, after an attack by Japanese aircraft, lay at the bottom of the ocean. The American historian, Samuel Eliot Morison, wrote of this disaster that 'The Allies lost face throughout the Orient and began to lose confidence in themselves.'[6]

In a system of representative government, disasters sooner or later lead to political difficulties. On 21 January, Eden and Beaverbrook tried to persuade Churchill that he needed to take steps to shuffle the government and throw his critics off guard, but they found him 'tired and depressed . . . inclined to be fatalistic about the House, . . . [maintained] that [the] bulk of Tories hated him, that he had done all he could and would be only too happy to yield to another; that Malaya, Australian Government's intransigence and "nagging" in House was more than any man could be expected to endure.' A long speech to Parliament, later repeated over the radio, seemed to stabilize the situation, but the toll was heavy.[7]

Field Marshal Smuts, to whom Churchill had complained of his burden, was pained

> to think of all his energy thus absorbed, . . . taken off the grim business of war which is his real job. Democracy does really involve a cruel waste. How can a man find time and proper concentration for some of the hardest and most fateful problems of all time, when he has continually to pause and prepare for and make speeches which surely involve an immense amount of physical and mental energy? I think not so much the war as his own people are consuming him, literally eating him up, and I fear he will not stand this cruel process for too long.[8]

On 15 February came the fall of Singapore, the much-touted Gibraltar of the Far East, to a relatively small Japanese attack force. Vast numbers of prisoners were taken and the evidence soon began to come in that there had been no will to resist. Eden's secretary, Oliver Harvey, was appalled at the '. . . deplorable behaviour of all responsible in Singapore. No preparations, troops refusing to fight, looting by troops . . . officials leaving their posts — 60,000 British troops beaten by 5,000 Japs. It must be hard to beat as a national disgrace. Many disturbing resemblances with the fall of France.' Sir Charles Wilson noted that Churchill was 'stupefied' by what he regarded as a disgrace. In Wilson's judgement the event left a scar on his mind. Churchill admitted that it was the most shameful moment of his life. Months later Wilson saw Churchill sitting in his bathroom enveloped in a towel, interrupting his drying to survey the floor gloomily and exclaim, 'I cannot get over Singapore.'[9]

When the Prime Minister's former private secretary, John Colville, then serving in the RAF, heard Churchill's address on Singapore over the radio, he noted the plaintive tone and 'the nature of his words and the unaccustomed speech and emotion with which he spoke'. He became immediately convinced that Churchill was being sorely pressed by critics and opponents at home. The Prime Minister's bodyguard, Inspector Thompson, who had been with him through numerous crises (such as an almost-fatal accident and near financial ruin), was disturbed by Churchill's condition at this time. 'During my period of guarding him — beginning in 1921 — I have never seen him so disheartened. He could take the worst sort of knock, but this seemed one that was beyond his control. It was almost as if, through an unexampled carelessness, he had caused the death of one of his own children. These were bitter days. He could not sleep or eat.' Beaverbrook later commented that this was 'Churchill's darkest hour.' The weight of the burden, Beaverbrook said, 'would have crushed any other man.' Indeed Thompson, convinced that Churchill was about to crack, succeeded where his physician had failed in persuading Churchill to take a rest.[10]

Churchill now began to play with the idea of resigning. In a discussion on Eden's earlier career, Churchill told Eden on 27 April that 'one ought not to be afraid to drop out for a bit. . . . It was a mistake to believe that if one had once played a great part one would be forgotten.' His flagging morale coincided with his increasing inability to produce new excuses for the continued setbacks. Malcolm MacDonald, who saw Churchill on the eve of the debate on Singapore, found the Prime Minister under no illusions about his plummeting popularity. Churchill complained: 'I am like a bomber pilot. I go out night after night, and I know that one day I shall not return.' But some still thought Churchill demonstrated all his old skills when he finally met Parliament in secret session over Singapore. Hugh Dalton felt the Prime Minister had said 'enough, but not too much, on Singapore. . . Many different persons and sections have been blamed, meanwhile it would do no good and would only divert active men from the immediate business of the war to hold an inquiry.'[11]

Most observers, however, were deeply alarmed at the prospect that Churchill's grip was weakening — particularly Franklin Roosevelt, who cabled a tonic message on 18 February:

> I realize how the fall of Singapore has affected you and the British people. It gives the well-known back seat drivers a field day but no matter how serious our setbacks have been . . . we must constantly look forward. . . . I hope you will be of good heart in these trying weeks because I am very sure that you have the great confidence of the masses of the British people. I want you to know that I think of you often and I know you will not hesitate to ask me if there is anything you think I can do.[12]

Churchill reshuffled his Cabinet in February and this produced an explosion with Beaverbrook, whose exclusion from the War Cabinet made him bitter and resentful — he refused to work with Churchill's new arrangement — and the clash took its toll. Averell Harriman, who saw Churchill frequently in this period, was particularly concerned. In March he warned the President that he was 'worried about the Prime Minister — both his political status and his own spirits. . . . Although the British are keeping a stiff upper lip, the surrender of their troops at Singapore has shattered confidence to the core — even in themselves, but more particularly in their leaders.' What really troubled Harriman was that the PM had 'not been able to stand up to this adversity with his old vigor'.[13]

Churchill surmounted the crisis, but only with difficulty. Rarely at a loss for words, or to conceive vast historical panoramas, he replied on 20 February to Roosevelt's cabled message of concern by confessing that 'I find it difficult to realize how gravely our British affairs have deteriorated since December 7. We have suffered the greatest disaster in our history at Singapore, and other misfortunes will come thick and fast upon us.' But he went on to reassure the President that 'everything is now solid' and asserted that the pressure 'has never been dangerous'. He proclaimed that 'Democracy has to prove that it can provide a granite foundation for war against Tyranny.' Although he admitted, 'I do not like these days of personal stress and I have found it difficult to keep my eye on the ball', he expressed confidence that he now had everything in hand. But this was just bold talk, designed to conceal his vulnerability. A week later Churchill's daughter, Mary Soames, noted in her diary: 'Papa is at a very low ebb . . . he is not too well physically and he is worn down by the continuous crushing pressure of events.' The next day Clementine Churchill wrote to her sister that 'These are . . . days of anguish for Winston so full of strength & yet so impotent to stem this terrible tide in the Far East.' She thought that part of the reason for her husband's depression was his over-dependence for moral support on Beaverbrook, who she felt should be dropped from the Cabinet. Writing to Churchill on 19(?) February, she revealed the depth of her concern: 'My Darling — Try ridding yourself of this microbe which some people fear is in your blood — Exorcise this bottle Imp and see if the air is not clearer and purer'.[14]

Churchill's state was no secret. In Cape Town, Smuts was deeply concerned, saying that it was his 'constant fear' that Churchill 'will break down and there is none to replace him.' Less than two weeks later Smuts was bemoaning 'our complete dependence on one man and he an old man.' In Washington, Roosevelt was sufficiently apprised of the situation to continue administering a twice-monthly dose of the Rooseveltian tonic. On 18 March the President sent another long cable that attempted to show how much he felt and shared Churchill's dilemma:

> I am sure you know that I have been thinking a lot about your troubles during the past month. We might as well admit the difficult military side of the problems; and you have the additional burdens which your delightful unwritten Constitution puts your form of government into in war times just as much as in peace time . . .

Roosevelt went on to add that he recognized that Churchill was getting a drubbing at the hands of the press and the so-called opinion-makers:

> Neither one of us is much plagued by the news stories which, on the whole, are not so bad. But literally we are both menaced by the so-called interpretive comment by a handful or two of gentlemen who cannot get politics out of their heads in the world crisis, who have little background and less knowledge, and who undertake to lead public opinion on that basis.

Roosevelt concluded by giving Churchill an intimate glimpse into his own presidential style and suggested it might help:

> I know you will keep up your optimism and your grand driving force but I know you will not mind if I tell you that you ought to take a leaf out of my notebook. Once a month I go to Hyde Park for four days, crawl into a hole and pull the hole in after me. I am called on the telephone only if something of really great importance occurs. I wish you would try it , and I wish you would lay a few bricks or paint another picture.[15]

Roosevelt could see what Churchill perhaps refused to recognize — that his problems were far from over. Though the editor of *The Times* called the Cabinet reshuffle a 'really . . . large sweep, capable of re-invigorating the conduct of the war and public confidence', in March public dissatisfaction with the Government's conduct of the war reached 50 per cent, while only 35 per cent said they were satisfied.[16]

What started as an oscillation in mood, soon became a crisis of government. Close advisers and cabinet members were appalled by the sudden deterioration in Churchill's work-habits. In March, Eden complained to Cadogan that '. . . there has been no direction of the war. War Cabinet doesn't function — there hasn't been a meeting of the Defence Committee. There's no hand on the wheel. (Probably due to the PM's health).' Meanwhile most observers continued to see nothing but drift. Two months later the complaints had grown. 'I have never thought so ill of the PM,' Hugh Dalton wrote in his diary in May, 'nor been so vexed by him before. He talks more than half the time, and has clearly not concentrated his mind on the details for the subject at all.'[17]

At the end of May, Churchill seemed to recover, but while he was in Washington in conference with the President, Roosevelt handed him a telegram that announced the fall of Tobruk. Churchill at first refused to believe that 33,000 Allied troops had surrendered after only a brief skirmish with half as many German troops. The American Secretary of War, Henry L. Stimson, a fierce adversary of the Prime Minister's in the strategic debate, was present and he noted in his diary: 'I was very sorry for Churchill. He was evidently staggered by the blow of Tobruk and showed it in his speech and manner, although he bore up bravely.' Churchill left the President, to mull the news over. Sir Charles Wilson 'found him pacing his room.' Turning on him, Churchill broke out: '"Tobruk has fallen". I am ashamed I cannot understand why Tobruk gave in. More than 30,000 of our men put their hands up. If they won't fight . . .' — his speech trailed off.[18]

Soviet officials were also aware of what was happening to Churchill. Ivan Maisky, Soviet ambassador to Britain, recounted his impressions in July 1942 when the Prime Minister, under the influence of 'bad news' or 'whisky', seemed unable to control his reactions. 'At times', Maisky noted, 'his head jerked in a strange sort of way, and then one felt that in reality he is already an old man . . . and that only a frightful concentration of will and consciousness maintains Churchill's capacity to act and fight.'[19]

A lesser man might have fallen from power. Not Churchill. His survival was later explained as stemming primarily from his indomitable spirit, from his ruthless honesty no less than from the effects of his stirring eloquence. His rhetorical gifts were given great prominence in the crucial volume of his war memoirs. In *The Turn of the Tide*, which includes long extracts from speeches and hundreds of pages of his minutes, Martin Gilbert has succumbed to this powerful but essentially misleading explanation of crucial events by quoting long stretches of the great man's witty, perceptive, and dramatic prose, ranging from maxims to cyclonic speeches. One does not, however, survive the wolves of politics by pretty phrases but rather by cajoling, disarming, and, if necessary, tricking one's opponents. And most of this sort of activity, in which Churchill excelled, is obscured both in Churchill's memoirs of the war and in the official biography.

Churchill was fertile in expedients as he clung determinedly to power, in ways that were not always above-board. At the most rudimentary level there was his claim to superior wisdom. Churchill had not made a mistake in Norway in 1940; on the contrary, Hitler had made 'a cardinal political and strategic error'. There was the technique of the rhetorical surprise. When everyone was extolling Dunkirk as a defeat turned into victory, Churchill chose to to confound his admirers by denouncing the fools who were glorifying the event. He called it instead a 'colossal military disaster' and soberly stated that 'Wars are not won by evacuations.' There was also the technique of simply being out of the country when things were likely to be going wrong. Admittedly his poor health partly explains the five weeks Churchill spent in the United States while large chunks of the empire came crashing down with Japan's first blows. But he was also out of the country in June 1942 when Rommel's offensive finally achieved its predictable goal of capturing the garrison at Tobruk. Then there was the technique of Jovian insouciance, as applied to the miserable fiasco of the expedition to Dakar in August 1940 when, as he later wrote, 'I decided that no explanations should be offered, and Parliament respected my wish.' There was also the technique of blaming the military. 'The decision to send the Army to Greece,' was, he asserted blandly, 'freely taken by the men on the spot without the slightest pressure from home.' He also used more complex strategies that tended to immobilize his opponents. In December 1941, in an attempt to prevent Britain's Ambassador to the Soviet Union, Sir Stafford Cripps, from carrying out his threat to resign and resume his seat in Parliament to criticize Churchill's Russian policy, he sent Eden to Russia to soothe Stalin's and Cripps' anxiety with words, even though Britain had nothing to spare at that time in the way of equipment or men to help the Soviet Union.[20]

But as disaster piled upon disaster, Churchill had to dig deep into his bag of tricks. The repercussions of the fall of Singapore in February 1942 required an enormously complex holding-action that defies any attempt at brief description. He had first of all to head off a possible cabal led by Eden and Cripps. Stealing their thunder, he now announced that he was prepared to assent to Stalin's territorial demands, at least so far as recognizing the 1940 Russian seizure of the Baltic states. He also accepted the necessity of paying lip-service to General Marshall's proposal of a sacrifice gesture on Russia's behalf across the Channel — Operation *Sledgehammer* — and recognized the need to appease Cripps by inviting him into the War Cabinet and turning over to him the leadership of the House. This last move was particularly crafty. It ensured Cripps' doom by obliging him to speak, and speak again, until nature had its way and his well-known capacity for malapropisms was abundantly demonstrated to the House. Then, for good measure, Churchill pounced on Cripps' interest in the Indian question, packing him off to India to deal with the prickly, not to say intractable, Mahatma Gandhi. Churchill was not, however, completely successful in his strategy of co-opting possible opponents. Try as he might, he could not get Attlee, Beaverbrook, and Cripps to work in the same Cabinet and so Beaverbrook resigned.

Beaverbrook was in a vindictive mood, telling his editors it was time to 'veer leftwards'. Churchill reacted characteristically with gestures of appeasement, one of which was his dramatic appointment of Beaverbrook's protégé, Lord Louis Mountbatten, to the Chiefs of Staff Committee. But Churchill did not delude himself that this would be enough to satisfy Beaverbrook. Though Churchill was himself determined to oppose Stalin's latest territorial demands, he let Beaverbrook believe that the real opponent was Roosevelt. Knowing how keen his friend was to plead Stalin's cause, Churchill played up to Beaverbrook's vanity, convincing him that he was the man to make Roosevelt abandon his firmly stated opposition to granting Soviet demands while the war was on. The resulting mission to Washington, which greatly puffed up Beaverbrook, had the not entirely coincidental effect of keeping him out of the country for months — chasing, to use Stimson's characterization of Roosevelt's intellectual processes, errant moonbeams bouncing across the walls of a darkened room.

Then there was the classic case of the motion for a Vote of Censure after the fall of Tobruk on 21 June. This debate book place on 1 July — the very day German forces captured El Alamein, 130 miles inside Egypt and 80 miles from Cairo. The mover of the motion, Sir John Wardlaw-Milne, felt that Churchill was interfering disastrously in military affairs. Churchill apparently confessed to him that maybe he *was* having a hard time and might give up the Ministry of Defence, but pleaded for gentleness; he was a monarchist and the Vote of Censure would be all the easier to accept if the mover proposed HRH the Duke of Gloucester as his successor. This proposal, the instant Wardlaw-Milne uttered it, brought howls from the house and a huge grin to Churchill's face. But such ruses could hardly be repeated indefinitely and, while admiring their virtuosity, his political opponents knew that a cat had only so many lives.[21]

What caused Churchill most concern was not the activity of his parliamentary critics but rather the possibility of defections from his immediate circle, a possibility that had been growing since June 1941 when Anthony Eden had spoken to his aides of the 'great need' for a Minister of Defence 'independent of the PM'. By October 1941 Harold Macmillan, the Parliamentary Secretary to the Minister of Supply, had written Beaverbrook to suggest that Churchill's monopoly of power, domestic and foreign, could be challenged. As Macmillan analysed the situation, 'The Political system is bad. The House of Commons is very restive. The press is hostile.' He attributed the mood first and foremost to 'our impotence to help Russia by direct military effort . . . compounded by a lack of grip by the government on internal questions, the continuance in office of the old gang which are unpopular along with some of the new gang who are largely regarded as failures.' Macmillan concluded that 'all the symptoms are developing which marked the end of the Asquith coalition . . . and the formation of the Lloyd George coalition'. Newspaper editors were beset by indications that Churchill's own ministers were 'highly critical' of their chief and were known to call him 'an old fool', apparently without much concern about who might hear. The catalyst was Cripps, who in the fall of 1941 had openly threatened to quit his post in Russia and come back to challenge Churchill's seeming indifference to the Soviet Union's problems. Beaverbrook was encouraged to challenge the Prime Minister on the same grounds. Already by January 1942 Harold Nicolson was attending cabals of Conservatives where all — save himself, he tells us — were agreed that Churchill 'must be brought down'. The group included close friends of Eden's: R.A. (Rab) Butler (Parliamentary Under-Secretary for Foreign Affairs) and Richard Law, Viscount Cranborne (Secretary of State for the Dominions). The possibility that such a group could work better with the Deputy Prime Minister, Clement Attlee, was widely commented upon. From a different side of the political spectrum Hugh Dalton, who headed the Board of Trade, joined in May those who sought to challenge Churchill. By July there were signs of a much more important defection — that of Attlee, who had given the Government important support during the Vote-of-Censure debate and had not hesitated to discipline Bevan and seven other Labour deputies who had voted for the motion. On 6 July he was convinced that the crisis could not be papered over and sent Eden a long memorandum on British military failures, with the suggestion that it might be made public. This was patently an invitation to a political alliance against Churchill. Even Brendan Bracken, who was given to suggesting that he was Churchill's un-acknowledged heir, wavered in his support. The list of defectors was growing ominously.[22]

The most direct consequence of the pressures building on Churchill was that he became ever more insistent on some convincing demonstration of Britain's fighting ability. His physician noted it well: 'My diary for 1942 has the same backcloth to every scene: Winston's conviction that his life as Prime Minister could be saved only by a victory in the field.' Brendan Bracken agreed: 'The Prime Minister must win his battle in the desert or get out.'[23]

In the light of this, Churchill might have given Mountbatten encourage-ment of a vague sort to undertake a raid on Dieppe. And being disappointed by the failure to embark on *Rutter*, after so much work had gone into its preparation, he might also have asked how soon another raid of that scope could be mounted. Given the intense psychological pressures that weighed on him, his unrecorded encouragement for the disastrous Dieppe raid might easily have disappeard into his subconcious.

But this conclusion still leaves unanswered many questions that we will have to try to deal with in the following chapters. Was Mountbatten responding only to pressures from Churchill, or did he have his own objectives? How could a raid at Dieppe have fitted into the calculations of one or the other — or both? Why a raid and why at Dieppe? Why, with military resources so tight, use them up in so hopeless a task? We can answer these questions more easily if we first examine the question that was uppermost in Churchill's mind in the spring and summer of 1942, which was how to put Britain on the offensive. But where? The little port of Dieppe did not figure in his initial plans, or for that matter in Mountbatten's.

4

# Three Powers in
# Search of a Strategy

That Churchill should gamble everything in 1942 on winning a battle in the Libyan desert does not appear at first sight to be a logical answer to the problem of how to strike a blow at Germany. The strangely winding road of his strategic thinking (which always kept in mind Moscow's expectations) led from France, to the desert, to Dieppe. Churchill's strategic vision and how he tried to sell it to his allies — a difficult task, since they found his proposals to be inimical to their own strategic priorities — is our subject in this chapter. Having explored this question, we will be in a better position to understand how Dieppe might have become enmeshed in the package he tried to sell to Stalin.

It was only after a long and tortured debate that Churchill and his government came to pile all their gambling stakes on the Libyan desert. It began in June 1940 when the French army lay broken under the murderous Wehrmacht, as it became apparent that inflicting real damage on Hitler's Germany had become virtually impossible. This should not have been Britain's problem alone, but until Pearl Harbor the United States clung desperately to the illusion of isolationism. The Soviets, until they were invaded, hoped they could continue to ride the tiger and pick the bones of Hitler's prey at little cost to themselves; while in both Britain and America, Communist-party members were supporting Stalin's professions of loyalty to the Molotov-Ribbentrop pact by sabotaging war industries. Although a solution to the strategic dilemma of how to hit out at Germany was beyond Britain's capacity to resolve, the public — steeped in the myth of imperial greatness — refused to recognize that Britain had been strategically defeated. As Basil Liddell-Hart put it, the British people were 'instinctively stubborn and strategically ignorant'. Listening only to Churchill's speeches and his ringing prophecy of ultimate victory, they were possessed of an utterly unfounded confidence. In matters of grand strategy, the British nation sank into a 'sublime stupidity'.[1]

It was, however, universally conceded that the French army was gone for good, and almost as widely recognized that no British army could defeat Germany without assistance. Churchill might talk very boldly — 'Britain will fight on, if necessary for years, . . . if necessary alone. . . . We shall go back.' But in fact he privately agreed with the consensus of the military professionals that the German army ought not to be challenged until it was on the verge of collapse. Still, a plan of action was needed.[2]

The only conceivable strategy was one in which the defensive element prevailed substantially over the offensive: Britain and the Commonwealth would try to set up a ring of air and sea power to contain the Axis and prevent its further expansion. At the earliest opportunity the ring would be gradually tightened and cause Germany's eventual collapse. Initially the offensive element would consist of free forces within occupied Europe — as yet very small in number — that were prepared to undertake guerilla activities against the occupying armies. This would be supported from without by Special Operations until, in the final stage, internal revolt reached its peak. Only then — and not before — would a relatively small British Army force land and administer the final thrust. This conception was succintly expressed in the fall of 1940 when an American admiral, Robert L. Ghormley, Assistant Chief of Naval Operations, asked the Chief of the British Air Staff, Sir Cyril Newall, how the war could be won. Newall replied that 'in the long run it was inevitable that the Army should deliver the coup de grâce. We hoped, however, for a serious weakening in the morale and fighting efficiency of the German machine, if not a complete breakdown, which would make the task of the Army much more easy.' This tendency to defer land offensives was not just an Air Force point of view. When asked late in 1941 for a plan to win the war, General Sir John Kennedy replied simply: 'We could not do it until America came in.' Churchill, thoroughly convinced of the merits of this policy, in the summer of 1940 instructed Section D of the Foreign Office, predecessor of the Special Operations Executive, to investigate every possibility of attacking potential enemies 'by means other than the operation of military forces'. As Major L.D. Grand later commented, 'one felt as if one had been told to move the pyramids with a pen.'[3]

Not everyone was sold on these rather fanciful constructions. Among the doubters, an alternate strategy was increasingly gaining acceptance, that of stimulating an economic collapse in a supposedly over-mobilized Germany. Churchill's scientific adviser, Frederick Lindemann, was for the most part an advocate of this concept, and the Chiefs of Staff in fact embraced it in their study of 19 May 1940 on future strategy. The economic collapse of Germany was to be induced by a bombing program that would concentrate on key resources, such as the oil fields. In essence, it was a strategy based on the notion that German rearmament had reached levels that no economy could long sustain; if external pressure were kept up, its weight would cause the collapse of the Third Reich. As A.J.P. Taylor has noted, this misjudgement was shared by many qualified observers. But the notion that every extension of the German empire increased the possibility of its collapse did not necessarily correspond to reality. Each extension raised the costs of occupation, but also brought new resources for the German war machine. Moreover, no policy of economic strangulation was going to work as long as the Soviet Union was under German domination, supplying it with essential war materials.[4]

A new situation was created on 22 June 1941 when Hitler, losing his patience with Soviet demands for compensation for German territorial gains, gave vent to his long-simmering hatred for the Soviet regime by unleashing a massive ground and air attack, Operation *Barbarossa*, all along the 2,000 miles from the White to the Black Sea. Stalin understood that there was much more behind Hitler's move than ideological hostility. It was Hitler's way of trying to crush hope, and thus resistance, in the West. At one and the same time Hitler would secure still more complete access to Soviet supplies and seal off forever Britain's hope of strangling the axis.[5]

The momentous events of 22 June thus increased both the dangers and the opportunities for Britain. If Hitler succeeded not only in defeating Russia but in keeping her in a satellite relationship, no conceivable military combination could defeat an axis so structured. Conversely, if the Soviet Union could simply impose a stalemate on Germany, then German wastage rates would climb enormously and the prospects for a strategy of attrition would improve greatly. Indeed, the better the Soviet performance, the more conceivable it became to re-establish the two-front strategy that had evaporated when Britain, the United States, and the Soviet Union unwisely allowed the defeat of France. It was clear, however, that a German collapse imposed at sea by Britain and on land by Russia would greatly redound to the benefit of the Soviets. Therefore, as a counterpoise to the Soviet Union, American participation seemed desirable. But in fact British officials had little confidence in Soviet chances of survival, and tended not to worry about distant prospects of Soviet territorial expansion. Entry by the United States was urgently sought, more as insurance against an imminent Soviet collapse than as a counterweight against what must then have seemed like a very remote political threat.

The essential consideration, however, was that *Barbarossa* made it possible for British strategists to return to their earlier conception of tightening the ring, to be followed by a relatively minor thrust at the end of the war. But what Churchill gained on one side, he was threatened with losing on the other, for the attritional strategy was becoming less tenable in terms of domestic politics. By the time of *Barbarossa* the proportion of national resources, public funds, and manpower devoted to the war had swollen greatly. Highly mobilized societies, particularly if they are democracies, develop a great impatience with anything that seems like a slow and indirect route to victory. As that impatience grew, it became evident that a strategy based on the gradual grinding down of the enemy might also wear down the political capital of the home government. Attrition was a sword that could cut both ways, a fact that by early 1942 had been brought home most forcefully by the record of increasing sacrifices with no end in sight.[6]

Equally important in forcing a reconsideration of grand strategy was declining public confidence — in British armies, in Churchill's war direction, and in British strategy — and this threatened to have momentous political consequences unless the drift was checked. The dynamism looked for in Churchill's succeeding Chamberlain as Prime Minister in May 1940 was proving to be evanescent, if not illusory. By the spring of 1942 it was evident that after so many British defeats, the appearance of simply sitting back and letting someone else destroy the Axis was just too humiliating for the British public to accept indefinitely. In short, the old strategy did nothing for the national image or for Churchill as Britain's war leader. Indeed, as early as 1939, when he was First Lord of the Admiralty, Churchill had explained to the First Sea Lord that 'I cd never be responsible for a naval strategy which excluded the offensive principle, and relegated us to keeping open lines of communication and maintaining the blockade.' That, of course, was precisely what Whitehall's official strategy postulated. But it is safe to say that by May 1942 any policy that could be interpreted as purely defensive, however sensible and necessary it might seem in Whitehall, would eventually be rejected by the British public.[7]

Churchill also had to worry about the views of his new ally, the United States. By April 1942 the Americans were also looking for ways of launching an offensive war strategy. This was an astounding development, for while the United States was still neutral, British planners had managed to co-opt American strategic thinking into accepting the attritional strategy of 'tightening the ring'. Even at the Newfoundland summit conference in August 1941, US representatives had accepted the British Chiefs of Staff's definition of the primary strategic objective as seeking 'methods of wearing down Germany's resistance'. Such a war of attrition would become, first of all, a war of industrial mobilization. At that time British planners had been saying: 'We do not foresee vast armies of infantry as in 1914-1918. The forces we employ will be armoured divisions. To supplement their operations the local patriots must be secretly armed and equipped so that at the right moment they may rise in revolt.' This strategy was acceptable to the United States because it accorded a vital role to America's greatest strength, her industrial productive capacity, while assuaging the worst fears of domestic partisans of neutrality, whose political clout was still very great in America.[8]

But shortly after the Newfoundland conference, American conceptions began to change as a result of studies initiated earlier in the summer to determine needs and resources should the United States enter the war. The 'Victory Program', which emerged from these labours in September, indicated that an army with an air corps totalling over 8 million men — which translated into something like a 215-division ground army and a two-million-man air corps — was an attainable goal. This was a much larger force than had ever been envisaged, but the accompanying strategic outline still echoed British military thinking because it relied essentially on the tactics of attrition: the application of a blockade, a heavy air offensive, aid to the resistance in Europe, propaganda campaigns, and any other effort that would wear down German morale. Nevertheless the possibility of a distinctly different approach to strategy now appeared on the horizon. According to the authors of the 'Victory Program': 'We must prepare to fight Germany by actually coming to grips with and defeating her ground forces and definitely breaking her will to combat.'[9]

Just as important as the Victory Plan in changing American strategic thinking was the gradual appreciation of the consequences of *Barbarossa* in June 1941. The War Department then recognized that the fate of the attritional strategy was hanging in the balance. If Russia were defeated, and Germany gained unlimited access to its resources, defeat of the Axis would be next to impossible. There would be no rope strong enough to tighten the ring in any effective way.[10]

The events of 1941 that brought the Soviet Union and the United States into the war — *Barbarossa* and Pearl Harbor — could only have reinforced British strategists in their determination to accumulate overpowering strength around an ever-tightening ring. At last American productive abilities would be fully mobilized. Even if Russia should prove unable to wear Germany down seriously, or even should it be defeated, there was now a new ally with the manpower and resources that might make the knock-out blow at the end of the attritional phase. The defeat of Britain in the ultimate sense no longer seemed possible. Churchill, while grieving for the losses suffered by the Americans at Pearl Harbor, could not hide his joy at the American entry, convinced as he was that the war was now as good as won. British armies might still meet reverses, and large areas might be lost. But with the luxury of double insurance, Russian and American, there was no longer any doubt about the ultimate outcome.[11]

Given these momentous changes, Britain ought to have been able to relax slightly the rigour of her mobilization and look after her own regional strategic interests, while allowing the inevitable weight of the larger forces at play to determine the broader strategic issues. But it soon became evident that the cost of doing so was unacceptable. The Roosevelt administration, which had to contend with a vocal and undisciplined public opinion, would demand immediate results on the battlefield — consonant with the established mythology of the First World War when, it was said, the mere appearance of the doughboys had been enough to make Germany collapse. This legend was impossible to argue against, and because of it American strategists were unlikely to allow Britain to rest on its oars.

The appearance of new allies also tended to make the British public impatient for some demonstration of British military activity, lest others claim victory on the battlefield and the right to determine the geopolitical consequences. In a war won principally by Russia and the United States, British interests were certain to receive short shrift; British armies must therefore produce results while their effort could still be appreciated.

Thus the situation by the end of 1941 was that the strategy of attrition, while more feasible militarily, was less so politically. Energetic prosecution of the war had become a political imperative for London. It was also perfectly understandable that whatever effort was expended should be made to serve those British interests that her allies were unlikely to protect. Determining the future contours of the post-war world was, in any case, beyond Britain's power; the most that might be achieved would be simply holding on to the Empire, itself a very tall order. Well might British strategists ask themselves: Why make enormous sacrifices elsewhere if that meant losing the Empire? Would America or Russia be the least bit grateful if Britain sacrificed her imperial efforts to their strategic conceptions? Even those British leaders who were realists about the nature of the Empire's evolution were convinced that for now it must be reclaimed *in toto*, if only to bargain from a position of strength.

Everything pointed, then, to a major offensive to protect Britain's Mediterranean lifeline, with all its legendary strongpoints: Gibraltar, Malta, Cyprus, and Alexandria. Victory along this path would signal British determination to remain a great power. To Churchill, one of the last great imperialists of his day, such a policy came as naturally as breathing; but it is hard to imagine any other Prime Minister adopting a different strategy in 1941 and 1942. The planners fully shared the old imperialist's vision. As Kennedy has recalled, he was convinced in mid-July 1941 that 'We would still have to hold the Germans on an outer ring, which must include India, the Persian Gulf, and the southern end of the Red Sea. . . . it is right therefore that we should fight on the inner ring, that is to say in the Middle East, so long as we can do this without too heavy a drain upon our resources.' This strategy, while deeply resented by American anglophobes, was not without its supporters even in the United States, such as Colonel W.F. Kernan, who in a popular book, *Defense Will Not Win the War* (1942), argued along much the same lines.[12]

It should not be thought that British leaders were so foolish as to believe that the Second World War could be won in the Mediterranean. It was simply that they thought Britain could win her war there while still making a significant contribution to winning the global war, given her resources.

Eden explained all this very carefully to the Chief of the Imperial Staff early in 1942. His conviction that this was the correct course was neatly summarized in his memoirs: '[It was] . . . in North Africa that our fighting must be done. Nowhere else could Britain get to grips with the enemy on land. We could not foresee when a landing in Europe would be practicable again, but our sea-power, using exterior lines, made it possible to build up our strength in Egypt and in the Western Desert. This was the theatre where the army must prove itself.' Just how deeply ingrained this strategy was can be easily seen in the minutes of the Defence Committee (30 January 1942), which concluded that 'nothing should detract from the maintenance of the Army in the Middle East which was so vital. Any adjustments should be at the expense of the United Kingdom.' Such a strategy was certain to infuriate the Americans because it seemed to commit scarce allied resources to the perpetuation of the British Empire and to the continuation of the slow attritional approach to the war.[13]

Churchill understood American attitudes very well indeed, and trying to overcome such resistance constituted one of his principal burdens in the first half of 1942. He could not afford a confrontation with the Americans because he needed their asistance in many areas. Much against his natural instincts, this most direct of all the great leaders of the war was therefore forced to dissemble by wrapping all the strategic issues in clouds of suitably vague rhetoric that would capture the imagination of the Americans while he pursued a different policy with calculating attention to detail.

As Churchill travelled to America on the *Duke of York* in December 1941, he briefed the British Chiefs of Staff very carefully on the attitude they should assume for their American colleagues:

> Most people outside our very limited circle would be horrified at the idea that all offensive action must be postponed till even later years [than 1943]; in fact, I am sure they would not put up with it. Still less will they do so if all the time Japan is 'running wild' in the East Indies and Northern Australia. I hope therefore, that we shall speak with confidence and decision upon the liberating offensive of 1943 and that we shall ask for the vessels, and tackle, and tanks to be prepared on this basis and that we shall hold out to the captive populations the hope of relief.

Anglophobic American military planners, of course, suspected the worst from the very first. One of Churchill's great worries, therefore, from December 1941 through to the end of July 1942, was how to throw the Americans off guard until some decisive feat of British arms had been executed in Libya. If none materialized, then Churchill must try to get the United States to consider a North African expedition. In nursing this hope he was counting on what he expected would be American impatience to get American troops into action. An awareness of this impatience was reflected in the President's comments to his military advisers on 23 December when he said that it was 'very important . . . to give this country a feeling that they are in the war, to give the Germans the reverse effect' and this could be done only by having 'American troops somewhere in active fighting across the Atlantic.'[14]

After June 1941 the Soviet Union also joined the strategic debate, though somewhat more sporadically. By 1942 it did not have many options. After *Barbarossa* Stalin's most important objective should have been to make good the great mistake of the Russo-German alliance and somehow secure the re-establishment of a Second Front in the West, despite the defeat of France. Many have held that this was Stalin's paramount objective beginning in July 1942 — a dubious conclusion. Real military collaboration under difficult circumstances implied a greater degree of trust than was ideologically possible for Stalin. Moreover, Stalin must have known that the establishment of a Second Front was well beyond Britain's capabilities. His mind turned to other objectives, such as obtaining supplies and, perhaps more important, retaining that part of Poland Hitler had accorded him, and securing recognition of the incorporation of the Baltic states into the Soviet Union and of other territorial adjustments in the Balkans. Stalin was not the least discomfited by knowing that these objectives placed the Soviet in an adversarial position with the West. This simply made the heirs of the Revolution more, rather than less, comfortable.

Why, then, did Stalin repeatedly ask for a Second Front in which he did not believe? Ivan Maisky, his ambassador in England, has explained this with a clarity that is as remarkable as the tendency of historians to ignore his explanation. After one interview, in which he complained to Eden about the failure to open a Second Front, Maisky observed:

> I was struck by one trait which I had never noticed before: the Foreign Secretary felt embarrassed at the refusal of the British Government to organize a second front in France, and strove to soften our disappointment at this by underlining British readiness to give us help on a large scale in the form of military supplies and otherwise. I felt the same note of apology in the statements of other highly-placed British people with whom I had to deal in the days that followed.

This was really only a variant of the Marxist-Leninist understanding of the weakness and contradictory character of bourgeois consciences, but it pointed directly to a strategy of exploiting British embarrassment by demanding an impossible Second Front and then simply cashing in on the compensations that were certain to be offered as a result of Britain's being unable to deliver. The strategy made all the more sense as Churchill's political woes multiplied and his principal rivals, declared and undeclared — chiefly, Eden, Beaverbrook, and Cripps — indicated that their likely platform, if they mounted an open challenge, would be that Churchill was gambling recklessly with the Soviet Union's commitment to the war by ignoring its requests for assistance.[15]

Maisky then proceeded to develop his already close relations with Cripps and Beaverbrook and the partisans of concessions to the Soviets. At the same time he told Moscow to increase its demands and convey its unhappiness with increasing imperiousness. As Maisky has explained in his memoirs, in August 1941 he advised the Soviet leader to ask for a Second Front and a massive program of supply for the Red Army. 'I warned Stalin that on the first question there would be no practical results, but it was important constantly to remind the British of the need for a second front. But on the [supplies] . . . question, I wrote, judging from the mood prevalent in London, there were chances to get something real.'[16]

This led to the cable of 3 September in which Stalin told Churchill: 'I think the only way is to open a second front this year somewhere in the Balkans or in France, one that would divert 30-40 German divisions from the Eastern front . . . ' Such an invasion, capable of diverting 30-to-40 German divisions, would have required many more troops than the 1944 Normandy landing (which pitted some 37 Allied divisions against some 60 German divisions but had only a negligible effect on the Eastern Front). Churchill tried to point out how impossible some of these requests were, but Maisky, who already knew this, simply turned up the heat. The gist of his reply is to be found in Maisky's memoirs: '. . . if Hitler would be victorious in the East, what would be the fate of Britain? It was not difficult to imagine . . . Therefore the duty of every individual, every Government, every country which wanted to see the progressive development of mankind, was, just at this moment, to strain all its forces and afford the maximum of assistance to the USSR.' Maisky preached this gospel throughout Britain in an attempt to pressure the government.[17]

Churchill was not able, then or later, to contain the combination of external and domestic pressures. He had to compromise continually by making some gesture that might indicate to the Soviet Union, and to his domestic critics, that he was not indifferent to Russia's fate. In August 1941 he turned over 200 Hurricane fighters as a gift, and shortly thereafter put all supplies sent to the Soviet Union on a lend-lease basis, with none of the strings and preconditions that the Americans had imposed on Britain. Then in September he and Roosevelt sent Beaverbrook and Averell Harriman on a mission to Moscow to draft the first lend-lease protocol. The intention, as Beaverbrook explained on the eve of their departure, was 'not . . . to bargain but to give. . . . It was to be a Christmas-tree party, and there must be no excuse for the Russians' thinking they were not getting a fair share of the gifts on the tree.' Harriman told his fellow delegates that the policy of the United States would be to 'give and give and give, with no expectation of any return, with no thought of a quid pro quo.' When Stalin met the first offers with the comment that the 'paucity of your offers clearly shows that you want to see the Soviet Union defeated,' Beaverbrook just redoubled his efforts, increasing the offers of aid, in some areas beyond his instructions, until Stalin warmed and the atmosphere at last changed. As Harriman put it, in the end there was the 'sunshine after rain.' But no effort at appeasement ever lasted for long, perhaps because the German onslaught on Russia never really subsided, but more likely because Stalin and Molotov did not know how to give up a diplomatic negotiating advantage.[18]

The string of Western concessions had no lasting effect. Time after time the apparent good will created by a particular gesture wore off with alarming rapidity. Scarcely more than a month after Beaverbrook and Harriman had left Moscow amid wide jubilation, Molotov was complaining to Cripps 'that we [the British] were not helping with any armed forces.' An offer to send a small British force (a couple of divisions) to the Caucasus was not accepted. Soon the Soviet government was indicating that the Anglo-Soviet accord signed just a few months before, in July, with smiles all around, was inadequate. Mistakenly believing that the Soviets were raising political demands in order to get military assistance, Churchill offered early in November to send his representative on the Chiefs of Staff Committee, General Ismay, to Moscow, together with General Sir Bernard Paget, the Deputy Chief of the Imperial Staff, to discuss military co-operation. This gesture had at least the merit of forcing Stalin to reveal his hand: he now stated that if the British generals could not sign a political accord (and by implication recognize the Soviet territorial acquisitions made in partnership with Hitler), there was no point in their coming to Moscow. The effect of this rebuff to Churchill was accentuated when Cripps chose this moment to say that he was in complete disagreement with Churchill's policy towards Russia as being dangerously negative, and asked to be relieved as Ambassador so that he could return to Parliament to lobby against the Government. At the very same time Beaverbrook was boring from within, challenging the Government's policy towards the Soviet Union and appealing directly to factory union leaders to push for a Second Front.[19]

Molotov came to understand, during the course of his trip to Washington in May 1941 — if he did not already know — that the Allies considered a Second Front in 1942 to be a very doubtful proposition indeed. He reported to both Moscow and Churchill on his return that the President had refused to give a firm commitment. Nevertheless Molotov insisted that a press communiqué should be released, as a measure of war propaganda, saying 'that complete agreement had been reached with regard to the urgent tasks of the creation of a Second Front in 1942.' When Molotov returned to London, he persuaded Churchill and Eden to agree to this wording in the interests of psychological warfare. But in order not to mislead the Soviet government, Churchill gave Molotov a confidential *aide-mémoire*, dated 10 June 1942, which had been drafted by the Chiefs of Staff and approved by

Churchill in its final form. This crucial document, while indicating all the things Britain was doing to wage war on Germany, carefully pointed out limitations, and concluded that 'we can therefore give no promise [on a Second Front] . . . .' But in a subsidiary paragraph — strangely ignored by historians studying the Dieppe raid — the Chiefs of Staff also stated that the British Government 'shall continue our policy of raids against selected points on the Continent. These raids will increase in size and scope as the summer goes on. By this means we are preventing the Germans from transferring any of their 33 Divisions in Western Europe to their Eastern front and keeping them constantly on the alert, never knowing at what point the next attack may come.'[20]

This assurance would assume great importance for the British because difficulties in implementing earlier promises to the Soviet Union had elicited repeated charges of bad faith from Moscow — and just a step away from such charges was the implied or assumed threat of another German-Soviet truce. Diplomats of all political persuasions were convinced by June 1942, if they had not previously been convinced, that extensions of promises of aid that could not be implemented must be avoided at all costs. The Soviet Union must not be given any more occasions to charge bad faith. The promised raids had to be implemented, especially because they were offered in a document whose ostensible purpose was to convey with rigorous honesty the true state of what the Allies could and would promise to do and what they could not do. The purpose of the clause was evidently to soften the blow of what could *not* be done. Under these circumstances the obligation to redeem the raid promise would have been difficult to contest — and never was contested. The obligations incurred with the *aide-mémoire* thus became a major factor in the Dieppe decision, more important even than the desire to demonstrate to the Americans British fighting spirit.

A North African invasion, and the fulfilment of the raiding program, might satisfy both allies. By the end of July, Roosevelt at least had bought the package. That left Stalin. As Churchill travelled to Moscow, he had high hopes that the Soviet leader could also be persuaded that a North African invasion (*Torch*, formerly called *Gymnast*), and whatever major raids Mountbatten could produce, represented the most feasible immediate program to inflict damage on the Axis.[21]

Churchill explained this to Stalin by using for the first time his crocodile metaphor. He referred to *Torch*, the focus of the discussions, as a blow to the enemy's soft underbelly. But he also spoke about striking at the snout of the beast — i.e. the Channel area, which was what Stalin kept asking about. Churchill thus confirmed that the promise on raids was being kept. He described at length, and in somewhat inflated terms, the Dieppe project, while also surrounding it delicately with some uncertainty about whether it would come off — but he was hopeful. He was understandably pleased, and probably grateful to Mountbatten, to be able to offer aggressive action in the Channel area, to which the Soviets attached such importance. This is undoubtedly why he cabled London inquiring about the status of *Jubilee* (mistakenly using the old code-name *Rutter*). Less than four days after his discussion with Stalin, the raid finally did take place.[22]

But why did the combination of American, Soviet, and domestic pressures lead to the raid on Dieppe, which had few prospects of success, rather than somewhere else where the prospects could have been better? To answer these questions, which go to the heart of the decision-making process, we must examine the other decision-makers besides Churchill: the Service Chiefs who, together with Mountbatten, formed the Chiefs of Staff Committee.

# 5

# General Sir Alan Brooke
# and the Prelude to Dieppe

Not the least remarkable aspect of the Dieppe affair was the fact that the decision to remount, after the July cancellation, took place on General Sir Alan Brooke's watch as Chief of the Imperial Staff (CIGS), while he was chairing the Chiefs of Staff Committee. That this major operational decision was never approved, as far as the records indicate, by the Chiefs in any of their formal meetings, and transpired without any formal assumption of responsibility, becomes particularly puzzling when we consider that the raid was carried out under Brooke's usually watchful eye. Brooke was a staff-officer's officer, shaped by long service as an instructor in the Imperial War College and known as a stickler for procedure. All his wartime colleagues have testified that in procedural matters he was crisp, precise, and orderly, and was not inclined to tolerate sloppy administrative procedures. Even Mountbatten noted that a red light from Brooke was unarguable. Generals who were inclined to act without proper authority soon found themselves rotated out to new commands and obliged to accept as their principal staff officer one of Brooke's minions dedicated to seeing that no other unauthorized action took place.[1]

How closely Brooke observed the formalities of careful decision-making and scrupulous record-keeping was made clear in December 1941 when the Prime Minister, acting as Minister of Defence, decided he would communicate directly with subordinate commanders. Brooke promptly warned the commanders that he would tolerate no deviation from established lines of responsibility. 'It is, of course, very desirable', Brooke wrote to one such commander 'that you should send private telegrams direct to the P.M. in reply to his and keep him informed as to the general course of events, yet I do not think that this should in any way affect the normal channels which should exist between you and the War Office. . . . I therefore hope that, whilst maintaining the necessary flow of information by direct messages to the P.M., you will insure that such a procedure does not affect the normal channel of communication to me which should exist between us.' When the Prime Minister developed a personal relationship with Mountbatten, regularly inviting him to weekends at Chequers, his country residence, Brooke would carefully brief Mountbatten before he left London and expect a detailed report on his return. This penchant for tight procedures is revealed in the minutes of Chiefs of Staff meetings where Brooke can be seen guiding the discussion briskly to specific points and clear decisions.[2]

How the Dieppe decision escaped his rigorous procedures remains a mystery. One explanation could be that it was taken in early August by his deputy, Lieutenant-General Archibald Nye, after Brooke had left with Churchill for Cairo and Moscow; but we have Ismay's testimony that Nye was furious to find out that he had not been informed of the decision, and learned of the operation only when the dispatches from Dieppe came back. There is no evidence to suggest anything to the contrary. Brooke himself later testified: '[Nye] was brilliantly able and full of character and . . . I could leave the country with absolute confidence he would do his level best to maintain the identical policies which he knew I wanted.'[3]

What is certain is that well before Brooke left for Cairo and Moscow, Combined Operations was issuing orders and requisitioning supplies for a raid on Dieppe as though there was no problem about approval. Indeed, the Combined Plan, including what amounted to an overall operations order, which presupposed prior authorization, was signed on 31 July, nearly two days before Brooke left London (on 1 August). Whether or not Brooke approved, he must have known the raid was going forward, for he was in frequent contact with General Andrew McNaughton, the Canadian Army Commander, whose troops would be used. Brooke's knowledge is also implied by his reaction, when he heard the raid had been carried out, as recorded in his diary and in that of Sir Charles Wilson, who was with him. The evidence suggests, then, that this was a decision that Brooke accepted tacitly, even though it was never recorded or subjected to the formalities of responsible decision-making. How Brooke came to tolerate such a breach in the tight procedures of the Chiefs of Staff requires some explanation.[4]

Since Brooke's opinion of the Dieppe plan was not recorded, save in one brief remark at a meeting on 30 June, his position can be derived only from examining the environment in the weeks preceding Dieppe — the long-festering political and military crisis of 1942 that swirled around the Prime Minister.

Brooke became Chief of the Imperial General Staff in November 1941. How formidable was the task of holding this position under Churchill may be gleaned from the fact that it had nearly broken his predecessor, Field Marshal Sir John Dill, a man of no mean accomplishments, whom Churchill hounded until he was able to post him off to Washington. The job, whether held by Dill or Brooke, was difficult, as it involved wearing several hats at once. As senior commander of the British Army, Brooke was responsible for ensuring that no plan that jeopardized the Army's integrity, its fighting efficiency, or its morale was approved by the Chiefs of Staff. Once a plan was approved by the Chiefs and the Minister of Defence, Brooke had overall responsibility for its execution. When he took over as Chairman of the Chiefs of Staff Committee he accumulated all the powers and responsibilities Dill had held. As the 'first among equals' where the Service Chiefs were concerned, he had to see that military plans were not adopted at the exclusive expense of any one service. At a time when British military fortunes were very low and Britain was scraping the bottom of the supplies barrel, this was a challenging task. It was all too easy for each Service to come up with a scheme for winning the war if only it were given everything it could possibly want. Brooke knew that to approve any such scheme would destroy the spirit of trust and collective responsibility that was the essence of the Chiefs of Staff structure and the only real source of confidence in ultimate victory. Keeping the Chiefs of Staff as a positive, constructive engine of the British war effort meant keeping a balance among the services within the particular global strategy that seemed most promising.

Brooke was perhaps the boldest, or at least the most optimistic, of British strategists, being virtually the only one who still thought it was possible for Britain to make the major contribution to victory. The essence of his strategy was to tighten the ring: while avoiding frontal attacks on the Axis powers, he would use air and sea power to confine them within their existing positions. Though the enemy might have the advantage of short lines of communication within the ring, Britain and her allies would be able to harass them from without and, as the enemy's power was worn down, force the Axis to retreat within an ever-shrinking base. But Brooke was very much aware that this would be ineffectual unless a decisive *coup de grâce* could be delivered at the conclusion. Like the American Chief of Staff, General George C. Marshall, Brooke was convinced that in the final analysis only ground troops could inflict ultimate defeat upon Germany. He believed that Britain could make her contribution only if great care was taken not to waste available resources. Like most experienced staff officers who had taught at the Imperial War College, Brooke was a great believer in the concentration of effort. He was convinced that the great mistake Britain had made in the First World War was the creation of so many 'subsidiary theatres and [the] frittering away [of] our strength'. Brooke recognized that in the Second World War victory would have to be won in Europe, but he was convinced that a premature landing 'could only result in the most appalling shambles which must . . . reduce the chances of ultimate victory to a minimum.' The idea that Britain should husband her resources very carefully indeed was hard to get across to the War Cabinet. ' Why', Brooke exclaimed at one point, 'will politicians never learn the simple principle of concentration of force at the vital point and the avoidance of dispersal of effort?'[5]

Where waste especially had to be avoided was in the use of shipping. The strategy of tightening the ring, whatever other advantages it had, certainly had this drawback: it conceded to the enemy all the advantages of working on interior lines, while Britain and her allies were obliged to work the vast distances of the periphery. Large quantities of shipping were going to be required, in addition to what was needed to feed Britain, to work these outside lines, and finally to transport Britain's armies from the periphery for the final stroke against Germany. These concerns fell primarily on the shoulders of Admiral Sir Dudley Pound, First Sea Lord, but Brooke also felt their full weight. From his first days as Chief of the Imperial Staff his mind had been drawn to the shipping problem as the key to all the stages of the war leading up to the final assault. Brooke later recalled that already, on his third day as CIGS: 'I had a clear-cut idea as to what our policy should be . . . it was plain to me that we must clear North Africa to open the Mediterranean, and until we had done so we should never have enough shipping to stage major operations.' He thought at least a million tons of shipping could be freed for offensive operations if the Mediterranean were made secure. Until then Britain had barely enough shipping to send troop replacements to its far-flung forces, and perhaps to one or two minor offensive operations. These later recollections of Brooke's are completely borne out in the record. Though Churchill was vitally interested in the disposition of the fighting forces, and even of the convoys to Russia and Malta, he had a hard time focusing on the seemingly mundane question of transporting supplies. While Brooke was convinced the shipping situation was 'most disturbing', he found it was a subject that the Prime Minister had difficulty facing.[6]

Brooke's ring strategy, which gave so prominent a role to the naval battle, did not neglect the important contributions the Royal Air Force could make. Brooke was convinced that modern ground armies could not operate effectively save under the protective umbrella of air superiority. Without such mastery of the sky, any attempt to strike the final blow against Germany would only create a death trap. He also recognized that the RAF had a major role in wearing down Germany in preparation for the final thrust. As a result, Brooke was much more willing than most generals to listen to the plans the RAF was always ready to propose for a massive air assault.

This balanced approach to strategy would take a long time to implement. First Egypt had to be secured, then the Mediterranean. Only when these goals had been obtained would it be possible to provide for the defence of India and the East at reasonable cost in shipping. Once North Africa was safely secure, then Britain could strike directly at Europe if Russia were still holding German armies. If Russia collapsed, Britain could only strike at the weaker Axis partner, Italy, and then re-examine the possibilities for a cross-Channel attack. Since there was so much doubt about Russia's ability to survive in both 1941 and 1942, Brooke naturally focused on the slower course of consolidating Britain's position in the Mediterranean by holding on to the Libyan coast in the centre, from which bombers might easily reach the entire rim of the Mediterranean basin. This was not a policy that he invented. As early as August 1940 the Chiefs of Staff had stated that 'We regard the elimination of Italy as a strategic aim of the first importance. The collapse of Italy would largely relieve the threat to the Middle East and free our hands at sea to meet the Japanese threat.'[7]

These hopes were promptly dashed by the crisis in the Far East. On 20 December 1941 Brooke noted in his diary: 'The more I look at the situation the more I dislike it. My hopes of carrying on with the conquest and reclamation of North Africa are beginning to look more and more impossible every day. From now on the Far East will make ever-increasing inroads into our resources.' Before the end of the year he was completely convinced that the North African project was out of the question. Britain did not seem to have even the minimum forces needed to prevent further disastrous defeats.[8]

It was easy to become depressed. Dill turned to General Kennedy at one meeting in March 1941, saying: 'Do you realize we are fighting for our lives?' The crisis only deepened through the rest of that year. There was certainly good reason for the sense of near-despair that repeatedly crept into Brooke's diary. He was simply counting the days that passed as days in which Britain managed to survive. But it was survival on an ever-slimmer margin. After the humiliating failures in Greece, Crete, Libya, and the Far East, Brooke remarked with sorrow to a friend early in 1942 that the last few months had been 'about the grimmest of my life'. 'We seem to lose a new bit of the Empire almost every day, and are faced with one nightmare situation after another.' It was all happening during his watch and he reacted with some bitterness even against his own service. He wrote on 17 February 1942: 'If the Army cannot fight better than it is doing at present we shall deserve to lose our empire.'[9]

But Brooke found a partial solution to the evident shortage of resources early in 1942 when he discovered how keen the Americans were on an early Second Front. In return for promises to attempt their cross-Channel (*Sledgehammer*) plan, the Americans were willing to take up an additional amount of Britain's defence burden both in the home islands and in the Indian Ocean, so that British forces could concentrate on future operations against the Continent. It was on this basis that Brooke secured the sending of American divisions to Australia and American naval units to reinforce the British fleet in home waters as well as in the Indian Ocean.[10]

This strategy, however, was constantly in danger of becoming unravelled. There was first of all the tendency of Churchill and others to talk too freely about the middle-range goals of Brooke's strategy, particularly the North African project (*Gymnast*). The Americans were sensitive, indeed overly so, to every hint of a diversion in the direction of what they regarded as British imperial interests. To calm their apprehensions it became important to cease talking about *Gymnast*, which in any case was not feasible yet. Ironically Brooke, who recalled — almost with a tinge of desperation in December 1941 — how hard he had to try to convince the Prime Minister of the 'advantages of a real North African offensive policy', now had to work manfully to unconvince him. For the time being Britain should concentrate on purely defensive measures. But as this was not likely to create much enthusiasm with the Americans, it was necessary to let them think Britain was planning a cross-Channel invasion so that they would continue to ship divisions, naval vessels, and aircraft to Britain, thus enabling the British Chiefs of Staff to send equivalent forces out of Britain to meet immediate dangers.[11]

In the first eight months of 1942 the situation was grave for Britain everywhere. The loss of Malta, the whole Mediterranean, Egypt, and India seemed imminent — and these just topped the list. Britain was on the defensive, and not surprisingly the question making the rounds was whether the new CIGS was too defensive-minded, too cautious to take the energetic measures to reverse the situation. Even if Brooke himself had the *sang froid* to ignore the gossip, he was painfully aware that Churchill hated to be on the defensive and was incessantly looking for some way to attack. Repeatedly he came back to his two favourites. One was *Jupiter*, the plan to seize portions of Norway and so provide flanking protection for the convoys sailing to the USSR. There was also his project to invade North Africa, where Vichy France held sway, and provide support from the rear for that seemingly hopeless British Army in Libya. Finally there was Churchill's occasional but still dangerous infatuation with the possibilities of an early attack in France. None of these offensive operations had very good prospects, and Brooke had to say 'No' to them — firmly and repeatedly — even at the cost of seeming to confirm a reputation for being timorous and defensive-minded. He knew Britain had absolutely no resources to waste anywhere.

Brooke's sense of acute crisis makes his acquiescence in Dieppe all the more mysterious. At no period in his career was he more aware of the shortness of means, of the absolute need to conserve and show maximum discipline. Yet it was in the midst of this very period that he allowed the largest raid in history to take place against very long odds, indeed near-certain disaster — a raid that would culminate in heavy RAF wastage and the effective loss for the better part of a year of a well-equipped and promising Canadian division, as well as the loss of many valuable landing-craft. Brooke's apparent willingness to fritter resources in this way is as surprising as his acquiescence in Mountbatten's circumvention of proper procedures.

Brooke's apparent acceptance of Dieppe seems even more puzzling when one considers that the raid was justified by many as an aggressive gesture to appease the Soviet Union and to a lesser extent as an attempt to impress the Americans. Brooke was not inclined to be greatly moved by either consideration. He viewed the American military with the most extreme form of condescension. And he had developed an immense distaste for the Soviet Union when, as commander of the British Expeditionary Force in France in 1940, he observed that France's ally of 1934, the Soviet Union, was supplying Hitler with war materials for France's destruction.

That experience left Brooke with little patience for those who imagined that 'Russia had only come into the war for our benefit.' His diary entry of 13 March 1941, speculating on the possibility that Germany would turn on Russia, displayed not the least bit of sympathy for Russia's dilemma. Nor did he ever state in any of his diary entries that the Western powers owed Russia anything. Social occasions with the Soviets left him profoundly uneasy. On 26 May, Brooke went to the Soviet embassy to witness the signing of the Anglo-Russian treaty. In his diary he wrote: 'Many toasts and many speeches. Somehow the whole affair gave me the creeps and made me feel that humanity has still many centuries to live before universal peace can be found.'[12]

Nevertheless Brooke could see that American desires and Churchill's political interests might coincide to force some desperate gesture towards the Soviet Union. He had been involved earlier in plans to appease the Russians. In September 1941, just before his elevation as CIGS, he was called in to discuss what he regarded as mad schemes (put forward by Beaverbrook) to try to relieve pressure on Russia by a feint attack on the Cherbourg peninsula. And a few weeks later he was asked to produce a viable plan for an attack on Norway after the Chiefs of Staff, supported by a considerable group of planners, had confessed their inability to produce anything workable. Again, the stated goal was to help the Russians. Brooke regarded this task as sheer folly and a great waste of time, since British forces would have to operate under the dominance of the land-based German Luftwaffe, with no hope of effectively challenging it. Early in December 1941 he was faced with Churchill's desire to send two British divisions to fight in southern Russia. Brooke refused to consider it, though he was doubtless aware that Dill's opposition to Beaverbrook's schemes for a sacrifice operation to help the Soviets had much to do with the loss of his position as CIGS. Brooke fought the idea because, as he noted, there were 'no troops that could be spared' and 'This [diversion] would probably mean having to close down the Libyan offensive.' In short, it would dash all prospects for implementing a Mediterranean strategy. Brooke succeeded in securing the defeat of the plan, but not without a 'most awful outburst of temper' from Churchill. After berating his staff for being able to do nothing but produce obstacles, the Prime Minister sat back for five minutes in silence, then slammed his papers together and walked out of the room.[13]

That experience introduced Brooke to the formidable difficulty of saying no to Churchill. On an earlier occasion, when Brooke had been forced to give Churchill a negative report on the Norway project in October 1941, Churchill exploded. When it was explained that a twenty-four-hour delay would make this Trondheim venture impossible, Churchill angrily demanded that the staff 'explain to me exactly how every hour of those twenty-four would be occupied.' When this was done he went on to complain in noticeably sarcastic tones that Brooke and the staff had produced 'a masterly treatise on all the difficulties and on all the reasons why this operation should not be carried out.' Churchill then proceeded to interrogate Brooke closely for two hours on every difficulty that he had advanced. For Brooke it was an unpleasant, gruelling session.[14]

He was only slightly less negative towards Churchill's wish to deliver large quantities of supplies to the Soviet Union. Roosevelt's and Churchill's tendency to give supplies and materials without asking the Soviets to justify their requisitions filled him with disquiet. He noted acidly in his diary on 25 February: 'Personally, I consider it absolute madness. We have never even asked Russia to inform us of the real urgency of these reinforcements.' After the war he would recall with some bitterness: 'We kept supplying tanks and aeroplanes that could ill be spared and in doing so suffered the heaviest of losses in shipping conveying this equipment to Arctic Russia. We received nothing in return except abuse for handling the convoys inefficiently.' The notion of sending British forces to fight alongside Russian forces he would later describe as 'wild'.[15]

Though Brooke did not believe that Russia would collapse, or that it would make a separate peace with Germany, he was prepared to accept either eventuality with equanimity. Indeed, his North African project, and seemingly much of his Mediterranean strategy was designed to place Britain in a strong position should the Soviet Union collapse.

Brooke was in a distinct minority in taking these positions. The British public would probably have been shocked to learn of his views. But he had little faith that the public could really understand the issues. As he noted in his diary: ' The universal cry to start a Western Front is going to be hard to compete with, and yet what can we do with some ten divisions against the German masses? Unfortunately the country fails to realize the situation we are in.' Brooke's views did not change as Soviet reverses and hints of a separate peace filled the air. The Russian winter offensive slowly ground to a halt and by April the situation on the Eastern Front was widely regarded as ominous. On 16 April, in the midst of general panic over the Russian situation, he noted in his diary that 'Public Opinion is shouting for the formation of a new Western Front to assist the Russians. But they have no conception of the difficulties and dangers entailed. The prospects of success are small and dependent on a mass of unknowns, whilst the chances of disaster are great and dependent on a mass of well-established facts. Should Germany be getting the best of an attack on Russia, the pressure for invasion of France will be at its strongest, and yet this is just the most dangerous set of circumstances for us.'[16]

Brooke was somewhat more sympathetic with the desire to get along with the Americans, but this too can be easily overstated. His predecessor, Field Marshal Dill, had been placed in charge of the British military mission in Washington and kept Brooke regularly informed of the growing American criticism of Britain's military effort — reports that usually left Brooke cold, but on occasion provoked his scorn or ire, even if he exercised self-restraint. Believing that British troops would have to undertake the most difficult combat on the Western side, he was still conscious of how dependent Britain was on others for the sinews of war. Without healthy aid from American war production, none of his plans were likely to come true. The Americans wanted some sign of offensive action. Brooke realized he would have to give it.

Conscious of the need to make some gesture in the direction of appeasing the American military, Brooke nevertheless was aghast when he found out what objectives they were setting. General Marshall, Secretary of War Henry L. Stimson, and a group of bright young staff officers — including General Dwight Eisenhower — all came to define the survival of the Red Army at or very near the top of their list of priorities. They were prepared, in principle, to sacrifice large numbers of men to ensure the survival of the Soviet Union in a 1943 cross-Channel invasion (*Round-Up*) and only a slightly smaller number in a 1942 version of that operation (*Sledgehammer*), which was widely regarded as a sacrificial gesture intended to prove to the Soviet leadership that the West cared.

Brooke's lack of enthusiasm for Britain's allies and their desiderata brought him into constant conflict with the Prime Minister. But they also disagreed — emotionally, if not intellectually — on the kind of strategy Britain should adopt. The disagreement stemmed from Brooke's conviction, dating from the summer of 1940, that for the time being an essentially defensive policy was mandatory and a Second Front in Europe was out of the question. Churchill, on the other hand, saw nothing save political disaster in such a course. Even if public opinion had not been clamouring for a Second Front, Churchill would have liked to do something for an ally in trouble. There was also the fact that he had based part of his opposition to Chamberlain in 1939 on the premise that Russia could have been courted and that success on that front might have made all the difference in restraining Hitler. If Churchill did not maintain his credibility on Anglo-Soviet solidarity, there were any number of possible rivals prepared to seize the opening.

Such considerations were of course political, but Brooke had to take them into account. After all, Churchill was not only Prime Minister but also his direct supervisor as Minister of Defence. Brooke could have ignored Churchill's political dilemma only if he was also prepared to accept with equanimity the replacement of Churchill as Minister of Defence. At times Brooke was tempted, saying rather incautiously that the P.M. was just like a 'child' who had lost his temper, and that at such times a nurse 'should come and fetch him away.' Churchill's pretensions of having inherited the strategic genius of his great ancestor Marlborough left Brooke cold, and he could scarcely resist poking fun at Churchill's attempts to demonstrate bayonet drill before his guests. But Brooke had invested an enormous amount of time in getting Churchill to appreciate the problems of the military. Like others who dealt with the 'Churchill problem', he felt 'Resignation is no answer. It is forgotten in a fortnight.' The fact that all Churchill's rivals for power were even more insistent advocates of help to Russia — not only Beaverbrook and Cripps, but also Eden — could only fill Brooke with apprehension at the thought of Churchill's being overturned, a possibility that recent scholarship has shown was less remote than has previously been thought. Brooke would have hated to start from scratch with anyone else.[17]

As a regular attendant of the Cabinet's Defence Committee meetings, Brooke was well placed to see how the political pressures were bearing down on Churchill. What these were like he recorded in his diary on 2 January 1942: '. . . most unpleasant remarks by various ministers in connection with defeats of our forces.' On 9 February he recorded, there was 'nothing but abuse for the army.' The humiliation of Singapore, and the German naval dash up the Channel, ended any reticence the War Cabinet might have had to criticize too directly British military performance. Brooke was a shrewd observer and very quickly developed an appreciation of the Prime Minister's troubles, noting anxiously, in his diary on 17 February, that he found the Prime Minister 'in a dejected mood', having just come back from dealing with a 'troublesome house' — adding with evident concern, 'I am afraid that he is in for a lot more trouble.' Months later, on 29 June, Brooke was still paying very close attention to these problems, recording in his diary a War Cabinet session at which the Minister of Labour, Ernest Bevin, was 'full of uneducated peevish questions about the Middle East operations, continually asking questions on points that I had just explained.'[18]

Increasingly Churchill had to join the critics of the services rather than appear to condone what appeared to be hopeless passivity. In the middle of one Cabinet meeting in 1941, Churchill turned to Brooke and said: 'Pray explain, C.I.G.S., how is it that in the Middle East 750,000 men always turn up for their pay and rations but when it comes to fighting only 100,000 men turn up. Explain to us exactly how the remaining 650,000 men are occupied.' After treating Brooke roughly on another occasion, Churchill approached him later '. . . with that astounding charm of his, . . . and said to me, "I am sorry, Brookie, if I had to be unpleasant about Auchinleck and the Middle East."' Brooke could understand. Indeed, from time to time Churchill made a point of keeping Brooke informed of the measures he had taken to handle political pressures, and as often as not Brooke was whole-heartedly in agreement.[19]

But there were also many times when Churchill's anger and disappoint-ment with the Eighth Army was real and very sharp. In an August 1941 Defence Committee meeting, the Prime Minister spoke once again of the troublesome problem of '600,000 useless mouths' in Egypt. On 10 June 1942 he exploded, as much with sorrow as with anger, to Brooke and Kennedy: 'I don't know what we can do for that Army. All our efforts to help seem to be in vain.' Nothing, he complained, '. . . seems to help them. And I am the one who gets his neck wrung when things go wrong. . . . Why are there not more men in the fighting line? They all come up for their rations, but not to fight . . . I doubt that Army's offensive spirit.'[20]

Fortunately for Brooke, Churchill was usually gentler with him than with the Admiralty — in part because Churchill was less confident of the technical basis of his Army criticism, and perhaps also because he recog-nized that the Army had not received much from the prewar defence budgets. But browbeat the Generals he did, though less vehemently than the Admirals. This began at the start of the war and greatly increased with the disasters of 1941. In April 1942 Churchill exploded when one of the Army planners, General Kennedy, dared to consider the prospect that Egypt might have to be abandoned. Churchill declaimed: 'Wavell has 400,000 men. If they lose Egypt, blood will flow. I will have firing parties to shoot the generals.' It was with great difficulty that Brooke managed to keep Churchill from sacking Kennedy.[21]

The Prime Minister's reaction to the general erosion of the offensive-minded spirit in the British armed forces was embodied in a general directive he issued on 28 April 1941: 'It is not to be expected that the British forces of the land, sea and air in the Mediterranean would wish to survive so vast and shameful a defeat as would be entailed by our expulsion from Egypt, having regard to the difficulties of the enemy and his comparatively small numbers . . . . No surrenders by officers and men will be considered tolerable unless at least 50 per cent casualties are sustained by the unit or force in question. . . . Generals and Staff Officers surprised by the enemy are to use their pistols in self defence.'[22]

During the difficult first months of 1942 the situation was so grave that even Churchill hesitated to propose anything that would divert British military resources away from the crucial danger-points. Churchill could only sit and wait hopefully for the best possible outcome from Auchinleck's planned offensive in Libya. By force of circumstance, therefore, the Prime

Minister and the Chief of the Imperial Staff found themselves in a truce. But Churchill was unhappy with the policy of restraint, and impatient to surmount the immediate crisis in Libya. Brooke therefore had his hands full trying to keep the impatient Churchill from prodding Auchinleck into a poorly prepared offensive.

But Churchill, though recognizing the necessity of husbanding every resource possible for Auchinleck's offensive, could not help asking, as the Russian situation deteriorated late in the winter of 1941-2, for some action that could help the Soviet Union. More precisely he demanded that Germany be made to keep resources in the West, a goal that he believed could best be accomplished by an attack on the Cherbourg salient. Brooke seemed to have defeated this project by agreeing to consider a large raid on the Calais front, but within weeks Churchill was back, seeking some more substantial landing.[23]

By April the combined pressures were so great that Brooke momentarily had to yield when General George Marshall came to London. On the eve of the General's arrival Brooke recorded in his diary that 'This Empire has never been in such a precarious position throughout history.' The proposal that enormous risks should be taken for the sake of the Soviet Union, for which Brooke cared not one whit, made it quite difficult to pay lip-service to Marshall's plans — what Brooke called 'castles in the air'. Nevertheless Brooke gamely agreed in principle with the American plan for a 1943 landing — and possibly even an emergency landing in 1942 — in Europe.[24]

Churchill, growing rebellious at the pressures coming from the combination of domestic and foreign critics, co-operated enough with Brooke during the spring and early summer of 1942 to extricate Britain from Marshall's plan for a 1942 cross-Channel attack (Sledgehammer). But Brooke and Churchill, while agreeing that so ambitious a project must be opposed, still differed about Churchill's demand for some offensive against Germany. Early in May, Churchill tried to get one started and refused to believe that so modest an operation as the recapture of the Channel Islands was beyond Britain's capabilities. He thoroughly bulldozed the General Staff and very nearly succeeded in getting the plan adopted while Brooke was temporarily out of London. But Brooke was soon able to note in his diary with some satisfaction, '. . . . returned just barely in time on morning of 6 May to turn down a landing in Alderney.' Brooke opposed the plan because it would simply tie down a British force and expose it to relentless German attack for no strategic gain. It took him another five days of difficult debate to get what looked like the definitive cancellation of the project.[25]

As the pressures for some sort of offensive operation began to accumulate, particularly from the Prime Minister's office, Brooke must have wondered whether Churchill was not trying to repeat what he had done to Dill: badger him until a dismissal could be justified. Brooke was vulnerable. He had not been Churchill's first choice for CIGS. Nye had been, and only

Nye's lack of seniority in 1941 had stopped that selection. Since then Nye had shown himself, as Brooke later admitted, brilliantly able. Just a few weeks before Dieppe, Churchill dangled before Brooke the invitation to take command of British troops in Libya. This was Churchill's subtle way of saying that he was prepared to replace him. To stay, Brooke had to work with the Prime Minister and appreciate his political needs at home and abroad. This he had done already, to a remarkable extent — otherwise the suggestion that he could be replaced would, one suspects, have been delivered a lot less sweetly. Nevertheless Churchill clearly wanted more support than he was getting from Brooke.[26]

In the summer of 1942, as Mountbatten pushed forward with *Rutter* and then *Jubilee*, Churchill demanded a major offensive against Germany and grew more impatient with those who explained that the time was not yet ripe. His scorn for Brooke's organization was reaching fever-pitch. It was clear that if Brooke resisted too much the demands for a Second Front, he — and perhaps even Churchill — might be out; while if he gave in uncritically to the demands for an offensive against France, the war might be lost. He had to find some substitute that would avoid these hazards and, given his conservative approach to force deployment, the cost would have to be kept to a minimum.

Brooke's obsession with keeping down the cost of any offensive military gesture was underscored when in March the Directors of Plans recommended a major sacrifice operation on the Continent for Russia's benefit. Brooke did not argue with the principle, only with the size contemplated, saying on 10 March that '. . . we could not afford to lose 6 or 8 or our best divisions in a diversion of this nature. We should be sending 4 or 5 divisions overseas in the next few months and the reduction of Home Forces by 11 or 12 divisions would leave us perilously weak in the event of an ultimate attempt at invasion.' He had also objected the previous December to the notion of sending two divisions to the Soviet Union, which he felt were more than Britain could afford. Still, the proposals kept coming, stimulated by the announcement on 9 May that Molotov, Soviet foreign minister, would soon be visiting London, apparently encouraged by the Americans to think a Second Front was possible. Churchill was under intense pressure to produce some gesture for the Soviets. As Brooke's biographer, Sir Arthur Bryant, noted, this was transmitted down to Brooke and was 'almost impossible to resist.' On 13 May a gesture that Brook could approve appeared on the horizon when Mountbatten presented his outline plan for an attack on Dieppe. In their relief the Chiefs of Staff seemed to pay scant attention to the apologies Mountbatten made for presenting a plan that still contained important unresolved problems. Brooke's approval of the outline, encompassing the use of one-and-a-half divisions of ground troops, probably indicates the maximum size of the gesture he was prepared to concede to parry the pressures that were bearing down on him and Churchill from the Second-Front-Now movement.[27]

This limitation on the size of the effort that could be made for Russia does not appear to have been stated categorically in any official document. Throughout the war there was discussion aplenty, in abstract terms, about the necessity of risking men and being prepared to take losses. Churchill had felt that a military operation should not be ruled out merely because of an expected loss of twenty per cent of the men embarking. Quentin Reynolds, in his 1943 book on Dieppe, attributed to Mountbatten the term 'expendables', meaning 'Not well-trained pilots, or navigators or specialists, but the ordinary soldier or sailor [who] is an expendable. It is true that he can only be expended at a certain rate.' These were of course abstract statements, and sensitive officers knew better than to say that the men in any operation were expendable — it would be corrosive to morale and offensive to families. But the fact remains that Churchill and his military advisers were all considering what would be the most inexpensive gesture in terms of manpower. Brooke's thinking seems clear. He considered two divisions excessive — though not (according to the record) a division and a half. Less than that was not likely to be noticed, and hence was regarded as insufficient.[28]

Such calculations could provide the answer to the puzzled German officer, interrogating prisoners captured at Dieppe, who remarked that *Jubilee* appeared to be too large for a raid and too small for a lodgement. The size of the operation was determined not by weighing the military objectives but by estimating what size operation might register with the Second Front movement as a decent gesture, while still not jeopardizing the integrity of Brooke's plans for waging war that summer.[29]

The process of defining such a gesture began in earnest in connection with Molotov's visits to London on his way both to and from a conference with President Roosevelt. Churchill's advisers all assumed that the top Soviet objective was to secure some offensive operation against German positions in France, which the Soviets, studiously ignoring the way the Western powers had provided one in the Far East, insisted on regarding as the only possible location for a Second Front. Anticipating Soviet demands, Churchill intensified the strategic debate. Though he agreed with Brooke that *Sledgehammer* was a most dubious proposition, he coaxed the Chiefs to approve something larger than *Rutter*. In his opinion Brooke, with his tight parameters, was cutting matters rather too close if he thought the raiding program by itself would meet the exigencies of the political situation. On 23 May, Churchill spent three hours with Brooke and Mountbatten discussing other invasion possibilities. Brooke staved off most suggestions, but not without leaving some opening for an even larger raid than Dieppe, *Imperator*, a massive super-raid involving four divisions that would stay in France for up to a week. Even that was not enough for Churchill, who turned once again to the Norway project as another gesture towards the Russians. Brooke found himself obliged to study it carefully once more.[30]

Most of Brooke's surrenders to Churchill's ideas for diversions proved to be only temporary. Despite the many times Churchill forced reconsideration of the Norway project in 1941 and 1942, and the many times Brooke seemed close to surrender, he always managed to get out at the last minute by imposing one condition or another — as in October 1941, when he approved a Norwegian expedition on conditions that the Admiralty was certain to refuse. By this device all of Churchill's major projects for Norway were defeated one by one. *Imperator* was also successfully killed in June 1942, with Mountbatten's help. What seems so surprising about Brooke's acquiescence in Dieppe is that it was not temporary but final.[31]

Brooke did not lack opportunities to kill the Dieppe raid, as he had managed to do with many other operations. He could have done this when Montgomery, after the cancellation of *Rutter*, opposed its revival. But Churchill needed — perhaps psychologically, certainly politically — some major offensive operation against the German occupation of Europe, and if an assault against the German front-line could not be arranged soon, he would focus on another even more dangerous project — an eventuality that Brooke wanted to avoid. It was becoming increasingly difficult to preserve the integrity of the planning process. As one key planner later recalled: 'Whenever an idea, however wild, was thrown up, he [Churchill] ordered detailed examinations, or plans, or both, to be made at high speed. Our stables were so full of these unlikely starters that we were hard put to it to give the favourites the attention they deserved.'[32]

While Brooke was working on Churchill's pet project, and the planners were exploring others, the pressures coming from the Soviets — along with their supporters in Britain, and increasingly from the Americans — were continuing to grow. At the end of May the Americans conceded to the Soviets a press communiqué that Molotov had drafted, not to say dictated, which said that full agreement had been reached about the 'urgent' need for creating a Second Front.[33]

In anticipation of Molotov's return after his first visit to London, the Chiefs of Staff recognized on 6 June that a gesture was required and proposed that 'if things go badly on the Eastern Front "Imperator" would be our response to a "cri de coeur" from the Russians.' For a while the planners seemed to agree that this was the best they could do. As for the Chiefs, they seemed fully resigned to the massive losses implied. But Churchill, who had studied the plans carefully, did not think any of the postulated military objectives could be attained, and complained that 'we should, in addition, have to face the odium of an evacuation and the probable loss of a considerable part of the force and its equipment.' He ruled out *Imperator* on 11 June. On Molotov's return to London, Churchill presented him with the confidential *aide-mémoire*, drafted in collaboration with the Chiefs of Staff, demurring to any notion of a Second Front promise, while still assuring the Soviets that a large raiding program would be undertaken. In his own mind Churchill still hoped to do more. He refused to consider that this was a substitute for a Norwegian campaign. Mountbatten's raiding program was merely a supplement, albeit an impressive one, to whatever package Churchill would ultimately present to the Soviets. For Churchill there were only two remaining operations worthy of consideration: an attempt to seize airfields in Norway (*Jupiter*), making more secure the convoys to the Soviet Union, and an invasion of North Africa (*Gymnast/Torch*), from which an allied force could strike at Rommel's rear. On more distant horizons was the possibility of moving from North Africa to strike at Sicily and perhaps even the Italian mainland.[34]

Surveying these prospects, the Chiefs had no difficulty in choosing the North African project — they considered the difficulties inherent in any offensive in Norway to be insurmountable. But Churchill could not see how a North African invasion, by itself, would appease the Soviets, or Second Front supporters in the West, for it was far from self-evident how action in North Africa could have any effect on the momentous events on the Eastern Front. It was most unlikely that any of Churchill's would-be successors — Eden, Cripps, or even Beaverbrook — would buy the notion that Britain could discharge her moral obligations to the Soviet Union with a North African operation. For all these reasons, Churchill insisted on some other substantial gesture towards the Soviets, even though he liked the North African project as contributing to his Mediterranean strategy. All through June and July he was locked in combat with his Chiefs of Staff over this requirement. As Churchill later reported in his memoirs: 'If it had been in my power to give orders I would have settled upon "Torch" and "Jupiter" properly synchronised for the autumn. . . . ' But the Chiefs were not willing to be pushed into this combination at so delicate a point in the war. Nor did Churchill dare to command them, knowing that another fiasco might spell the end of his government. He must coax the Chiefs into *Jupiter*, so that if worse came to worst he would be in a position to say, as he had after the Crete defeat, that the decision had been 'freely taken' without the slightest pressure from him.[35]

As part of his effort to get the Chiefs to accept both *Torch* and *Jupiter*, Churchill decided to go to Washington, following closely upon Mountbatten's June trip, to kill *Sledgehammer*, which he knew was the bugbear of the Chiefs of Staff. Brooke was relieved to hear of Churchill's determination and as a reciprocal gesture the Chiefs dutifully promised to study the Norwegian project. It seems clear that they were playing for time until Churchill had done the dirty work of undoing the apparent commitments made to Marshall in April. But when Churchill returned two weeks later he brought nothing but bad news. He had failed in his mission to get

*Sledgehammer* cancelled outright. Moreover, he was depressed and in poor humour, having been humiliated in the President's office when he had suddenly been confronted with the news of the Tobruk surrender, which was followed swiftly by news of the tabling of a Motion of Censure in Parliament. Churchill had been forced to cut his trip short. He had already made up his mind — and the Cabinet had confirmed this, on the morning of 30 June — that this challenge in the House should be taken up immediately. That would mean a vote on 2 or 3 July. The *Rutter* force was due to begin boarding the ships on 2 July. The two things, a potential Dieppe disaster and the Vote of Censure, were thus placed in perilously close proximity.[36]

Under these conditions, that same day, 30 June, Churchill called in Mountbatten and Brooke for a private re-examination of the Dieppe project. No Canadian was present, as Churchill could not have wanted many witnesses if he was going to cancel for reasons of domestic politics. Only Ismay and Hollis, from the Chiefs of Staff Secretariat, were present. Nor for that matter could Mountbatten have wanted his Force Commanders present if Churchill was becoming apprehensive. Thus Mountbatten brought with him only one of the Force Commanders, Hughes-Hallett, the chief architect of the raid — who, one would have thought, would stand firmly by the project. Churchill opened the meeting by obliquely referring to the political crisis, explaining that this was no time to learn through adversity. He was suggesting that he no longer needed such an operation if it would turn out badly. He then asked whether success was certain. That should have evoked a reply about how uncertain it was, which would have given Churchill the opportunity to cancel it. Indeed, Hughes-Hallett did not think he could give Churchill the assurances he requested; according to his later recollection, he replied by saying that '. . . so far as I knew every ship might be blazing with 15 minutes of the beginning of the engagement.' But Brooke jumped in to save the Dieppe raid, saying, as Hughes-Hallett recalled, 'that he thought the question was one of the most unreasonable ones he had ever heard, observing that the object of the operation was precisely to find out whether or not success [in a cross-Channel attack] would result.' He insisted that no military leader would ever agree to plan such an attack unless this operation was attempted.[37]

Brooke was either showing his complete ignorance of the *Rutter* plan and its inadequacy as a test of cross-Channel invasion tactics, or he was simply hiding his real reasons for supporting the project. Certainly he knew better than to dismiss Churchill's perfectly reasonable question. One could forgive a less-experienced staff officer's not seeing the defects of the plan — such as the Canadian, Colonel Churchill Mann, who, when asked to study the outline plan for feasibility, had concluded on the basis of his limited experience that 'such a plan, on the face of it, is almost a fantastic conception of the place most suited to land a strong force of A.F.V. [Armoured Fighting Vehicles, i.e. tanks]', and then went on to explore it, as he said, with an 'unbiassed mind'. But what was Brooke's excuse, with all his knowledge of the importance of fire support in frontal attacks, not to mention his long experience of the theoretical side acquired in eight years at the Staff College, Camberley, and at the Imperial Defence College — not to mention his time as Director of Military training and as Commander of the First Mobile Division, Britain's first armoured division? Coming from a man of his enormous professional competence — from the non-pareil, really, of the British military establishment — his rationalization of the Dieppe raid at this meeting seems scarcely credible.[38]

What Brooke was doing was buying time while he sorted out his strategic priorities. It was the same policy that the Naval Commander in the Mediterranean, Admiral Sir Andrew Cunningham, had recommended to the First Sea Lord: 'With a man like [Churchill] . . . it is not good policy to present him with a brick wall. . . .' That Brooke was temporizing became evident the next day, when the Chiefs of Staff, under his direction, reassured the War Cabinet by proclaiming that they were 'definitely committed both to the Americans and to the Russians to prepare for offensive operations in 1942.' As Brooke's diary shows, he did not believe that there existed any obligation to make a major gesture on behalf of the Soviets. More evidence of the Chiefs' playing for time was reflected on 6 July, when they accepted Mountbatten's recommendation that if *Rutter* were cancelled, 'consideration' should be given later to remounting it. The wording seemed innocuous enough, committing the Chiefs to nothing more than keeping open minds, which in Whitehall parlance meant very little indeed. But it avoided giving Churchill the bad news all at once — a goal of some importance to Brooke inasmuch as the Chiefs were preparing another negative response on Norway. The issue that was weighing uppermost in their minds was how to tell Churchill once and for all that nothing could be done in Norway. That very day, on 7 July, they finally worked up the courage, formally reporting that after mature consideration they were absolutely convinced that *Jupiter* was not a workable military proposition. Only a few hours earlier the depressing news of the forced cancellation of *Rutter* arrived and the utility of Mountbatten's temporizing resolution of 6 July was made manifest. It is not surprising, therefore, that when Mountbatten revealed in the coming days that his intention was to remount *Rutter*, the Chiefs made no effort to stop him. The pattern is clear. They were waiting until Churchill slowly came to accept the inevitable; that the sole military initiative of 1942 would be *Gymnast*, combined with whatever raiding project Mountbatten could still work up. The danger they were trying to avoid was the same one that General Pownall had recognized as early as October 1941, when as Vice-Chief of the Imperial General Staff he observed that ' . . . if he [Churchill] were allowed a free rein . . . he would get himself into a series of disasters sufficient to lose us the war.'[39]

The degree to which the Chiefs were now positively involved in a campaign of dissimulation with Churchill can be seen in the way they handled *Jupiter* in the same period. When Churchill refused to take 'no' for an answer, and proposed that a 'more flexible and fertile brain' (General McNaughton) should restudy the question of the feasibility of *Jupiter*, the Chiefs accepted. Though Brooke ostentatiously said that McNaughton would not have access to the previous negative studies so that he would not be prejudiced, he took the Canadian aside at the first opportune moment, and, as Brooke noted in his diary, '. . . informed him privately how matters stood' — that is, that the Chiefs of Staff considered *Jupiter* to be an impossibility. McNaughton loyally proceeded to mark time as much as he could. Churchill no doubt divined the truth, for he later commented somewhat acidly in this memoirs: 'I did not hear from the General for a long time.' And as he observed when McNaughton's report came in: '. . . [it] certainly does not err on the side of underrating the difficulties before us.' Nevertheless, the ploy worked, for by then *Jupiter* was no longer feasible — if it ever had been — by reason of the imminent autumnal storms. Dieppe had probably served the purpose of helping to pacify Churchill by suggesting that at least one offensive operation was pending.[40]

If *Jupiter* had been feasible, Dieppe might never have occurred because Churchill did not really like frontal attacks against high odds whenever he came to examine them closely (*pace* his bloodthirsty rhetoric). *Sledgehammer, Imperator,* and *Rutter* were all of that variety. When the 30 June meeting occurred, he had already managed to cancel *Imperator,* was well on his way to vetoing *Sledgehammer* (the cable to Roosevelt went out one week later), and evidently intended to do the same with *Rutter* unless he received iron-clad guarantees, which in the nature of things were impossible to give. But it is not hard to reconstruct Churchill's thinking behind his inclination to cancel *Rutter.* If, as he hoped, he would get his way with *Jupiter*, Dieppe was no longer needed as a gesture towards the Soviets, or as evidence of an aggressive spirit. The fate of Dieppe was thus intimately tied to the fate of *Jupiter.* The same conclusion is reached if one examines the situation from the Canadian perspective. McNaughton would not have wanted to risk the bulk of his force in two daring expeditions in the space of a couple of months, nor would the Canadian Government have allowed it. Thus, if the Canadians had been tapped for Norway, as Churchill intended, McNaughton would have had to give up Dieppe. Of course McNaughton must have hoped that the converse would prove true: that supporting Dieppe would more easily allow him to refuse *Jupiter*. The problem from Brooke's point of view was that if the Dieppe raid were to be dropped, Churchill would take this as evidence of a spirit of negativism, not to say defeatism, and would redouble his efforts to force *Jupiter* on the Chiefs. To prevent this from happening, Brooke was prepared to keep Dieppe alive, and from this perspective the disaster that resulted may be said to be part of the price paid for the slow strangulation of *Jupiter*.

Why the Chiefs should try to avoid an impression of negativism is not hard to fathom. As Generals Kennedy and Dill explained, even in the best of times it was difficult '. . .for a soldier to advise against a bold offensive plan. One lays oneself open to charges of defeatism, of inertia, or even of "cold feet". Human nature being what it is, there is a natural tendency to acquiesce in an offensive plan of doubtful merit rather than to face such charges.' This observation had even more force when the government was under siege. On 3 July, one day after the Vote of Censure was defeated (three days after Churchill's conference on Dieppe), Kennedy noted in his diary: 'In spite of what one may feel about Winston's methods and his judgement, I do believe that, on balance, it is best that he should continue as Prime Minister.' The studied detachment of this statement expressed both a perception of Churchill's precarious position and the degree to which Churchill's increasingly difficult behaviour had caused the military to entertain doubts about his value. Of course the final balance was still believed to be positive. But if Churchill was to stay, he had to be helped to defuse the Second Front movement and satiate the public's demand for some evidence of offensive military spirit.[41]

The conviction that something must be done for the Soviet Union, which seemed so acute in the days just before the Vote of Censure, continued to grow after it. On the same day as the vote, Sebastopol fell to the Germans, and on 7 July Vornezh followed. In the United States, *Time* warned on 13 July that Hitler was well on his way to victory in Russia and that if he succeeded, '. . . the Allies will then have lost their best chance to defeat Germany and win World War II.' *The Times* echoed these warnings nine days later, editorializing that 'those who watch and wait are well aware that another adverse turn of the wheel would have its instant if unpredictable consequences.' Rostov fell the next day, which was a crushing blow, not just to Russia but to the Allies. In that atmosphere no one wanted to cancel Dieppe for good — which would amount to breaking the promise, contained in the 10 June *aide-mémoire*, about raids of ever-increasing scope and frequency — for according to Mountbatten there was no other large-scale plan on the boards for that year. It was convenient, from this perspective, that *Rutter* had not been ruled out.[42]

First on 30 June and then again on 6 July, when he appears to have been temporizing, Brooke accepted Mountbatten's proposition that even if *Rutter* were to be cancelled, consideration should be given to remounting it. He did this not because he thought it had good prospects, but rather because it was the least costly effort that could be undertaken to reduce the political pressures acting upon the Government. That may seem a difficult conclusion to make about so very professional an officer as Brooke. But he was not the only one who was forced to make such unpleasant choices. A comparison with the American Chief of Staff's surrender on the *Gymnast/Torch* project is illuminating. General Marshall, in his rigorous conception of military professionalism and the importance of strict procedures, was very much like Brooke. He too made a religion of concentrating military effort, and accordingly despised the North African project, completely agreeing with his superior, Secretary of War Henry L. Stimson, in considering it the worst sort of 'diversionary debauch', which could only detract from the urgent task of beating Germany in Europe. But as Marshall later explained, he was faced ultimately with the necessity of choosing *Torch* as the least-damaging diversion, and he sadly concluded that all the others were worse. The reasoning was not pretty. The way Marshall would tell the story to the official army historians was that 'We failed to see that the leader in a democracy has to keep the people entertained.' This should be compared with Brooke's apprehensive assessment of the impact of public opinion on military strategy, recorded as early as March 1942:

> To begin with a democracy is at a great handicap when up against a dictatorship when it comes to war. Secondly a government with one big man in it, and that one a grave danger in many respects, is in a parlous way. Party politics and party interests still override larger war issues. Petty jealousies colour decisions and influence destinies. Politicians still suffer from that little knowledge of military matters which give them unwarranted confidence that they are born strategists. As a result they confuse issues, affect decisions, and convert simple problems and plans into confused tangles and hopeless muddles.[43]

The tangles increased over the next few months as *Jupiter, Imperator,* and *Sledgehammer* — all non-starters — were debated. Brooke's strangely cool and detached reaction to the grim denouement of Dieppe suggests that he had long since written off the entire force. Sir Charles Wilson, who was with Brooke in the Egyptian desert, recorded in his diary: ' "It is a lesson", the CIGS grunted, "to the people who are clamouring for the invasion of France." ' On 19 August, after an evening spent with Montgomery, who filled him with confidence about the prospects for dealing with Rommel, Brooke wrote in his diary — in which he habitually penned morose entries whenever he was surprised by reversals or defeats: 'Very comfortable. Very lovely night with the sound of the waves only a few yards away.' He later recalled: 'I went to bed that night with a wonderful feeling of contentment.' A third of the globe away, similar waves were lapping on the blood-stained beaches of Dieppe, littered with the sad evidence of a brief and hopeless battle.[44]

# 6

# The Royal Navy on
# the Eve of Dieppe

The views on Dieppe of the First Sea Lord, Admiral Sir Dudley Pound, like those of the other Service Chiefs, went largely unrecorded. What is known of Pound's position is scarcely more than a tantalizing hint, contained in the papers of Rear-Admiral Baillie-Grohman, that makes little sense. As usual we must fill in the outline by examining the context. According to Baillie-Grohman, when he arrived from Cairo early in June to join Combined Operations Headquarters, he looked at the plans for the Dieppe raid and immediately asked why a battleship had not been requested. Mountbatten called him aside and told him that it had been requested but that a firm 'no' had been given by the 'highest authority' (almost certainly Pound). The reason, Mountbatten reported, was that '. . . should the battleship be sunk, we could never claim Dieppe as a victory: it was highly important at this period to be able to report a victory (Russia, our own morale, etc. etc.).' The remark bears much similarity to Pound's complaint made earlier that year in a letter to Admiral Cunningham expressing puzzlement at the treatment his Service was receiving from public opinion: 'I do not know why but both the House of Commons and the Public seem to think that the sinking of an important ship is a crisis, while nobody takes any notice of the loss of 30 or 40 bombers in one night.'[1]

That Pound should want to avoid a major public-relations reversal is understandable. A battleship operating off Dieppe would have been vulnerable because perfect air-cover was impossible until the Luftwaffe was decisively defeated. (In the actual Dieppe raid, German planes managed to score a direct hit on one destroyer off Dieppe, which had to be sunk to prevent its capture, while another barely limped home.) Battleships, though having much better armour plate, present larger targets, and the possibility of a sinking could not be excluded, particularly as the narrow confines of the Channel do not allow the manoeuvering space necessary to take evasive action from hostile aircraft. But if all this was true, then why did Pound not veto the Dieppe raid, as he certainly knew that eight destroyers could never replace the firepower of one battleship? Why did he seem to accept a raid whose objective was to secure a morale-boosting victory if he was also ruling out the firepower without which victory was doubtful? There was in Pound's position a *non sequitur*, inasmuch as he was on the one hand denying a battleship for fear of a morale-depressing casualty, while on the other increasing the likelihood that Dieppe itself would be a morale-crushing defeat for want of a battleship. Baillie-Grohman himself called this 'pretty feeble' reasoning. What could have made Pound take such a logically inconsistent position? The explanation lies in the situation the Royal Navy found itself in on the eve of Dieppe. Put briefly, it was simply that in the months preceding the Dieppe raid Pound, the First Sea Lord, though well supported by his civilian chief, A.V. Alexander (the First Lord of the Admiralty), was under pressure so intense — the most severe the Admiralty faced throughout the long war — that he felt powerless to object to the preparations for Dieppe, however bad, indeed illogical, they might appear. Such ineffectualness will seem implausible to anyone familiar with Pound's reputation as an unshakable, eminently logical, Service Chief, thoroughly grounded in sound common sense.

The crisis for the Navy in the summer of 1942 — from which stemmed Pound's concern over morale — was due in large measure to an accumulation of problems dating back to the beginning of the war. The Admiralty had started out on a shaky footing because everyone expected so much from the premier service. When war broke out, the British naval preponderance over the German fleet was staggering because Germany had only two modern commissioned ships with guns of eleven inches, the *Scharnhorst* and the *Gneisenau*. It was therefore expected that such superiority, coupled with the geographic advantages Britain had over Germany, would ensure victory in any naval contest. It should have been relatively easy to deny the German navy access to the Atlantic, the most important objective of British naval policy. A strong fleet at Scapa Flow, off northern Scotland, would box in the German battle fleet and prevent it from leaving its bases via the North Sea. The British Navy was strategically well placed, and had the force to spare.

The advantage gained by Britain's superiority in capital ships, though great, was nothing compared to the advantage now conferred by the ability of British long-range aircraft to maintain surveillance of the German fleet right up to the German bases in the North Sea and the Baltic — something that had not been possible in the First World War.

The German navy might also have been expected to draw some benefit from innovations in the air, using long-range aircraft to guide submarines to targets. But German attempts to capitalize on these possibilities came rather late, and were on a modest scale: they required resources that Hermann

Goering, who headed the Ministry of War Production as well as the Luftwaffe at the start of hostilities, was not inclined to allocate to the navy. Where Germany should have been able to redress the balance a bit was with technological advances in underwater weapons, the torpedo and the mine. But here too fortune seemed to smile on the British Navy, for the surface-launched torpedoes developed by the Germans had so short a range that their use was impossible without attacking suicidally at close range. Underwater torpedoes were of course the key, but the Germans were plagued for a long time by a faulty form of percussion detonator, which meant that a very high proportion failed to go off at all.

As for the mine, Britain managed to deal effectively with moored mines by means of running paravanes — a mine-deflecting device — early in the war. The magnetic mine, which proved deadly for a short time, was also overcome by the beginning of 1940, thanks in part to the chance discovery of one dropped on an English mud-flat; it was seized, the mechanism was defused, and its secrets revealed. Britain simply degaussed her ships, and by March 1940 virtually all allied ships had been degaussed. The Asdic U-boat detector was also an undeniable technological advantage, but it had severe technical limitations as it did not reveal the depth of an enemy submarine and was useless in detecting craft on the ocean's surface. Thus in actual use it failed to live up to expectations.[2]

But it was primarily to the size and power of the British Navy that everyone looked. Before the war it had been receiving the better part of the defence budget but had not been wisely managed. As Churchill, then First Lord of the Admiralty, learned to his horror, the budget for 1938 had not included provision for any destroyers, and only 32 were in construction from previous budgets. This was hardly adequate in the face of an enemy that was certain to resort to a major submarine attack.[3]

The British public's expectations of an early Naval victory were dashed almost at the start of the war by a German coup. In October 1939 Lieutenant-Commander Günther Prien managed to bring a German submarine inside the main British base at Scapa Flow, sinking the battleship *Royal Oak*, and leave unmolested. The British public were shocked, and until war's end it was hard to shake the belief that somehow the deed had been made possible by traitors within the service. This exploit in fact merely demonstrated the weakness and carelessness that characterized defences at the base, a condition the Royal Navy would have liked to veil from public notice. But alas, just three days later German bombers were again able to penetrate its defences at Scapa Flow and succeeded in damaging the old *Iron Duke*.

These two attacks succeeded in putting the Royal Navy in a state approaching flight from its home base, with part of the fleet being transferred to Loch Ewe on the west coast of Scotland. But it too was penetrated by a German submarine, which badly damaged the battleship *Nelson*. Soon the

Navy was being based in the Firth of Clyde. Not until March 1940 was the British fleet back and relatively secure within the revamped defences of Scapa Flow. Even then the conventional forces of the German navy, greatly outnumbered though they were, managed to wound the Royal Navy's pride, most notably by superior gunnery in the Norwegian campaign, when the *Scharnhorst* sighted and then hit the aircraft-carrier *Glorious* from 28,000 yards with only her second salvo. Soon the vessel was out of control and afire, sinking rapidly with a loss of 1,500 servicemen.

Humiliations of this kind did not sit easily on the shoulders of the First Lord of the Admiralty, Churchill, who was beside himself — alternately bristling with indignation or showing signs of deep depression. Though he acted resolutely on becoming Prime Minister, going to Scapa Flow on 31 October to plan improved defences there and at Rosyth, he seemed unwilling to accept any personal responsibility. Showing signs of stubbornness and inflexibility, he refused to accept intelligence estimates indicating that the German navy was in fact operating with meagre resources. So unwelcome was this information that Churchill posted to sea the officer in naval intelligence who had developed the profile.

This smell of defeat and humiliation put Churchill under considerable strain, with consequences that would be serious for the Navy. Refusing to accept any further losses that would attract public attention, Churchill sent major portions of the fleet to chase every reported sighting of a German raider. This threatened to play into German hands by dispersing the Royal Navy. Opposing the Prime Minister's folly was the conservative but sensible First Sea Lord, Sir Dudley Pound, who was determined to concentrate on protecting the great bulk of Britain's commerce travelling in convoys, and to chase raiders only when they attacked convoys or when there was an unusual excess of unoccupied cruisers. Only twice did Churchill's more aggressive policy of seeking out German ships pay any dividends. The first was when the German pocket battleships, *Deutschland* and *Admiral Graf Spee*, broke out into the Atlantic. Churchill insisted on action at just about any cost. With some luck a small cruiser detachment was able to force the scuttling of the *Graf Spee* in December 1939. The other occasion was in May 1941, when Churchill ordered a disproportionately large force — two battleships, one battle cruiser, one aircraft-carrier, three cruisers, and nine destroyers — to hunt the *Bismarck* with what the British naval historian Stephen Roskill has called the most extraordinary signal of the war: that the *Bismarck* had to be sunk at any cost, even if it entailed the possible loss of the largest and most modern of British battleships. This wild gamble nevertheless paid off and on 27 May 1941 the destruction of the *Bismarck* was accomplished. The fact that on these two missions Churchill turned out to be right only encouraged him to think he was right every time and to insist on his strategy.[4]

The sinking of the *Bismarck* thus paradoxically began a long period of tension between Churchill, who became Prime Minister in May 1940, and Pound. This was hardly the first time there had been friction between Prime Minister's Office and Admiralty, but Pound was at a great disadvantage because Churchill knew a lot about Admiralty matters. It was hard to put off a Prime Minister who had the interest and the knowledge to write the First Sea Lord that he had spotted a major defect in the stocking of torpedo supplies — telling him that while the stock of type 21 torpedoes was fairly good, that of type 18 'leaves very little margin'; or who was able to talk as knowledgeably on naval construction as almost anyone on the Admiralty Board.[5]

The major dispute between the two men — the one that set off the sparks between them — had to do with the question of how offensively the British Navy should operate. Churchill could not bring himself to accept a policy that seemed merely defensive. He believed firmly in demonstrating naval strength. As he later explained:

> Amid the torrent of violent events one anxiety reined supreme. Battles might be won or lost, enterprises might succeed or miscarry, territories might be gained or quitted, but dominating all our power to carry on the war, or even keep ourselves alive, lay our mastery of the ocean routes and the free approach and entry to our ports.

Though Churchill understood the reasons for Pound's conservative, essentially defensive, deployment of naval force, he solemnly warned Pound that the truth must be veiled from the public. He told him: 'I could never be responsible for a naval strategy which excluded the offensive principle.' Pound had to put up with minutes from Churchill that accused the Admiralty of being unable to understand that 'Time is the essence of success', and the planning staff of 'negativism and undue yielding to difficulties and a woeful lack of appreciation of the time factor.' A failure of a raid on the Italian-held island of Castellorizo off the Turkish coast in March prompted him to ask the First Lords of the Admiralty: 'What disciplinary or other measures are going to be taken on this deplorable piece of mismanagement after we have had eighteen months' experience of war?'[6]

Pound and Churchill never entirely settled their argument about naval strategy, and it would flare up acutely whenever raiders were active. At such times Pound would feel the pressure from Churchill as keenly as did any other commander in the war. When it became extreme, Pound would yield, detaching destroyers from convoy escort duty to search for submarines or raiders as much as 100 miles away from the convoys — almost always fruitlessly, and frequently to the serious detriment of the convoys. Whenever Churchill's attention was focused elsewhere, Pound not surprisingly reverted to his highly conservative employment of naval force.[7]

By the end of May 1940 the diversion of 31 U-boats to the German campaign in Norway virtually suspended Germany's attack on convoys, and this gave the impression that the first phase of the war at sea had ended with at least some modest success. But in the light of the great advantages the Royal Navy possessed, and of the exposed position of German ships in the Norwegian campaign itself, this was illusory.

The German conquest in May and June of Norway, the Lowlands, and France ushered in a new period of crisis for the British Navy as Germany's occupation of a large zone of French territory dramatically changed the naval situation. While hitherto Britain's ability to box the German navy in close home waters had dominated the picture, this advantage suddenly disappeared, as the Germans could now place both naval and air bases from Scandinavia to the Spanish border. German submarines could be spared the outbound voyage of 1,000 to 1,500 miles, allowing them to spend much more time in active service relatively close to their stations. This began to tell when 58 Allied ships were sunk by submarine and another 44 ships by air or mines within one month, June. Gone for Britain was the possibility of close surveillance or easy interception of German craft seeking the Atlantic. As Churchill later pointed out: 'Never before in her history had Great Britain found herself faced by enemy forces on all sides except the west, a loophole which the German Navy attempted to close and thus isolate this country from the rest of the world.' Indeed, Britain's coastal waters now became imperilled. Convoys had be routed around Scotland. The use of London as a port had to be seriously curtailed.[8]

With the Fall of France, Britain also lost the support of the French fleet, one of the world's most modern navies, which had once been a powerful adjunct to the Royal Navy. So grave was the situation that Britain felt obliged to neutralize the French fleet, going so far as to attack it at Mers-el-Kebir in North Africa on 3 July 1940. The only compensation for this loss was that Britain took control at the same time of most of the merchant fleets of the occupied countries — including France, Holland, and Norway — giving her 7 million tons of additional shipping over the 1939 shipping pool. Britain's display of determination also prompted Roosevelt to agree to turn over 50 old destroyers to the Royal Navy and assume the defence of Britain's bases in the western hemisphere. But this hardly compensated for the added burdens imposed on the Admiralty in protecting imports on new routes, defending Britain against a possible invasion, and trying to deal with the German navy's new easy access to the Atlantic — which required keeping a sizeable fleet both at sea and in home waters.[9]

Added to all these challenges was the entry of Italy into the war, which accompanied the Fall of France. The Italian navy had considerable strength, and Britain now was faced with the threat of a closed Mediterranean, with all that would mean for Malta, Egypt, and the Indian Empire. With Spain and Vichy France as unfriendly neutrals, and Italy hostile, any and all

British ship movements in the Mediterranean were likely to be reported immediately to Germany. It was a difficult or impossible situation for the Royal Navy.

Churchill, however, refused to accept that the odds were turning greatly against Britain. In opposition to naval advice, he insisted on maintaining every naval position in the Mediterranean, a decision that would later be called one of the boldest and most critical decisions of the war, but which obliged the Navy to stretch its forces so thin that there was less chance than ever of mounting the offensive operations he was constantly demanding.

The Royal Navy was now on the defensive. Though it was meagre comfort to Pound, Churchill gradually began to face this reality and understand the danger the Navy was facing. At the end of 1940 he wrote to Roosevelt:

> The danger of Great Britain being destroyed by a swift, overwhelming blow has for the time very greatly receded. In its place there is a long, gradually maturing danger, less sudden and less spectacular, but equally deadly. This mortal danger is the steady and increasing diminution of sea tonnage . . . . Unless we can establish our ability to feed this island we may fall by the way . . . . It is . . . in shipping and in the power to transport across the oceans , particularly the Atlantic Ocean, that in 1941 the crunch of the whole war will be found.

The other Chiefs of Staff also seemed to understand that every military plan now hinged on the question of supply. As Brooke put it, the Chiefs wished to know what 'was the bare minimum of imports into this country . . . ' that would enable them 'to see what could be spared for important military operations.' But understanding the primacy of the Navy's defensive role was one thing, Churchill's acceptance was another.[10]

While the Admiralty seemed to have the crisis well in hand, managing for a while to keep supplies flowing in at a more than acceptable rate, there was little grumbling. But this was due less to the Royal Navy's success than to Goering's conflict with the German Naval Command over armaments production, labour, and raw materials. Goering had the clout to ensure that the Luftwaffe's needs were met first and the navy's last. U-boat production actually fell during the second half of 1940 to two a month (German plans had called for 29 per month). German successes to date had in fact been achieved with amazingly meagre forces employed in the new pack tactics. In September 1940 the grand total of U-boats was 57, of which never more than 8 or 9 were kept on active patrol west of Ireland. The submarine threat Pound faced might have been much more severe. Mercifully, in the Mediterranean the structural shortcomings of the Italian navy in defensive armour became evident as it tried unsuccessfully to ward off naval bombardments, weaknesses that helped to produce a British victory in March

1941 at Cape Matapan off the Greek coast. But its positive effect was more than counterbalanced by the reappearance of a major submarine menace. Beginning in February merchant shipping lost to enemy submarines climbed steadily. As Churchill put it later, 'This mortal danger to our lifelines gnawed my bowels.' The Cabinet then established, on 6 March 1941, the Battle of the Atlantic Committee to co-ordinate anti-submarine efforts.[11]

Some results were soon evident. The proportion of ships lost to submarine action began to decline. But the overall losses of shipping continued to climb early in 1941. As Churchill's anxiety increased, so also did his wish to interfere in the day-to-day operational decisions of the Admiralty, which was foreshadowed by his writing in March: 'I'm not afraid of the Air. I'm not afraid of invasion, I'm less afraid of the Balkans — but I'm anxious about the Atlantic.' The high losses in May and June — a two-month record of 1.2 million tons lost — was ominous and Churchill took them as proof of the Admiralty's incompetence.[12]

If that were not enough, there was now also the problem of handling the increasing German air presence in the Mediterranean when, in early 1941, the X-Fliegerkorps was moved to it its new base in Sicily. Malta's agony now began as Mediterranean convoys became the victims of devastating air attacks. Attempting to protect the convoys was increasingly proving costly for the Royal Navy's Mediterranean forces, a fact that was brought home when the aircraft carrier *Illustrious* suffered severe damage.

In May there was ample evidence of what the new circumstances implied when the Royal Navy found itself unable to support the defenders in Crete because of inadequate air cover, and was forced to retreat. This humiliating operation severely damaged the Royal Navy's reputation. The Admiralty was blamed for leaving the defenders in the lurch, vulnerable to sea attack.

Churchill was furious, complaining that 'The enemy has completely established himself in the Central Mediterranean. We are afraid of his dive-bombers at every point. Our ships cannot enforce any blockade between Italy and Cyrenaica or Greece and Cyrenaica, apart from submarines.' Pound naturally pointed out that many of the shortcomings were caused by a shortage of anti-aircraft fire and RAF support, which left both Army and Navy positions vulnerable to attack by the Luftwaffe, particularly its Stuka bombers.[13]

Having so analysed the problem, Pound then proceeded to enter into a protracted struggle with the Royal Air Force for control of Coastal Command's bomber craft, a struggle that would last into 1942 and undoubtedly weakened the ability of the Chiefs of Staff to work effectively as a committee. That Pound needed to fight the sister services so fiercely for scarce aircraft is open to some doubt. After all, Washington had already announced in April 1941 that German U-boats crossing 26' longitude west would be considered hostile. By July the US Navy was taking over some of the convoying duty to Iceland. With the advent of *Barbarossa,* much of the Luftwaffe's strength was transferred to the east, reducing the pressures on the Royal Navy. But for the conservative First Sea Lord the only thing that mattered were the statistics of submarine construction and shipping losses, and these did not look very good in the summer of 1941.

Pound was obliged to tell Churchill in July that the Admiralty's estimate of German submarine construction for the balance of the year was too low — it was off by something between a third to a half. Churchill's reply was scathing:

> It is disconcerting to have such a violent change introduced into the figures. That the Admiralty should be out by no less than 51 boats, makes me desire to know more about the new evidence which has led to this most serious conclusion. . . . I must say that I feel this very decisive change and aggravation of our dangers should have been reported to me as a major event, and not simply be elicited as result of the inquiry I made. . . .. I had been reassured by the figures as epitomized in your returns, but now feel very anxious indeed, especially if there are going to be any more surprises of this kind.

Churchill also asked if Pound would mind if Professor Frederick Lindemann (later Lord Cherwell), the Prime Minister's science adviser, went through Royal Navy records to find out 'when these facts first dawned upon the Admiralty.'[14]

Pound was also faced at this time by a much more specific challenge from the Royal Air Force, which was now looking to whittle down still further the Admiralty's demands on aircraft, on the grounds that the RAF was the only really offensive arm and could make the greatest contribution to winning the war. The Secretary of State for Air, Sir Archibald Sinclair, had launched just such a campaign in February 1941 with a program that Pound interpreted as meaning that both the Navy and Army would have 'to go short of their requirements.'[15]

Pound was at first inclined to grant the Bomber Command of the RAF offensive priority on the apparent assurance that minimal naval and military requirements would be required. But he was soon forced to change his position when the venerable British expert on air warfare, Lord Trenchard, entered the debate at the end of May with a long and tightly argued memorandum calling for the drastic reordering of priorities that amounted to an attack on the Admiralty:

> It must be recognized that to-day the sea is a source of weakness to us as well as a source of strength. Germany has been able to turn the weapon of blockade against us, and it is we, owing to our sea approaches who are being increasingly blockaded while Germany owing to her land frontiers is enabled to draw on the resources of the whole of Europe and the vast resources of

Russia beyond. We cannot therefore find that weak point which we should attack either on the sea or by blockade.

From that conclusion Trenchard went on to argue the case for strategic bombing.[16]

Much to Pound's relief, even Churchill thought that Trenchard was flogging a 'good horse to death'. But in a memorandum of 7 June, the Chiefs of Staff accepted much of Trenchard's memorandum: '. . . subject . . . to the requirement of security [of Britain, including the Battle of the Atlantic].'[17]

Trenchard's memo signalled to Pound the dangers the Admiralty was facing as disappointment with its performance spread. A grand strategy relying on strategic bombing, such as Trenchard advocated, would leave the Navy with little more than a defensive role. Pound, much against the grain, now attempted to go on the offensive, arguing in a memorandum to Churchill that the Admiralty deserved a greater allocation of resources because of its past role in the defence of the British Isles and its continuing role in transporting men and *matériel*. But this only brought a rebuke from Churchill, who accused Pound of overstating the case: 'An Admiralty which says: "We secured the United Kingdom from invasion," runs the risk of being thought to overlook the part played in 1940, and indeed at the present time, by the R.A.F . . . .'[18]

But Pound, feeling his service was under attack, went ahead with his demand for more resources, presenting to the Cabinet a somewhat toned-down version of the memorandum on 21 October. After indicating the great damage being done by Germany at sea, he argued that if Germany exploited the present opportunities in the Atlantic, 'our whole war effort including our bomber offensive itself may well be jeopardized.' The memorandum, however, failed to shift priorities away from the strategic bombing offensive.[19]

Still, the last six months of 1941 must be considered a relatively easy time for Pound. There were some promising developments. First there was an increase in the sinking of U-boats. In 1940 there had been only 23 sinkings, whereas there were 35 in 1941, of which 25 were in the last six months of 1941. Moreover, British and Canadian shipyards were now producing destroyers and corvettes at substantially increased rates. The submarine scare seemed to be hastening the day of American entry into the war, and the Americans had, as the Germans themselves estimated, the capacity to build 5 million tons of shipping per year, or nearly twice the amount of current Allied net shipping losses.

Though Pound was still carrying the unsolved problem of the Mediterranean, and though he had been badly frightened in the first half of the year by the situation in the Atlantic, he could feel in the second half of 1941 that his insistence on a conservative employment of force was correct. Shipping losses in June 1941, though they were still high (109 ships, 432,025 tons), showed a fall from May, and there was a sharp drop in July to 120,975 tons, and even in August no more than 130,699 tons were lost. There was a brief alarm in September when the losses hit 285,942 tons, but then calm returned when the total fell in October to 218,289 tons, then to a low of 106,640 tons in November. (This was what has often been called the false dawn of 1941.) But these somewhat more positive results were no insurance against the criticism of Churchill, who seemed only to notice what was going wrong. In November 1941 he wrote the First Lords to say that he was much disquieted by the submarine losses: 'The failure of our methods, about which so much [was] proclaimed by the Admiralty before the war is painfully apparent.' In December he unburdened himself of his disappointment over the failure of operation *Anklet* against the island of Vaagsö in Norway, noting sarcastically that the Admiralty seemed more adept at carrying out the deception plans to cover such operations than in executing them. Rebuttals by the military staff only produced from Churchill a brutal summation: 'If the fact of the enemy assembling a certain number of aircraft within striking distance of *Anklet* was to be held a good reason for an immediate retreat this operation should never have been undertaken. The *Anklet* episode must, therefore, be judged a marked failure as it was abandoned hastily and without any facts being apparent which were not foreseen at the time of its inception and preparation.'[20]

But Churchill and Pound soon had other things to worry about when a crisis developed in the Pacific every bit as serious as the one in the Atlantic. Within days of the Japanese entry into the war British strength in the Pacific had been decimated, and blame naturally was assigned to the Navy, the traditional guardian of those distant interests. The perilous situation had been much compounded by Churchill when he forced Pound, much against his will, to send the new battleship *Prince of Wales*, together with the *Repulse*, to Malaya, where they were quickly sunk. Churchill had been the moving force behind this decision, arguing on 25 August 1941 that just as the only capital ship left to Germany, the *Tirpitz*, had caused endless preoccupation to a British Navy with 15 battleships and battle cruisers, 'a small but very powerful and fast force in Eastern waters' would have a great restraining force on Japan. He returned to the argument on the 29th, saying that sending one or two modern battleships would have the effect of the *Tirpitz*, which 'exercises a vague, general fear and menaces all points at once. It appears, and disappears, causing immediate reactions and perturbations on the other side.' The appearance of a *King George V* class ship, he argued, 'might indeed be a decisive deterrent.' He had boasted to Roosevelt that 'There is nothing like having something that can catch and kill anything.' When the *Prince of Wales* and the *Repulse* were sunk on 10 December, Churchill gave no signs of accepting responsibility.[21]

Much later in his memoirs he did so, but only indirectly, saying that 'I was thankful to be alone. In all the war I never received a more direct shock.' But at the time he insisted on regarding the episode as a terrible illustration of the Navy's incompetence. He demanded the most complete reports and even after he had these, he remarked: 'This is really not good enough.' For months he continued to churn over the loss of the *Prince of Wales*, seeking to find a scapegoat for the disaster. Why, he asked the First Sea Lord in March, could *Tirpitz* escape torpedo bombers while the *Prince of Wales* and *Repulse* had clearly not been able to do so: '. . . kindly let me have a report on the Air attack on *Tirpitz*, explaining how it was that 12 of our machines happened to get no hits as compared with the extraordinary efficiency of the Japanese attack on the *Prince of Wales* and *Repulse*.' Interim replies he judged unsatisfactory, and on 24 March 1942 he again complained that he had not yet received a satisfactory written report.[22]

Churchill, now alert to Intelligence failures, began to criticize the Admiralty regularly for shortcomings there. But of course the problem went beyond Intelligence. The British Navy had lost valuable ships and had now been placed in a position of absolute inferiority in the Far East. The tension took its toll on Churchill. In February 1942 he had a major tantrum when the commander of the Home Fleet, Admiral Sir John Tovey, failed to include two major warships in the list of those available for immediate action. Rather than accept that they might not be ready, Churchill asked testily whether the Admiral had lost or misplaced the vessels. Despite Churchill's best effort to get every ship into action, it became necessary in April 1942 to allow Admiral Somerville to withdraw his ships from Ceylon to East Africa, creating for the first time a real opportunity for the Japanese to take India. The greatest crisis for the British Empire now loomed before Churchill and Pound. As the Prime Minister explained to Roosevelt:

> . . . the consequences of this may easily be . . . the loss of Ceylon [and the] . . . invasion of Eastern India with incalculable internal consequences to our whole war plan and including the loss of Calcutta and of all contact with the Chinese through Burma. But this is only the beginning. Until we are able to fight a fleet action there is no reason why the Japanese should not become the dominating factor in the Western Indian Ocean. This would result in the collapse of our whole position in the Middle East, not only because of the interruption to our convoys to the Middle East and India, but also because of the interruptions to the oil supplies from Abadan, without which we cannot maintain our position either at sea or on land in the Indian Ocean area. Supplies to Russia via the Persian Gulf would also be cut. With so much of the weight of Japan thrown upon us we have more than we can bear.

In short, it was no longer quite so certain, as Pound had said in August 1941, that 'The Atlantic is the vital area as it is in that ocean and that alone in which we can lose the war at sea.' There was now a crisis of similar magnitude in the Indian Ocean.[23]

Almost any attempt Pound made to redress the naval balance in one area aggravated the naval situation in another. To protect shipping between Calcutta and Ceylon, it was now found necessary to send flying boats to the Indian Ocean, which meant there were fewer for anti-submarine warfare in the Atlantic, just when the peril there was at its height.

Worse still, the situation in the Mediterranean was also deteriorating in an alarming way. In March, Admiral Cunningham had to admit that his fleet was shattered. In the next month the Navy was forced to the long-anticipated but much-dreaded decision to abandon convoys to Malta, thus laying open the possibility that Malta would fall and that the enemy would enjoy an uninterruptable supply to North Africa, with all the immense consequences this might have in the Middle East. Alexandria was in fact virtually abandoned as a naval base in this ominous period.

Pound now came under tremendous pressure. He certainly knew which service would be blamed should Malta fall. Churchill made this very clear in an 'Action This Day' minute he sent to Pound, Alexander, and Ismay: 'It will be necessary to make another attempt', he warned, 'to run a convoy into Malta. Gort [the Governor] must be able to tell the population "the Navy will never abandon Malta."' It is equally clear that the Admiralty would also be blamed for the loss of India were that to follow a major failure by Admiral Somerville.[24]

How acute the crisis was may be seen in the flood of 'Action This Day' minutes Churchill now unleashed on the hapless Pound, asking where this or that ship was and why any given ship could not sail at once into action. Churchill was now using these red-flagged documents, which required response and action on the very day received, for questions that, while important, did not concern issues on which immediate action could in fact be taken in any operational sense. Such was his 'Action This Day' request on 14 April asking for an explanation of why the Japanese could transport more aircraft on their carriers. Another of the same date asked for the latest information on the repairs to a number of ships, sarcastically adding, 'You surely do not propose to send *King George V* for refit in the present stringency?' At the same time Churchill demanded to know why Admiral Somerville was complaining about the readiness of the defence of Malaya, and asked if her guns were cocked up. For good measure Churchill tossed in another barb, noting that he had found an Admiral who did not agree with one of the readiness estimates Pound had given him earlier. It was hardly a model of efficiency to require the staff to drop whatever they were doing to make thorough investigations on this fistful of nettles and report back within hours.[25]

Whether a staff so harassed could work efficiently on operational matters is open to question, particularly as the most carefully drafted replies during this period rarely satisfied Churchill. He routinely shot back further re-quests, typically including such stock demands as 'Please let me have dates and further particulars.' Any minute that began 'Pray do inform me' sent staff scurrying. Informal replies rarely satisfied Churchill. On 24 April he called to ask the Vice-Chief of Naval Operations what the status of *Valiant* was. Though he received a reply, Churchill found it necessary to write the next day to ask him to 'Please report officially today.' One can sympathize with Brooke's sardonic comment to younger staff officers: 'The more you tell that man about the war, the more you hinder the winning of it.'[26]

In June 1942 Churchill complained to Pound that 'No satisfactory explanation' had been given by Somerville 'of the imprudent dispersion of his forces' in the early days of April, which resulted in the loss of HMS *Cornwall*, *Dorsetshire*, and *Hermes*. Pound, who had ordered an informal inquiry and sifted through the findings to his satisfaction, recognized in Churchill's minute a challenge to his authority and that of the civilian chief of the Navy and quickly wrote Alexander, the First Lord, to point out Churchill's usurpation of their collective responsibilities, adding that 'I do not think this can be allowed to go unchallenged.'[27]

But it soon became clear that Churchill was interested not so much in the fate of these lesser commanders as in preparing a dossier against the respective Service Chiefs who retained the 'deficient' commanders in place. In July he wrote the First Lords to complain that he should have been informed that they could not meet their promised date for the return of *Valiant* to duty, adding for the record: 'I must regret that I was not told when this grievous failure occurred.' In July, Churchill wrote the First Lords to say that he could not help having the impression that 'Admiral Harwood and the Navy are doing very little in this fight. . . .'[28]

It was during this period, while Dieppe was taking shape, that Pound's relations with Churchill began to deteriorate precipitously. That something had changed in their relationship was evident when on 7 March Pound sent Churchill a remarkably frank and transparently honest recapitulation of their differences. Implicitly taking note of the reason why he was being replaced in the chair of the Chiefs of Staff Committee, Pound tried to reason with Churchill, and fearing that the repercussions of their disagreement would be 'great', he explained at length his objection to Mountbatten's promotions. Churchill was not moved and Brooke replaced Pound on the 9th. Moreover, it soon became known that Churchill was contemplating Pound's replacement as First Sea Lord, possibly with Mountbatten. The correspondence between Pound and Churchill in the spring of 1942 certainly gives the impression that Churchill was trying to build a dossier of incompetence against him. Alexander was so fearful of the strain on Pound that he virtually begged Churchill for mercy, asking that Pound be permitted to appoint a Deputy First Sea Lord, 'having in mind the heavy and increasing load of work and responsibility falling upon him'. But as it was clear that the real purpose of this request was to insulate Pound from the Prime Minister's badgering, Churchill, not surprisingly, refused.[29]

It would be no exaggeration to say that by June and July 1942 Churchill was not far from the breaking-point, and he was driving much of his staff there too. Pound wrote Churchill on 3 May to say that the burden of the convoys to Russia 'is cruel upon the Fleet, and in all my experience I have never seen the strain so great.' The strain was also upon Pound personally and, indeed, on all those around Churchill.[30]

The growing evidence of Churchill's discontent with Pound coincided with a series of bad turns in the war at sea, particularly the new phase of the submarine threat. In the spring and summer of 1942 a substantial growth of Germany's submarine force seemed to be predicted. Three new classes of U-boats were now becoming operational, including a large long-range attack vessel. Sinkings once again began to mount ominously: 863,164 tons in March, 834,196 tons in June. By November, three months after Dieppe, they would still be in the 800,000-ton range. But more important, the proportion of the loss due to aircraft attack was declining, while an ever-increasing number of losses were due to U-boats. Though the crisis peaked after Dieppe, the outlines of the problem had been visible since March. On July 27, scarcely three weeks before Dieppe, Admiral Doenitz made a broadcast to the German people announcing an imminent increase in U-boat activity. And indeed by August, Doenitz was able to field a force of over 100 boats, more than double the number that had so terrorized the Atlantic little more than a year earlier. Instead of only one or two sub-marines attacking a convoy, it was now possible for the Germans to use a dozen or more. As one historian has noted, 'The remainder of 1942 was a nightmare for Britain.' It was clear that large armies could not be safely transported across the Atlantic for a sizeable cross-Channel operation, be it *Sledgehammer* or *Round-Up*, while these conditions obtained.[31]

Doenitz's greatly increased resources were not the only element in this deadly equation. In the spring of 1942 the Royal Navy received a serious blow to its Enigma code-breaking program, though it was fortunately hidden from the public. Hitherto, Naval Intelligence, using Enigma inter-cepts, had been one of the key elements, if not the principal one, in directing the Admiralty's tactical dispositions. But now German U-boats received their own Enigma (sometimes referred to as Ultra) code-machine settings. Though it was hoped and expected U-boat signal traffic could be soon tapped again, it was not until December that any significant success was achieved. The sudden inability to decode intercepts, at a time when the number of German operational U-boats was increasing, constituted a heavy blow to the Royal Navy.[32]

This corresponded with the great success of the German code-breaking service, B Dienst, in breaking, at about the same time, some of the key British convoy codes, so that the most important intelligence advantage had now shifted to the other side. Churchill later referred to this changing aspect of the Battle of the Atlantic as a 'terrible event in a very bad time.'[33]

As the losses mounted, so also did Churchill's anxieties, and his ceaseless prodding of the Navy increased apace. Churchill demanded more and more frequent reports until he was forcing the Admiralty to give him highly detailed technical reports daily. It could never be said that he did not know how to inflict punishment.[34]

There was another problem of much concern to Pound, one that had great impact on the way he approached the Dieppe project: that of getting supplies to the Soviet Union. There was good reason to believe that by 1943 he would have the submarine problem licked. But Churchill had to ask himself what was the use of being able to ship millions of tons of supplies to Russia in 1943 or 1944 if in the meantime Russia had been defeated or had quit the war? The need was immediate, but in 1942 getting supplies to the Soviet Union was extremely difficult. A Mediterranean route was unlikely. Churchill could not even get supplies to Malta, and in any case the Crimea was certain to fall into German hands. The westward route through the Indian Ocean was also imperilled, so that it would be difficult to get supplies to Russia via Iran; and in any case the Soviets were inclined to discourage the use of this route. Supplies therefore had to be moved up through the Iceland gap between Iceland and Norway and around the northern tip of Norway (the North Cape) under the very noses of German air and naval stations. This attempt to keep open a life-line via the North Cape was arduous, risky, and expensive. Nor was there any way to profit by the return voyage. Ships might go out laden, but there was little they could carry back in return. This meant keeping a large number of ships under-utilized, something Lord Cherwell calculated Britain simply could not afford. Moreover, the casualties and losses, proportional to the size of the convoys, proved staggering. Nevertheless some convoys would get through. By June 1942 German intelligence estimated that Russia had received 2,800 American and British tanks and large quantities of American 2.5-ton trucks (which in fact became the basic transportation vehicle for the Russian army). The United States alone would ship 360,000 long tons of war materials in the second half of 1941, and in the first half of 1942 that amount would climb to 1,226,000 long tons. But as Soviet officials quickly pointed out, owing to what they described as the 'inefficiency' of the British Navy, nearly 300,000 tons were lost at sea.[35]

In his frustration Churchill blamed the Navy, convinced as he was that the convoy problem would not have existed had Pound and others not failed him in the Norwegian campaign of 1940, thus giving Germany, by default, the perfect position from which to interfere with supplies to the Soviet Union. The Prime Minister kept pressing for a new campaign — the capture of Norwegian bases and airfields — to unroll, as he said, the map of Europe from the top. Hitler too regarded Norway as a possibly decisive theatre. In a curious way Hitler and Churchill saw each other's intentions much more clearly than did their staffs. Churchill was convinced that

Hitler's real objective was to break the Anglo-Soviet alliance. As German forces were deep in the Soviet Union, one of the principal hopes of the Allies had to be that Russia would hold. The Allies did not have the shipping for a cross-Channel attack, hence the only help they could offer Russia was to send her supplies. If the convoys could be stopped, the effects might be enormous.

Convinced that Norway was the 'zone of destiny', Hitler insisted, beginning in the fall of 1941, on posting a significant part of Raeder's small force there, thus casting down the gauntlet to Churchill. After the failure of German armies before Moscow, Hitler redoubled his efforts to find victory in the waters off Norway. Early in January the recently commissioned *Tirpitz*, sistership of the *Bismarck*, left for Norway. On 22 January 1942 Hitler insisted that six U-boats also be sent there. Very shortly thereafter he decided to send his remaining capital ships to Norwegian waters rather than leave them in port as targets for the RAF. Soon the *Gneisenau*, *Scharnhorst*, and *Prinz Eugen* were all headed towards Norway. To these were added, in March, the *Admiral Hipper* and the pocket battleships *Lützow* and *Admiral Scheer*. Virtually the whole German surface navy was now congregated where it could threaten the convoys to Russia.[36]

The passage of three German warships up the English Channel on their way northwards under the nose of the Royal Navy was a severe humiliation that greatly damaged the credibility of Britain's wartime government. Since Pound frequently argued that British capital ships could not operate in the narrow waters of the Channel, the ability of the German navy to use the Channel, even after Britain had received ample prior warning, was particularly embarrassing. Undoubtedly this increased Churchill's suspicions about the Admiralty's inefficiency and led him to redouble his efforts to ferret out all the indications of rot that he believed Pound was covering up. The German feat gravely damaged Pound's credibility and probably contributed to Churchill's decision to rotate Pound prematurely out of the chair of the Chiefs of Staff Committee.

Naturally the reinforcement of the German fleet made Pound all the more opposed to any Norwegian campaign, but Churchill's plans were already well advanced. Eden's return from Moscow earlier, on 30 December 1941, with first-hand news of the delicate state of Anglo-Soviet relations, had increased Churchill's determination. But even without this inducement he was certain to want action, for the victor over the *Bismarck*, on whose destruction he had risked so much, smelled blood again and was determined on another chase, writing excitedly that 'crippling this ship [the *Tirpitz*] would alter the entire face of the naval war and that the loss of 100 aircraft and 500 airmen would be well compensated for.' Soon Churchill's sense of urgency had grown by leaps and bound and he now wrote that the 'whole strategy of the war, turns at this period on this ship which is holding four times the number of British capital ships paralysed to say nothing of the two new American battleships retained in the Atlantic. . ... I regard the matter [the need to cripple the *Tirpitz*] as of the highest urgency and importance.'[37]

The Admiralty had no ships to spare for that purpose. A failed attempt involving the loss of any of Britain's capital ships would greatly increase the chances that the German force might break into the Atlantic, where it could wreak enormous damage on the precious convoy traffic. Better to conserve strength and be content with containing the German fleet in Norway. Even this conservative policy would strain the Royal Navy, as it required Pound to beef up the Home Fleet at the expense of convoy protection in the Atlantic. Pound, therefore, was caught in a vicious circle, made particularly acute by the fact that the German ships in Norway were largely new and powerful, so that he could not safely continue his policy of keeping an ageing Home Fleet — most noticeably the old and slow *Rodney* and the very lightly armoured *Renown* — on guard against the Norwegian flotilla. The only real strength lay in the powerful but as yet untested and untried *Duke of York*. In these circumstances Tovey, the Commander in Chief of the Home Fleet, found himself arguing against Churchill's more ambitious conceptions of how the naval war should be fought, and the Prime Minister was soon making clear that he wanted that commander removed. Thus it was that the differences between Churchill and the Admiralty were gravely accentuated by their disagreement over the wisdom of deploying huge naval forces in Norway.[38]

In this dispute over how much naval force to put behind the convoy effort, the Cabinet tended to back Churchill very decisively, perceiving the question as vital to the Soviet Union, whose survival seemed in doubt. As Beaverbrook, the ex-Minister of Production, explained in April 1942:

> First, Russia will have to bear the brunt of Germany's attack in 1942. In order to keep her confidence and sustain her morale, we must supply her with munitions to the limit of our ability . . . To do less would increase the dangers, if there are any, of Russia's making a separate peace.

Russia's military position had begun to deteriorate in March 1942 and the consequences bore down hard on Pound, who was urged to redouble his efforts to run convoys through the treacherous North Cape route. The same considerations incited Churchill to press all the harder for his project to seize Norwegian bases and airfields, to which Pound was absolutely opposed because the RAF would not guarantee adequate air cover for capital ships. At the very least, therefore, Hitler was succeeding in setting Churchill at odds with the Admiralty.[39]

The First Lords responded by pressing the Americans for reinforcements for the Home Fleet, which would liberate more British vessels for the North Sea. This effort succeeded to a considerable extent because the US Navy sent two battleships, the aircraft carrier *Wasp*, two heavy cruisers, and a number of destroyers. Some of this force was assigned to distant protection of the eastbound convoy PQ 17, but with little benefit.

The real problem was that the Germans did not even have to send out their capital ships to prey on convoys headed for Russia. Though the *Tirpitz* ventured out to inflict heavy damage on one pair of convoys, identified as PQ 12 and QP 8, she generally stayed in her fiord. It was the increasingly powerful German air force, combined with the numerous submarines, that took a devastating toll. PQ 12, at the start of March, and PQ 15, at the end of April, occasioned the loss of two cruisers, the *Edinburgh* and the *Trinidad*, as well as severe damage to the new *King George V* (though the latter was mostly self-inflicted damage). Not surprisingly, the loss of freighters grew apace. In PQ 16 seven ships were lost in May 1942 carrying valuable cargo destined for Russia: 147 tanks, 77 aircraft, and 770 transportation vehicles.

These losses underlined the fact that there was not enough naval force to run the Atlantic, Malta, and the Russian convoys. Faced with this situation, the War Cabinet decided to reduce drastically convoys to Malta. As Oliver Lyttelton noted, this was 'cutting things very fine . . . [as] Malta would probably be lost . . . if the one convoy for June met with disaster.' The Cabinet agreed to risk losing Malta for the sake of the Russian convoys, but many were unhappy.[40]

Pound wanted to draw the line with this gamble and he told a War Cabinet meeting on 13 April that 'it was important . . . [to] make the Russian government realize the extent of the risks that were being run and the efforts being made' so that they would understand if the convoys to Russia had to be curtailed — a policy he was in fact recommending. Pound not only told the War Cabinet bluntly that the planned cycle of northern convoys to the Soviet Union was the absolute maximum the Navy could handle, but also warned that 'serious losses were likely to be incurred if we continued the effort to sail convoys to Russia on the present scale throughout the summer months.' How heavy the burden would become was soon apparent when Pound was obliged to strip the Home Fleet further in order to protect the next convoys, thus negating much of the impact of the American contribution. All that was left to the Home Fleet at Scapa Flow were six capital ships; below this figure no naval authority was prepared to go. It was during these readjustments, while the first plans for Dieppe were taking shape and the question of naval support was being decided, that Pound confessed that the Navy was now bearing 'a far greater strain than at any time since the war began.'[41]

By 24 April Pound had managed to convince Eden, though not Churchill, that the cycle of convoys to Russia would have to be reduced to no more than six over a two-month period. Even this schedule, Pound ventured, could not be sustained unless the Soviets were to help more in their defence of the convoys.[42]

Predictably, both the Soviet and American governments tried to influence the outcome of the debate in London. At a time when the United States, by its slack defences off the Eastern seaboard, was more of a liability than an asset in the Battle of the Atlantic, Roosevelt intervened, asking Churchill to make a greater effort to get supplies to Russia. The whole issue reached a boiling-point in a crucial Cabinet session on 18 May. Churchill began by summarizing Pound's views that the convoys scheduled for May and June had to be cancelled, though he left open the hope that the convoys for July might be increased correspondingly. But having presented Pound's views, Churchill intoned that 'The Russians were engaged in a life and death struggle against our common enemy', for which correspondingly great sacrifices were necessary. Churchill then proceeded to minimize these, recalling that Pound had predicted great losses for the last convoy, which in Churchill's view had survived reasonably well. The War Cabinet upheld Churchill and ordered the departure of the next convoy.[43]

With Molotov due to arrive in London to discuss aid to the Soviet Union, the decision was understandable. Pound was put under increased pressure to send out another convoy when the Soviets promised to meet it with better support. Pound reported this assurance to the War Cabinet on 20 May, saying that, 'The Russians are going to treat the arrival of this convoy as a special operation. Two hundred aircraft of the Red Army would be employed on protective measures and 50 Bombers would attack the enemy aerodromes in Northern Norway.' Soviet destroyers were also expected to meet the convoy. Pound thus nailed Russian assurances of support to the record. If they were not honoured, Pound would come back to the attack.[44]

In fact PQ 16 was not supported by Russian destroyers until 28 May, seven days after it sailed and two full days after it had suffered its greatest casualties. As for the Russian aircraft, there was no sign of them along the route. Only as the convoy approached Murmansk, long after the danger zone had been passed, were any in evidence.

Given this performance, and given the fact that Malta desperately needed a convoy, Pound tried to persuade Churchill to cancel the next North Cape convoy, PQ 17. But Churchill, knowing that Molotov was once again expected on his way back from Washington, and knowing that the British Cabinet had just decided against any large sacrifice-landing on the Continent, could not see giving the Russians such a dose of bad news and instead opted only for a delay in the sailing of PQ 17.

PQ 17 finally sailed for Russia at the end of June, a mission that was destined to bring relations between Churchill and Pound to a crisis. In the Cabinet War Room, and at the Admiralty, attention became rivetted on this convoy, which everyone recognized would be doomed if the *Tirpitz* or *Hipper* came out after it. In addition to the standard escort of six destroyers and a swarm of corvettes, minesweepers, submarines, and anti-aircraft vessels, the Home Fleet had been ordered to sea with two battleships (one

American), as well as an aircraft carrier and fourteen destroyers, as a gesture to confuse German naval intelligence. The American Atlantic fleet was put on alert for possible assistance during the earlier part of the convoy's journey.

When in fact the convoy was discovered by the Germans on 1 July, some 300 miles away from Murmansk, there was understandable concern, though Pound still refused to risk his Home Fleet and declined to issue it any new orders. On 4 July it was discovered that the *Tirpitz* and *Hipper* had left their berths, and something close to panic struck the Admiralty, as it was now too late to order the Home Fleet to assist, even if Pound had wanted this. He ordered the convoy to scatter, which left each ship defenceless. There now began a long agony that spread out over a two-week period. Every day brought news of some new sinking.

The piecemeal destruction of PQ 17 gave Churchill an opening to carry out his earlier threats to replace Pound. The First Sea Lord was now quite vulnerable as severe criticism of the disastrous order to scatter the fleet surfaced from the convoy commander and was widely echoed in the Admiralty. The Russians, faced with the virtual certainty that the convoys would now be curtailed, could scarcely conceal their scorn for the decision and for the Admiral who gave it. Churchill, however, defended the Admiralty, eventually telling the Russians that 'If the ships had not dispersed . . . every ship including escort vessels would have been sunk by the Tirpitz.' But he knew better.[45]

Churchill's initial decision to stand by Pound was perhaps not all that surprising. Replacing Pound would have given substance to the charge that British naval incompetence was responsible for the loss of so much *matériel* destined for the Soviet Union. That, Churchill knew, was in the main false and he did not want to lend credence to such a charge. Now under considerable pressure himself, Churchill must have sympathized with Pound, who was clearly under the greatest strain of his career. Churchill would later write with immense sympathy of the 'heart-shaking decisions' Pound had been forced to take. But even though Churchill was surprisingly restrained in his response, Pound could not have felt very secure after the PQ 17 fiasco. As more reports drifted in, Cabinet debates over PQ 17 continued for nearly a month. Meanwhile Pound still had to cope with the loss of the intelligence advantage and the ominous statistics of the submarine war. In sombre tones Pound summarized the situation in mid-July:

> We are now approaching a crisis in the war and we must face the facts. Apart from the areas now conquered by Japan, we have lost control of sea communications in the Mediterranean, on the route to North Russia, and we use the Bay of Bengal only on sufferance. . . .
>
> Our whole power to wage an offensive by sea, on land , in the air, both at home and abroad is now being undermined by our weakness at sea both in

ships and in the air . . . we have reached the point at which we are unable to face the risks that an offensive strategy demand . . . slowly we are being forced into a position such as we have never faced whilst our enemies have gained where we have lost.[46]

Though Pound was persuaded to withdraw this memo as being too alarming, and duplicating overmuch his earlier warnings, it accurately conveyed his feelings as the Dieppe decision was being reached.

Meanwhile the debate over PQ 17 and its consequences was proceeding. In a stormy Defence Committee meeting on 10 July, when only the first reports had arrived, Pound argued that PQ 17 had made manifest the risks that had always been implicit in sending out convoys. In his view they could not be reduced by deploying any practicable number of heavy ships for cover. Even if they had been available, sending more capital ships would be to 'court disaster, having regard to the scale of enemy shore-based air and submarine attack to which our ships would, in present circumstances, be subjected in these waters, and might lead to the loss of naval control in the North Atlantic . . . [which] would prejudice the whole of the 'Bolero' plan [to gather supplies for a cross-Channel attack].' Though Pound urged the suspension of the convoys, and Churchill showed dismay at Pound's grave prognostications, the Committee supported Churchill, saying that 'We could not afford to abandon the running of the next Russian convoy when the great battle was raging on the Russian front. Some method must therefore be found [to continue the convoys].'[47]

A suggested method for keeping the convoys going had been circulating in Whitehall for some time in the form of a memorandum by S.M.Bruce dated 7 July and addressed to the Prime Minister. It argued that as the convoys were crucial, and as they were not getting through adequately, it was now necessary to use 'battleships and adequate carrier borne fighter protection.' Bruce added: 'No doubt this involves risks, but they must be taken if they are reasonable ones. The Germans took a risk in bringing the Tirpitz out in [the] face of a submarine screen. . . . They felt the risk was worth it and took it. Surely we must do the same.' Alexander loyally supported Pound who, in opposing this proposal, pointed out that the Germans 'have nothing to lose and everything to gain'. He added:

We on the other hand, have everything to lose, if with our many commitments such as the Malta Convoy and the Troops Convoys in the Atlantic and the Indian Oceans, our Home Fleet were to be mauled in an engagement. This would have the most serious effect both on the control of the North Atlantic, the passage of Convoys from America and on the preparations for either Bolero [a cross-Channel attack] or Gymnast [a plan for the invasion of North Africa].[48]

But as the full story of PQ 17 became known, many joined the ranks of those demanding greater use of capital ships for the protection of convoys, even though Pound continued to believe the result would be catastrophic.

It was in the midst of this debate on detaching part of the Home Fleet to protect the convoys that the decision to renew the Dieppe raid was taken after the cancellation of *Rutter* on 7 July. Though the continuation of the convoys was infinitely more important than the preparations for Dieppe, the two policy questions obviously influenced each other.

At about that time the final tally on PQ 17 losses became available, and it indicated that of the 35 ships in that convoy only 11 made it. The ocean floor had received a precious cargo of about 500 trucks, 430 tanks, 2500 aircraft, and some 3,350 transportation vehicles. 153 seamen had lost their lives. Churchill now confessed to the Defence Committee that, although he had taken the position that 'if 50% of the ships of a convoy got through it would be justifiable to sail the next one', the losses had been heavier than that and it would be wrong to continue: 'The loss of so many ships and so much material meant that the convoy, far from helping Russia, constituted a disastrous loss to the whole Allied cause.' With the Russian front going badly, and the naval situation as grave as it had ever been, one of Churchill's most trusted confidants, the South African Prime Minister Field Marshal Smuts, now sent a cable strongly supporting Pound's objections:

> I assume we cannot afford to continue incurring such losses and must either abandon assistance to Russia along the Northern route, or increase our escorts to battleship and air-carrier scale, capable of meeting large enemy forces. Whether enemy preoccupations elsewhere justify us in making such heavy naval concentration on Northern route is for naval authorities to say, but if their decision is adverse we may be forced to abandon that route with proper explanations to Russia. . . . While we should be prepared to make very great sacrifices for Russia . . . our vital interests elsewhere [should also be kept] . . . well in view.[49]

Churchill now granted Pound something of a respite by agreeing to send Roosevelt and Stalin cables informing them that the convoys would have to be suspended. Challenging the politically powerful supporters of the Soviet Union in this way was an extraordinarily bold gesture, considering that only a couple of weeks before a motion of non-confidence had been defeated. Eden was leery, saying that it was '. . . worrying to give negatives to the Russians at this critical time.' He had in mind the string of recent Red Army defeats in the Crimea, but he must also have been thinking of the restlessness he still sensed with Churchill's leadership. The cable to Stalin, however, was duly dispatched. In it Churchill reported that '. . . my naval advisers tell me that if they had the handling of the German surface, submarine, and air forces in present circumstances, they would guarantee to complete destruction of any convoy to north Russia.' Churchill also intimated that the prospects of a Second Front in 1942 were growing dimmer. Stalin's response, which Churchill later characterized as 'rough and surly', took issue at every point with Churchill, 'Our naval experts', Stalin wrote, 'consider the reasons put forward by the British naval experts to justify the cessation of convoys . . . to be wholly unconvincing. . . .' In so many words, Stalin signalled that the Soviet Union had lost confidence in Pound and the Royal Navy. The very day Churchill approved the cables he sent Pound an Action-This-Day minute, saying that in spite of his message to Stalin, '. . . a further intense effort must be made to solve the problem of running convoys by the Northern route.' Churchill then went on to propose the most extravagant use of the Royal Navy he had conceived to date:

> Let the following be examined. . . . If all goes well [with the attempt to resupply Malta] bring *Indomitable, Victorious, Argus* and *Eagle* north to Scapa and collect with them at least five of the auxiliary aircraft carriers, together with all available Didos and at least 25 destroyers. Let the two 16-inch battleships go right through under this Air umbrella and destroyer screen . . . and thus fight it out with the enemy. . . . If we can move our armada . . . under an umbrella of at least 100 fighter aircraft we ought to be able to fight our way through and out again, and if a Fleet action results so much the better.

To remind Pound that he was under a heavy cloud and should co-operate, Churchill added another paragraph, asking some very pointed questions about who gave the order for the destroyers to quit PQ 17. 'What did you think of this decision at the time? What do you think of it now?'[50]

Pound, however, only dug in his heels more firmly, refusing to be blackmailed into supporting Churchill's flights of fancy. But he placed no objections on the record when, by mid-July, it became clear that Mountbatten would go forward with an attempt to relaunch Dieppe unless he received a red light.

In trying to decide what position he should take on Mountbatten's project, Pound had to consider the broader context, the debate over a Second Front. Pound's approach to that question is fairly clear. He favoured a cross-Channel attack in theory, since it was predicated on gaining mastery of the Atlantic and on an open-ended commitment for that purpose, but he could not support any assault on the Continent until that objective had been assured. In the meantime, other immediate problems would have to be resolved. The Admiralty would have to meet the threats in the Mediterranean, secure Malta, reinstate Alexandria, make the Indian Ocean once more secure, and satisfy the War Cabinet that everything possible was being done to get supplies more effectively to Russia. Given these demands, Pound's position in the strategic debate during 1942 is easy to understand. While he was not averse to keeping cross-Channel strategy alive, talk of an early attempt filled him with apprehension, if not horror. The Chiefs of Staff minutes reveal he was vocal in opposition to any attempt at a bridgehead on the Continent at an early date — indeed, to anything that 'involved . . . sustained operations on the Continent.'[51]

But if an early Second Front was unthinkable, what was Pound's reaction to the raiding policy in general and the Dieppe raid in particular? Pound was generally so silent on secondary matters at Chiefs of Staff meetings that an answer can only be conjectured, though it is not hard to reconstruct his perspective. If keeping alive a cross-Channel strategy that gave the Navy a vital role was his objective, then a raiding program that bought time, and sidetracked other more impetuous operations, had to be considered very favourably by Pound — provided always that it was not too wasteful of scarce resources. By the end of June 1942 the choices had narrowed drastically and Pound could see that if the Cabinet wanted to give the Russians evidence of good will, it would have to be through continuation of the convoys, a Norwegian campaign, or raids. Conservative tactician that he was, Pound had no difficulty in deciding that an ambitious raiding program was the least wasteful option. It would shift the burden of making gestures to Russia from his hard-pressed convoy forces to the Army. If the Dieppe raid been cancelled for good, with no alternative raid in view, all Pound's difficulties would have continued to mount.

Even if Pound had wanted to oppose the Dieppe raid, he would have experienced great difficulty in doing so. Since the war began his strategy had been, as we have seen, cautious and defensive, and this had led him to a rather unseemly clash during the fall of 1941 with the fire-eating Director of Combined Operations and Admiral of the Fleet, Sir Roger Keyes. The doughty admiral made known to all and sundry that the basis of the dispute had been the naval staff's, and particularly the First Sea Lord's, opposition to taking risks or allowing Combined Operations to proceed with any plan that required naval support of any significance. Pound won that test of strength and Keyes had been duly eased out (only to take a seat in the House of Commons). Pound then allowed himself the luxury of scoffing at his opponent, saying that 'Keyes never had much brains and whatever he has got left is quite addled.' In handing over the reins to Mountbatten, Keyes made the mistake of saying the real problem was that 'the British have lost the will to fight'. It was the sort of comment Mountbatten could and did use in order to boost his own position at the expense of the discredited Keyes.[52]

With Keyes gone but not silent, Pound could not afford to be seen as repeatedly throttling the only organization, Combined Operations, that seemed able to put on an offensive show, particularly after the Navy had been humiliated in the escape of the Scharnhorst and Gneisenau. Thus he was obliged to give at least token support to the Combined Operations plans of Mountbatten, Keyes' attractive and energetic successor.

It was a hard line to follow. When Churchill announced in March 1942 that he wanted to make the very junior Mountbatten a Chief of Staff, Pound indiscreetly wrote to Churchill opposing the Mountbatten proposal, pointing out that Mountbatten did not have experience commensurate with the proposed promotions, while pretending that he 'did not feel very strongly about it'. But the truth was clearly otherwise. Pound resisted, and in the end was forced to relinquish the chair of the Chiefs of Staff Committee on 9 March, embarrassingly soon after the furor over the passage of the German battle-cruisers up the Channel. Sensitive to the dangers implicit in his quarrel with the proposed Mountbatten appointment, Pound complained in April to the Commander-in-Chief of the Mediterranean, Admiral Cunningham, that Churchill was out to replace him as First Sea Lord and that Mountbatten was being groomed as the successor. Cunningham advised Pound, in Pound's words, to 'glue himself to his chair', and though the First Sea Lord might feel tempted to resign, particularly as he was already beginning to feel the effects of illness, he was obliged to follow Cunningham's advice, since he was convinced that the next Churchill appointee might yield to political intervention and fritter away whatever remaining strength the Royal Navy had left. Pound in fact signalled that he would fight to stay early in June when Churchill proposed that Admiral A.B. Cunningham be called to command the Home Fleet and that Admiral Sir John Tovey be eased out. These were sweeping changes that seemed to herald more and could be seen as nothing less than an attack on Pound's system. Since relations with Churchill were so strained, Pound sent his protest to Alexander, but obviously the words were for Churchill's ears. 'It is most unwise', Pound warned, 'to attempt to fight a war with a Navy which has lost confidence in the Admiralty administration.'[53]

Pound at first showed great skepticism towards Mountbatten's projects when they were presented to the Chiefs of Staff committee, but his opposition diminished at the end of March when Combined Operations pulled off its great morale booster, the highly successful raid on the St Nazaire drydock facilities. Though the raid was a hollow victory as regards its stated purpose (there was not much point in denying drydock facilities to a German fleet that had already escaped to Norway), it had nevertheless forced Doenitz to move his headquarters from Kernevel, near Lorient in southern Brittany, to Paris. In the public's eye there was no question but that St Nazaire was a glorious feat of arms. Mountbatten's staff worked tirelessly to keep that impression alive.

St Nazaire made it clear to Pound that a direct confrontation between him and Mountbatten contained great danger, as the public might easily form the opinion that one was dashing and daring and the other was old and timid. Because he was determined to stay, Pound had to be careful in challenging Combined Operations and avoid confirming his public image as too timid a leader. Nor could he afford to give the appearance of being jealous of Mountbatten, having taken the strongest stand against his promotion.

If opposing the Dieppe project was unthinkable for fear that it would boost Mountbatten's image as an aggressive leader while seemingly confirming Pound's as too old, too sleepy, and too cautious, opposition was still more unthinkable in the light of deteriorating Anglo-Soviet relations, which had soured over the convoys question, when Pound gave the disastrous order to PQ 17 to scatter in flight. Pound had taken the leading role in urging their suspension and so enraged a segment of the public that felt not enough was being done to help the Soviet Union. He could ill afford to offend this group because, by reason of its growing power and dynamic leaders, it was increasingly showing its political clout. Cripps and Beaverbrook, most prominently, marched to its drum beat, but Eden could hear it too. Nothing would have pleased its drum major, Maisky, more than to be able to prove the strength of the lobby by driving from office so powerful a figure as Pound, upon whom Stalin had implicitly poured scorn. Such a demonstration of the power of the pro-Soviet lobby would send a signal to Parliament, and through Parliament to Churchill, to redouble efforts to help the Soviet Union. That he was out after Pound's head Maisky more or less admits in his memoirs, saying that after PQ 17, 'Both I and Admiral N.M. Kharlamov, the head of the Mission, as well all our leading personnel, did not conceal our indignation in talks with British politicians, journalists, sailors, and soldiers. In the end there was such an atmosphere in the capital that Churchill was forced to react. . . .' The Soviet Ambassador's campaign dovetailed perfectly with Stalin's 'rough and surly' cable of 23 July on the suspension of the convoys, which Churchill wanted to pass over in silence, or so he claimed in his memoirs. In fact he was in a fever trying to find some way of appeasing Stalin.[54]

On 29 July Maisky and his military attaché were invited to hear Pound's excuses at a meeting that was also attended by Eden and the First Lord, Alexander. It was something of a precedent-shattering affair, as it involved a Service Chief giving an accounting of himself directly to the representatives of a foreign government. Churchill and Eden, in their memoirs, pass over this humiliation of the Royal Navy in utter silence, as does Stephen Roskill in his official history, *The War at Sea*. (It would appear that Air Marshal Harris was also asked to give explanations later that week to Maisky.) We have Maisky's word for it that 'feelings at this meeting ran very high' as they raked over the history of the convoys. The First Sea Lord was put on the defensive and kept there. 'Pound grew . . . more furious,' Maisky tells us. At one point he said 'angrily' to Maisky: 'Tomorrow I shall ask the Prime Minister to appoint you instead of me to command the British Navy.' When the meeting broke up, Maisky made it widely known he was dissatisfied with the responses and continued to complain loudly about what he considered was Pound's apparent incompetence, which, the Ambassador hinted, must be masking some sinister motive.[55]

The delicacy of Pound's position in subsequent weeks was reflected in the retort Maisky got from Lord Vansitart, former Permanent Under-Secretary at the Foreign Office, whose memoranda Churchill still read attentively: 'What are you surprised at?' Vansitart asked. 'Who is Pound? . . . A poltroon and a sluggard. . . . If he has to take any action he will find ten arguments not to do it. . . . Do you know what his nickname is on the lower deck? "Don't do it Dudley" . . . that's Pound all over.' The remarks indicated how badly Pound's stock was plummeting in the summer and early fall of 1942. As late as September, two months after the PQ 17 affair, Cripps was still trying to get Pound fired.

For Pound to have opposed *Jubilee* — which was being defined by Mountbatten as a gesture to placate the Soviets — would have been asking to be pilloried. Nor for that matter did Pound necessarily want it cancelled. The giant raid had a positive side for Pound inasmuch as it promised to shift for a while some of the burden of appeasing the Soviets, which had hitherto largely fallen on the shoulders of the Navy in the form of the murderous convoys, onto COHQ's shoulders. Appeasing the Soviet Union on the French coast might also cool Churchill's passion for an attempt to provide protection for the convoys by seizing bases in Norway — a nice idea in the abstract, but one that was certain to be prohibitively costly in capital ships. His own interests, then, as well as those of the service, urged Pound not to veto Dieppe, even though he must have known its prospects were poor, at best.

The repercussions of Stalin's explosion at Churchill also influenced the remounting of *Rutter* in a very specific way. At the meeting on 23 July, when Maisky delivered Stalin's message, Churchill outlined the gestures Britain was making to reduce the pressure on the Soviet union, including heavy raids in the air and on the ground. Maisky is completely silent on Churchill's promise of significant ground raids, probably not wishing to have the pressure he placed on the British government used to explain Dieppe. But Churchill reported the offer of raids to the War Cabinet the next day, at the same meeting in which he announced that Pound and Harris would be asked to make their explanations to the Soviet Ambassador. Churchill also decided, on 27 July, that the Soviets should be told of the strategic decision made that day to abandon *Sledgehammer*, save as deception, in favour of *Torch*. Informing Roosevelt of how he planned to reply to Stalin, Churchill cabled the President: 'We must establish a second front this year and attack at the earliest moment. As I see it this second front consists of a main body holding the enemy pinned opposite *Sledgehammer* and a wide flanking movement called *Torch* (hitherto called *Gymnast*).' These are practically the identical words Churchill used to preface his discussion of *Torch* and Dieppe (defined as a raid suggestive of a *Sledgeham-*

1. General Andrew McNaughton and Winston Churchill ponder the perennial question: when, where, and how to employ Canadian troops? (Courtesy the National War Museum, Ottawa.)

2. In the midst of crisis, in December 1941, William Lyon Mackenzie King poses with Winston Churchill on his arrival in Ottawa. Behind, on the train platform, is Air Marshal Sir Charles Portal, and descending the steps is Sir Charles Wilson, Churchill's physician. (Courtesy the National War Museum, Ottawa.)

3. A worried Churchill, having cut short his visit to Washington to return to face a Vote of Censure over Tobruk, is greeted by his daughter Mary Soames on 27 June 1942. (Courtesy the National War Museum, Ottawa.)

4. The Chief of Combined Operations, Lord Louis Mountbatten, doing what he did best, delivering a pep talk (to the *Jubilee* force). (Courtesy the National War Museum, Ottawa.)

5. General H.D.G. Crerar, the man who fought for and obtained the assignment of Canadian troops, despite British reluctance, for the largest raid in modern military history. (Courtesy the National War Museum, Ottawa.)

6. General McNaughton, cigarette in mouth, with senior British military officers: General Sir Alan Brooke (far right) and General Bernard Paget. (Courtesy the National War Museum, Ottawa.)

7. King George VI and Queen Elizabeth visit the set of *In Which We Serve* in the summer of 1942. The unidentified man with his back to the camera standing next to Noël Coward would appear to be Mountbatten. (Courtesy the Mountbatten Archives, University of Southampton, and the Mountbatten Estate.)

8. Mountbatten gives a morale-boosting talk in 1942 to one of the Canadian Scottish regiments off the Isle of Wight, where they were in training before seeing action at Dieppe. (Courtesy the Imperial War Museum.)

9. The aftermath of the battle. The heavily pebbled beach was the worst of all possible surfaces for tanks, but the main reason for their immobilization was that they, and the engineers accompanying them — who had means of facilitating their passage — came under devastating fire. (Courtesy the National War Museum, Ottawa.)

10. The Germans come out from their defences, through barbed wire, to survey the aftermath. (Courtesy the National War Museum, Ottawa.)

11. Puzzlement at the folly was the initial German reaction. The casino is visible in the background. (Courtesy the National War Museum, Ottawa.)

12. Nearly 1,900 Canadian prisoners being marched off for internment until the war's end. (Courtesy the National War Museum, Ottawa.)

13. A portrait by Lawren Harris of Major-General J.H. 'Ham' Roberts, Military Force Commander at Dieppe — with the raid that effectively destroyed his career in the background. (Courtesy the National Gallery of Canada and the National War Museum, Ottawa.)

14. Mountbatten, his career apparently untouched by the Dieppe disaster, continued to take centre-stage in the High Command of the war. He is shown here with Churchill and Roosevelt and the US and British Chiefs of Staff at Casablanca on 18 January 1943. From the left, seated: Lieutenant-General Arnold, Admiral King, the Prime Minister, the President, General Sir Alan Brooke, Admiral Sir Dudley Pound, and General Marshall. Standing: Brigadier Jacob, General Sir Hastings Ismay, Mountbatten, Brigadier-General Deane, Field Marshall Sir John Dill, Air Marshall Sir Charles Portal, and Harry Hopkins. (US Army photograph, courtesy the Franklin D. Roosevelt Library, Hyde Park.)

15. Mountbatten being interviewed in July 1967, by John Secondari of ABC, for a television program on Dieppe. (Courtesy the Mountbatten Archives, University of Southampton, and the Mountbatten Estate.)

*mer*-type attack) to Stalin approximately two weeks later in Moscow. The connection between appeasement of the Soviets and the Dieppe raid, whose execution was evidently being taken for granted, was made clear on the 29th when Churchill again cabled Roosevelt: 'In the meanwhile we are explaining to Maisky in detail nature of problems of Russian convoys and latest position about bombing attacks on Germany and plans for commando raids.'[57]

In this formulation can be seen Churchill's intention to reassure the Soviets that the subsidiary paragraphs of the *aide-mémoire*, about what Britain would promise, were being implemented. The reference to commando raids was clearly equivalent to the earlier mention of a simulated *Sledgehammer* and could scarcely have referred to anything save the centrepiece, Dieppe. The President, who had been briefed on Combined Operations' plans in June by Mountbatten, must have understood it as such, because he replied on 29 July: 'I think that without advising him of the precise nature of our proposed operations [in plural] the fact that they are going to be made should be told him [Stalin] without any qualifications.'[58]

One can thus understand somewhat better Mountbatten's report to General McNaughton on 25 July: '. . . the Prime Minister and the War Committee of the Cabinet had approved Operation J[ubilee] in general principle.' Though at first glance it would appear that Mountbatten was playing a little fast-and-loose with the record, as the discussion had been couched in generalities — no operation in particular had been intimated — it is true that the War Cabinet had raised no objection to Churchill's general statement that Britain would try to undertake heavy raids in the near future. So Mountbatten's assurance, while misleading, was not wholly inaccurate. McNaughton was given to understand that it was the problem with the convoys and Stalin's reaction that had prompted the discussion. But what is most revealing to the historian is the fact that Mountbatten, even on this late date, did not claim that the Chiefs of Staff had approved. McNaughton certainly had some inkling of Mountbatten's problems because earlier, on 16 July, Mountbatten had tried to enlist McNaughton's help in expanding his authority, so that in future the Chiefs of Staff Committee could be bypassed, suggesting that he (Mountbatten) should be 'made the Supreme Commander', responsible for launching all raids. McNaughton had refused to be drawn in, indicating that this was not for him to say but was 'a matter' for the C-in-C Home Forces and the Chiefs of Staff Committee. As we know, Mountbatten had not got the Chiefs to approve. Though the Combined Operations after-action report later claimed he received this approval at a meeting of the Chiefs of Staff Committee on 27 July, he did not, and the suggestion in the report that authorization was implicit in the minutes of that meeting was mistaken, not to say fraudulent.[59]

But seeing that Dieppe was now so very important in the context of Anglo-Soviet relations, why, one must ask, did not Mountbatten get

Churchill to intervene and press the Chiefs of Staff for specific approval of *Jubilee* or accord him the increase in authority he was seeking? Why not bring the weight of the War Cabinet and Churchill to bear on Mountbatten's problems? The answer, it seems safe to say, was that Mountbatten feared involving Churchill too directly, for any confrontation over Dieppe would lead to too many questions being asked and ultimately to formal rejection of the plan. After all, Churchill himself had twice come very close to ordering its cancellation. He had to be kept at a distance. All of this makes clear that Mountbatten was serving not his superiors' interests but his own, for in the case of the former he would not have cared particularly whether it was cancelled or not. Believing that cancellation was against his interests, Mountbatten let sleeping dogs lie and went ahead with remounting, confident that so long as he avoided raising controversial questions he would not be stopped. Certainly Pound, who was under attack for a long string of disasters and since July was being portrayed as indifferent to Russia's agony, could not afford to veto the project.

At the same time the very pressures that induced Pound to hold his peace about the project also militated against acceding to Mountbatten's request to assign something larger than destroyers for naval support. Though the Germans had risked three capital ships in the Channel in February, Pound did not feel he could risk one in August in support of the Dieppe operation. The explanation for this timidity is in part technical. The Luftwaffe had been able to concentrate much of its strength in France on the one task of providing massive cover. But Pound knew that one of the purposes of the Dieppe raid was to provoke an air battle, and that the RAF would have its hands full in waging that battle while simultaneously providing fighter cover for the ground forces, a dual mission that would produce the greatest air battle of the war. With that load it was unlikely that the RAF would also be willing to undertake the extra protection that a capital ship would require. But there is no evidence that Pound ever bothered to put the question to the RAF, though he had everything to gain by doing so, since he was still trying to establish that the Air Force did not provide the Royal Navy with adequate support. One must conclude that for Pound, consulting the RAF was never in question because the use of a battleship was effectively precluded by other considerations. These, surely, were the long shadow of the *Prince of Wales* disaster; the humiliating German passage up the Channel that resulted in the establishment of a formal Board of Inquiry to explain the success for the German feat; and finally the PQ 17 disaster, leading to Stalin's indictment of the Royal Navy — all of which had raised questions about the wisdom of keeping Pound in office. He could not afford to chance any further disasters, such as the loss of a battleship in the Channel, which would undoubtedly have inflamed public opinion. There was no arguing the reality of the public's routine acceptance of the loss of scores of bombers on every monster raid, while panicking over the loss of a capital vessel. Rightly or wrongly the loss of a capital ship, when he was already under so heavy a cloud, would have given his critics a field day. They would have asked why he had thrown away a battleship when all the experts knew that no more should be risked, and were in agreement that the worst place to risk one was in the Channel.

Very present in Pound's mind must have been the sweeping strategic survey presented in March by the great Lord Hankey, one of Britain's most eminent civil servants (five times secretary to Imperial Conferences — though shabbily dismissed from the War Cabinet by Churchill in 1940), in which he argued that the greatest danger faced by Britain was not the loss of any particular area but rather that 'the number of [Allied] . . . capital ships may gradually be whittled away until their present margin of superiority disappears.' With this problem in mind, Hankey had gone on to oppose any thought of reinforcing the Mediterranean fleet with capital ships, and similarly inveighed against risking capital ships in the Channel area. As he explained: 'In the narrow waters of the Mediterranean, as in those of the Channel and the North Sea, the operations of capital ships are proving dangerous and costly both in casualties and damages.' It would have been madness for Pound to ignore such an opinion, with which he was in full agreement anyway. Hence Pound's illogical position, as Mountbatten reported it to Baillie-Grohman. There was no opposition from the 'highest authority' [Pound] to the Dieppe project, only to risking the loss of a battleship that might have a grave effect on 'morale'. Similarly understandable was the briefer remark that Mountbatten often quoted as Pound's response to the request for a battleship at Dieppe: 'A capital ship in the Channel, you must be joking!'[60]

These considerations also explain why Pound did not insist that the project to remount *Rutter* be submitted to the Chiefs of Staff Committee. A formal request for specific approval based on a submission of Mountbatten's plan might easily have put Pound in the position either of having to meet requests for more naval support or of opposing the project, despite its political importance. Hence Pound did not push for a formal decision on Dieppe.

Baillie-Grohman, to his credit, kept pressing for more naval support. Shortly after he arrived at *Rutter* headquarters at Cowes he was informed that the preliminary heavy bombardment had been cancelled. His first reaction was that the battleship about which he had earlier inquired was now all the more imperative, and signalled back to London, asking if under these circumstances a battleship might be made available, or failing that 'one or two cruisers'. The reply, Baillie-Grohman has recounted, was that none was available and that we 'must depend on surprise'. He seems not to have been satisfied with these declarations, for the Combined Operations Staff minutes for the next day show that those in attendance advised that the Dieppe operation be combined with a small naval demonstration in the

Boulogne area. Baillie-Grohman promised to take it up, but he still had not overcome Admiralty resistance a month later. The demonstration he had wanted never materialized.[61]

Thus it was that whereas the German navy had boldly risked not one but three capital ships in the Channel under the very noses of the Royal Navy and the Royal Air Force — admittedly not without damage — Pound would hazard nothing of significance within his own protective umbrella five months later. A Canadian division was being risked with patently inadequate fire-support, and Pound clearly acquiesced. It was not his most brilliant moment. The only excuse one can advance on his behalf is that Churchill's constant prodding and plotting, and the campaign waged by his critics, had reduced Pound practically to the breaking-point. It was under these pressures that he refused to hazard the naval force that might have spelled the difference between a miserable failure and a marginal success.

# 7

# The RAF on the Eve of Dieppe

Air Marshal Sir Charles Portal was by general reputation the most militarily perspicacious of the Service Chiefs. As Chief of the Air Staff he skilfully balanced the conflicting interests of the RAF's many commands, of which the three principal ones were Bomber Command, by 1942 the most vital, Fighter Command, and Coastal Command, whose supervision he shared with the Admiralty. Why he too should have acquiesced in the Dieppe raid is something of a mystery. That he knew of the decision to carry it out seems certain. On or about 31 July 1942 the Air Ministry received copies of the Combined Plan, which included the overall 'orders' for Operation *Jubilee*. These would not have been kept from him. Nor is it plausible that the Air Marshal did not know on 19 August that hundreds of his planes were taking part in what became the largest air battle of the war.

About the actual contribution of the RAF to the events of that day there is some controversy, not so much about the role of the fighters in warding off the Luftwaffe but about the serious lack of heavy- and medium-bomber support. The original outline plan had called for heavy preliminary bombardment. As Walter Skrine, one of COHQ's military planners, later recalled, he and his fellow planners had felt the original plan was feasible only under cover of a heavy bombardment, and then only if the leading landing-craft 'arrived very close behind that bombardment.' The bombers originally envisaged could have neutralized, at least initially, German defences, and to that extent would have redressed the imbalance in fire-power between the force attacking from the sea, trying to get onto the wide beach, and the defenders firing from what amounted to an amphitheatre of caves and cliffs on either side and the fortified former houses and hotels in the centre on the esplanade. Without heavy air bombardment, the disparity in fire-power proved fatal to the Canadian and British invaders. Battleships, which were also absent, might have helped redress the balance, but the risk to them in the confined space of the Channel would have been considerable. The risk to bombers, however, would not have been particularly great.[1]

The role of the RAF in Dieppe appears, then, to have been a strange combination of heavy investment in fighter effort with almost complete indifference to the necessity for bombardment. Since air operations almost always call for a balance in the mix of aircraft used — in achieving which Portal was an acknowledged master — the imbalance in the effort over Dieppe seems surprising, not to say shocking. Portal certainly knew better. The reason why he allowed this deficiency, and why he acquiesced in Mountbatten's operation, are tied up in the intense strain and sense of crisis that had been building for years and that was to reach its peak around the time of Dieppe, most visibly within what was defined at the time as the cutting-edge of the RAF, Bomber Command. Portal had been its Chief before his elevation to the pinnacle of the RAF, and he still believed firmly in its capabilities. Though his later successor, Air Marshal Sir Arthur Harris, was as hot-headed as Portal was cool and controlled, they nevertheless forged a very close partnership, so much so that it was often impossible to say where the policy of one ended and that of the other picked up. As the Dieppe raid was moving forward, both had a sense of impending crisis in the course of the war. Harris expressed this memorably in August 1942 when he said that a great juncture had been reached, a historic turning-point in the war, an opportunity to hit Germany at the 'solar plexus of her whole-politico military organism'. Few, if any, historians would agree that in 1942 Germany lay open to defeat by air bombardment, or even that such a possibility was in sight. German fighter forces were still very powerful and had shown an ability to inflict massive casualties on every bomber detachment that went in against German cities. German anti-aircraft defences were being strengthened after every attack. RAF fighters still had so short a range that the bombers had to go unprotected for most of their voyage. It would take more than a year before some of these limitations on the bomber offensive were lifted. August 1942 was in no meaningful sense a turning-point in the air offensive. And yet this perception was clearly present in the top echelons of the RAF and we must try to understand what was behind it, for this perceived crisis has much to do with the detrimental imbalance of the RAF's contribution to the Dieppe fiasco, and forms the essential context.[2]

At the time the Dieppe raid was launched the Royal Air Force was desperately trying to prove that Lord Trenchard, the father of the service, was right when he said in 1916 that 'the aeroplane . . . as a weapon of attack, cannot be too highly estimated.' In the 1930s, even though Stanley Baldwin warned that 'The air was the first arm which the Germans will start to build up,' Britain found herself outstripped, and by 1938 was without a bomber force comparable to Germany's, and precious few resources with which to try to keep Trenchard's faith in aircraft alive. At the time of Munich the inadequacies of Britain's bomber force produced near-panic because it was commonly assumed that there was no limit to the damage Germany could wreak from the air. We now know that the great disparity of forces believed to exist at the time was something of a myth, but it is undeniably true that the British bomber program that began in 1937 was woefully under-funded, so that it was unlikely ever to attain its stated objectives. In June 1939 Chamberlain announced to Parliament that in the event of war Britain would not bomb anything save strictly military targets. So concerned was he about German's ability to retaliate that he proceeded to place innumerable restrictions on RAF bomber activity; even purely military targets that might result in collateral civilian casualties were forbidden, making it doubtful that heavy bombers could be employed at all. Fear of Germany's bomber force was also great across the Atlantic. President Roosevelt appealed to both sides to refrain from unrestricted air warfare. Chamberlain did not intend anything else, and Britain's first bomb cargoes consisted of nothing more than propaganda pamphlets. Not surprisingly, it was hard to get substantial allocation of resources when nothing more serious was envisaged than a propaganda war. Morale in Bomber Command was accordingly low. The lack of offensive purpose was also reflected in the British Government's stress on fighter as opposed to bomber production. The resulting disparity in offensive capability was masked for a while by the Luftwaffe's concentration on Poland. By the summer of 1940 Germany was accelerating its bomber production at so fast a clip that fear once again gripped all those who contemplated the possible outcome of a bomber duel.[3]

With the savage fury of Germany's attack on France in May-June 1940, public attention was rivetted not on the RAF but on what the Luftwaffe was accomplishing, particularly with the Stuka dive-bomber's startling capabilities. Many uninformed observers thought the moment had come to unleash a strategic-bombing offensive against Germany 'before the defences were fully efficient', when a 'crippling blow might be struck at the outset.' But the experts knew better. In fact on 28 April the Vice-Chief of the Air Staff, Air Marshal Peirse, concluded that a German bomber effort on Britain would be four times as heavy as anything that Bomber Command could throw back. This was surely disappointing news to Portal, who at the time was chief of Bomber Command.[4]

When shortly thereafter the Germans broke the so-called Roosevelt moratorium with the bombardment of Rotterdam on 14 May, followed by the collapse of Holland and the breaking of the French line at Sedan, it was clearly time to get serious about unleashing whatever capabilities Bomber Command had. And in fact the Cabinet soon authorized a bomber offensive against Germany. But severe restrictions were issued, and with only limited resources this first offensive could not possibly have fulfilled the expectations that had been entertained. Trenchard's disciples nevertheless continued to urge the removal of target limitations and the launching of a major offensive.[5]

With Churchill's advent as Prime Minister, the prospects for unrestricted air attacks on Germany improved. He might describe himself as a former naval person, but he was capable of nursing the most extravagant notions of what bombing could accomplish. On 8 July he wrote:

> The blockade is broken and Hitler has Asia and probably Africa to draw from. Should he be repulsed here or not try invasion, he will recoil eastward, and we have nothing to stop him. But there is one thing that will bring him back and bring him down and that is an absolutely devastating exterminating attack by very heavy bombers from this country upon the Nazi homeland. We must be able to overwhelm them by this means, without which I do not see a way through.[6]

These beliefs were deeply held by Portal, who claimed on 17 July that in Bomber Command 'We have the one directly offensive weapon in the whole of our armoury, the one means by which we can undermine the morale of a large part of the enemy people, shake their faith in the Nazi regime . . . .' Portal's hope that the restrictions would be slowly lifted by Churchill were not disappointed, and the process was accelerated during the invasion scare in July, when a wider list of targets was approved for Bomber Command. But given the limited resources they had been allocated, the bomber effort could not have much effect.[7]

Because the RAF was employing relatively heavier bombers, it was unable to produce results comparable to those the Germans were achieving with the Stuka dive-bomber. General Edward Spears, chief British liason officer to the French Army, vividly recorded his reactions: '. . . the dive-bomber emerged in my consciousness as a really serious danger. I soon became accustomed to hearing it described as a nerve-shattering, irresistible weapon, attacking vulnerable points with uncanny pertinacity. Guns were helpless against it , so was the infantry.'[8]

Britain did not in fact have a comparable aircraft and thus there was some embarrassment when Churchill and Lord Halifax, the Foreign Secretary, pushed early for a retaliatory bombing campaign against Germany. The lack of aircraft types, however, and concern for civilian casualties limited the authorization in 1940 to a campaign against oil.[9]

Successive attacks in May, when 535 tons of high-explosives were dropped, achieved none of the hoped-for objectives. The oil targets were too small and too difficult; and as they were often at some distance from population and industrial centres, the German populace seemed unaware of the attacks. Soon the RAF indicated that it wanted the restrictions on bombing urban centres lifted.[10]

Two events helped bring about this change. The first was the Luftwaffe's accidental bombing of London on 24 August 1940. It was caused by a combination of navigational and operational difficulties, but Churchill apparently did not know this and ordered retaliatory bombing of Berlin for the next night. While the raid succeeded in shocking German leaders, it also revealed to experts in Britain that a successful attack required more than aircraft; navigational aids, skilled crews, and sophisticated targetting technology were also needed. In 1940 these were all lacking. But hopes waxed considerably in September when it became evident that Hitler could not invade Britain that year, which meant that Bomber Command could be relieved of some of its defensive obligations so as to experiment with offensive operations. Since no other service was able to contemplate any significant offensive, a most attractive opportunity to win new support was now on the horizon if only the RAF could make a convincing demonstration of its capability. Those who had earlier regarded the theories of strategic warfare with skepticism now entertained extravagant hopes. Reflecting this new optimism, Churchill wrote the Chiefs of Staff in September:

> The Navy can lose us the war, but only the Air Force can win it. Therefore our supreme effort must be to gain overwhelming mastery in the air. The Fighters are our salvation, but the Bombers alone provide the means of victory.[11]

Bomber Command was anxious to please the Prime Minister and to keep such hopes alive. Berlin was again added to the list of targets in September, even though it did not meet the requirements that all targets must contain strategic resources. The goal for the attack on Berlin was stated to be the creation of 'the greatest possible disturbance and dislocation both to the industrial activities and to the civil population in the area.' Churchill continued to press for this broader definition of possible objectives, writing to the Secretary for Air, Sir Archibald Sinclair, on 20 October that though strategic targets would continue to have priority, when these could not be hit 'the nearest built-up areas' should be attacked. At the War Cabinet meeting on the 30th he expressed the view that 'the civilian population around the target areas must be made to feel the weight of the war.'[12]

This increasing emphasis on civilian targets coincided with the elevation of Portal to the pinnacle of the RAF structure on 25 October. As Chief of the Air Staff, Portal was much more willing than his predecessor to admit that something besides purely military targets was being contemplated. With Portal's support it became possible to work morale-breaking raids on twenty or thirty German cities into a package of targets that included communications lines, marshalling yards, submarine bases, and the continuation of attacks against Luftwaffe bases in France. But in fact, out of this package only two of these goals could possibly produce significant results

— the destruction of the German oil industry or the devastation of cities, though what industrial damage might be produced by the latter was anyone's guess. Not surprisingly, more sober minds on the Air Staff preferred oil as offering a finite list of clearly defined targets, thus allowing the more precise monitoring of the bomber attacks that was so essential if procedures were to be refined. Misleading data soon became available to support expectations that such objectives were possible, and on 31 May 1940 the Lloyd Committee (set up to study the most efficient use of RAF bomber capability) reported that if the RAF could destroy some 350,000 tons of German oil by 1 September, Germany 'would then be on the danger lists as regards her oil supplies.' On 13 January 1941 the Air Staff endorsed the attempt to knock Germany out of the war with such an attack.[13]

With woefully inadequate resources and minimal successes, however, the implementation of this plan soon looked more like a parody of what Trenchard had advocated, and the paucity of results did not escape Churchill's notice. Though he had earlier joined the ranks of those advocating strategic bombing, he felt no compunction in promptly joining the critics — devil's advocacy being a major ingredient of his leadership. He now pressed Portal for evidence that strategic bombing would work and that it deserved a major share of Britain's war resources. Portal, still new to the job, gave unrealistic assurances that half the numbers the planes dispatched would reach their targets.[14]

While Portal was wrestling with having to support the overly ambitious program to bomb oil installations, he also had to deal with the implications of the growing crisis in the Atlantic. This prompted the Admiralty to mount a double-edged campaign to force the assignment of more long-term bombers to Coastal Command and, when this was resisted, to demand that control of Coastal Command be taken away from the RAF. In this campaign Pound had the powerful backing of Lord Beaverbrook, the Minister of Aircraft Production, who wrote the First Lord, A.V. Alexander, that 'We will never get a satisfactory solution to our trouble until the Navy is in charge of reconnaissance over the Sea.' Portal naturally resisted transferring control of Coastal Command to the Admiralty. Nevertheless, in the summer and fall of 1940 Pound succeeded not only in shifting plane-production schedules, but also in taking control of Coastal Command away from the RAF and placing it virtually under Admiralty control. With Pound's victory, the number of bombers available for duty over Germany's heartland was drastically reduced.[15]

The defeat Portal suffered in the matter of Coastal Command proved, however, to be fortuitous. By December 1940 evidence began to appear that the successes Portal had predicted for Bomber Command were not being achieved. On 31 December Churchill wrote Portal about one of the reports, saying that 'this is the most serious and precise of many melancholy reports ... the matter causes me a great deal of anxiety, and also the cabinet.' But the RAF now had what looked like a valid excuse when it claimed that the inroads made on bomber strength by the Admiralty's demands for the release of bombers to Coastal Command were responsible for the meagre destruction wrought on Germany. This, however, was not a complete explanation for the difficulties being experienced by Bomber Command. Shortcomings in fighter protection and navigational technology were causing casualty rates to soar in the fall of 1940. By November, Churchill was so concerned that he gave instructions for a suspension of the bombing program, writing Portal on 17 November: 'Painful as it is not to be able to strike heavy blows after Coventry, yet I feel that we should for the present nurse Bomber Command a little more.'[16]

In fact it was not until April 1941 that the RAF began to re-establish control over Coastal Command and secure a more favourable production allocation. By then the seemingly fickle Churchill was back to his old enthusiasm, asking Portal on 15 April:

Is not too much emphasis being put on the Battle of the Atlantic, and too little on the forthcoming battle for our vital industries and the staying power of our civilian population?. . . Our only defence is the counter attack in Germany. We ought now to be piling up the damage in Germany.

Soon momentum was gathering for a renewal of a bomber offensive. But by now Portal was convinced that the existing projects, particularly the campaign against German oil resources, required more precision than Bomber Command could achieve. The remaining bombing missions attempted for the Admiralty, particularly the costly attempt to sink German capital ships at Brest, only underlined this fact. The conviction was gaining strength that the strategic bomber was useful only against very large targets — that is, large built-up areas.[17]

As Portal campaigned for licence to strike German cities, a certain measure of British nationalism came to his aid. Since Germany had been able to wreak so much devastation in bombing British cities, it was all too easy to conclude that British pilots should be able to create even more destruction and break the resolve of Germans, who, it was assumed, were much less attached to their political regime than Britons were to theirs. Portal soon made clear that his evolving strategy was focusing on the cities themselves with the object of breaking German morale. But few wanted to admit that this morally questionable ambition was all that was left of strategic-bombing doctrines. One who did was Air Marshal Harris, who had commanded Bomber Group No. 5 prior to his appointment in December 1940 as Deputy Chief of the Air Staff. 'Bert' Harris would pick up other nicknames, including 'Bomber' for his unrestrained advocacy of heavy bombing against urban areas. In a minute of 1 April 1941 he stressed that the objective of a bombing campaign must be to show that Britain had its own way of returning fire for fire: answering the blitzkrieg with a death-dealing bomber counter-offensive in which precision was irrelevant. Harris proposed that key German cities should be selected for the 'maximum damage and destruction to the populated areas, as a demonstration of that ruthless force which we shall have to employ . . .' This evolution towards massive bombing of German cities appealed to Churchill, who, like most Victorians, focused on the will to fight. He wrote to the Army's principal planner, Major-General Sir John Kennedy, at the end of April 1941: 'My plan for winning the war is this . . . 1,000 tons of bombs a night on Germany — we are only averaging 50 now — and 20,000 tanks or so, ready to land all along the coasts of Europe.'[18]

Portal took advantage of the swinging pendulum to present as forcefully as he could the case for strategic bombing. He told the Chiefs of Staff on 21 May:

> Our aim is to win the war by building up a crushing measure of superiority. Meanwhile the Navy must keep open the sea routes and all three services must defend the home base and vital overseas territory against invasion. The Army has no primarily offensive role. . . . We aim to win the war in the air, not on land. Undoubtedly we must build up land forces as well . . . but as far as the continent is concerned these forces will be used as an Army of Occupation after the bombing offensive has crushed the enemy's will to resist.

A great boost to this strategy had just recently issued from the apostle of strategic bombing himself, Lord Trenchard, who on 19 May submitted a powerful memorandum to Churchill, arguing that 'The most vulnerable point' in the German nation was 'the morale of her civilian population under air attack.' While the current list of objectives resulted in ninety-nine per cent of the bombs missing their target, concentration on German cities and morale would produce ninety-nine-per-cent success. Soon even Army planners — including General Kennedy — were looking to the air, arguing that as the Germans had not prepared their population for a massive aerial attack, there was the possibility of strategic surprise.[19]

In Portal's view the new strategy not only provided an alternative to precision bombing (which he had favoured, but which he now recognized was a long way off); it would also have broad public appeal and promised to increase the visibility of the RAF. Perhaps not incidentally it would require an even greater allocation of productive capacity to bomber production. (One of the main yardsticks of an organization's vitality in wartime was its hold on production priorities.) Everything seemed to argue in favour of a new definition of strategic bombing.

These trends were well launched even before Hitler's great gamble, the attack on Russia. But *Barbarossa* served to solidify support around the bombing program, since the bomber offensive might now be one of the few ways the Soviet Union could be offered immediate help. If the bomber attacks were successful, Hitler would have to bring some of his air force back to the west, or at least stop sending reinforcements east. These were attractive notions and the Chiefs of Staff, now coming under pressure to help Russia, rallied to the notion of strategic bombing aimed at destroying German morale. Shortly after *Barbarossa* a coherent program was being developed to reap the full benefits of this strategy. In the first stage the RAF would begin a series of attacks to waste the remaining fighter defences over Europe in preparation for a major escalation of the bombing. To challenge the Luftwaffe and give succour to the Russians, a series of fighter sweeps over France, 'Rhubarbs', and a series of bomber and fighter sweeps, 'Circuses', were to be launched. The new campaign began with an attack on Brest on 1 July and soon included Cherbourg, Lorient, Le Havre, and the Seine shipyards. Two days later, on the 3rd, a series of night bomber-raids was launched covering a host of targets, including Bremen, the Ruhr region, Cologne, and much of the Rhineland. But the Germans, operating close to their bases, in fact had the advantage, and as John Terraine has shown, the advantage in kills lay with the Luftwaffe by 4 to 1.[20]

*Barbarossa* also led to a new directive to Bomber Command on 9 July 1941, which noted the situation created by Germany's offensive and ordered an attack on nine rail targets in the Ruhr as being 'suitably located for obtaining incidental effect on the morale of the industrial populations.' The new orders to Bomber Command cited a plethora of targets, but the intent was clear: '. . . you will direct', the Chief of Bomber Command (Air Marshal Sir Richard Peirse) was told, 'the main effort of the bomber force, until further instructions, towards dislocating the German transportation system and to destroying the morale of the civil population as a whole and of the industrial workers in particular.' It was another step down the dark road to terror bombing.[21]

The gathering consensus was formalized by the Chiefs of Staff on the eve of the Riviera Conference in Argentia, Newfoundland, when they noted, on 31 July, that 'We gave the heavy bomber first priority in production for only the heavy bomber can produce the conditions under which offensive forces can be employed.' The Chiefs now thought it was possible that strategic bombing might by itself 'be enough to make Germany sue for peace'. This new doctrinal consensus found expression in a plan calling for the destruction of 43 German cities with a population totalling 15 million, including the majority of towns with a population of over 100,000. As Trenchard had foreseen, this would require 4,000 first-line bombers, which certainly would consume much productive capacity. But as the effect was now predicted to be 'decisive', few took issue with the barbarous implications.[22]

The extent of the RAF's doctrinal victory may be seen in the role the Chiefs now allotted to the Army. If, as they hoped, the bombing program would force the Germans to sue for peace, '. . . the role of the British army on the Continent will be limited to that of an army of occupation.' The combat mission assigned to the Army was very limited. It should be prepared in the final stages of the war, the Chiefs suggested, 'to accelerate victory by landing forces on the Continent to destroy any elements that still resist, and strike into Germany itself.' But this could hardly be described as a decisive role.[23]

As this strategy gave pride of place to the Royal Air Force, Churchill did his best to soften the blow to the other services. He sent Portal a series of minutes, urging co-operation and reminding him that the Army had long been starved for the sake of RAF development, and that there were a number of long-standing grievances that needed to be addressed. 'If the Army is not well treated in the future the Air Ministry will have failed in an essential part of its duties.' Such solicitude was all the more important, Churchill recognized, as the new bomber program would probably make it 'necessary to slow down the Admiralty program or to reduce the flow of equipment for the army.'[24]

Even before the air offensive got started, however, Churchill's principal scientific adviser, Professor Frederick Lindemann — now Lord Cherwell — was shrilly blowing the whistle on the new doctrines. Pointing out that much of the program was based on untested theories, Cherwell proposed an investigation of Bomber Command's real as opposed to claimed efficiency, to be conducted by the War Cabinet Secretariat with full access to ministerial documents and surveys. The devastating conclusions of the Butt Committee, presented in August, revealed that in full-moon conditions only forty per cent of the planes reporting successful attacks actually got within five miles of their targets. When there was no full moon, something like seven per cent got within this distance. These statistics looked only at those claiming successful attacks. If one factors in the pilots who were honest enough to admit failure, the result is a very sorry picture of Bomber Command's effectiveness. As Churchill said, 'It is an awful thought that perhaps three quarters of our bombs go astray.' He was, in fact, aghast, and minuted to Portal in his most delicate style that this study was a 'very serious paper', which 'seems to require your most urgent attention.' It was now evident to most readers of the Butt Report that nothing could be salvaged out of the original doctrine of strategic warfare based on careful identification of precise targets; that strategic bombing either had to be abandoned or redirected towards the blanket bombing of cities, aiming directly at the German will to continue the war.[25]

The Butt Report also had the effect of making painfully clear how high RAF casualty rates were when measured against the bomb-load delivered on the targets. Excessive loss rates, such as those experienced in the attacks on Rotterdam, made agonizing reappraisals imperative. Churchill now took the opportunity to write Portal to urge caution, as 'The losses in our bombers have been very heavy this month, and Bomber Command is not expanding as was hoped. While I greatly admire the bravery of the pilots, I do not want them pressed too hard.' But when the Air Staff reminded Churchill that he had asked for any help that could be offered to the Soviet Union, Churchill said: 'Good. The devotion and gallantry of the attacks on Rotterdam and other objectives are beyond all praise.'[26]

In fact both Cherwell's criticism and the Butt Report helped put Churchill on his guard, triggering once again that natural oscillation of his temperament from daring conception to sober calculation. He drew back from the kind of official commitment to the strategic-bombing campaign Portal and Harris wanted, without which it would be impossible to impose the resource-allocation priorities the doctrine of strategic bombing seemed to require.

Portal, recognizing the threat, chose to fight hard for those priorities, taking up the Prime Minister's challenge on 2 October. He reminded Churchill of the Chiefs of Staff paper at the Riviera Conference on 31 July, and that 'production has already been planned to conform to this strategic conception and we are already committed to it.' In effect, he was telling Churchill that he should either stick with the decision, or if he had doubts look for a new strategy. Trying to win Churchill back to an unquestioning adherence to strategic bombing, he again laid before the PM the decidedly rosy vistas that had proved so alluring in the past. If Germany had been able in 1941 to cause 93,000 deaths or serious injuries in Britain with a fraction of the bomb-load planned for Germany in 1943, there was no reason why Britain should not be able to match or exceed those rates. The effect ought to be decisive.[27]

Churchill, who never gave himself wholeheartedly to any single doctrine for long, reacted neutrally to Portal, saying: 'One has to do the best one can, but he is an unwise man who thinks there is any *certain* method of winning this war, or indeed any other war between equals in strength. The only plan is to persevere.' He also advised Portal to retain an open mind and never to lose sight of the changes that would accompany America's entry into the war — changes that would create the opportunity of supplementing the bombing program in 1943 'by simultaneous attacks by armoured forces in many of the conquered countries which were ripe for revolt.' Portal nevertheless continued to press until he could claim that the Prime Minister had acknowledged 'the primary importance of our bomber operations' and the need to build up the bomber force 'on the largest possible scale'.[28]

Though Portal managed to hold his own in the battle for priorities, it was much harder to win the battle in the skies. He still had to deal with the stubborn facts contained in the Butt Report. Though there had been much criticism in RAF circles of the methods and the data used in this report, Bomber Command soon began to receive its own indications that its sorties were both inaccurate and costly. During the second half of 1941 a raid on

Berlin produced a no-return rate of 12.5%, while the one on Mannheim produced a rate of 13%. A subsequent raid on the Ruhr produced a no-return rate of 21%. The ratios for planes that actually reached the target were even more disheartening. Considering that many of the aircraft that did return were damaged beyond salvaging and those that returned relatively unscathed often carried many dead and wounded, these were indeed grave casualty figures such as no air force could sustain for long.[29]

When Churchill learned of the losses he was naturally very upset, and though he was anxious to help Russia, he told Portal in November 1941 that since such rates could not be sustained any longer, Bomber Command should save its strength for the spring. This was humiliating but good advice, since it was much beyond the power of the RAF to prove the effectiveness of the bombing program with the technology and the numbers at hand. But such a policy of restraint was not easy to follow. While Portal was conserving RAF strength, British workers and the entire British war machinery would have to be geared to produce the sort of bomber force Portal and Harris wanted. Inactivity by Bomber Command was certain to lead to disaffection and loss of public support. So there was here the makings of a vicious circle: the continuation of raids to build public support would so weaken the force that a concentrated offensive might be beyond reach for a long time, but conservation and a period of prolonged inactivity would have a corrosive effect on the support needed to prepare for a great offensive. Moreover, any pause in the campaign would leave an opening for Pound to argue that if the bombers did not have work to do in Germany, there was work for them to do in the French ports. Indeed, in the brief period between 10 December 1941 and 20 January 1942, Portal was obliged to expend 37% of Bomber Command's efforts in largely futile attacks on the three German battle cruisers at Brest, succeeding only in demonstrating the RAF's inability to hit precise targets.[30]

Amid these distractions Portal was obliged to resort to a very delicate balancing act, one that would have a significant impact on the way he would react to the raiding program in general and to Dieppe in particular. To keep alive the prospect of massive strategic bombing, he decided to alternate periods of tactical inactivity, spent on preparing for the longer term, with short bursts of intensive bombing attacks designed to retain public support for strategic bombing, while hoping for the least possible wastage of his forces. Even at the best of times this was trying to square the circle, as he was always short of resources and really could not even afford the few offensives he mounted.

This basic dilemma was greatly complicated at the end of 1941 and the beginning of 1942 by two developments that threatened to demolish permanently Portal's hopes for a real strategic bombing offensive. The most important was the American entry into the war on 8 December 1941, less than six months after the Soviet Union's entry. As Churchill noted, while there had been no hope of victory save by air power in the early part of the war, there were now other possibilities. Why wait for a far-off victory by strangulation and bombing when a land victory might be possible a lot sooner by co-ordinating Russian and American military efforts? This prospect, of course, meant devoting industrial plants not to the production of bombers but of fighter aircraft capable of close support, as well as of tanks and the myriad necessities associated with large armies.[31]

The Soviet Union's entry into the war brought the western democracies into an ambiguous alliance with an ideological opponent whose resources on the ground were great, but whose resources in the air were limited. The Soviets were soon urging the Western powers to wage the heaviest bombing campaign possible, no doubt for the immediate relief this provided the Red Army. But there might have been other longer-term considerations as well. Americans, and some Britons, began to ask themselves if it was wise strategy to reduce the air support available to their own armies for the sake of an air offensive that would pave the way for the Red Army. Might not the strategy of tightening the ring, with its reliance on strategic bombing, be playing into the hands of a great land power like the Soviet Union? How far strategists were looking down the road is not clear, but the truly perspicacious might have noted that intensive bombing would bring with it indiscriminate destruction, which civilian populations would find difficult to understand and sometimes more difficult to forgive. In due course, liberation by land armies would bring the bombing to an end and would become one of the welcome reliefs to Europeans at the end of the war. In short, those who manned the bombers, with their relentless rain of inaccurate destruction, would be resented a lot more than those who, in one decisive thrust, smashed down the gates of beleaguered towns. These questions were not yet addressed with the attention they deserved, but there was some symptomatic uneasiness about the long-term consequences that was reflected in periodic re-examinations of overall strategy.

In fact by February 1942, when Arthur Harris took over Bomber Command, it was becoming evident that the forces tending towards a new strategy were gathering momentum. With Sir Stafford Cripps, back from Moscow, taking up the campaign for a Second Front, Lord Beaverbrook now stepped forward with a major assault on the strategic-bombing policy, which he saw as consuming the resources required for a cross-Channel attack, and he tried to diminish the priorities that had been accorded to bomber production. Complaining on 7 February that Bomber Command's results were not commensurate with expectations, Beaverbrook declared: 'The policy of bombing Germany, which in any event can yield no decisive results within any measurable period of time, should no longer be regarded as of primary importance.' A few weeks later Cripps, now the Leader of the House, openly questioned the efficacy of the bomber offensive and suggested that the time had come 'to reallocate war productive capacity.'[32]

This rejection of strategic bombing could not have come at a more awkward time for Portal and Harris, who were in the midst of converting their force away from reliance on Blenheims, Whitleys, and Hampdens to the new generation of Lancasters and heavier bombers that were just now becoming available. These new aircraft — together with Gee, a new navigation technology, and new techniques of target-marking — were at last giving the RAF hope that they were within grasp of demonstrating that what they had long promised was possible. Tests of some of these techniques had already been planned in mid-January. Portal secured a new charter for the bombing program on 14 February, which indicated that the 'primary object of your operations should now be focused on the morale of the enemy civil population and in particular on the industrial workers.' What Portal needed was time to weave all the new elements together, but the combined attack on strategic bombing by Beaverbrook and Cripps — echoed increasingly in the press — threatened to decide the issue before the renewed Air Force could even get off the ground. The fact that Cripps was supposed to be speaking for the Government could not be ignored, and Portal knew that Churchill might soon add his voice to the attack. Indeed, on 25 February Churchill forwarded to Portal a memorandum from Clement Attlee, now Deputy Prime Minister, complaining that the Air Ministry were 'too rigidly' devoted to the policy of bombing Germany. There now opened up before Portal the spectre of a major reallocation of resources away from the bomber program.[33]

Portal could only hope that the tests of new procedures the RAF had been developing would remove the growing doubts. A trial of target-marking techniques took place on the night of 3 March and achieved new levels of accuracy against a Renault plant outside Paris. The Secretary of State for Air, Sir Archibald Sinclair, pointed to the results with pride in the debates in Parliament the following day. He told the House that it was decided 'to resume the bomber offensive against Germany on the largest possible scale at the earliest possible moment,' noting that this was the 'only force upon which we can call in this year, 1942, to strike deadly blows at the heart of Germany.' This was a most maladroit intervention, because the very point Beaverbrook and Cripps were contesting was that the bomber program should take precedence over attempts to help Russia. The tenor of the ensuing debates made it amply clear that one attack on a factory was not going to end the argument with critics of the bombing program.[34]

Harris was beside himself with anger as he watched these debates. He saw in the anti-bombing campaign the work of Beaverbrook and Cripps, whom he described as 'certain Members of Parliament with axes to grind, and of 'other influential people of such standing [Attlee?]' who 'ought to know better.' He was certain action had to be taken. Portal should see Beaverbrook and ensure that public attacks were stopped. In Harris's view: 'The gutter Press, which deserves a full share of the blame in this matter, can presumably only be got at through the sensation mongers, circulation hounds and irresponsibles who run it . . . .' More subtle was Portal's approach when he admitted to Churchill that the Air Ministry was indeed guilty, as charged, of putting great emphasis on the bombing program. But he added that this 'seems to us the only immediate way to help Russia, to hearten our own people during the present bad patch and to affect the German war effort and morale.' For all these reasons Bomber Command did not intend to reduce its efforts; rather it was waiting for the first opportunity to redouble them. Thus it was that an immediate major display of Bomber Command's capabilities would have to be grafted, and quickly, onto the list of demonstrations that had been planned before the Parliamentary debate took place — even though larger demonstrations would involve greater wastage and would delay the launching of a really decisive offensive, now effectively being pushed forward to the first third of 1943 at the earliest.[35]

Nor were the prospects for immediate demonstrations very promising, as the Luftwaffe had an abundance of fighters that could be used to decimate British bombers and inflict very high casualties. Portal's solution, with which he plunged ahead without a moment's hesitation on the morrow of the debate in the House, was to prepare the way for bomber demonstrations by challenging the Luftwaffe to a duel in the sky, even though this would mean sacrificing many RAF fighters. Portal justified his gamble by claiming that Intelligence showed that the Luftwaffe, hurt in earlier offensives, had been conserving its strength more effectively. It was time, therefore, to lift the restrictions and try to inflict greater wastage rates. Portal also stressed the Soviet side of the equation, writing that 'One of the ways in which we could best help the Russians would be to weaken the German fighter force and so reduce the adequacy of the air support given to the German armies. If by our air operations in the west, we can succeed in further weakening the G.A.F. or at least preventing its recovery, the chances of the enemy launching a successful offensive against Russia and particularly towards the Caucasus or Iraq will be reduced.' Portal thus came to recommend the renewal of daylight 'Circus' operations — that is, the sending of bombers in daylight over France — to attack targets that would oblige the German fighters to respond. Churchill was worried: 'You are terribly short of fighter aircraft now . . .'; but he added that 'it pays us to lose plane for plane.'[36]

Two contemporary developments on the high seas gravely imperilled this strategy. The most serious was the growing crisis in the Battle of the Atlantic. The other was the sorry state of the British position in North Africa and the Indian Ocean. By the spring of 1942 losses in the Atlantic, particularly off the North American seaboard, were reaching monumental proportions and would not diminish until a rigorous convoy system was established. It was also clear that the pace of German technological innovation in submarine warfare was very great indeed. In the Libyan desert the Eighth Army continued to be the cause of repeated British defeats. And in the Far East, Japanese forces were still very much in the ascendant and their navy was dominant in the Indian Ocean, so that an attack on India was a real possibility.

In circumstances such as these, the Admiralty once again put great pressure on the RAF to provide long-range bomber assistance and demanded that more resources be allocated for the battle at sea. This was particularly disappointing to Portal, as the escape of the three German battle cruisers at Brest up the Channel had relieved the RAF of the terribly costly and largely ineffectual bombing programs directed against them. Now the Admiralty was renewing demands for the allocation of more bombers to Coastal Command, insisting once again on the placement of Coastal Command under the unrestricted control of the Admiralty, and demanding as well RAF reinforcements for the defence of India. Joubert de la Ferté, the RAF officer in charge of Coastal Command, strongly supported the Admiralty in February. The Americans, who were greatly criticized for not imposing a convoy system, also tended to support the Admiralty and Coastal Command. They complained that 'those of us who are directly concerned with the combating of the Atlantic submarine menace are not at all sure that the British are applying sufficient effort to bombing German submarine bases. . . . It seems that the RAF is not fully cooperative.'[37]

Pound's demands for more bombers to be put at the service of the Admiralty grew in the early part of 1942. It was evident by March that if he could have had his way Bomber Command would have been stripped and left with three fewer operational squadrons than it had at the outbreak of the war. Portal bitterly summarized the situation in April, noting that the Admiralty's demands 'cover some 2,000 first line aircraft'; taken together with simultaneous demands by the Army in Libya, this would 'automatically extinguish any hope of development of that bombing offensive which has been postulated . . . as one of the essential measures for winning the war as opposed to merely not losing it.' As Portal later recalled, '. . . they [the Admiralty] would gladly have abandoned the whole of the bomber offensive in exchange for a twenty per cent reduction in the scale of the U boat attack.'[38]

Portal had other problems as well. As pressure from the Navy was growing, so also was that from the Army, which was experiencing defeat after defeat in the Libyan campaign. These reverses were increasingly being blamed on the RAF, which it was alleged was both reluctant to provide the necessary air support and opposed to the creation of a British dive-bomber because it would lead to a separate Army Air Arm. The Army also claimed that German ground forces frequently had better air support. It seems hard to avoid the conclusion that this assertion — though it had some validity — was meant to veil the Army's deficiencies and gain time to institute the real improvements in the management and maintenance of equipment and supplies that were really required.[39]

Brooke, however, was prepared to do more than complain. He wanted action, and on 10 March he called for the formation of a separate force of 109 air squadrons to be operated by the Army as 'an integral component' for Army support. Brooke's reasoning was brisk and cold. He minuted on 1 April that events in the Far East 'have shown only too clearly that our land forces have once more been inadequately provided with air support.' His proposed solutions had the effect, as he noted in his diary, of making Chiefs of Staff meetings increasingly 'difficult' — they were producing 'heated arguments'. An attempt by Portal to ward off such sweeping proposals, with a promise that the Army would henceforth have the full support of Bomber and Fighter Commands when needed, brought a scathing reply from Brooke: 'The General Staff', he wrote on 2 May, 'do not in any way wish to infer that the Air Staff have deliberately withheld support from the Army. They consider, however, that had the role of the support of the Army been placed in the same order of importance by the RAF as is the case with the Luftwaffe, the Army would not have had to operate with such inadequate air support as has been the case up to the present.' Brooke's diary entries show that he was determined to get better air support for the Army even if that meant a major confrontation with Portal. Churchill too was determined to get the Air Force to give the Army more support, telling the Air Ministry, as Brooke recorded, that it should 'devote more love and affection to those Air Forces destined for Army requirements.'[40]

At the centre of the RAF effort to develop its air-support capability was Fighter Command, and more particularly Group 11, commanded by Air Marshal Trafford Leigh-Mallory, who would become the Air Commander for the Dieppe raid. Since its days of glory in the Battle of Britain, Fighter Command had continued to grow in numbers even though it had little occasion to see combat. Experimenting with new missions in search of a *raison d'être* was Group 11. It was given the principal responsibility for the 'Rhubarb' and 'Circus' operations, which sought to impose combat on the Luftwaffe. Because the Dieppe raid was being envisioned by Portal as pursuing the same end, it was only natural that Group 11 should be assigned to that operation, all the more so as Leigh-Mallory was among the most experienced RAF commanders in providing air support for ground forces, having pioneered in that mission during the First World War. He was anxious to build on that experience, and Dieppe would obviously provide a brilliant demonstration of the possibilities of air support, for the raiders could hardly hope for much support from the destroyers. If anyone could give the lie to Brooke and the RAF's Army detractors, it was Leigh-Mallory and Group 11.

Dieppe thus fitted into Portal's defence of the RAF from its critics. As Portal saw it, the cumulative effect of Pound's and Brooke's efforts would lead to 'the division of the Air Force into three separate services.' He was fighting for nothing less than the very survival of the RAF as an organization, with Bomber Command as its principal component. By May 1942, at the time the Dieppe project was being approved, Brooke's and Pound's combined assault on the RAF was wearing his patience thin, particularly as it was accompanied by evidence of Churchill's growing annoyance with the performance of all the Services. The criticism from virtually every quarter was so strident that airmen were convinced they would be blamed for every piece of bad news no matter what the facts were.[41]

If Portal and the RAF were able to hang on, this was because the public, by and large, maintained some residual hope in strategic bombing relative to the greater disappointments produced by the efforts of the other Services. But Churchill seemed to have abandoned his former faith in the bombing program. He was no longer even interested in hearing the arguments, telling Portal on 13 March: 'You need not argue the value of bombing Germany, because I have my own opinion about that, namely that it is not decisive but better than doing nothing.' This was slim comfort, particularly as Churchill was now siding with Pound on shifting production priorities to produce more of the torpedo-bombers the Navy wanted and fewer of the heavier bombers Harris was asking for. Churchill's shift was understandable after all the false hopes Bomber Command had raised. It was also understandable in terms of the pressures Churchill was placing on Pound to keep the convoys to Russia going; making such unreasonable demands, he had to give Pound something.[42]

Help for Portal and Harris came at the end of March and the beginning of April from a surprising source. Lord Cherwell — who in 1941 had been one of the principal critics of strategic bombing — intervened with a memorandum to Churchill reversing his earlier negative appraisal of the bombing program, agreeing now with the RAF's old argument that it should be able to inflict damage on Germany commensurate with what the Luftwaffe had rained on Britain, and that with greater resources more decisive results could be expected. Even after reservations were expressed by one of the deans of the British scientific establishment, Sir Henry Tizard, Cherwell concluded that it should be possible to subject leading German towns to a weight of attack three or four times as heavy 'as that which had fallen on Hull and Birmingham'. An attack on this scale, he predicted, would be 'catastrophic' for Germany.[43]

Cherwell's intervention did much to prevent the division of the RAF feared by Portal. But support also came from Anthony Eden, whose discussions with the Russians, beginning in Moscow in December 1941, had convinced him that they highly valued the bomber offensive and wanted it continued at any cost.[44]

But in its way, Cherwell's and Eden's new enthusiasm was as unhelpful to the RAF as Beaverbrook's and Cripps's disappointment. Portal was only then beginning to receive heavier bombers and knew that he was far from finished with Pound's and Brooke's calls for extra assistance. Under such circumstances Portal was unwilling to commit himself too deeply to the renewed calls for an early bombing offensive. He threw cold water on Eden's most ambitious suggestion, that the RAF should publish a list of 'doomed' German cities that were then to be knocked off one by one.[45]

Portal and Harris were hatching their own plans, with the important objective of winning Churchill back to the strategic-bombing doctrine. Indeed, that effort was underway even before the Cherwell memorandum. On 22 March, Churchill, anxious to become acquainted with the controversial new chief of Bomber Command, invited Harris out to Chequers. That first *tête-à-tête* must have been a clash of titans, but Harris clearly came out on top, for a few days later Churchill cabled Roosevelt: 'I find it very hard to take away these extra six squadrons from Bomber Command in which Harris is doing so well. Our new methods of finding targets is yielding most remarkable results.'[46]

But there was soon new evidence that the doctrinal victory that Portal and Harris sought might still elude them. No sooner did Cherwell come out for the bomber offensive than his long-time rival Sir Henry Tizard, often an adviser to Beaverbrook, renewed the debate with a memorandum of 20 April — addressed to the civilian chief of the RAF, Sir Archibald Sinclair — arguing that aircraft production even on the highest priorities would never produce the numbers that Bomber Command required to carry out a massive bombing campaign. He also doubted that, even with all the technical advances then available, more than 25% of bombs would reach their target, a figure too low to justify the massive allocation of resources Bomber Command desired. Priority, Tizard felt, should go to the Navy. His memorandum had a great impact, coming so soon after the February attacks on the bombing program by Beaverbrook, Cripps, and Attlee and the growing public restlessness. In fact the War Cabinet had already decided (in mid-April) to set up still another independent inquiry on the prospects for strategic-bombing under Mr Justice Sir John Singleton. Bomber Command would go on trial once more.[47]

Portal was leery, as he knew that on the existing data the report was likely to be unfavourable and he would then lose the struggle for production priorities; but he did not yet have the resources to mount a sustained campaign that might produce different data. Still, something had to be done if he was to maintain the integrity of the RAF and the credibility of its mission. Under intense pressure he decided it would be necessary to make an enormously ambitious demonstration — to take advantage of the new Gee navigation techniques before the Germans became wise to them — of what city bombing could accomplish.

In March and April trial attacks on Essen and Cologne took place. Churchill was soon back to his old optimism about strategic bombing, saying in mid-March that the bomber offensive was 'the only offensive action we could take'; he hoped that 'in the next few months, we should give the Germans treatment on a scale that they had never received before.' Gone was the moral outrage he had expressed when German bombers first struck at civilian targets. On the eve of a massive attack on Lübeck on 28 March, Churchill was urging the United States to lend all the support possible and move forward the date for the arrival of American bombers. 'Never was there so much good work to be done,' Churchill wrote, 'and so few to do it. We must not let our summer air attack on Germany decline into a second rate affair.'[48]

On 28 April, one month after the successful attack on Lübeck, Rostock was subjected to the first of a series of devastating raids that used many of the new methods. Harris's luck held as the four-night assault on Rostock succeeded almost completely. Vast fires consumed much of the city and came very close to Harris's aim of demonstrating that an industrial town of moderate importance could be utterly destroyed with a brief series of raids. The cost to the RAF was only 12 aircraft from 521 sorties. This was certainly an acceptable price for taking out a city. But such attacks did not really prove much. Both Rostock and Lübeck were best known as medieval centres of historic significance and therefore had been lightly defended. Attacks on industrial centres were bound to meet much greater defences. But this did not seem to matter. Churchill now embraced the RAF's new program, not so much because it proved that strategic-bombing was feasible, but rather because it promised to offer comfort to the Soviet Union. He wrote Roosevelt to explain:

All now depends upon the vast Russo-German struggles. It looks as if the heavy German offensive may not break until after the middle of May or even the beginning of June. We are doing all we can to help and also to take the weight off . . . Only the weather is holding us back from continuous heavy bombing attack on Germany. Our new methods are most successful. Essen, Cologne and above all Lubeck were all on the Coventry Scale. I am sure it is most important to keep this up all through the summer, blasting Hitler from behind while he is grappling with the Bear.[49]

Here was a feasible equivalent to a Second Front! In Britain the attacks were given very wide publicity and the Cabinet was regularly kept abreast of the bombing offensive with triumphant reports, such as the one presented on 30 April that described Rostock as completely enveloped in clouds of smoke from the successive attacks, the damage 'was heavy and widespread', and direct hits were claimed on the railways station, the gasworks, and a Heinkel factory. Indeed, it would seem that not a single target of significance had been spared.[50]

Singleton now had new facts to consider and admitted in his report that he was greatly impressed with these raids. But while he shied away from supporting the negative implications of a bombing offensive suggested earlier by Tizard, he did not see anything in the most recent raids that would allow the Government to embrace Cherwell's hopes. It was an indecisive report; the RAF's battle for priorities was far from won.[51]

Even as Singleton was making this limited progress against domestic critics, a new threat to Bomber Command appeared from the quarter Portal had most feared: the United States. On 1 April, Roosevelt and Stimson decided that the policy of supplying planes for foreign air forces, before the American air force had met its quotas, had to stop. In May the Americans began to hint that allocations of bomber craft made before the United States entered the war could not be maintained, now that the US air force was to be expanded. On 19 May Roosevelt notified Churchill that the US would have to keep more of bomber production than had originally been foreseen. The President asked Churchill to understand 'our great desire to make the most effective contribution to our combined war effort in every appropriate theater to the limit of our growing capacity.' This reasonable preamble led to a painful conclusion: 'We are anxious that every appropriate American-made aircraft be manned and fought by our own crews. Existing schedules of aircraft allocations do not permit us to do this.' Roosevelt now proposed to reduce American aircraft deliveries by 5,000 planes, equivalent in Portal's eyes to the loss of over 100 front-line squadrons. In Washington it was announced that General Henry 'Hap' Arnold, the Commanding General of the US Army Air Force, would be leaving for London on the 23rd to settle the revised allocation schedule. Churchill's answer on the 20th revealed that he had been expecting this notice, though hoping that it would not materialize.[52]

In anticipation of an American cut-back, Harris had already proposed launching vastly larger air attacks on Germany involving forces of 1,000 bombers per attack, or four to five times as many craft as had been used in the boldest previous attempts. The ambitious nature of the program was fully conveyed by the code-name chosen, 'Millennium'. Given the shortages of planes, given the pressures coming from the Admiralty and the Army for greater air support, and the demands for more air support from the whole Pacific quadrant from Australia to India, this decision to gamble with such abandon does not seem reasonable. Nevertheless Portal and Churchill immediately accepted the proposal. Harris in fact had only about 400 serviceable commissioned bombers in the first quarter of 1942, and an insufficient number of qualified crews, so he had to scrape very hard to reach the figure of 1,047 'bombers', which took to the air on the night of 30 May. Portal was obliged to use both training crews and crews in training, so that the plan imposed enormous strains throughout the RAF. As the number of hours crew-members would have to serve before rotation was markedly increased, Harris and Portal were gambling with the whole force, its future and their own. And yet there was some logic behind the program. How else could the RAF resolve the questions left unanswered by the Singleton report? How else persuade the Americans that the first bombers coming off the lines should go to Britain instead of waiting until American units were organized and trained? What better way to define the RAF's unique mission and thus prevent the tendency of the other services to seek the division of the RAF and Parliament's inclination to shift resources to other efforts? If successful, the 1,000-bomber raids would firmly establish the RAF's unique character and mission.[53]

Of all these objectives, the most pressing may well have been parrying the attempt to cut back plane allocations to Britain. The Americans must be shown how far advanced the British program was and how far the American Air Corps still had to go. Air Vice-Marshal Baldwin, the senior officer flying on the first 1,000-bomber raid against Cologne, told the crews as they prepared to depart on 30 May that their performance would be watched by the world, particularly by 'our friends overseas', who, it was said, needed a bit of jogging up. General Arnold, who was in Britain to persuade the British to accept reductions in deliveries, could not help musing about his bad luck: 'As Commanding General of the U.S. Army Air Forces, I happened to be on the spot at an ironic time. Of all the moments in history when I might have tried to sell Mr. Churchill and his R.A.F. advisers on the future of American precision bombardment by daylight, I had picked the night when they were selling their own kind of bombardment to the world.' It was less of a 'coincidence' than Arnold imagined. But Harris and Portal made their point. If the objective was the earliest possible victory over Germany through strategic-bombing, the thing to do was to give the lion's share of aircraft production to the RAF. Impressed the Americans certainly were. Arnold later spoke of that evening as the real beginning 'in the world's eyes and in Germany's eyes . . . of the "round the clock" destruction of Germany from the air.' In fact Portal and Harris realized that by committing their resources prematurely with the Millennium raids, they were postponing the day when the great offensive could really take place because they knew that, for the time being, they could launch only a very limited number of these show-pieces.[54]

The ulterior motives behind the project concerned more than just the Americans. The first 1,000-bomber raids — one on 30/31 May against Cologne and the second on 1/2 June against Essen — were also advanced and accepted as a useful antidote to the pessimism that had been gripping the British public since the beginning of the year. Churchill was ecstatic, saluting these raids as a 'remarkable feat of organization . . . proof of the growing power of the British Bomber Force' and a 'herald of what Germany will receive, city by city, from now on.' A memorandum by the Minister of Information to Cabinet reported nation-wide satisfaction: 'There is much feeling that the public have been asked far too long to admire Russian resistance, American production and Empire fighting qualities.' From General Arnold came fulsome praise. He called the program 'bold in conception and superlative in execution', though he hinted that he did not think the raids meant that the US Air force should not get its allotment of planes, and he volunteered that 'Our air forces hope very soon to fly and fight beside' the RAF. No one seems to have thought about the hapless German civilians caught up in this maelstrom.

Harris did everything he could to extract the maximum advantage from the results, and his staff claimed that at Cologne Bomber Command had at last won an unqualified victory against a major target. Bomber Command's Quarterly Review boasted that the raid on Cologne constituted the 'greatest air operation ever planned and undoubtedly achieved the greatest single success in aerial warfare.'[55]

Having stripped every command to reach the magical thousand-bomber figure, Harris now responded to the greatly intensified conflicts among the Services by setting his sights on the still-more-ambitious program of two Millennium raids a month; he even indicated an interest in four. This could not be done without a frontal attack on the other Services. On 17 June Harris unleashed his campaign with a long memorandum in which he complained bitterly of having to supply bombers for a Combined Operations raid that he called a 'side show'. This was mild compared to the words he had for Coastal Command, which he attacked as an 'overswollen' defensively minded organization that could achieve 'nothing essential either to our survival or to the defeat of the enemy', and indeed constituted an 'obstacle to victory'. Every effort, he felt, should be concentrated on exploiting the opportunities created by Bomber Command. It was time to press the Americans for an increase in bomber shipments rather than acquiesce in reductions; time also to recall the bombers from Coastal Command and, as soon as the situation had stabilized in the Middle East, to recall the bombers assigned to Army support there. Most important of all was the need to assign the highest possible priority to the production of bombers in Britain. He made these demands against the backdrop of his highly personal, typically grandiloquent review of grand strategy. Entering into the debate then being waged over the future of *Sledgehammer*, Harris told Churchill that a 'premature landing before the bomber has done its work and the landing becomes a mere police action, spells disaster.' It would mean at the best slaughter in the 'mud of Flanders' on a scale comparable to that in the last war, and might even lead to another Dunkirk. It was 'imperative to abandon the disastrous policy of military intervention in the land campaigns in Europe . . .' The answer lay in the weight of the air attack that Britain could now bring to bear on Germany, such as 'no country . . . could survive'.[56]

The conflict among the Services was thus fully engaged. For the third raid Harris had asked Portal on 14 June to get from Pound, 'if necessary with the assistance of the P.M.', approval to use Coastal Command bombers. Pound must have resisted the request, for the next day Churchill dispatched a stiffly worded Action-This-Day minute in which he put the matter very bluntly to Pound: 'I must ask definitely for compliance with this request.' Pound complied, but brought the matter up for discussion at the next meeting of the Chiefs of Staff, making clear that, while he had 'no wish to stop the bombing program', he was 'anxious that priority be given to the improvement of our position at sea', the urgency of which was clear and immediate. Overcoming Pound's resistance to lending back planes assigned to the Navy was to be a continuing problem for the rest of 1942, in no small measure because Pound too had his solid reasons for calling on Coastal Command bombers. American shipment of men and materiel to Great Britain was now assuming substantial proportions, and serious losses in British zones of responsibility, or any slackness in prosecuting the Battle of the Atlantic, would have grave consequences for the alliance and for Britain's fortunes.[57]

Under these circumstances there was no desire on the part of the RAF to provide Combined Operations with any bombers. Every request between the inception of the Millennium program in May and the execution of *Jubilee* met with fierce resistance from Portal and Harris. On 11 May, just days before the outline plan for *Rutter* was presented to the Chiefs of Staff Committee, Harris made clear that his bombers could not be used closer to daylight than 30 minutes before civil twilight because of the German concentrations of day fighters. This rule was formalized as a result of the cancellation of an important raiding project, *Blazing*, planned for August, for which the preliminary bombardment would have extended well into the twilight, when his bombers would have been exposed to Luftwaffe daylight fighters. When Harris realized this, he quickly moved to have the operation cancelled for good. Portal too was furious that the risk to his force had not been explained to him sooner. The incident also revealed how Churchill viewed the respective merits of the bombing campaign and commando raids as gestures to offer consolation to the Soviets. In deciding against *Blazing*, he minuted on 11 May that 'we could not, in present circumstances, afford the risk of heavy casualties to our bomber forces which this [raiding] operation would entail.' The cancellation of *Blazing* undoubtedly served as a warning to the supporters of *Rutter*: if there was a conflict between Bomber Command and Combined Operations, the former would carry the day.[58]

As a result, the rule that the bombers could not be employed closer than thirty minutes to the start of morning twilight was firmly in place. It came to play an important role in the outcome of *Rutter*, as the attacking force was scheduled to make the main assault just before twilight, which would mean that, following Harris's injunctions, the bombers could be used for only five minutes or less. Given these conditions, it hardly seemed worth the co-ordinating effort required to lay on the heavy bombers, a conclusion Harris did his best to get accepted. He also made clear in May that not all the Wellingtons previously scheduled for dropping parachutists would be available if more pressing missions arose. Admittedly Harris stopped short of taking all the Wellingtons away — he would still guarantee enough lift for one battalion of parachutists, or about two-thirds of the force originally stipulated in the outline plan. But as this was well below the threshold considered necessary, it inspired in COHQ the feeling that here too the game was scarcely worth the candle; eventually for *Jubilee*, commandos would replace the parachutists.[59]

In the days immediately before the presentation of the outline plan to the Chiefs of Staff Committee, the support offered by Bomber Command had already begun to shrink to insignificance. This grave development un-doubtedly explains why Mountbatten, at his formal presentation of the plan on 13 May, was forced to be apologetic to the Chiefs of Staff about it, admitting that it was less finished than he would have liked. The source of the problem was delicately alluded to when Mountbatten suggested that if the Force Commanders did not insist on the heavy preliminary bombard-ment, it might be done away with, inasmuch as there was a War Cabinet rule against causing unnecessary hardship to the French populace. Ismay, as Churchill's military chief of staff, seems not to have been convinced of the wisdom of doing without this bombardment, for he requested authori-zation from Churchill and Eden to carry it out, and he had obtained permission by 1 June. Ismay might as well have spared himself the effort, for over the next two weeks what was left of the plan's preliminary bombardment component would collapse.[60]

This occurred as an outgrowth of the first 1000-bomber attack, which Harris and Portal were able to carry out on 30 May only by scraping together every possible craft, including about 50 Blenheims of 2-Group and Army Co-operation Command, which had been designated to provide bombers for *Rutter*. On 1 June the second Millennium raid, with slightly less than 1,000 bombers, left for Hamburg (they would be diverted to Essen). Some time before 4 June there came a day when, according to Montgom-ery's liason officer with COHQ, Goronwy Rees: 'Admiral Mountbatten, handsome and breezy, like Brighton at its best, announced that Mr Church-ill had decided that, for political reasons, it would be inexpedient to under-take the bombing of Dieppe.' This was just another example of Mountbat-ten's tendency to invoke the Prime Minister's name whenever things went badly. In fact at the time, when Mountbatten made his announcement to Rees, the Prime Minister and the Foreign Secretary had already authorized the bombing of Dieppe. The reason for the misleading presentation was probably that Mountbatten did not want it known that he, titular member of the Chiefs of Staff Committee, did not have the clout to make Harris, who held him in complete disregard, bend.[61]

Breaking the news of the decision to the Force Commanders was a problem because they would be greatly discouraged by it. As they had the right to refuse the mission, cancellation was being risked. This is why, at the meeting of Force Commanders on 5 June, the refusal to use the bombers was only lightly alluded to. Instead there was much emphasis placed on the advantage of the cancellation of heavy bombardment. In short a charade was about to be played out.

Terence Robertson in *The Shame and the Glory* seems to have stumbled upon the explanation for the decision. According to his account, Leigh-Mallory, as Air Force Commander, had discussed the problem of the bombers with Harris, who had been intractable, explaining very candidly that he had no bombers to waste. That this was indeed Harris's position we know also from other sources. Leigh-Mallory could not have been in any doubt that the Millennium program, which was now underway, was in fatal conflict with the plans for Dieppe, for the simple reason that Harris needed every bomber he could possibly scrape together for nights of near full moon — exactly the same condition that had been set for *Rutter*. Hence Leigh-Mallory's conviction that if the raid was made dependent on the availability of bombers, it might never come off. Certainly this was Hughes-Hallett's impression, for he later admitted that dispensing with bomber support was 'the price paid' for making sure that the raid took place. The minutes of *Rutter* Force Commanders at the meeting of 5 June, shortly after Mountbatten had left for the United States, do not show that Leigh-Mallory said this explicitly. Nevertheless he began the meeting with a presupposition that an adequate bombing effort to precede the main attack would probably be unavailable; therefore it was up for consideration whether the minor bombing effort that had been offered was worth the difficulties it would cause. As presently planned, he explained, it would serve only to alert the defenders, and cause rubble and bomb craters etc. that would impede the progress of the tanks. In short, he emphasized the positive side to cancelling the heavy preliminary bombardment, but not without hinting that in any case Bomber Command would make no more than a token effort.[62]

One would have thought that if Montgomery — who took the chair in Mountbatten's absence — were hearing this for the first time he would have expressed surprise. In his capacity as supervisor for Home Forces he had originally considered the bombardment to be an important part of the plan because this was one of the few essential elements he mentioned when first briefing Goronwy Rees. That it was vital had certainly been Rees's perception. As he later recalled: 'The original intention of the plan . . . had been that the bombing of Dieppe . . . should be so devastating in its effect that any opposition would be merely nominal. . . . It was an integral and essential element in the plan.' The fact that Montgomery registered no surprise must be taken to mean that he had already known before Leigh - Mallory spoke that the bombing was out, that nothing could be done to get it back, and that Mountbatten had approved.[63]

Because of the controversy surrounding the abandonment of heavy bombing, at the time and later, the reasons that were given against it merit some attention. Leigh-Mallory's contention that the rubble caused by the bombing would have made it difficult for the tanks to penetrate Dieppe on their way to destroy the airfield (an objective that bombers could have accomplished) was at best a prescient guess on his part because this result of saturation bombing, *vis-à-vis* the progress of tanks, was not actually experienced until a year later. None of the Army planners — who had examined the plan for more than two months — raised this as an objection. Even if they had seen it as a problem, the abandonment of heavy bombing might have been debated in the light of whether it was more important to create the conditions necessary to enable the men to traverse the open beaches and the wide esplanade (requiring heavy bombing) or to enable the tanks to start out for the airport. The folly of sacrificing a thousand lives for the sake of easy passage for 30 Churchill tanks seems not to have been discussed — perhaps because Harris had made clear he would never provide the bombers in the quantity the infantry needed to make its frontal attack. Getting the tanks into the town — and, it was hoped, beyond — therefore became the single paramount objective.

Very much after the event Leigh-Mallory said that it would have been impossible to time the arrival of the heavy bombers accurately enough to precede (and thus not to impede) the landing. But this is scarcely credible because the flights were very short and really posed no problem of synchronization. Leigh-Mallory also said that a heavy bombardment would lose the element of surprise. But Dieppe had been bombed from time to time by the RAF without the follow-up of an amphibious raid. Roberts understood that a few more such raids would be carried out on a heavier scale to lead the defenders of Dieppe to miss the significance of the actual attack. Those on Combined Operations Staff closest to the ground plan were convinced that an air bombardment could easily have been fitted in without seriously compromising the element of surprise.[64]

(Subsequent historians — including C.P. Stacey, who later wrote that the failure to work out an adequate air plan was fatal — have been mystified by the abandonment of heavy bombing and by the reasons advanced for it. Noteworthy is the studied understatement of the official historian, Stephen Roskill, who stated that the reasons for eliminating the bombing '. . . were not altogether sound' — an unusual admission to appear in an official history. It may be that the problem of softening up the ground defences from the air was insoluble, but in retrospect what is so disquieting is that there is no evidence of any real attempt to confront and solve it.)[65]

But all rationalizations for the virtual withdrawal of adequate bombing support from Dieppe simply obscure the essential reasons for this: Harris's refusal to use his bombers on 'side shows', the RAF's desperate commitment to win production priorities for its Millennium raids, and finally the stringent limitations of weather conditions laid down by Bomber Command, which as a precondition of the raid only increased the possibility of its cancellation. In Hughes-Hallett's mind, this was probably the decisive consideration.[66]

Two months before Dieppe, Churchill was strongly leaning towards Harris's position. So sympathetic was he to the Millennium project that in mid-June he asked Harris to draft a memo on the 'Role and Work of Bomber Command', so that Cabinet could be informed about the great value of the program — implicitly to rationalize why the other Services would have to make do without much bomber support. Harris was only too eager to comply, and sent a particularly biting memo to Churchill on 28 June, beginning with the suggestion that 'Those who advocate the breaking-up of Bomber Command for the purpose of adding strength to Coastal and Army Co-operation Commands and overseas requirements are like the amateur politician who imagines that the millennium will arrive through the simple process of dividing available cash equally between all.' Harris followed this angry opening with every argument he could muster to urge a maximum effort in support of Bomber Command. He pointed out that operational bomber squadrons amounted to no more than 11 per cent of the front-line strength of the RAF and the Fleet Air Arm, and that over half its effort was devoted to naval and military targets other than strategic bombing. This, he felt, was disproportionate, and he decried the wasting of so much bomber effort on targets of no strategic significance. As he put it: 'Whilst it takes approximately some 7,000 hours of flying to destroy one submarine at sea, that was approximately the amount of flying necessary to destroy one-third of Cologne, the third largest city in Germany in one night, a town of vast industrial import . . ..' But some of Harris's other arguments bordered on hyperbole. He claimed, for instance, that it was Bomber Command that had saved England from invasion. Of like character was his denigration of the efforts of the other Services, which he said were all defensive in nature and 'are not intended to do more, and can never do more, than enable us to exist in the face of the enemy.'[67]

Despite the hyperbole, Churchill liked the argument, asking some time later that the memorandum be shown to Roosevelt, to whom he explained that 'Out of zeal he [Harris] has no doubt over-stated a good case,' but that 'None the less the paper is an impressive contribution to thought on the subject.'[68]

Churchill knew that this memorandum was likely to enrage the sister Services and did not work up the courage to distribute it for another two months. Meanwhile the other Services continued to resist every one of

Bomber Command's new demands. As Portal repeatedly moved to overcome this resistance, he must have wondered how long he could continue to expend his bureaucratic capital in this incessant warfare on behalf of what Harris himself, in a more candid moment, called 'travelling-salesman's samples', for Harris and Portal both knew that Bomber Command's best efforts of 1942 were unlikely to dent the German war effort by much.[69]

Harris found his own reasons to back off from the ambitious language contained in the 28 June memorandum. There was first of all the problem of false expectations to which he was now awakening. In July he complained to Churchill that while the other Services fought only half-a-dozen battles a year, people were expecting a massive raid every night, and when weather gave Bomber Command a respite and 'we fail to stage and win a major battle, the critics rise in their wrath and accuse us of doing nothing yet again.' Harris thus came to see the importance of being more candid and of slowly deflating excessive expectations. But the more fundamental reason for scaling down his monster raids was the fact that they were terribly costly, particularly of training units sent into combat with a consequent reduction of new pilots. As well, it soon became painfully clear that past a certain point in crew attrition, the whole program was self-defeating. By taking their toll of the most experienced crews, these raids were wreaking havoc on units already stripped to the bone. It was only a matter of time before Portal and Harris would have to suspend the experiment or accept the complete disintegration of RAF unit structures in England. This imminent possibility caused sadness all round. In a general review of the war on 21 July, less than three weeks before Dieppe, Churchill noted with 'sorrow and alarm the woeful shrinkage of our plans for bomber expansion.' But even he had to accept that it was impossible to continue with the 1,000-bomber raids.[70]

Another factor that Harris could no longer ignore was the mounting criticism from those known to be his supporters in the other Services, such as General Kennedy. Kennedy too found it hard to justify the enormous expenditures of men and resources when the effect on Germany could only be temporary. In June he complained that the bombing raids had given rise to 'much jubilation and wishful thinking in both the American and the British Press . . . [but they do not realize] what a big price we were paying for the bombing of Germany.' Kennedy estimated that 'if even ten per cent of the effort devoted to bombing could be diverted to the air support of the Navy and the Army, the war situation would be greatly improved.'[71]

These were telling considerations, but Churchill made clear in his policy review of 21 July that he would retreat only so far in his support of Bomber Command. Picking his words carefully, and indulging in what for him was a bit of understatement, he said: 'We must regard the Bomber offensive against Germany at least as a feature in breaking her will second only to the largest military operations which can be conducted on the Continent until that war-will is broken.'[72]

The situation in July — as the plans for reviving the Dieppe raid were going forward — was that Harris, while over-extending himself, had still managed to retain a lot of support even in the Dominions, judging by the memorandum that S.M. Bruce, the Australian representative to the Cabinet, distributed, which asserted that only in the air was it possible to create 'an overwhelming and decisive strength.'[73]

Portal was still trying desperately to gather every bomber he could. To theatre commanders overseas who needed more bombers, he counselled restraint, as Harris's program was 'beginning to have great results.' And he freely gave out assurances that strategic bombing would make a victory possible in 1944 with an offensive by 'a relatively small land force.' Churchill advised Roosevelt: 'We know our night bomber offensive is having devastating effect.' The most recent raids had shown a greater degree of accuracy than had ever been demonstrated before. After a raid over Hamburg, Harris had been able to tell Cabinet that 'most crews found their targets', a claim he had never been able to make before. But high casualty rates, the shortage of aircraft, and soon the weather all dictated the inevitable: the monster raids were scaled down. Unfortunately the smaller bomber forces now ran much higher risks because the monster raids had provoked an improvement in German defences and there was no way of turning back the clock to the relatively smaller casualties of an earlier period.[74]

Hence the crisis in which Harris and his Chief found themselves in August 1942. It was not, as Harris claimed, that 'Germany now offers . . . a target to defeat by Air bombardment at the solar plexus of her whole politico-military organism. . . .' That was hyperbole. Germany would not be vulnerable in that way for years. Nor was it, as he stated, that 'Opportunity . . . knocks NOW, and knocks loud. . . .' There was indeed a 'knock', but what it was announcing was the imminent defeat of the RAF's battle for strategic priorities. Bomber Command had done all it could by way of demonstrations, and in the immediate future there was little save diminishing returns and increasing casualties. It was an awareness of this prospect that had forced Harris to try to collect everything he possibly could for the first Millennium raids, beginning with the raid over Cologne. The enormous destruction rained down on that city — which Harris insisted on seeing as a triumph for Bomber Command — did not delude him into forgetting that his battle for priorities was on the verge of being lost. By the time of Dieppe, Harris had still not secured Cabinet's agreement to give Bomber Command first call on resources; indeed, the prospects for it were slipping away. But Harris was not one to give up easily. He was driven by the thought that if he could only mount one more raid, perhaps he could still win acceptance for his program.[75]

Though Portal, at Harris's prompting, did his best to keep the heavy bombers out of the Dieppe plan, he could see some utility in Dieppe, most obviously in buying time by quieting the Second Front movement. A real effort to establish an early Second Front would drain resources away from the strategic-bombing program. Bomber Command needed time to show what they could do and so win the inter-service battle over priorities. If, in the meantime, the raids showed the difficulty of cross-Channel operations as opposed to bomber offensives, so much the better. Harris certainly made no effort to hide his scorn of the pressure for a cross-Channel invasion, saying that it was devoid of thought and reasoning and could be explained only as 'a blind and even pathetic urge' to do the only thing, in their ignorance, that its proponents could imagine. Portal, though more re-strained, was not unsympathetic to this view. In April, when the COS had 'approved' Marshall's *Sledgehammer* invasion plans, he had been among the most outspoken in expressing reservations against any attempt to stay on the Continent. He told his colleagues at the time that it was necessary 'to bear in mind the differences between air operations across the Channel and the landing of an Expeditionary Force. The former could be continued or stopped at will.' In the latter case, however, 'we could not take as much or as little as we liked. We should have to maintain the air effort for as long as the troops remained on the Continent.' Since air support was so critical, it followed that no landing should be attempted unless Britain was certain that its air resources 'were sufficient to enable operations to be carried through to the end.' But raids were another matter for Portal, who — like Churchill and Mountbatten — saw them as a way to defuse pressure for an early Second Front. In Chiefs of Staff meetings he therefore regularly supported such operations.[76]

There was an additional attraction for the RAF in *Rutter* because it was certain to provoke an air battle. The nemesis of Harris's program was the Luftwaffe's large supply of fighters. While the Germans tended not to attack British bomber groups within the range of RAF fighter cover, as soon as squadrons moved beyond that range the German fighters moved in and had an easy time picking off British bombers. Inflicting wastage on Luft-waffe fighter formations was thus a vital goal for both Portal and Harris during the summer of 1942. This had been the principal objective of the Circus operations launched by the RAF early in the summer, though the results had been disappointing because the Luftwaffe often refused to rise to the challenge except in conditions distinctly favourable to themselves.[77]

The idea of using one or more large-scale ground raids as a means of promoting an air battle seems to have occurred to both Portal and Sir Alan Brooke at about the same time. The minutes of the Chiefs of Staff meeting of 21 March show Portal taking a strong position in favour of raiding opera-tions. He suggested that 'we might be able to bring on a series of air battles in advantageous conditions by dropping detachments of paratroops behind the coast defences in the Calais area and then launching a series of small sea-borne raids with the object of bringing off our paratroops.' Though Portal noted that this would require some of his precious fighters and equipment, he was 'prepared to divert the necessary aircraft from other operations' if a prompt decision was reached. As the Chiefs of Staff Committee noted, to 'compel her [Germany] to fight we must either simulate a sustained operation or carry out a major raid.'[78]

In April, Portal again spoke of the need to bring on air battles, saying that it would probably prove necessary 'to use more aggressive tactics and to bait the trap with more tasty pieces of cheese.' The minutes later clarified what he meant. Under the rubric 'Decoys', it was noted that the Committee had discussed 'various suggestions for bringing about air battles in conditions favourable to ourselves.' The suggestions put forward included 'a daylight raid' on the coast of France, or the threat of such a raid, under cover of smoke, and 'the towing of barges to and fro in the channel.'[79]

In discussing the possibility of some sort of a sacrifice landing in 1942, as a response to Russian reverses, Portal favoured the Pas area (from Dunkirk to the Somme estuary), not because it was less fortified than Normandy (the contrary was the case), but because a landing there was bound to draw the Luftwaffe into an area where the odds would favour the RAF. Dieppe clearly fitted into this concept. Indeed, Goronwy Rees understood that *Rutter* was designed primarily with this air battle in mind. As he later recalled: 'We were assured that a landing in France on the scale of *Rutter* would compel the Luftwaffe to react violently.' An unstated additional advantage to a large commando raid within fighter range was that it would give the RAF an opportunity to confound its critics, who were saying that the RAF did not want, or was not technically competent, to give British ground forces adequate air support. Portal was deeply concerned by these charges, telling his commanders in March: 'If the Army do not ask for cooperation, we must "sell" it to them, the deal being that no Army unit is without an offer of cooperation during the next few weeks if it is stationed anywhere within reasonable distance of the RAF.' But wasting the Luftwaffe, not support of the Army, was Portal's primary objective in approving commando ground raids.[80]

There were some — Churchill among them — who doubted that the RAF would do so well in these encounters. In his memorandum of 23 March, Churchill noted that 'No air battles are less advantageous to us than those fought tip and run over coastal towns. We have a greater advantage the farther inland the raiders come.' He was right in thinking that the closer the RAF went to Luftwaffe bases, the more the advantage went to the latter. At other times Churchill spoke very differently. He had told Portal just ten days earlier that 'it pays us to lose plane for plane'. In August, when he broached the subject of Dieppe to Stalin, Churchill assured him that the most important feature would be the air battle.[81]

At first Leigh-Mallory, commanding the key fighter sector in south-eastern England at Uxbridge, shared all the optimistic hopes that an important raid might produce an air battle of considerable value. In a closely reasoned paper on 25 May he argued that the pressure — from both the Russians and the British public — to do something for Russia could be met by an attempt to capture Boulogne and hold it as an enclave, or alternatively he suggested a raid on Le Touquet-Étaples, on the French coast northeast of Dieppe. He favoured such projects on the grounds that an 'operation of this nature would be sure to be met with strenuous opposition from the German Air Force, and it would have the advantage of being in an area favourable to the employment of our own fighters.' At the same time he clearly intended to do all he could to help the ground forces, telling the *Rutter* Force Commanders in mid-June 'that he was anxious to play a full part in this exercise and that he would try to fit the fighter sweeps over the enemy coast so as to cover the period during which close support was being given to the landing craft as they came inshore.' But before long he was having doubts, writing on 29 June to his superior, Air Marshal Sholto Douglas, commanding RAF fighter forces in Britain, to say that after careful review and detailed calculations the prospects did not look so good. 'The casualties will, I expect, be relatively high and we can, I suggest, be well satisfied if our losses do not exceed, say 60 to 70 pilots, and 120 aircraft in the Squadrons providing fighter cover.' This, he explained, was all because 'we cannot yet claim to have attained air superiority in North West France.' He was particularly concerned because 'once our plan is clear to the enemy, the initiative is his, and he can choose his moment to concentrate his forces.'[82]

Sholto Douglas, knowing full well the pressures being exerted for some action on Russia's behalf, which Leigh-Mallory himself had singled out in his memorandum of 29 May, replied somewhat coldly:

> ... I do not know however quite what you expect me to do about it. I certainly do not propose to call the operation off. If I may say so, I think that you are worrying too much about these possible casualties. Unfortunately one cannot often win a battle without considerable casualties, however much one would like to do so.[83]

On 19 August five squadrons of Hurricanes approached Dieppe at 5:20 in the morning, strafing the beaches and firing 20-mm cannon at the town front just before the main force landed. Cannon of that modest firepower, while useful against the planes of the day, were of little use against a well-protected position. The fire was pathetically brief, over in minutes. Men on the beach looked up and asked: 'Is that all?' It was obvious that the defences of Dieppe were virtually intact after this brief assault. A heavier and more prolonged bombardment of the town front might have made a very considerable difference by disconcerting the defenders long enough for the assaulting force to get to the town. But as it was, by the time the Canadians landed on the main beach, the Germans had got over their surprise. Within minutes the Germans regained the initiative and never lost it. Thereafter the bombers were mainly used to screen the beach from the East Headland and for such miscellaneous missions as could be carried out in response to requests from General Roberts. But as the time between the request and the execution took an average of one hour and 26 minutes, the effect of these could not have been great. The Boston bombers expended much effort on dropping 500-pound bombs on the major gun emplacements, but there were no direct hits, and this size of bomb could not seriously damage the well-constructed defences.[84]

From the RAF viewpoint, what was much more important was the massive fighter battle in the skies. 66 fighter squadrons, equivalent to approximately 730 single-seater fighters, flew 2,111 sorties, making this the largest air battle of the Second World War, indeed of history.[85]

The air casualties were somewhat lighter than Leigh-Mallory had feared (106 lost planes, 88 of which were fighters). Convinced that a great air victory had been won at Dieppe, and that at last a way had been found to inflict severe wastage on the Luftwaffe, Leigh-Mallory wrote Mountbatten shortly afterwards urging more raids of the same kind, making only one common-sense observation, which perhaps Combined Operations needed to hear: 'When attacking the enemy on land, one does not generally strike at his strongest point.' Less than a month later, Mountbatten was suggesting to the Chiefs that it should be possible to deceive the Germans — with a combination of deceptive exercises and real operations — into believing another Dieppe raid was under way, 'whereby another advantageous air battle could be induced.' The only one who seems to have been a little embarrassed by this notion of using men as bait was Portal. Though he had leaned on this rationalization himself earlier, he now said that he did not want the press to get the idea that Dieppe had been staged primarily for the air battle.[86]

Embarrassment would indeed follow if attention were drawn to the unevenness of RAF support. The disparity of fighter versus bomber effort was glaring. While 2,111 straight fighter sorties were flown by the RAF and RCAF in the Dieppe area, bomber sorties were composed of 288 dual-purpose craft and 62 bombers, mainly Boston bombers carrying bombs of 500 pounds or less.

The explanation for this disparity can be traced back to the time when *Rutter* was cancelled. Harris wrote Portal to complain strenuously of what he called the Army's insistence on getting what he called a pound of 'bomber flesh'. He pointed out that the two Wellington squadrons reserved for the parachutists during the period assigned to *Rutter* could have flown 304 sorties against Germany and drop over 400 tons of bombs. 'Whatever the effects of Rutter might have been on the war situation as a whole',

Harris wrote, '. . . you will appreciate that there will be more than one opinion! . . . we cannot afford to ignore the repercussions of such operations on our other activities.' Harris concluded by asking, in effect, that a similar call on his bombers not be made again. Portal replied, saying that Harris's figures were indeed 'most useful ammunition' and that he was working to see that similar calls on his bombers would not be made a second time.[87]

This was not the only occasion on which Harris expressed the opinion that he could make much better use of the bombers than could Combined Operations. In June he had minuted: 'What shouts of victory would arise if a Commando wrecked the entire Renault factory in a night, with a loss of seven men! What credible assumptions of an early end to the war would follow upon the destruction of a third of Cologne in an hour and a half by some swift moving mechanised force which with but 200 casualties, withdrew and was ready to repeat the operations 24 hours later! . . . All this and far more, has been achieved by Bomber Command.' The raids, he made clear, were about as worthless as the other suggestions that Mountbatten sent to Bomber Command, of which Harris complained: 'C.C.O. [Mountbatten] sends us one wild idea after another for dispersing the bomb lift. About once a fortnight.' In this unwillingness to lend his bombers, Harris was displaying a certain amount of ingratitude. One of the reasons Mountbatten pushed the Dieppe raid was to produce an air battle such as the RAF was demanding. When he went to America in early June to explain the raiding program, he expressed Portal's point of view, saying (as he recalled later) that 'The chief German shortage lay in fighter aircraft and all our efforts were being bent towards provoking fighter battles in the West.'[88]

The strange mix of aircraft over Dieppe is thus easy to explain. In accordance with Portal's theory that fighter battles in the Pas area would favour the RAF, there was an enormous amount of fighter power assigned to Dieppe. The wastage inflicted on German fighters would hopefully make the task for the bombers flying to Germany easier, while the RAF fighters over Dieppe would also prove that the RAF could give ground forces close support and vindicate Leigh-Mallory's experiments in that direction. (Indeed, within three months of Dieppe, Leigh-Mallory would be promoted to succeed Sholto Douglas as Commander-in-Chief of Fighter Command.) On the other hand, bombers that could be used in the massive raids needed to win priorities for strategic-bombing were, in effect, withheld from the Dieppe operation. If the plan to revive the Dieppe raid had been formally presented to the Chiefs of Staff, Portal might have been obliged to lend some heavy bombers, for any detailed discussion would have raised questions about the wisdom of dispensing with both the airborne troops and bomber support. But as far as Portal was concerned, if Mountbatten was prepared to go forward without raising all these difficult questions, he was certainly not going to stop him.

There was a degree of callousness in Portal's allowing the largely Canadian force to go in without the bomber support they needed — particularly when Canadians at home were turning out huge numbers of the bombers he and Harris wanted. Admittedly when he first spoke about baiting the trap 'with more tasty pieces of cheese', he was permitting himself the luxury of being flippant because he fully intended to give the raiding force every measure of protection the RAF could provide. It was only after the Millennium project was conceived that the expression assumed a sinister meaning. Goronwy Rees, who observed both the preparations and the terrible dénouement, later wrote: 'Thus the military forces employed in the operation [Dieppe] were not only guinea pigs. They were also bait. What did it matter if the bait was devoured whole so long as the fish, or rather the Luftwaffe, was properly hooked'. That is a harsh way of putting it if one accepts Portal's and Harris's view of the future: that destroying Luftwaffe fighters, winning production priorities, and opening the door for the strategic bomber program represented the quickest road to victory and hence the surest way of saving lives. Were they here today, Portal and Harris would surely tell us that the compromises they made with *Jubilee* in order to keep alive the hope of a strategic bomber offensive were, in the harsh logic of warfare, the price that had to be paid to save the far greater number of lives than were lost at Dieppe. But what an appalling way to save lives.[89]

One might say in Portal's defence that he, like his colleagues, may have assumed that others — perhaps the Canadian commanders, the Admiralty, or Brooke — were attending to the questions of risk and responsibility for Dieppe. In the absence of a formal decision these assumptions were easy to make — but they were deadly.

# 8

# Mountbatten the Strategist

General Sir Alan Brooke, Admiral Sir Dudley Pound, and Air Chief Marshal Sir Charles Portal — the Chiefs of the Army, Navy, and Air Force — were implicitly responsible for having acquiesced in the Dieppe operation, but Mountbatten's responsibility was much more direct. They could feign ignorance of the plan's details or of its prospects, but he could not. As Chief of Combined Operations he presented and explained the outline plan to the Chiefs of Staff Committee; kept it alive when, time after time, cancellation seemed probable; nominated the Force Commanders; and was responsible, personally or through his delegated officers, for securing from the Royal Navy and Air Force the highest degree of available fire support. Finally, on the fateful day he was at the Uxbridge command post of the Air Commander, able to direct additional support and, if he desired, to communicate with the command ship of the Navy and Army Force Commanders. Mountbatten was the highest-ranking officer whose responsibility for launching the operation could be proved. He was the most ardent and persuasive exponent of an ambitious raiding program in general, and inevitably of Dieppe, and had much to do with raising Churchill's hopes and expectations for such offensive operations.

No such responsibility, however, seemed even remotely possible just fifteen months before Dieppe. In early 1941 Mountbatten, approaching his forty-first birthday, a cousin of the King and long known as one of the Duke of Windsor's close friends, was nowhere near Combined Operations. He had just lost his ship, HMS *Kelly*, and was looking for a new vessel to command. In June 1942 Montgomery commented to one of his staff officers, Goronwy Rees, on Mountbatten's qualifications to command: 'Yes Admiral [Mountbatten] . . . had three ships under him . . . three ships sunk under him. *Three* ships sunk under him [pause] doesn't know how to fight a battle.' Despite what many would regard as an indifferent naval career until then, Mountbatten was sure he was destined for greater things. He had been offered command of a new cruiser by Admiral Sir Neville Syfredt, Naval Secretary to the First Lord of the Admiralty, but felt that something more impressive was in order, though he had never commanded a cruiser before. As he explained to his wife Edwina, he still had hopes of getting an aircraft carrier and would await committing himself until he had seen the First Lord in person. By August 1941, having used his name and connections for all they were worth, he had been assigned command of the carrier *Illustrious*, then being fitted out in an American port.[1]

It was in America that Mountbatten began to weave the makings of his great career, for President Roosevelt had inherited from his mother an unusual fascination with royalty. (Sara Delano Roosevelt's piano in the Hyde Park house was covered with silver-framed inscribed photographs of European royalty.) In October 1941 Mountbatten was invited twice to the White House, where one self-styled genius of the naval theatre regaled the other with tales of derring-do and royal shindigs. Enchanted, Roosevelt invited Mountbatten to be a house guest, and made sure that he saw anyone in the American naval establishment he wished to see. Between meetings at the highest level, Mountbatten regaled the press. His skills at public relations, undoubtedly his strongest card, now came through. The effect was impressive. One British embassy official noted: 'I have seen Mountbatten in action on several occasions since he arrived in the United States, and, in my opinion, he has done more than anyone else to instil and to encourage American admiration for Britain.'[2]

These reports inevitably reached Lord Beaverbrook, who was at this time a member of the War Cabinet and was as anxious as the Americans to see some offensive spirit put into British military efforts. There is evidence to suggest that it was Beaverbrook who first encouraged Churchill to give Mountbatten a prominent role in the war effort. This was still the period of American neutrality when the Prime Minister was, as he said, courting the United States for his 'harem' and, being anxious to impress the Americans, saw merit in the suggestion that Mountbatten be pushed ahead. Beaverbrook's pressure was probably decisive. Though Mountbatten's official biographer passes over all this in silence, the evidence is unmistakable. Early in September 1941, in obvious preparation for his trip to Moscow, Beaverbrook advocated an early Second Front on the Cherbourg peninsula, or at the very least a super-raid to give the Soviet Union proof of good will. He returned from Moscow on 9 October, convinced of the rightness of the advice he had given Churchill before his departure. The topic must have come up when the Prime Minister saw him that same day. The next day the Prime Minister wired Mountbatten to say that he would not get HMS *Illustrious*, explaining in a separate communication to Harry Hopkins, the President's adviser, that Mountbatten was being recalled for a 'very active and urgent job'. On the 15th the directive for Mountbatten was drafted. On the 19th Beaverbrook submitted to the War Cabinet an attack on the Chiefs of Staff, saying that when it came to helping Russia all they did was 'point out the difficulties but make no suggestions for overcoming them.' A few days later Mountbatten's new position as Adviser on Combined Operations was officially confirmed. Mountbatten would be asked to further the projects Beaverbrook was recommending. Roosevelt and his advisers were enthusiastic and supportive. Admiral Stark, probably at Roosevelt's instigation, wrote the First Sea Lord, Admiral Pound, a most adulatory letter about Lord Louis that found its way to Churchill's desk. And so great was the enthusiasm for the appointment that the President himself sent a glowing report on Mountbatten to the Prime Minister.[3]

Immediately upon his return to London, in October, Mountbatten was briefed by Churchill on his new mission. He was to take over as Adviser of Combined Operations from the very much more senior, indeed overly senior, Admiral of the Fleet, Sir Roger Keyes. Mountbatten was many ranks and 27 years junior to Keyes, but all this was reckoned an asset. The young Captain of destroyers was given a remarkable opportunity, since the only serious prospect on the whole British military horizon for offensive operations and headline-catching opportunities lay in raids launched on the European coast. The fact that Mountbatten had virtually no prior contact with Combined Operations, or even any prior staff responsibilities of significance, was not reckoned a liability by the Prime Minister. In desperate times Churchill was not much interested in military credentials. Mountbatten seemed to confirm Churchill's late-Victorian belief that the fates smiled on the young and dashing, a view that was especially appealing to the depressed Prime Minister, who was surrounded by the masters of negation in Whitehall and by his would-be successors in Westminster. The same complex of emotions accounted for Churchill's attraction to General Orde Wingate, a young, seemingly daring figure fighting in Burma who offered positive proposals for impossible situations, and whom the Prime Minister extravagantly promoted, defying much of the military establishment. Indeed, provoking their ire and stirring them to action may have been Churchill's object in appointing Mountbatten.[4]

Beaverbrook warmly applauded the appointment and the *Daily Express* was soon giving prominent attention to the commandos and asserting that action on the Continent was still possible in 1941. Neither Beaverbrook nor Churchill seems to have realized that Mountbatten could do real harm and cost lives in a position for which he was utterly untrained. All Churchill could see were Mountbatten's undoubted qualities: an engaging manner, a zesty enthusiasm, and above all an ability to project dynamism to the Americans. In being swayed by these considerations, Churchill had set foot on the path that would lead to the Dieppe disaster.

How high Churchill's ambitions were soaring and how difficult it would have been for the young Mountbatten to resist them, even if he had wanted to, became evident when Churchill called Mountbatten in to inform him of his promotion. As Mountbatten recalled, the 'P.M. gave me staggering orders on my new job.' When Mountbatten modestly suggested that the carrier command would be enough, Churchill replied: 'You fool. The best thing you can hope to do there is to repeat your last achievement and get yourself sunk.' According to Mountbatten, Churchill then outlined what he had in mind. It was a 'two-fold job. The first was to continue the raids, so splendidly begun by Keyes, in order to keep the offensive spirit boiling and harass the enemy. Second, to prepare for the invasion of Europe, without which we could never win the war. "I want you to turn the south coast of England from a bastion of defence into a springboard of attack."'[5]

But his most important mission was left unarticulated: Mountbatten was to provide a showpiece for the Americans, using the raiding program to dispel the impression of passivity and defensiveness that was doing so much to erode the good opinion of British fighting resolve that Americans had formed during the Battle of Britain. Churchill and Mountbatten both knew that his every action would be watched by Roosevelt and the American brass. Nothing less than a sterling performance would do. 'You are to give no thought to the defensive,' Churchill told him, 'your whole attention is to be concentrated on the offensive.'[6]

If Mountbatten represented youth, he also represented brashness and more than a touch of immaturity and inexperience. Having received his mission from the highest level of government, he would have no need to acknowledge debt or service to anyone else. 'Winston had told me what he wanted, and now it was up to me to carry it out.' For thus turning the young Mountbatten's head, Churchill was in no small measure responsible.[7]

Not surprisingly, Mountbatten acted as though no one had ever held the post before — though Combined Operations was an unknown territory to him. While publicly lauding Keyes' work, he semi-privately scowled, making it known that he thought Keyes had left him with absolutely nothing of value. Mountbatten's tendency to disparage the work of his predecessors extended to his staff. This is amply reflected in the unpublished memoirs of his chief naval planner and staunchest supporter, John Hughes-Hallett, who wrote of Keyes: 'So far as I can make out the vision of C.O.H.Q. during the Keyes "Regime" never went much beyond a bigger and better Zebrugge-type raid. Moreover the Admiral and many of the older officers at C.O.H.Q. had great difficulty in grasping the need for close co-ordination between all three Services.' Of the first Director of Combined Operations, General Bourne of the Royal Marines, Hallett wrote that he was 'over anxious to carry out tiny raids, chiefly, I suppose, on account of their stimulating effect on morale. Nevertheless these operations achieved nothing, and a number of very gallant young officers, such as Commander Congreave, lost their lives to little avail.' These observations came, it should be noted, from an officer who himself had only limited administrative experience and even less of Combined Operations. It was easy to criticize, as Mountbatten and Hughes-Hallett would learn, but they seem never to have realized that there was a price to be paid for captious criticism: the more they found fault with the work of the Keyes organizaton, the more that would be expected of them. Raising expectations is always very dangerous business.[8]

Admittedly the early performance of the Mountbatten team looked good. They were largely benefiting, however, from what Keyes and his staff had prepared. This was the case with the raid on Vagaasö, Norway, which was carried out early in Mountbatten's administration; though its objectives were limited, it proved successful in every way. Keyes had also left in semi-finished state plans for a parachute raid on the German radar station at Bruneval, France, to secure vital intelligence and communications data and equipment. This would also be carried out with success under Mountbatten.

Though these plans were on the boards in various stages when Mountbatten became Adviser on Combined Operations, it was clear that something more would be required if he were to convince observers that greater things were being accomplished than Keyes had ever dreamed possible. Accordingly Hughes-Hallett and David Luce, a key COHQ planner, sat down in January 1942 to plan for the rest of the year, quickly producing the outlines of a suitably ambitious program. One of the most important decisions was that of turning away from Norway as the principal area for raids. Transporting a raiding party that far away posed considerable difficulties and greater vulnerability to the vagaries of weather. A lot of cancellations would never serve the purposes of the ambitious organization-builders at Combined Operations. The Channel area did not actually provide better weather, but because it was closer, delays and postponements could be more easily managed so that more raids would be possible. It was also apparent that raids in the Channel area would be more visible, grab more headlines, provide greater encouragement to the public, thereby helping the Government — and greatly annoying the German High Command.[9]

But such calculations seem to have played little part in Hughes-Hallett's choice of targets. As he later admitted: 'We were not so much concerned at this stage with the intrinsic value of objectives on a particular raid, but rather with the feasibility of reaching the place undetected.' These were the words of a technocrat, interested only in overcoming existing limitations to possible operations; the military objectives could be worked in later. The only problem was that raiding in the Channel area had been assigned to a different command, Home Forces, so that carrying out Hughes-Hallett's experiments promised long jurisdictional disputes. But it was expected that this would be exactly where Mountbatten, with his powerful social and political connections, could be useful.[10]

The upshot was a schedule — only gradually unveiled over many months — that called for the execution of the Keyes plan for Bruneval in February, a raid on a Luftwaffe rehabilitation centre at Ostend for early March, a raid on St Nazaire for later that same month, and a raid on Bayonne for April. In May there would be an attempt to seize and hold the Channel Island of Alderney. In June there would be a major raid (*Rutter*) by a division on the small Channel port of Dieppe, in July a repeat raid on Dieppe. For August a somewhat hare-brained scheme for a raid on the German Headquarters in Paris was proposed.[11]

The choice of Dieppe was motivated by a number of factors. In exploring the possibility of some gesture to aid the Soviets, the Joint Planners working for the Chiefs of Staff Committee had also focused on the Channel ports. Naturally wanting to get some benefit out of any attack that was made, they thought it might be useful to test whether a port could be captured in usuable condition. (After a little study, they became convinced that it probably could not.) Hughes-Hallett was particularly attracted to this technical problem, as he had written a paper in 1940 on defending small ports and was curious to see the offensive side of the problem. Designating a port as the target would also give something for a division of men to do, besides attacking grazing cows. Of the ports within the range of fighter-cover, Boulogne and Calais were perhaps too large for a division to attack, as they had more than twice the population of Dieppe. Moreover, there was an understandable desire to spare the French population in the larger ports more aggravation than was necessary. That left Dieppe. There was not much conviction behind the project. As Hughes-Hallett later recalled: '. . . Dieppe was chosen for no particular reason originally except that it was a small seaport and we thought it would be interesting to do — to capture — a small seaport for a short time and then withdraw. . . . It was not thought to be of any particular military importance. . . . And it appeared . . . that it would be about the scale of objective that would be suitable for a divisional attack. . . . But I must impress that we were raiding for the sake of raiding. . . . There was no particular significance attachable to the places that were chosen.' Mountbatten, not knowing much about the raiding opportunities, did not question Hughes-Hallett's choice of Dieppe as a centre-piece for the raiding program.[12]

Dieppe and the other projected raids, if carried out successfully, would have represented something of a *tour de force*. But the chances of success were slim and Mountbatten's organization wisely kept the whole list pretty much to itself, bringing forth one or another scheme as the circumstances warranted. In this way it avoided, for a while, promising more than could be delivered

While these ambitious plans were being hatched, Keyes was letting all and sundry know that he had been dismissed because he was too offensive-minded, and because Churchill had been stingy in his support. With singular indiscretion, Keyes had told Mountbatten that the 'Chiefs of Staff are the greatest cowards I've ever met,' words that Mountbatten did not keep to himself. Here too luck smiled on him, for Keyes' accusations forced Churchill to prove Keyes wrong by giving Mountbatten unqualified backing. The Chiefs of Staff, who shared a dislike for Keyes, understood what Churchill was doing and were consequently more indulgent towards Mountbatten than they might have been in other circumstances.[13]

Mountbatten concentrated at the beginning of his tenure on developing a large staff rather than a policy. He knew that the Chiefs would be more likely to slap him down for administrative failures than for what the raiders on forlorn missions actually accomplished, particularly as the Commander in Chief of Home Forces, Sir Bernard Paget, was still the principal officer responsible for raids in France. Thus the months that followed Mountbatten's promotion were, in terms of military operations, rather quiet. But this relative inactivity was not what Churchill had in mind. Before Mountbatten could become too professional or too conventional, Churchill once more intervened in his career. As late as 3 March 1942 Mountbatten was still a rather junior Captain in the acting rank of Commodore. By the end of the month, in one of the most meteoric promotions in British military history, he was made Vice-Admiral, with the further honorary ranks of Air Marshal and Lieutenant-General. Soon he was insisting that he have an appropriate staff, with a Major-General as Vice-Chief of Combined Operations, an Air Vice-Marshal as Deputy Chief of Staff, and a Commodore as Assistant Chief — permanent ranks that exceeded his own of just a few weeks before. As part of the new regime, Mountbatten was now to sit on the Chiefs of Staff Committee whenever Combined Operations or the general conduct of the war were discussed. His title was to be changed, as soon as the Chiefs of Staff and the two First Lords of the Admiralty approved, from Adviser to Chief of Combined Operations. As Mountbatten noted in a family letter: 'The youngest Vice-Admiral since Nelson was Lord Beatty who became one at 44. Does that stagger you or (as the Americans say) does that stagger you?'[14]

About these promotions, called 'miraculous' by one historian, there is considerable mystery that is not much illuminated by Philip Ziegler, Mountbatten's official biographer, who says the promotions occurred on 4 March. What really happened can be pieced together from a careful examination of the official records, and from an interview given by Hughes-Hallett three years after the fact and echoed in his draft memoirs, prepared two decades later. Churchill had just gone through (in mid-February) a difficult Cabinet shuffle to bring in Stafford Cripps and elevate Clement Attlee to the vice-premiership. Keeping Beaverbrook in the War Cabinet had proved impossible, and like a loose cannon he threatened the political future of this new combination, accusing the Cabinet of indifference to Russia's fate and of unconscionable military passivity. On 3 March,

Churchill attempted to mollify Beaverbrook by suggesting that they go together to see Stalin, presumably to explain the military necessities. Almost immediately Churchill thought better of the suggestion and began to cast about for some other way of appeasing the press lord. Placing Beaverbrook's protégé, which Mountbatten certainly was in the fall of 1941, inside the Chiefs of Staff Committee probably seemed the easiest way of reassuring Beaverbrook that he would be kept abreast of the military situation and have a chance to present his views. At the same time the Mountbatten promotions neatly met the requirement of showing the Americans that something would be done about launching an offensive operation, a gesture that became imperative early in March when the Joint Staff Mission reported from Washington that the Americans were very anxious to start some military offensive, which the Mission suspected would probably cut deeply into the military supplies being sent to Britain. So from this perspective too it was important that Britain seize the initiative. Accordingly, Churchill urgently requested the Chiefs of Staff, the Commander in Chief of Home Forces, and the Adviser on Combined Operations to make proposals in case it became imperative to carry out a sacrifice operation in France in July 1942 in order to keep Russia in the war.[15]

The respondents were all unenthusiastic, save Mountbatten, who came up with the very idea of opening a front on the Cherbourg peninsula that Beaverbrook had championed the previous September, though it was now considerably developed as a result of some work Montgomery had done the previous fall for Brooke. Whereas Churchill's other respondents had proposed sacrifice bridgeheads or super-raids — or, worse still, claimed that nothing could be done — Mountbatten had the temerity to propose seizing the Cherbourg peninsula and holding it as a bridgehead indefinitely, which, he said, could be done by flooding the marshes connecting it with the rest of Normandy. It was the very next day, according to the majority of sources, that Churchill announced to Mountbatten his new position as Chief of Combined Operations and the intention to confer on him the whole series of extraordinary promotions. Thus it was that he became the first person in memory to hold simultaneously three commissions from the King: Vice-Admiral, Lieutenant-General of the Army, and Air Marshal.[16]

Mountbatten threw himself into the bridgehead project with all his formidable energy, boasting that he was prepared to act immediately on the Cherbourg plan. On 7 March he reported that his headquarters had already forwarded to the Admiralty the specifications for a properly equipped headquarters ship. He also completed a plan to initiate RAF squadron training in ground-support tactics; instituted a program for the training of landing-craft crews; and would be submitting to the COS a list of what had to be done to get ports in southern England ready to handle a major offensive. In order to continue these efforts he requested an immediate expansion of his own staff as well as *carte blanche* to select particular officers for his command. Demonstrating the unbounded ambition that was to make him so many enemies, Mountbatten went on to argue, evidently thinking of himself, that the real potentialities of the situation could only be realized if overall responsibility was turned over 'without delay to a man of exceptional ability, and [armed] with exceptional powers.' He seemed to be saying that he would be the Marshall Foch of this war.[17]

Churchill ignored Mountbatten's cheek. The explanation for this tolerance clearly lies in the Beaverbrook connection. Churchill had been interested not so much in promotions for Mountbatten as in concessions to the former minister. Indeed, in an amazingly candid moment — really a slip of the tongue — Mountbatten admitted Beaverbrook's role: 'He [Beaverbrook] saw me as the young man who would make Winston change his mind about the date of the invasion.' It was a sort of exchange arrangement. Beaverbrook told Mountbatten: 'The Chiefs of Staff need my help, and you as a young man can let me know what you hear.' Several times he said, 'Stick to me!' In recounting this exchange Mountbatten immediately added, 'Of course I could do nothing of the kind, and told Max so.' Whether Mountbatten spoke bluntly to Beaverbrook is open to doubt. All through the summer of 1942 Mountbatten fought for his Cherbourg idea and Beaverbrook's press remained remarkably well informed about what the Chiefs of Staff were doing.[18]

But Mountbatten's appointment also served Churchill's American objectives particularly well. Far too many Americans tended to characterize the leaders of the British armed forces as a lot of Colonel Blimps, inherently passive and defensive-minded. Now the darling of the American President and the media would be given star billing. That should keep the American press quiet for a while. Indeed, as established backers of Mountbatten, Americans could take pride in his promotion. Churchill jubilantly cabled Roosevelt on 1 April:

> I made him Vice-Admiral, Lieutenant-General, and Air Marshal some few weeks ago, and have put him on the Chiefs of Staff Committee as Chief of Combined Operations. He is an equal member, attending whenever either his own affairs or the general conduct of the war are under consideration. He will be in the centre of what you mention about the joint attack on Europe.[19]

Within Combined Operations there was much rejoicing at the promised increase in power and influence that was expected to come with the new Chief. As one of the key naval planners within Combined Operations, John Hughes-Hallett later recalled: 'My own reaction was one of exhilaration, almost exultation. At one stride our organization had penetrated the very centre and citadel of Power. We were now to work for a man with access to all the secrets, and for one who could, and would be an advocate at the top level for any plan.'[20]

Elsewhere, as Hughes-Hallett recognized, this startling upgrading of COHQ in general, and of Mountbatten in particular, aroused jealousy and opposition from the Service departments and delayed the formal announcement of the appointments until later in March. More than mere Whitehall corridor gossip was involved. The Chiefs were understandably aghast at the prospect of taking into their ranks, to weigh the most sombre issues of the war, someone who so recently was only a substantive Captain. Even after the war, Brooke's scorn for this notion blazed out from the pages of his draft memoirs: 'There was no reason for his [Mountbatten's] inclusion in the COS Committee where he frequently wasted his own time and ours.' Brooke also had good reason to suspect that Mountbatten would simply be the Prime Minister's stalking horse, in a position to disrupt the Committee's solidarity. Had he realized that Mountbatten was in a sense Beaverbrook's agent, Brooke would probably have been still more opposed. Nevertheless, Churchill deftly handled Brooke's potential opposition by asking him to be sporting enough to announce the promotions to Mountbatten.[21]

The most strenuous opposition came from Pound, the First Sea Lord, who sent a direct written protest to Churchill, saying that he thought this elevation would be put down to Mountbatten's being royalty or 'as another supposed case of your overriding my advice'. When Pound continued to oppose, Churchill promptly announced to the Chiefs in a single message that Pound had asked to be relieved as Chairman of the Chiefs of Staff Committee and that the government would insist on Mountbatten's promotions. The linking of the two in a single document amounted to a loud blast of the Churchillian trumpet — a reminder to the Chiefs that they served at Churchill's pleasure and that he would allow no interference with his plans for Mountbatten.[22]

Whether Portal also complained is not certain, but Churchill warned the Chiefs of Staff as a group against obstruction, telling them that that they were welcome to discuss the proposal but that he expected they would find themselves 'generally able to agree'. Churchill was even blunter with Ismay, to whom he wrote that he was prepared to hear amendments from the Chiefs, 'but I cannot have the plan seriously affected.' Months later the controversy was still echoing in the corridors of Whitehall.[23]

Though the promotions could not be defeated, the Chiefs had ways of making their position known. One way was to make certain that Mountbatten's mistakes, minor as well as major, received fairly sharp rebuke. When Mountbatten travelled to Washington in June 1942 and spoke a bit beyond his instructions to the American Chiefs of Staff, disclosing more of the British position than had been authorized, Brooke and his colleagues insisted on pointing this out to the Americans and putting it on the record that Mountbatten had misspoken. And the Chiefs took every occasion to show confusion over Mountbatten's rank and standing in the Chiefs of Staff Committee. Indeed, at some of the early meetings after Mountbatten's appointment, the minutes regularly noted unanimous agreement among the Chiefs even when Mountbatten had strenuously gone on record on the other side. For the first two months they recorded his presence as something of an exception. Not until the end of June was it accepted in the minutes that he was a regular member like the others.[24]

The resentment of Mountbatten's colleagues also found expression in the long time it took to define his jurisdiction as head of Combined Operations. His responsibilities for raiding on the Continent were not spelled out until May, when it was decided that Combined Operations should identify the target, prepare a draft plan, and ensure that there was agreement with the commanders-in-chief, who would provide the forces and submit the plan to the Chiefs of Staff. If it was approved, Force Commanders would then be appointed to produce precise orders; these would be reviewed once more by the commanders-in-chief and returned to the Chiefs of Staff for final approval. All this added up to no more than a secondary role for Mountbatten and he was most unhappy. During the summer of 1942 he was engaged in an unsuccessful campaign to get full authority to launch large operations without review by the Chiefs of Staff.[25]

The frequent administrative defeats Mountbatten suffered indicated that he was finding it difficult to carve a niche for himself in the British military empyrean. The opposition he had provoked among the Chiefs meant that he would still have a very difficult time reconciling the basis for his promotion as the apostle of the possible. And before him lay the formidable task of trying to flesh out the Cherbourg idea into a feasible plan in order to please Beaverbrook and justify his promotion.

The most serious problem with Cherbourg lay in the threat posed by the Luftwaffe in an area where RAF fighters could not remain overhead for more than 10 to 15 minutes before they had to return to refuel, leaving the ground forces exposed. Neither Beaverbrook nor Montgomery seems ever to have explained how he would deal with this. Landing and defending a bridgehead in such circumstances would be difficult, if not impossible. Even if the forces on the ground could be protected, the cost in the air would be heavy, for the Luftwaffe could easily muster a decisive superiority, while the RAF spent most of its time sending squadrons out and back for refueling and rotation. The result would be a terrible waste of fighter power (with heavy consequences for the bomber offensive, which was so dependent on the size of the fighter force available for protection). Though Mountbatten continued to argue for a Normandy assault, none of the Chiefs thought the Cherbourg idea had any merit at all, unless the German military machine cracked or longer-range fighters became available in quantity. And it is hard to find a military historian who does not agree. Indeed, it is hard to say why a recent Captain of destroyers, with no experience of land warfare, was immersing himself in this debate. Pressing for a Cherbourg bridgehead, however, served Mountbatten well because he achieved a reputation for boldness without having to pay the price.

Mountbatten could not have failed to see that an impractical plan that would never be implemented did not reflect well on his professional competence. He had to look for new ways of proving to the Prime Minister that he was still worth the yards of gold braid that had been bestowed on him. The first and obvious step was to emphasize raids. Less than a month after his promotions Mountbatten, prompted by Hughes-Hallet, brought out of the cupboard some of the plans conceived in January and others that had already been underway in the Keyes regime.

On 25 March he presented to the Chiefs a plan for a raid on Bayonne called *Myrmidon* and the final version of the *Chariot* plans for Saint Nazaire. When, on the 30th, he was able to give details of the successful attack on Saint Nazaire, the Chiefs were easily persuaded to approve *Myrmidon*. (They seem not to have pondered the meaning of the high casualty rates at Saint Nazaire.) The very next day, on 31 March, in preparation for the visit of the American Chief of Staff, General George C. Marshall, Mountbatten rushed forward the plans for *Abercrombie*, a raid on Hardelot on the French coast that was intended to test coastal defences south of Boulogne, using about 100 men. Two of these raids, *Myrmidon* and *Abercrombie*, shared the fate of most of COHQ's projects in the spring and summer of 1942; they were aborted short of realization. But even had they been carried out successfully, this would hardly reconcile Mountbatten with the other Chiefs or win their acceptance of him as a colleague despite his special ties with the Prime Minister. The arrival in April of General Marshall and his advisers, who were determined to keep alive the possibility of an emergency landing in Europe in 1942, gave Mountbatten his opportunity by reopening the question of what operations should be undertaken in that year. What followed turned out to be the most important strategic debate of the war.[26]

At Marshall's first meeting with the COS, the three Service Chiefs plied him with invitations to visit their principal installations, but Marshall indicated that the command he most wanted to visit was Combined Operations Headquarters. Basking in mutual admiration, Marshall and Mountbatten began to plan long-term collaboration by placing American service personnel on Mountbatten's staff and opening the way for American troops to join in the more important raids.[27]

In the meetings with Marshall, Mountbatten did what he was supposed to do: show his loyalty to the position of the other Chiefs by voicing his colleagues' doubts on the Second Front proposals. He declared that a bridgehead was not possible. This must have been a surprise to the Americans and news to Churchill, but as a fervent believer in Cabinet solidarity the Prime Minister could understand that Mountbatten was bound to take the majority position of the Chiefs of Staff in open conference. His doing so seems not to have diminished the Prime Minister's belief that Mountbatten was more endowed with an offensive spirit than all the rest, perhaps because Mountbatten chose that very moment to unveil his full program of raids to impress the Americans. The minutes captured the spirit of Mountbatten's verbal gymnastics in giving both yeas and nays to the Americans. His goal, he announced, '. . . was to stage as many raids as possible along the enemy occupied coastline, seeking always to find the soft spots.' He would endeavour 'to execute operations which promised a high degree of success.' These he described in some detail. But with regard to a large-scale landing on the Continent, he drew attention to the transportation and logistical problems. The ports on the French coast were only small ones and could not handle the supplies that would be required, and attempting to bring supplies over open beaches would be 'extremely difficult'. The shortage of landing-craft would also be a problem. Mountbatten thus drew a line at large-scale raids. Operations of that scale, he explained, were doubtful at best and would require much improvisation, given the shortage of landing-craft. But anxious not to lose his standing with Marshall, he held out great hopes for 1943, pointing out that 'by the Spring of 1943 we should have some 80 TLCs [tank landing-craft] and 5000 other landing craft and the position would be easier.'[28]

Thus, under the cover of solidarity with the other Chiefs, Mountbatten managed to begin dissociating himself from the position that had helped secure his promotions: his advocacy of an assault on Cherbourg in 1942. Though the Americans had been smitten by that prospect, Mountbatten, by embracing their plan for a 1943 Second Front, retained the backing of the American military when he might so easily have lost it.

That Mountbatten had not done himself any harm with the Americans could be seen from the agenda General Eisenhower, European Theater Commander, set for himself when he came to England a few weeks later. High on his list of priority items was extending an invitation to Mountbatten, from General Marshall, to come to the United States and explain raiding techniques. Eisenhower also wanted to discuss the selection of the 'picked men' who would be detailed to Mountbatten's headquarters and see if Lord Louis would increase their number over and above the original proposals. By the end of his trip Eisenhower was suggesting that 'possibly the assault echelon of *Bolero* [by which he meant the initial cross-Channel assault] should be under a single commander, who would be a direct subordinate of the supreme commander.' Eisenhower said to Brooke that Mountbatten could serve in either capacity. This notion of a further extraordinary advancement for Mountbatten, much gossiped about in both Whitehall and Washington in June and July 1942, hovered in the background as the Dieppe project went forward.[29]

Though Eisenhower's trip confirmed that Mountbatten's relations with the Americans were as good as ever, Mountbatten still had a way to go before he had sorted out his relations with the Chiefs of Staff. But they had put themselves in a very false position with their American colleagues, appearing to approve General Marshall's plan for a cross-Channel invasion in 1942 (*Sledgehammer*) or 1943 at the latest (*Round-Up*) when they really saw no merit in this at all. This situation created another perfect opening for Mountbatten. For the British Chiefs had just recently told the Americans that they accepted, in principal, *Sledgehammer*, the American plan for a 1942 assault on the heavily fortified Pas de Calais, which was a much more questionable operation than anything he had proposed. Mountbatten demonstrated the soundness of his military thinking during Marshall's visit by denouncing *Sledgehammer*, in effect taking the position the other Chiefs would dearly have preferred to take but could not, for fear of the political and diplomatic repercussions.

This opposition was quite safe for Mountbatten, who knew that he was simply voicing aloud what the British Service Chiefs were all muttering under their breath. He could attack *Sledgehammer* with greater authority than they, since he was one of those charged with planning the operation and had been suggested as one of its possible commanders. There was only one problem standing in Mountbatten's way before he could announce his true position: he had encouraged his colleagues on the cross-Channel planning committee, the Commander-in-Chief of Home Forces (Paget), and the Commander-in-Chief of Fighter Command (Air Vice-Marshal W. Sholto Douglas), to think positively about a cross-Channel attack in the report they were preparing for the Chiefs of Staff. Suddenly veering away from them might be costly, as they were well-regarded commanders who carried considerable weight in their respective services. But Mountbatten plunged ahead. His colleagues had unwisely carried the burden of writing the report. In setting forth their ideas on how a bridgehead could be secured in 1942, they proceeded on the assumption that Mountbatten, though very busy, was still the most enthusiastic advocate of a 1942 Second Front. They were mistaken. When the report was presented to the Chiefs of Staff Committee, Mountbatten excused himself for not having got to it earlier, and then launched into an exhaustive critique, which must have left his erstwhile colleagues gasping.[30]

They had proposed a date in mid-August. That, Mountbatten asserted, was too late to be of any use to the Russians. They thought a bridgehead could be held for weeks; he could not see the faintest possibility of that. 'Even if the initial assault were successful, the shortage of suitable craft would make it very difficult to maintain the minimum force' over the beaches in the absence of a suitable port. 'We could not rely', Mountbatten added, 'on getting the use of either Calais or Boulogne, as these were almost certain to be blocked by the enemy in an emergency', because they were particularly easy to put out of action.[31]

His argument was sound; but in making this critique he was serving both his personal interests and the interests of his organization. He was ingratiating himself with the Chiefs by showing the soundness of his thinking on *Sledgehammer*. In fact Mountbatten could see positive advantages in the cancellation of *Sledgehammer*. It would release large numbers of landing-craft for his raiding program and for the training they required. The possibilities of other offensive operations were spelled out by Mountbatten in a three-hour conversation he had with Churchill and Brooke on 23 May, about which Brooke noted in his diary: 'He [Mountbatten] was carried away with optimism . . . and established lodgements all round the coast from Calais to Bordeaux with little regard to strength and landing facilities.' In presenting a positive and aggressive façade, as well as in handling the intricacies of bureaucratic politics, Mountbatten was exceptionally gifted.[32]

The other Chiefs, who had been opposed to the *Sledgehammer* scheme from the start, must have admired, perhaps envied, Mountbatten's skill in spiking American plans. That his colleagues were prepared to take advantage of the opening he had given them and reward him is perhaps indicated in a decision they reached on the morning of 27 May. They ruled that if German civil or military morale showed signs of cracking, they would consider executing *Sledgehammer* as an assault on the Cherbourg peninsula, as Mountbatten had proposed, despite its being outside an effective air umbrella. Since evidence of the crack in German morale was nowhere in view, and the immediate prospects for it were virtually non-existent, this was a rather empty victory for Mountbatten. But it did give him a little more credibility. As for *Sledgehammer*, that was clearly going nowhere. But he also knew that despite its probable demise, those who helped plan it might well be in line for command of a real cross-Channel operation, whenever that came. And he did not want to be cut out of that.[33]

In order to remain on the cross-Channel planning staff, Mountbatten once again shifted position dramatically at an afternoon meeting with Churchill. The Chief of Combined Operations, who had risen on the assertion that a landing in 1942 was possible, now completed his abandonment of *Sledgehammer* by denouncing the whole concept as impossible and pronouncing himself very doubtful of the substitute that was being increasingly discussed — *Imperator*, a large three-day raid on France, which might penetrate as far as Paris. Significantly, however, Mountbatten now came out as an unqualified defender of *Round-Up*, a full-scale Second Front on the French coast for 1943. But it was not so much the position he took against *Sledgehammer* that his colleagues found so valuable as the rationalizations he presented. Brooke had opposed *Sledgehammer* on the grounds that the gain to Russia would be nil, or next to nil, while the cost would be so high that it would probably jeopardize the defence of Great

Britain — all very arguable points that could not be maintained without the most serious political complications, as they implied confronting the friends of the Soviet Union. Mountbatten had a much more antiseptic rationale. There simply were not enough landing-craft, and reserving large quantities for *Sledgehammer* would leave none for raiding operations and the training exercises that were necessary for a 1943 cross-Channel attack. Indeed, the number of available landing-craft was so limited, as was also the number of airborne troops, that it would take '21 days to put ashore the requisite force, during which time it would be exposed to extremely high risks.' Mountbatten thus presented himself as an opponent of *Sledgehammer* precisely because he was a believer in a 1943 operation, resolutely refusing to waste much-needed landing-craft prematurely.[34]

Though his principal adviser, Hughes-Hallett, already believed that a 1943 invasion was a very doubtful proposition, Mountbatten, by shifting attention to that distant prospect, *Round-Up*, could keep his hand in cross-Channel planning, while continuing to exercise his accumulated powers as CCO. All he was forced to give up was potential designation as Naval Force Commander for the moribund *Sledgehammer*. But this was effectively replaced by his increasing credibility as assault chief for the 1943 operation he seemed to be defending so stoutly. At the same time Mountbatten deferred to the political realities of the Prime Minister, which required that he appear to be doing something, by arguing that *Sledgehammer* should still be prepared, primarily to deceive the Germans, but also on the off-chance that it might yet prove both possible and necessary in case the Soviets found themselves *in extremis*. His argument was couched in terms vague enough to avoid any strong protests from Brooke or the others. Hypothetical preparations for *Sledgehammer* should go forward, Mountbatten urged, and such shipping as was not needed for raiding should be gathered to make the Germans think an invasion was imminent. At the same time Mountbatten made clear that the operation itself should never actually be carried out. This was squaring the circle: both killing the hope of a Second Front and keeping it alive. It was said of Roosevelt that he was a chameleon crossing plaid; this could also be said of Mountbatten.[35]

One would imagine that such a *volte-face*, with such clear implications of opportunism, would have alienated Churchill, and to some extent it did. About this time Churchill reproached the CCO with being most negative on *Sledgehammer*, but Mountbatten had provided well against this contingency by coming out as the most vocal champion in the Committee of a landing in Europe in 1943. This restored the appearance of vigour and kept him still viable as a bridge to the Americans.[36]

Nevertheless Churchill showed some reluctance to accept Mountbatten's overall scheme encompassing the demise of *Sledgehammer*. COS minutes for an afternoon meeting on 27 May indicate that 'The Prime Minister said that he was not prepared to accept the view that it would take as long as 21 days to put a force of 6 divisions ashore in the Calais area. The Chief of Combined Operations should consider what could be done to improve on this time-table by the use of floating piers and other forms of landing devices.' But by the end of the meeting Churchill accepted that *Sledgehammer* was virtually dead. The minutes had Churchill declaring that 'It would, however, be looking for trouble to attempt to force a bridge-head on the narrow frontage which was imposed on us by our limited number of armoured assault craft. The fact that we had made a gallant but fruitless attempt to open a Second Front in this area would be no consolation to the Russians. An assault in this area would probably cause a patriot uprising in the north of France and failure on our part would result in terrible consequences to our French supporters. In view of the military arguments which had been put forward he was not prepared to give way to popular clamour for the opening of a Second Front in Europe in these circumstances.'[37]

Churchill's reasoning reflected Mountbatten's success in turning him against *Sledgehammer*. Mountbatten merely had to flesh out the arguments for Churchill and together they would kill *Sledgehammer* once and for all. But as this would mean confronting the Second Front advocates, procrastination ensued. By the first of June, Mountbatten was ready with presentable arguments for burying *Sledgehammer*, while still championing a cross-Channel assault in 1943.

He now explained that there were simply not enough landing-craft for both *Round-Up* training purposes and the execution of either *Sledgehammer* or *Imperator*, the super-raid designed to last up to a week on the Continent. *Sledgehammer* would require tying up all available landing-craft six weeks in advance of zero-hour, which would force the suspension of training for *Round-Up*. Virtually the same effect would result from any attempt to carry out *Imperator*. Keeping a 1943 assault viable therefore implied ruling out *Sledgehammer* and almost certainly *Imperator*. Mountbatten concluded: 'We are however so short of landing craft that the training of the assault forces earmarked for *Round-Up* will require the use of every available specialized craft from 1st July onwards, including those released from *Rutter*.' The Chiefs readily accepted Mountbatten's formulation.[38]

The Prime Minister, too, seemed to accept wholeheartedly Mountbatten's suggestion that *Imperator* as well as *Sledgehammer* should now be regarded as unlikely, saying on 8 June that he agreed with the proposal that '*Sledgehammer* should be planned to take advantage of a crack in German morale' [an indirect way of saying it was probably not feasible], and adding that he 'doubted whether *Imperator* would serve any useful purpose.[39]

While Mountbatten had ably assisted the Chiefs in taking a stand in London against *Sledgehammer*, there still remained the difficulty of how to break the news to the Americans of *Sledgehammer*'s cancellation and of finding a substitute to offer them. Mountbatten's solution was to embrace Churchill's North African ambitions, a much-less-dangerous course than his earlier championing of the Cherbourg attack because the Chiefs saw more merit in this Mediterranean project (which was originally called *Gymnast* but would soon be renamed *Torch*). They had favoured *Gymnast* before the Japanese attacked Pearl Harbor, and could favour it again under the right conditions. If Mountbatten could get the American Chiefs to give up *Sledgehammer* and gamble instead in North Africa, thereby greatly improving the prospects for the British Eighth Army, he might still earn the regard of the other Chiefs. This was an ambitious and daring program that ran the the the risk of alienating the American military who had been his most fervent supporters. Had the American planners not been mesmerized by Mountbatten, they might well have asked how he could find the landing-craft for *Torch* and *Rutter* but not *Sledgehammer*? However, he had solidly established his reputation as the strongest advocate of an early Second Front with the Americans, who had no reason yet to doubt his good faith. Eventually they, like Churchill, would have to learn that the man they boosted for one set of considerations could move on to another. He would still have something to offer them — the development of a vigorous raiding program. Indeed, the more Mountbatten deviated from the American position in the strategic debate, the more important it became to expand the scope and frequency of the raids.

Mountbatten was given an opportunity to work out this new strategy in the course of a trip to Washington at the beginning of June 1942. The British Joint Staff Mission there, acutely sensitive to the increasing scorn shown by the American media for Britain's fighting abilities, had been anxious to have some of the heroes of Saint Nazaire visit the United States, preferably with some of the higher staff of COHQ, who could be presented to the Americans as experts in the most exciting new form of warfare on the immediate horizon. Marshall had repeatedly invited Mountbatten, and the British Joint Staff Mission seized on this visit as a golden opportunity to get some favourable press for Britain.

Mountbatten should have confronted the problems inherent in the Dieppe project before he departed. Instead he allowed it to go forward, even though he had previously marshalled sensible arguments against any attempt on Calais and Boulogne. His objections to these as attack sites were equally applicable to Dieppe. Such Channel ports offered too many opportunities for defence, too few for surprise — and, as he pointed out, were unlikely ever to be captured in usable form, as the Germans could easily block their harbours, particularly Dieppe's confined inner harbour. Nevertheless Combined Operations were still claiming that a Dieppe raid was necessary to get experience in capturing a Channel port and for a lodgement in France. But even if they believed that Dieppe, rather than Calais or Boulogne, was more likely to be captured in usable form, why point this out to the Germans with a brief raid? One did not have to know much about the German army to realize that once weaknesses — if any existed — were revealed, the defences would be strengthened to the point of impreg-nability and this would close all possibility of *Sledgehammer* in this coastal sector. Logic was not always Mountbatten's strong suit.[40]

The first meeting of the *Rutter* Force Commanders was scheduled for the beginning of June and important decisions would have to be taken. But Mountbatten set aside these considerations — even though they were intimately linked to his responsibility as Chief of Combined Operations — and flew off to Washington with six of his key staff officers, including the architect of the Dieppe plan, Hughes-Hallett. While a Canadian, the inex-perienced General John Hamilton Roberts, the designated ground com-mander, was making fateful decisions under RAF promptings to drop the preliminary bombing, Mountbatten, surrounded by the heroes of Saint Nazaire, was renewing his contacts with the Americans in Washington. While basking in the glow of Saint Nazaire, he would tell the Americans that *Sledgehammer* was out. As Mountbatten expressed it, 'The British Chiefs of Staff paid me the compliment of suggesting that I was the only person capable of convincing them [the Americans] that *Round-Up* [mean-ing almost certainly *Sledgehammer*] was quite impractical.'[41]

Churchill saw much to be gained from Mountbatten's trip. Burying *Sledgehammer* was going to be a dangerous business. The American Chiefs of Staff might resist and, with their influence on war production and weapons allocation, they had ways of registering their displeasure. More-over, a fundamental disagreement over grand strategy could not be kept secret. A public Anglo-American dispute would give Churchill's rivals a great opportunity. They might be kept at bay if the expected victory materialized in Libya, but Churchill's hopes had been dashed so many times by the Eighth Army that for his own protection he had to undertake some other offensive. Accordingly he authorized Mountbatten to explore with the President two of Churchill's favourite projects: the invasion of North Africa (*Gymnast/Torch*) and a Norwegian expedition. Thus Church-ill would have room to manoeuvre. And who better to carry out this delicate mission than the King's cousin, who had been such a smashing social success on his previous trip to America?

Mountbatten arrived in Washington with a complex set of objectives, hoping to meet the requirements not only of his personal position but those of Churchill and the Chiefs of Staff. If he succeeded, even his severest critics in Whitehall would have to think twice before challenging him again. And of course his achievement would improve his chances of commanding the major assault when it finally came.

Mountbatten's arrival in Washington did not catch the American military entirely off their guard. Aware of Roosevelt's infatuation with Mountbat-ten, and having picked up the hints thrown out by Churchill that a new strategy was in the making, American advocates of an early Second Front were filled with foreboding. One of Marshall's chief planners, and one of the strongest proponents of an early Second Front, Colonel Albert Wedemeyer, was particularly concerned: 'Now we had an extremely articulate Britisher endeavoring to raise bogies about the hazards of a cross-channel operation.' When Mountbatten spent five hours closeted with the President, Wedemeyer was near despair: 'After all, I had been exposed to his charm, plausibility and enthusiasm when I was in London.' This anxiety was shared by the Secretary of War, Henry L. Stimson, who knew the President's weakness for royalty.[42]

Mountbatten lived up to expectations by giving a virtuoso performance. Though it would be nearly two months before the idea of an invasion of North Africa, Operation *Torch*, officially replaced the program for a sacrifice assault on the Continent, Mountbatten was remarkably successful in convincing the President that *Torch* was at least a viable alternative to *Sledgehammer*. His explanation of the raiding program and its star piece, the plan for a raid on Dieppe, undoubtedly fascinated the Americans; but what most impressed them was Mountbatten's powerful and seemingly unshakeable advocacy of a major cross-Channel assault in 1943. Nevertheless, Roosevelt was not about to let Britain off the hook quite so easily. He confronted Mountbatten with a claim that Churchill had committed himself to an early emergency landing in France should Russia be in mortal peril. Mountbatten did not argue the point. In fact he left the Americans a crack of hope by saying that the preparations for *Sledgehammer* could still go forward and the venture might be launched if there were overriding imperatives or startling new opportunities. But he carefully stressed to Roosevelt the value of a landing in North Africa, which alone held promise as a major substitute for *Sledgehammer*. In short, he covered nearly all possible bases, as he had done in London. The President, whose mind tended to go off in all directions at once, was as always very impressed with 'Dickie', and seemed persuaded.[43]

Predictably Mountbatten's success in Washington increased his credibility in London. However, he characteristically overestimated his achievement: he reported back that he had single-handedly convinced the American President and his Chiefs of Staff of the soundness of the overall British strategy, presumably including its raiding component. Large governments do not change well-developed policies that easily, and Churchill chided his over-enthusiastic protégé by saying that most ambassadors at least know when they fail. But since Mountbatten knew he had not failed, he could take the ribbing in stride.[44]

It would take a trip to Washington by Churchill shortly afterwards, and one by Marshall to London, to formalize the new grand strategy for 1942 around *Torch* and what was left of the raiding program. Nevertheless Mountbatten had done much to prepare the shift in the American position away from *Sledgehammer* towards this new combination. He had indisputably consolidated his position at home, where his promotion had aroused so much displeasure. He had proved himself indispensable as a salesman to the Americans. Even the Chiefs of Staff could see Mountbatten's usefulness. Most surprisingly, he had pulled off the feat without losing his American support. If anything, it had increased.

This success may have encouraged Mountbatten to do another pirouette on policy. The other Chiefs had reluctantly concurred with Mountbatten's proposal at the end of May that although *Sledgehammer* would hencefor-ward be considered unlikely, it should be partially mounted; that is, pre-pared, as though it would take place. (This sop had also been offered to the American planners.) The British Chiefs were still clinging to the hope that the pretense of an invasion could be mounted, even though it was costing them a lot in terms of shipping and equipment tied up for an expedition that would never sail. But shortly after his return to England, Mountbatten came out against this waste, recommending cancellation of almost all the *Sledgehammer* preparations still slated for purposes of deception. In taking this position Mountbatten was not at all embarrassed by his having fa-thered the idea of converting *Sledgehammer* to a program of deception. He had technical reasons for this new position all in order. The Secretary of the COS Committee recorded that Mountbatten now 'held the view strongly that it would be very wrong to mount an Operation which we had no chance of carrying out. There was always the danger that, if the Operation were mounted, we might be ordered to carry it out. . .' Mountbatten sug-gested that no military advantage would be gained by carrying out large-scale exercises in 1942 or by the assembly of craft and troops for this purpose. If it was essential to mount an operation, then it should be one that if executed had a good chance of success and that would not prejudice training. One major problem remained. If all the preparations for both *Sledgehammer* and *Imperator* were abandoned, what would be left to con-vince the Germans that a Second Front was imminent? And if the German High Command concluded that it was not, wouldn't they transfer more of their ground and air reserves for combat on the eastern front?[45]

The COS minutes record Mountbatten as emphasizing that the decision not to mount *Imperator* or *Sledgehammer* '. . . made it all the more important to do at least one more big raid. Operation *Rutter* [Dieppe] was due to take place at the end of June and could be launched over a period of six days. There was every chance therefore of this operation coming off.' If, however, weather conditions were unfavourable for the whole of the six days, he suggested that the operation should be remounted a month later. 'The locking up of the craft required for this operation would not have an unduly serious effect on training.' At the same time, he assigned maximum priority to *Round-Up*, the full-scale Second Front on the French coast planned for 1943, and its training program, which meant that there was not sufficient capability to prepare *Sledgehammer*, only enough to carry out *Rutter* as a substitute for *Imperator*. In this way Mountbatten managed to extricate himself from the false position in which his bold talk of March, about a 1942 bridgehead, had placed him.[46]

# 9

# Mountbatten on the Eve of Dieppe
# — and After

While Mountbatten was spending hundreds of hours on the endlessly sterile *Sledgehammer* debate, the plan for Dieppe was taking form. According to his later recollection, he was shocked to find on his return from Washington, on 9 June, that under Montgomery's supervision the heavy preliminary bombardment had been dropped from the plan. This, together with an earlier decision of Montgomery's in favour of a frontal attack, over flanking attacks preceded by heavy bombardment, made a shambles of the original conception. Though Mountbatten said he protested — it is not on the record that he did so — nothing was done about the changes. Mountbatten's immediate concern in this period was to expand his authority as Chief of Combined Operations, while making himself appear credible as the assault chief for the eventual cross-Channel attack.[1]

Before departing for Washington he had attempted to tighten his control over raiding operations, particularly over the final planning phases when COS approval was sought, and detailed planning, following British tradition, was turned over to Force Commanders. Resorting to time-tested formulas for wearing down superiors, he made a nuisance of himself during June and July, inundating the Chiefs with requests for approval of the most minuscule raids — in effect, 'working to rule'. To a degree this strategy worked, for the Chiefs soon told him he need not present each individual project in the meetings. He had only to submit the plan in advance to the Chiefs and, if none of them raised objections in the meetings, the minutes would simply note approval without discussion. All through the summer Mountbatten was hard at work trying to get the Chiefs to increase his general authority for raiding operations, arguing at the end of July that 'he should be vested with the executive responsibility for mounting and launching the next large-scale raiding operation'. (In fairness to Mountbatten, much more was at stake than an increase in personal power. It was becoming ever more evident that the prospect for successful raids was rapidly diminishing because force-level commanders were becoming balky, tending to deny final agreement to the execution of the plan. As a result, raid after raid was being cancelled, after substantial investments of time and resources. Mountbatten had to work at increasing his authority if he was going to convert plans into action and maintain some credibility for the raiding program.) The other Chiefs, while prepared to discuss his latest request, chose to refuse most of it. Brooke ruled that, while the CCO should be responsible 'for the marshalling and launching of large-scale raids', Mountbatten's powers should end when it came to the 'actual execution of the raid to the extent of signing the operation orders'. In short, Force Commanders still had a veto, as did Admiral Sir William James, the Naval Commander at Portsmouth.[2]

The failure of Mountbatten's end-run around commanders and the Service Chiefs indicated that to increase his authority and control he would have to build his reputation slowly and carefully with an impressive record of raiding operations, which, after all, were his primary area of responsibility. Judging Mountbatten by performance made particularly good sense after all his bold talk. But by the summer of 1942 there were signs that he was not building the record he needed. Increasingly he succumbed to the temptations of public-relations manipulation.

In July 1942, around the time when the first proposed Dieppe raid, *Rutter*, was cancelled, Mountbatten and his close friend Noël Coward were heavily involved in making a film, *In Which We Serve*, on Mountbatten's exploits as the commander of HMS *Kelly*. It will be recalled that in the formation of his staff Mountbatten had included Jock Lawrence (a protégé of the Hollywood mogul Samuel Goldwyn), Darryl Zanuck, Twentieth Century Fox's most successful director, and the actor Douglas Fairbanks, Jr. Coached by the best Hollywood advice, Mountbatten threw himself into the film project, carefully going over details of the script and the production.

Noël Coward had originally met with great resistance when he first proposed the project in the summer of 1941. He later testified repeatedly and at considerable length about 'the irritations, frustrations, and tiresomeness' caused by the opposition, which led inevitably to 'crises, triumphs, despairs, [and] exultations.' But Mountbatten refused to be discouraged. As he explained to Coward, all that was needed was a script to take to the King and Queen. When 'sneering articles, contemptuous little innuendoes in the gossip columns, [and] letters of protest' appeared, focusing particularly on the notion of Coward's playing the Mountbatten role, even the Admiralty became restive. Nevertheless the hero-presumptive went to work defending the production, with both the Admiralty and the Minister of Information, Brendan Bracken. But what must have been really decisive was the appearance on the film set of Britain's sovereigns, escorted by Mountbatten himself. Such a visitation was virtually unprecedented, and on the heels of all the press gossip it seemed to underline that this was a 'family affair' that brooked no interference. By late spring 1942 production difficulties were mounting and Mountbatten threw himself whole-heartedly into the project as the principal consultant. It was hard work, requiring frequent visits to Denham Studios, whenever Coward could not make it in to Mountbatten's offices at Combined Operations Headquarters. Even the casting of minor roles received Mountbatten's attentive supervision. His interference seems not to have been resented, partly because film production was difficult in wartime and Mountbatten was willing to pull strings, managing even to secure special permission for the use of 60 tons of steel for a life-size replica of the long-gone *Kelly* (named HMS *Torin* in the film). For the big scenes there was no difficulty in securing hundreds of British sailors or Coldstream Guardsmen instead of paid extras. Mountbatten extracted a promise from the King and Queen to host an unofficial première of the film to coincide with the visit of Eleanor Roosevelt and Field Marshal Smuts. This gala affair was held at Buckingham Palace on 12 October 1942, attended also by a long list of English and American dignitaries. Commentary was by the hero himself. Shortly afterwards the King authorized Mountbatten to convey to Coward the possibility of a knighthood in the New Year's Honours list.[3]

All this was going on at a time when Mountbatten was complaining to military colleagues that he was overworked, and when Admiral Ramsay was rebuking Mountbatten — raising serious questions about the competence of his organization and criticizing its discipline as unacceptably poor. Contemporaries and later historians alike were shocked by the chaotic organization of his Headquarters. Mountbatten, however, was undeterred by any number of raised military eyebrows and proceeded unabated in his efforts to make himself the glamour-boy of the British armed services. (Indeed, on 20 August, shortly after the first reports of the Dieppe disaster arrived — and after he sent a cable to Churchill in which he said he would make no further reports until he had interviewed the returning commanders — he replied to Noël Coward's request of the 19th for help in securing favourable distribution for their film, saying: 'Your letter . . . caught me on my busiest day . . . but since the matter . . . is so pressing I am dealing with it before most of my service duties.')[4]

Mountbatten's efforts to glorify COHQ extended well beyond the media. Within the military establishment he worked assiduously to build up the mystique of Combined Operations, doing everything he could to project an image of a dynamic and aggressive organization prepared to redeem the honour of British arms. He was available to speak to graduating naval cadets, convincing them easily that their first choice, if they were ambitious and forward-looking, should be to become attached to Combined Operations. If Mountbatten was not available for a speaking engagement, there were substitutes from his staff ready to convey the sense of being in on something not only 'tremendously exciting' but also 'tremendously important'.[5]

As always, a prime audience for Mountbatten was the American military, to whom he was a positive symbol. Eisenhower was given special tours of Mountbatten's installations and invited to the exercises for Dieppe. As a result, one of Eisenhower's trusted young deputies, General Lucien Truscott, and about fifty other uniformed Americans would be present at Dieppe. Truscott would never have been made available had not Mountbatten succeeded in convincing the Americans that the work being done by Combined Operations was of great value.[6]

Despite evident signs that the raiding program was disintegrating, Eisenhower continued to press, with Marshall's support, for Mountbatten to be put in charge of *Round-Up* and the eventual invasion. 'Here is where Lord Louis fits in,' he told Marshall at the end of July. 'I should like to see him assigned, with the bulk of his staff, as the assault *Chief of Staff. . . .*I think there is little need to point out the several advantages of the scheme. . .. No other trained land-sea-air staff exists, and already there is good American representation on it. Moreover, the individuals in the group are *friends*, and work in a single building of their own (no small item).' This tribute to Mountbatten — who had inculcated a co-operative spirit in a highly diversified staff — was well deserved. But Eisenhower might have been less effusive had he known just how instrumental Mountbatten had been in defeating *Sledgehammer*, or had he stopped to analyse how the raiding program was slowly disintegrating. Mountbatten was keen on an invasion for 1943, and that seemed to merit Eisenhower's unqualified support.[7]

Under the twin pressures of rising expectations and the desire to mount an offensive, COHQ had been forced, by mid-July, to put forward all its major raid projects. But for one reason or another most had collapsed. As we have seen, the two first originally conceived under Keyes — the raids on Bruneval and Saint Nazaire — came off successfully enough in February and March respectively , and contributed to Mountbatten's growing reputation. Although small and limited in scope, they took place at such a dark time for Britain that they meant much. In the general rejoicing there was a tendency to overlook the fact that the casualties at Saint Nazaire were very high: 25 per cent of those who sailed were fatalities, and of the rest, half were captured. Admiral James, the commander at Portsmouth, noted after Bruneval: 'It seems rather silly to crow over this relatively unimportant affair when so much is going awry elsewhere, but even a tiny success lightens up the dark clouds.' The perspicacious correspondent for *The New Yorker*, Mollie Panter-Downes, pronounced the effect of the Norwegian raid 'better than a case of Mumm's to the spirits of [the] multitudes'. The Bruneval raid, she told her readers , might be 'only a small straw in the wind, but it was the best-looking straw that vastly cheered Britons had seen for some time.' The effect of the raid against the large drydock at Saint Nazaire was even more impressive. It was, as Churchill told Roosevelt, 'tremendously bracing'. This was more head-turning adulation for Mountbatten; and as one historian has noted, it led him to indulge in a fever of projects 'while the true challenge of developing modern combined operations was accorded second place'.[8]

But soon everything began to unravel. In April an ambitious long-range raid on Bayonne was mounted and launched. After travelling a great distance, the party arrived off Spanish waters essentially undetected, but at the last moment it was held back by the Force Commander, who thought the water conditions were not favourable. The dejected party slowly made its way back up the full length of the French Atlantic coast to Britain. The next scheduled raid called for the seizure of the Channel Island of Alderney in May, but the plan slowly disintegrated: it had originally been dependent on intensive preliminary bombing, but Bomber Command refused to operate save in conditions of darkness, and the commander of the airborne troops refused to allow his men to be dropped before there was sufficient daylight. Because the conflict could not be resolved before the forces had to quit the Isle of Wight to make room for the *Rutter* units that were to use the same installations, the Alderney operation was reluctantly cancelled. Then *Rutter*, originally scheduled for June, was postponed because of the poor performance shown in the trial exercises. The notion of a Paris raid was finally abandoned at the end of June. On 7 July *Rutter* was abandoned. If a raid on Dieppe were to be cancelled entirely, as Montgomery recommended, this would leave nothing significant on the program before the fall weather forced suspension of raiding operations. Thus the only significant raids of 1942 would have been those on Bruneval and Saint Nazaire, each of which the Keyes organization could claim as its own. In knowledgeable circles it would be asked: What had Mountbatten achieved with his vastly swollen staff and brave talk?[9]

Still, cancellation of the Dieppe raid might well have seemed the safer course, given the poor prospects for success. Proceeding with an operation that was likely to fail would simply confirm the charge that Mountbatten and his organization were incompetent, or callous butchers. But it was easier for Mountbatten and his advisers to defend themselves against such charges than to answer the criticism of having been all talk and no action. The blame for a failed raid could be attributed to bad luck or be shifted onto the Government, or onto the Canadian troops who carried it out. There was no plausible way, however, to shift blame for not having attempted to carry out a significant series of raids, when Mountbatten had been given such a vast increase in rank, authority, staff, and manpower. He was forced to choose between cancelling once again — and thus looking ridiculous — or carrying out a raid that, because thousands of men had been briefed and released to the pubs, might already have been compromised. Even if it hadn't been compromised, its chances of success were very poor. But Mountbatten, who was spreading himself thin with his myriad activities, may not have really understood the full dimensions of his dilemma. The Joint Planners had said that he had too many responsibilities (they presumably did not know how much time he was putting in at Denham Studios). Evidence of his inattention to detail abounds. Mountbatten later made some grossly inaccurate claims about the way the Dieppe plan had been developed, such as his story that General Roberts and his staff had changed the plan to a frontal assault. This has been put down to dishonesty. But like Montgomery, who sat passively by and allowed the preliminary bombing to be dropped from the plan, Mountbatten may simply have been inattentive to the details of the operation, even though it risked 10,000 lives.[10]

As long as a month before *Rutter*, Mountbatten was given several opportunities to cancel Dieppe had he wanted to do so. His first major opportunity came in June when the Chiefs of Staff seemed determined to cancel it because security had been compromised by the premature briefing of the bomber crews two weeks before the original target date. But he shied away from cancellation because it was tantamount to admitting he had failed to maintain a reasonable level of security. This would have reflected on his command, and he preferred to work hard to resolve the most obvious doubts and to slur over the lesser ones. A second opportunity arose on 30 June when Churchill called a meeting at 10 Downing Street. He was looking for an excuse to cancel. All that Mountbatten needed to do was to give a candid assessment of the high risks and it would have been cancelled. The third occasion arose the following day when General Montgomery, who was exercising overall supervision of the Canadians, reported to general Sir Bernard Paget — Commander-in-Chief, Home Forces — that there was some apprehension on the part of General 'Ham' Roberts, Commander of the Canadian 2nd Division. Montgomery concluded: '. . . there was a moment when certain senior officers began to waver about lack of confidence on the part of the troops — which statements were quite untrue. They really lacked confidence in themselves.' Though Montgomery's recollections about Dieppe are notoriously faulty, this contemporary report lends credence to his later comment that 'I'd never been happy about this difficult operation being done by such inexperienced commanders and troops.' But as he somewhat sheepishly admitted, '. . . if I'd once suggested to Roberts that the thing was a bit funny, it wouldn't have been done.' Paget immediately communicated Montgomery's report to McNaughton, who sent Crerar the next day to brace Roberts. It does not take much reading between the lines of Crerar's report to McNaughton to see that Roberts still had his doubts. Crerar stated that Roberts and his brigadiers expressed full confidence if 'given a break in luck'. Addressing the possibility that the landing-craft might not be able to keep to the critical schedule of the plan, Crerar had told Roberts that '100% accuracy should never be expected in any human endeavour, and that some error might be expected, and should be then solved by rapid thinking and decision.' It was most unlikely that the consequences of any mistimings in such a complex military undertaking could ever be overcome by any amount of rapid thinking. Having reassured himself more than he did Roberts, Crerar concluded his report to McNaughton by saying: 'I should have no hesitation in tackling it, if in Roberts place.' Mountbatten must have heard of Roberts' own apparent hesitation — at least from Montgomery — but if he did he took no notice.[11]

The men were loaded on the ships for *Rutter* on 2 and 3 July. The weather forecast was not promising and on the 3rd Mountbatten sent the Deputy Chief of Combined Operations, Air Vice-Marshal Robb, to notify the Prime Minister that cancellation was likely but that an attempt might be made later to remount the same operation. Here the record shows that Churchill was cool to the idea; remounting, after all the men and been briefed, would mean running grave security risks. Churchill suggested that perhaps Mountbatten should try to find some way around the weather problem; but if he could not, the raid should be definitively cancelled. The bad weather continued and with each passing day the possibility of cancellation increased. Ignoring Churchill's advice to cancel outright, Mountbatten went before the Chiefs of Staff on 6 July to request that if the operation were cancelled, consideration should be given at a later date to mounting it again. Something must have made him fear that a revival of the raid would be bitterly contested. Perhaps he had heard of the hesitation of Roberts, or of Montgomery's incipient criticism. Or it may be that he already anticipated the recommendation made on 7 July by Baillie-Grohman's staff that cancellation of the mission would have to be definitive. But if Mountbatten could get the Chiefs to go on record as supporting the idea of remounting, such doubts would be neutralized. Mountbatten's appearance before the Chiefs — and their acceptance of his proposal — accomplished this, and must be considered his most brilliant tactical move in defending the Dieppe project. He no longer had to reply to criticism before the other Chiefs of Staff until he was ready to ask for actual approval to relaunch. In the meanwhile, whenever anyone questioned why he was preparing to remount — holding ships, assembling landing-craft, or arranging for RAF assistance — he could say that the Chiefs had ordered him to prepare. For with the Chiefs-of-Staff minute of 6 July, saying that consideration should be given to the possibility of remounting, Mountbatten was now armed with all the authority he needed until the final moment. When that time came, who could say whether he would be able to consult the Chiefs in time or what encouragement — perhaps even orders — he could claim to have received from Churchill?[12]

Tactically brilliant though the 6 July approach to the Chiefs was, Mountbatten never mentioned it in subsequent historical discussions of

Dieppe, nor did Hughes-Hallett. Their remarkable silence is easily explainable. The minute did not square with their explanation of why they had gone ahead with Dieppe despite all the professional advice offered in the next two days — by General Montgomery, Baillie-Grohman's Combined Operations staff, and by Churchill himself — against remounting. Mountbatten's and Hughes-Hallett's story was that their decision to remount was a response to the Prime Minister's demands, *after* the force had disbanded on 8 July, and after an initial post-mortem that day. About this, Hughes-Hallett reminded Mountbatten in 1950 that 'later the same day you [Mountbatten] and I had a private talk at which you told me the Prime Minister was bitterly disappointed and regarded the cancellation of two successive large operations as tantamount to a defeat.' According to Mountbatten and Hughes-Hallett, it was after this that they explored the idea of remounting in an attempt to satisfy the Prime Minister's wishes. But behind the earlier minute of 6 July lies an awkward truth, which is that Mountbatten and Hughes-Hallett were already working to revive *Rutter*, even before it was cancelled — indeed, before Churchill had been informed. Perhaps Mountbatten was simply anticipating what he expected would be Churchill's response. Having in hand negative recommendations from Baillie-Grohman and his COHQ staff as well as from Montgomery, any responsible commander would have seriously considered cancellation; but there is no evidence that Mountbatten ever did. The determination to remount, it seems safe to say, came more from Mountbatten, and from Hughes Hallett's office, than it did from 10 Downing Street. As Hughes-Hallett later recalled in his draft memoirs, they were all distracted in the days after the cancellation '. . . by a strong rumour that General Marshall was about to be appointed as Supreme Commander in the U.K. and Channel area, with Mountbatten becoming his Chief of Staff.' These were heady thoughts.[13]

As of 6 July, when he approached the Chiefs, Mountbatten had not given up hope that *Rutter* could still be carried out under current authorization, that is before 8 July. His determination to see it through can be deduced from his reactions on 7 July when the Luftwaffe bombed the assembled craft. Even Bernard Fergusson, one of Mountbatten's strongest defenders in print, has observed that 'It seems crazy in retrospect to have mounted it again, when the attack on Yarmouth Roads [where the landing-craft had been bombed] seemed to afford clear indication that the enemy had wind of it.' Mountbatten, as far as the records show, was not troubled. He pushed on relentlessly; the affected units were disembarked and loaded onto alternative craft, and everything was made ready for departure. But it soon became evident that not everyone shared his determination, for cancellation of the raid was ordered by Admiral James, commanding at Portsmouth, apparently at the insistence of the Naval Force Commander, Baillie-

Grohman. Montgomery's superior — the Commander-in-Chief of Home Forces, General Paget — also urged cancellation.[14]

The actual cancellation on 7 July became a signal for those who had long nursed misgivings about the plan to speak their minds. On 9 July Baillie-Grohman forwarded a letter to Mountbatten, which he and Roberts signed, pointing out that there had been no full military appreciation — to assess how well integrated the various parts of the plan were and what the prospects for success were — accompanying the original COHQ plan, and that this deficiency had gravely affected subsequent planning. This letter addressed very directly the dilemma in which Roberts had been placed. As a junior officer he had found it difficult to reject a plan that Generals Montgomery, McNaughton, and Crerar had all supported (apparently in violation of the fundamental axiom that general officers should never comment on the soundness of plans without the full advice of their own staffs). It is of course true that the original plan for *Rutter* had been evaluated for General Roberts by Churchill Mann, a brilliant but somewhat eccentric staff officer, whose mind had been attracted mainly to the landing of tanks on the beaches without analysing the complex components of the plan, as he should have done. Roberts would have had difficulty rejecting a plan approved by Mann, reputedly the best and brightest officer in the Canadian Army; but he could never have stood alone against the opinion not only of Mann but of Montgomery, McNaughton, and Crerar as well. Though the possibility of reviving the raid was not addressed directly in the scorching letter, the clear implication was that before proceeding further, a comprehensive appraisal by a team of land, air, and sea experts was required; indeed, the letter correctly asserted that such an appraisal was the normal prerequisite for any combined operation. It may be doubted that the plan would even have survived such a review, for the process would have given Baillie-Grohman and Roberts an opportunity to challenge their superior officers, who saw no difficulty in remounting *Rutter*. As all the contemporary sources are unanimous in saying that Roberts was very loyal and brave — not the sort 'to put the break on anything' — his willingness to add his signature to Baillie-Grohman's letter bespoke grave concern.[15]

But though it probably had no more ambitious intention than helping Roberts out of his difficulty by forcing reconsideration of an improbable plan, the letter could also be interpreted as an attack on the professional competence of Mountbatten's organization in implying that the combined appraisal found wanting was a routine requirement for any combined operation, and by suggesting that proceeding without such an appraisal had imperilled the whole operation. It must have embarrassed Mountbatten, for it also drew attention to the touchy question of his inflated rank, and the way he had leap-frogged over senior, better-experienced officers, such as Baillie-Grohman himself, who had been Mountbatten's commanding officer for two-and-a-half years. Being taken to task by his former superior must have been hard for Mountbatten to swallow. Though Baillie-Grohman claimed that he and Mountbatten were on terms of intimate friendship at the time, if truth be told Mountbatten had been very touchy about having his former boss become Rear-Admiral Combined Operations. He had tried to avoid taking him on but had not succeeded because Baillie-Grohman had considerable experience of amphibious operations. In addition to being a highly valued member of Admiral Cunningham's command in the Mediterranean, he had commanded the Combined Operations Training Headquarters in the Mediterranean. He would clearly have been a natural candidate to succeed Admiral Keyes as Chief of Combined Operations had not Mountbatten been so much better connected. Though Cunningham had not wanted to give Baillie-Grohman up, Pound ruled that he should go to Mountbatten, evidently to compensate for Mountbatten's perceived shortcomings. The presence of Baillie-Grohman on Mountbatten's staff invited comparisons of professional qualifications — not, one must say, to the latter's benefit. Baillie-Grohman was himself embarrassed and tried his best not to be too critical of what Combined Operations was doing. He later generously admitted in his draft memoirs that he had failed to speak out as bluntly as he should and assigned to himself a measure of responsibility for the Dieppe fiasco.[16]

There is no reason to doubt Baillie-Grohman's sincerity. After all, he had kept his mouth more or less shut right up to the cancellation of *Rutter*. He probably would have continued to hold his peace had he not seen the evidence that Mountbatten still wanted to go ahead. When Baillie-Grohman's staff at COHQ recommended on 7 July against any attempt to revive the raid — and even more so when Montgomery reached the same conclusion — he was obliged to try to blow the whistle. But the letter could have been worded more diplomatically. Some sentences were positively patronizing, such as the assertion that '. . . it is presumed that before a combined operation is embarked on, it is the rule for a joint appreciation to be made and signed by a Senior Officer in each of the three services.' An embarrassed Mountbatten quietly asked Baillie-Grohman to show him a copy of the appreciation form. Baillie-Grohman did not help matters when he pointed out that it was not his creation but standard procedure in any combined command.[17]

Privately Mountbatten and Hughes-Hallett were seething, suspecting that behind the 7 July cancellation was, in Hughes-Hallett's words, 'the preoccupation of the Admiral [Baillie-Grohman] with the need for "appreciations", and all that sort of rot', as opposed to the view of Mountbatten who, Hughes-Hallett later recalled, was '. . . a man who refused to be put off by irrelevancies and trifles.' But more galling than the personal embarrassment was the fact that Baillie-Grohman lent weight and authority to Roberts' misgivings and without Roberts and his Canadian troops no divisional-size raid was possible that summer. Immediately before, and several days after, receiving the letter Mountbatten held two meetings of the Combined Operations staff — on 8 and 11 July — to get a consensus for remounting the raid. As this attempt failed utterly, we can safely assume that his top staff, Major-General Haydon and Brigadier Wildman-Lushington, did not support the initiative.[18]

After the meeting of 8 July, Hughes-Hallett recalled that he went off in search of allies outside of COHQ who could help bring Roberts back into line. On 10 July he first went to General McNaughton. What then transpired we must reconstruct from an analysis of the context, as the meeting was not noted in the official war diary (which routinely listed all McNaughton's military visitors), nor did McNaughton ever refer to the meeting subsequently. Hughes-Hallett clearly wanted McNaughton to persuade Roberts to co-operate in re-mounting the operation and cease raising objections. It may also be that Hughes-Hallett wanted McNaughton's help in spiking Baillie-Grohman's ability to work through Admiral James, the commander at Portsmouth, who held a final veto over the decision to sail and was suspected of having been Baillie-Grohman's tool in ordering cancellation on 7 July. Though there is no record of this conversation, it should be noted that it was at about this time that Hughes-Hallett first began to suggest that a formal inquiry be conducted under some eminent personage, such as Sir Stafford Cripps, into the reasons why so many raids had been cancelled on the insistence of Force Commanders — an idea that A.B. Acheson, of the Cabinet's Historical Office, later classed as 'absurd'. Though every historian has tended to dismiss Hughes-Hallett's threat as being nothing more than an intemperate expression of his disappointment, it in fact represented a calculated attempt to browbeat *Rutter*'s critics and intimidate Roberts. It may have been McNaughton who suggested that Hughes-Hallett should deal with the critics by threatening a judicial inquiry into the cancellations. In any case Hughes-Hallett went later that day, 10 July, to see Cripps. Here too silence has settled over the record, for there is no indication of this meeting in the Cripps papers. All we have is a brief entry in Hughes-Hallett's chronology of his activity that week. But Cripps probably gave Hughes-Hallett some encouragement, for the next day, 11 July, Hughes-Hallett invoked Cripps' name when he threatened the Force Commanders by saying that the *Rutter* cancellation should be the subject of an inquiry. The intent was fairly clear: Force Commanders had better be prepared to be raked over the coals if any were contemplating scuttling the attempt to remount *Rutter*.[19]

Not surprisingly, the meeting of 11 July became stormy; it was described later by Hughes-Hallett as 'acrimonious' — the atmosphere was heavy with 'acid'. He and Mountbatten seemed genuinely surprised that their attempt to blackmail the Force Commanders should cause such bitterness.[20]

Judging by the minutes, which survive in the Baillie-Grohman papers, they never got to the point of actually discussing the possibility of remounting. Baillie-Grohman, well known for his forthright candour, refused to take back any of his criticism. Worse still from Mountbatten's and Hughes-Hallett's point of view, Leigh-Mallory approved the letter of Baillie-Grohman and Roberts, saying that 'not to have such an appreciation' was 'fundamentally unsound'.[21]

After some mutual recrimination, the meeting broke up. But somehow a signal was passed telling some to stay back. Mountbatten's deputy, Haydon, and his chief of staff, Wildman-Lushington, were allowed to drift away. (Evidently the tenor of the discussions at the first post-mortem on 8 July had led Mountbatten to suspect that he could not count on their full support.) The small group that remained, which included Roberts, waited 'until Baillie-Grohman was safely off the premises', as Hughes-Hallett admitted later. Hughes-Hallett and Mountbatten had already decided they would bypass Baillie-Grohman, even though they had not yet worked out the details of how they would get him assigned elsewhere. In the meeting that followed the hapless General Roberts, with no supporter other than Leigh-Mallory, was left to face the very determined Mountbatten and Hughes-Hallett. The latter has given us some idea of what was running through his mind: 'There were many of us, certainly I myself, who felt that this [cancellation of *Rutter*] was really the equivalent to a great defeat . . . it was the third time in succession that a big operation had been mounted, ships held for training, troops held for training, great dislocations of the operations of Fighter command — all for absolutely nothing, and I remember I felt so strongly that I thought we ought to have a judicial enquiry.' Neither Mountbatten nor Hughes-Hallett, our principal source for the meeting, had any recollection of Roberts' intervention — from which we can safely assume that Roberts either continued to express reservations or, more likely, held his peace. Certainly his approval would have been recorded. So Mountbatten still had a problem. The first invocation of Cripps' name by Hughes-Hallett, and the possibility of an inquiry, had not been enough to make Roberts cave in.[22]

There was also the problem of joint appraisal that all three Force Commanders — Roberts, Baillie-Grohman, and Leigh-Mallory — had demanded, the production of which would have threatened the revival of the Dieppe project. Considering that Mountbatten had claimed that he did not like the *Rutter* plan as it had emerged under Montgomery's patronage, with the substitution of a flanking for a frontal attack and the abandonment of heavy preliminary bombardment, the preparation of the joint appraisal would have given him the perfect opportunity to reopen these questions. But such an appraisal was always followed by offering the Force Commanders an opportunity to reject the proposed operation. Needless to say, neither Mountbatten nor Hughes-Hallett wanted to risk this, and as soon as

Baillie-Grohman was out of the room all Mountbatten's talk about wanting a joint appreciation ceased. It was never produced. But getting Baillie-Grohman and his joint appraisal forms out of the way still left the problem posed by Roberts' misgivings as a signer of the letter. Who could tell how far he might still go?[23]

The solution, of course, was to have one of Roberts' superiors order him to carry it out, but as of 11 July that was still General Montgomery and as we have seen, he had recommended most strenuously against remounting. There was apparently even some question about Paget's being willing to give such an order. It would have to be McNaughton. On the evening of 16 July McNaughton met with Roberts. McNaughton, one suspects, had no intention of letting Roberts off the hook, because the meeting took place in Mountbatten's presence. They reviewed the operation. One would expect that there was some allusion to the problems inherent in the project and the recommendations against remounting, which had come from the Naval Staff and Montgomery. According to McNaughton's memorandum of record (our only source), Roberts finally said that if McNaughton 'instructed' him to carry it out, he would do so. McNaughton said he would, and the deed was done — Roberts would loyally attempt to fulfil his promise. After the disaster Roberts took full responsibility for accepting, and attempting to carry out, the raid. He never once suggested that he had any reservations, believing that McNaughton, to whom he owed his promotion to the command of the 2nd Division, still had great services he could render Canada.[24]

One can scarcely leave the story of the revival of *Rutter* as *Jubilee* without looking far ahead to what happened to Roberts, who had acted as a loyal officer. In the months that followed the Dieppe raid he accepted without protest the artfully disguised effort to make him a scapegoat for Dieppe. He was removed from the command of field units and sent to replacement and training units, but he kept his peace and never revealed the inner history of the decision to remount. Though interviewed several times, not once did he mention his reservations, the letter he had signed with Baillie-Grohman, or McNaughton's virtual order. Shortly after the war he lived out his life in self-imposed exile, serving on the War Graves Commission and then retiring to the Isle of Jersey, not far from the graves of those men from his 'grand division' who had given their lives under his command. In silence he suffered the humiliation of the packages he regularly received in the mail on each anniversary of Dieppe. Bitter veterans who thought they remembered him giving a pre-raid pep-talk describing their mission as a 'piece of cake' sent him a stale piece on several anniversaries to say that they had not forgotten or forgiven. The only time Roberts let out the barest of hints that he had been ordered to carry out the Dieppe raid, over his reservations, was a remark he made during a 1962 interview on the Canadian Broadcasting Corporation, in which he said: 'I could have refused, I suppose, but it wouldn't have done any good, from the point of view that somebody else would have taken it on. . . .' With so many eminent military men having gone on record saying that it was a good or workable plan — from Brooke, through Montgomery, McNaughton, and Crerar — no one was going to take the word of a division commander like Roberts, who had never before commanded a division, that it was no good. And since his division was the only one trained for Dieppe, the most likely outcome of any further protest on his part would have been that his division would be taken away from him. By all accounts he had done an exceptionally good job of training his men and could not abandon them. He could have given excuses to the Chiefs for withdrawing from the operation. The preceding October his wife had died under tragic circumstances; he had four children to worry about. But as he demanded courage of his men, he could not ask less of himself.[25]

How badly Roberts was treated may be seen from the list Mountbatten handed to McNaughton of the COHQ staff officers who knew of the 'project' to remount and could offer assistance to the Canadians. Commander David Luce of COHQ's naval planning staff was there to help Hughes-Hallett, and Group Captain A.N. Willetts was there to help Leigh-Mallory, but there was no one from COHQ who had been associated with the ground plan who could have helped Roberts. The COHQ officer who had been most intimately associated with that plan, Major Walter Skrine (whose papers later came to form the heart of the official COHQ *Rutter* files), was cut out. Skrine later recalled: 'I was horrified to hear the thing was on. I knew nothing about it until the day before. I was not allowed, although I asked to go on it, they wouldn't let me go. Of course, my mind was very confused at that time. I was horrified by the whole thing. I didn't know why it had been remounted or anything about it.' The only man who tried to help Roberts was Baillie-Grohman, who had been transferred to the command of Admiral Ramsay, the designated naval commander for any cross-Channel assault. Baillie-Grohman was probably behind the letter Ramsay wrote Mountbatten on 25 July, trying to get him to give up the current raiding program and threatening to go to the Chiefs of Staff. Mountbatten coolly replied that '. . . there are political reasons why I feel certain that they will not cancel [the raids].' Nothing, it would seem, could stop Mountbatten.[26]

Hughes-Hallett, one of the raid's most insistent defenders, later observed: 'Looking back after thirty years I still consider that the most remarkable thing about the Dieppe raid was that it did in fact take place, and for this the chief credit must go to the constancy of purpose of the Prime Minister, Mountbatten, Leigh-Mallory and General Roberts.'[95]. He should really have added his own name to that list.[27]

Hughes-Hallett's burning determination to carry out a raid on Dieppe was also evident in the way he engineered his own appointment as the designated Naval Force Commander for Dieppe in place of Admiral Baillie-

Grohman, who was increasingly critical of the project and of the professional competence of COHQ. It is not clear who approached the Admiralty first about his removal: Baillie-Grohman with the request to be given a new posting, or Mountbatten with the request for a new Naval Force Commander. Alden Hatch is almost certainly correct when he says that Baillie-Grohman 'wanted out' and that this was more than acceptable to Mountbatten. The same mutual disregard would lead to Montgomery's being cut out of the chain of command lest he think of other objections to reviving the Dieppe plan.[28]

The removal of Baillie-Grohman was a bold decision indeed if Mountbatten intended, as seems certain, to retry the operation by mid-August, less than six weeks after *Rutter*. A Force Commander had to be briefed and trained with his men. A possible solution was to name Hughes-Hallett, who knew the operation backwards and forwards. But Force Commanders were supposed to be of roughly equivalent rank, and Hughes-Hallett's rank as captain of destroyers was far below that of the other commanders — a Major-General and an Air Vice-Marshal. At this time the competence of Mountbatten's organization was coming under severe criticism, but Mountbatten did not wither. It was Hughes-Hallett who insisted on sailing on 18 August, despite what he called 'a more than doubtful weather forecast', a decision for which Mountbatten also assumed responsibility. Both Hughes-Hallett and Mountbatten preferred attempting the difficult to finding excuses for not taking action. Whether this resolve was courageous or irresponsible must be assessed in terms of the information they had at their disposal.[29]

Had they believed in the validity of their plan, their determination to carry it through would have been commendable. But they knew it was not good. According to Hughes-Hallett's later commentary, he had originally conceived the attack on Dieppe as requiring two battleships. He had never got them, or anything like their equivalent fire-power — a serious defect. Nevertheless he plunged ahead. His recollection of his thoughts on departing is striking: 'Of course, I was aware that there were shortcomings in the plan and also in the forces made available to carry it out, but the moment of sailing was no time for jogging backwards and I put my fears behind me.' Mountbatten always claimed that he had strongly disagreed from the outset with the decision to abandon the flank attacks in favour of a frontal attack, and that he had argued against it at the time. He made the same claim about the decision to eliminate the preliminary bombing, asserting that he had repeatedly pressed for more bombing support. He also subsequently argued that he regarded the naval support as marginal to inadequate and had asked for a capital ship (a major warship). It can hardly be called a virtue to have pressed hard to execute a plan when all these defects, deadly in their cumulative effect, were supposedly known to him, and his every request to strengthen the plan was turned down. The same may be said of Hughes-Hallett, who later observed that there was a need for heavier support from the air and that '. . . this had been fully realized by those taking part in the operation even before it took place.' The fact that Hughes-Hallett expected heavy casualties is evident in the memorandum he dictated just before sailing. Outlining the conditions under which he would abort *Jubilee*, he stated that had there been heavy bombing '. . . his conclusion as to the number of losses he would accept would have been modified' — i.e. the lack of bombing by itself greatly increased the chances for high casualties. If this was so, why force through the execution of the raid against such reasonable doubts?[30]

It might be argued that in having persevered, they learned valuable lessons. But this would be valid only if the plan's defects had not already been known, or if the lessons could not have been acquired some other way. Hughes-Hallett himself has said: 'I would concede that the same lessons could have been garnered more cheaply had we been able to resist the pressure to make a frontal assault.' Admiral Baillie-Grohman, who had extensive experience with Combined Operations in the Mediterranean theatre, put it less charitably; on reading the after-action report, he declared that it should have been titled 'Lessons learned by Captain Hughes-Hallett', adding that virtually all of them could have been acquired by anyone reading Admiralty background pamphlets on Combined Operations.[31]

Philip Ziegler has suggested that to disavow the plan for Dieppe — which he elsewhere admits was patently faulty — would have required 'remarkable moral courage, if not a dangerous degree of insubordination'. But neither was required. A responsible administrator would have seen to it that some other plan was prepared in case *Rutter-Jubilee* could not be executed. After all, COHQ had nearly a month and a half between the cancellation on 7 July and the fateful 19th of August to produce an alternative plan to raid some other less well-fortified point — and in fact they had even more time, counting from the second week of June, when Mountbatten claimed he first became critical of the *Rutter* plans. Considering his vastly expanded staff, the inability to produce a fresh project seems particularly blameworthy. Mountbatten's great record is irreparably marred by his neglecting this obligation, while spending so much time in the months before Dieppe on the fine details of a movie glorifying himself and the men of the *Kelly*. No other general — not even Montgomery or MacArthur — showed quite such poor judgement (not to say bad taste) during the war. The fact that the film was an excellent morale-booster scarcely mitigates his culpability.[32]

It must be admitted, however, that Mountbatten probably did not see the Dieppe raid only in terms of his own bureaucratic position. He knew that the other Chiefs of Staff had reasons for wanting or at least accepting it, as did Churchill. But he should have used them to extract greater resources to overcome the plan's known defects. Mountbatten, we are told by his biographer, always knew the right string to pull, and never flinched from pulling it (as he did in the case of the film). By his own accounts he did ask Pound on more than one occasion for more naval support. But he seems to have left the matter with Pound. Indeed, as Nigel Hamilton has observed, 'there was almost no attempt, between March and August 1942, to assess, rehearse, or improve such support as could be given' to the small craft that had been assigned to Mountbatten.[33]

In view of Mountbatten's slack supervision of the preparations for Dieppe — he was in Washington when important decisions were made — the fulsome praise he won from Noël Coward should have been embarrassing: '[His] . . . militant loyalty, moral courage and infinite capacity for taking pains, however busy he is, is one of the marvels of this most unpleasant age. I would do anything in the world for him.' Few veterans of Dieppe would agree. Mountbatten should have urged Churchill to lean on Pound, the way Portal and Harris often did. At the end of June he had the perfect opportunity. When Churchill, worried about the prospects for *Rutter*, called a meeting at 10 Downing Street on 30 June to ask for assurances that the plan had a fair chance of success, Mountbatten could easily have stated that without stronger naval support the operation was questionable. That, however, would have raised the possibility of cancellation, should Pound refuse to budge. Mountbatten dared not risk it.

Perhaps Mountbatten was too inexperienced to see the possibility of exerting real leverage. His failure to record the alleged insistence that he execute such a raid and the absence of any suggestion of final approval in the records suggests that at age forty-one he was a very immature young officer. He compounded these mistakes by later putting out the unbelievable story in subsequent interviews that the Chiefs thought the operation would be more secure if the decision to approve it was never recorded. This was not the work of a master schemer. Nothing should have been easier for him than to put on record that Dieppe was being carried out in deference to those who believed an attack in the general area of the Pas was feasible; or that he would never have recommended the operation had it not been for the pressing political needs communicated to him. It is most likely he feared that if he pressed for a delineation of responsibility, the Service Chiefs might order its cancellation — which, quite evidently, he did not want. Dieppe represented for Mountbatten pretty much the same thing that it represented for the other Chiefs: among the possible projects on the horizon, the one that could be attempted with minimum effort.

It is also possible that Mountbatten really did not care too much whether the Dieppe raid was a success or a failure. In objecting to *Sledgehammer* he had argued against an attack in that area. It was Brooke and the others who thought it was feasible in the Pas; if a disaster resulted, they were the ones who would be embarrassed, along with all the advocates of an attack at any price. But if Mountbatten was thinking along these lines about Dieppe —

this is doubtful — he should have been careful to establish the responsibility of others.

Beyond the charges of bureaucratic self-interest, for which we have seen some evidence, another still graver charge against Mountbatten is clearly false. Beaverbrook was surely wrong in thinking, after Diepppe, that Mountbatten was plotting vengeance against him by making Canadians, on whom his press doted, pay the price for the same papers' intemperate demands for an immediate Second Front. Mountbatten was vain and he was clever in bureaucratic skirmishes, but he was not base.[34]

What Mountbatten should have been held accountable for was his undertaking Dieppe without formal authority, misleading his staff all the while. The evidence indicates that by mid-July he was already in the process of deceiving his own staff about what the Chiefs of Staff had approved. The records clearly show that Hughes-Hallett believed on the 17th that the Chiefs had approved the relaunching of the raid, an opinion he could only have derived from Mountbatten. Nevertheless Hughes-Hallett was worried that there was no document specifically authorizing *Jubilee*. As he explained to Mountbatten on the 17th, there would be difficulties in dealing with the Admiralty and Bomber Command unless 'the Chiefs of Staff put out a conclusion' that they had authorized the operation. This suggestion, reflecting Hughes-Hallett's belief that the decision had already been taken and required only formalization, was made more than two weeks before Churchill's departure for Cairo and Moscow. Had Hughes-Hallett been correct in his assumption, there was no reason why Churchill should not have been informed of the plan and its new code-name before he left England.[35]

Though Mountbatten was prepared to go forward, on the mere supposition that the prior designation of Hughes-Hallett as the commander of the next large raid was tantamount to approval by the Chiefs of Staff of his plan to remount *Rutter*, he could see the point of Hughes-Hallett's observation that something on paper was needed. So he submitted a request to the Chiefs that they include in their minutes a sentence suggesting that they had ordered COHQ to mount a substitute for *Rutter*: in this back-handed way, Mountbatten was in effect asking for authorization to remount *Rutter* as *Jubilee*. This request is missing from virtually every relevant file in British Government records, presumably to cover Mountbatten's story that he had never asked in writing for approval of Dieppe. It exists, however, in the files of General Hollis, the Senior Assistant Secretary (Military) to the War Cabinet. In the form used to request a COS decision, the proposed minute, dated 17 July, states: 'The CCO is directed to mount an emergency operation to replace Rutter . . . using the same forces. . . .' Hollis was a meticulous record-keeper of the Government's military secrets and he invariably entered every decision taken by the Chiefs, either by attaching an extract of the formal conclusions or, in more sensitive cases, by noting the approval by hand. There is no such notation. The fact that the proposed minute was submitted contradicts the interpretation of Stacey and others that the planned appointment of Hughes-Hallett as Naval Force Commander of the next large raid was by itself equivalent to approval of the decision to revive Dieppe.[36]

Mountbatten, apparently nervous about proceeding on such an assumption, made one more indirect attempt to get something that looked like authorization. On 27 July he asked his colleagues for broad sweeping powers that in effect would relieve him of the need to request Chiefs-of-Staff approval for launching a large raid like Dieppe. In response they slightly widened Mountbatten's authority but insisted that the key procedures for formal approval remain in force. Though Mountbatten had again failed to get authorization, Hughes-Hallett refused to accept defeat and proceeded to organize the raid as though approval had been given. He seems never to have asked himself why he was meeting resistance. All he knew was that the resistance must be overcome. He was one of those most dangerous of men who, once committed to a course of action, seem constitutionally incapable of abandoning his project. Hughes-Hallett later recalled his frustration in a letter to Terence Robertson, author of *The Shame and the Glory*: '. . . one of the lessons of the raid was the need to make clear cut and irreversible decisions . . . weeks before an operation of that complexity. . . . Only by that means are the commanders and their staffs free to give their undivided attention to fighting the enemy rather than fighting obstructions and delays on the home front.'[37]

In the absence of such a clear-cut decision, one may ask: How did Mountbatten plan to get over the still-formidable problem of issuing operation orders, which usually contained a paragraph indicating the approving authority? As issued on 31 July, the cover of the Combined Plan — in effect the overall operations order for Dieppe — made a vague reference to the most recent directive on procedures for approving operations. In the after-action Combined Report, which implied that this directive constituted sufficient authority — after the discussion of the cancellation of *Rutter* — there is the rubric, 'New Directive to the Chief of Combined Operations'. Following a passage that is misleadingly made to appear as a quotation from a Chiefs of Staff directive, the statement is made: 'It was under this Directive that the Chief of Combined Operations launched the operation.' But this reference, like that in the operation order, is to the 27 July minute on procedures Mountbatten was to follow. The passage cited in fact refers only to a broad directive defining the Chief of Combined Operations' authority. It clearly did not give authorization to remount *Rutter* but spelled out the conditions under which Mountbatten could obtain approval to launch such operations. In post-war discussion Mountbatten never openly claimed that this or any other directive allowed him to launch on his own a raid the size of Dieppe. As he later admitted, when speaking of the decision to revive

*Rutter*: 'Of course we [Mountbatten and the three Force Commanders] had no authority to do more than put a proposal on these lines through me to the COS committee and then to the P.M.' This was also Churchill's belief when, in his memoirs, he stated: 'It was a major decision of policy.'[38]

The spuriousness of the claim to authority contained in the operations order and the after-action report indicates that on the 17th, when Hughes-Hallett was assuming the existence of authorization, there was none. Far from complying with the 27 July directive, Mountbatten acted the very next day as though he had authority. Annex 12 of the after-action report indicates that on 28 July the Deputy Assistant Quartermaster General (for Raids) was informed that *Rutter* was being remounted, under the code-name *Jubilee*.[39]

In acting without authority Mountbatten had to keep his intentions as quiet as possible. But failure to inform his most important staff officers was dangerous. They, particularly Major-General J.C. Haydon — who was Mountbatten's deputy and principal liason with external intelligence and deception agencies — and Wildman-Lushington, COHQ's Chief of Staff, regularly decided what information should be brought to Mountbatten's attention. For example, if unauthorized persons had found out about the first Dieppe plans, Mountbatten's Chief of Staff and his deputy would have had to decide whether such reports should be brought to Mountbatten's attention. Thinking the Dieppe raid was off, as they apparently did, they might have decided that their very busy chief should not be disturbed, especially since breaches in security — and there were many — now had only minor relevance. There is no telling how much information pertinent to Dieppe Haydon might have held back from Mountbatten on the basis of conserving his time. But it is certain that the Chiefs would have been horrified to learn that Mountbatten was flying solo, without benefit of advice from his principal staff officers, on an operation of such size and risk.[40]

The failure to inform his most trusted staff officers may also explain one of the most troubling aspects of the Dieppe raid, which is how the Germans might have received raw intelligence about *Jubilee*. But C.P. Stacey has established that German defenders at Dieppe were not forewarned. More recent studies suggest that this was principally because German intelligence did not *bother* to warn them (for reasons that are still not clear). The German scholar Günther Peis has recently claimed that German intelligence received four warnings, of which two came from agents operating under British control (the so-called Double-Cross system). This suggests that British agents had been, in fact, planting the story, or as Peis puts it, 'Dieppe . . . was the deception operation par excellence.' His findings have thus unfortunately lent some credence to the previously discredited view that the raid, as Anthony Cave Brown has argued, was deliberately compromised by British Intelligence. Peis has concluded that 'Churchill had knowingly, though not lightly, delivered up five thousand men, mostly Canadians, to the German bayonets waiting for them.' We are asked to believe that the whole affair was part of an elaborate deception to convince the Soviets that a Second Front was impossible.[41]

Either conclusion is too heinous and too illogical to be taken seriously. The operation might, however, have been given away inadvertently. Since Mountbatten's principal staff officers did not know that *Rutter* was to be revived, this would lead to the possibility — which one historian, Nigel West, reluctantly admits — that in their ignorance the Intelligence community might have thought they could now give away this operation to the Germans, on the assumption that it was dead. West interviewed many of the key survivors from that community; all denied that they ever made such a mistake. But even if West got to the right handler, asking him to admit to such an egregious error is expecting too much. Fortunately for Mountbatten's reputation, there is abundant evidence that even if the Germans received advance warning, they utterly ignored it.[42]

In any case, the crucial admission that *not one* of Britain's Intelligence Service chiefs was forewarned about Dieppe's revival has been made by the official historian of British Intelligence during the war, Professor F.H.Hinsley. Nor was the Inter-Service Security Board, the agency charged with surveying security for such operations, informed either. These were inexcusable omissions, considering the prior security breaches associated with this operation, and all the more so if one bears in mind that Mountbatten was proceeding on the assumption that the Germans might have learnt about *Rutter*! It was absolutely vital that other departments operating in the area, and having special knowledge of the conditions, be notified and consulted. The failure to do so went clear against the most fundamental tenets of modern warfare. The Intelligence Services could have provided a cover or vital intelligence. Of course, if Mountbatten was acting without proper authority and hiding this project from his key staff officers, he could hardly tip his hand by soliciting help from the Intelligence Services. Normally he would not even have had to ask for such help; the Secretary of the Chiefs of Staff Committee, General Hollis, would have ensured that the necessary intelligence co-ordination was under way. But there is no evidence that even he knew of Mountbatten's decision. The most outstanding aspect of all this is that Mountbatten should have thought — after Churchill, Montgomery, and Baillie-Grohman's staff had all pointed out the enormous security risks in remounting — that he did not even have to consult the security experts, choosing instead to run the operation on his own hunch. Even Hughes-Hallett later admitted that '. . . the main problem which faced us was [the lack of] security.' Ignoring the professionals in the intelligence field was an appalling example of Mountbatten's brashness — which was not in the least redeemed by his beginner's luck in escaping the total destruction of the force before it even reached the Dieppe coast. The

Germans might well have accomplished this, given the information that was generally available in southern England, and perhaps beyond, after the cancellation of *Rutter*.[43]

Sir John Masterman, who presided over the most important aspect of British counter-intelligence during the war, wrote: 'It is sad, but interesting, to speculate whether the Dieppe raid might not have been more successful or at least less costly, if it had been effectively covered [by the Intelligence Services].' The official record makes only one comment on this bizarre aspect. At a meeting in December 1942 the Chiefs of Staff were clearly shocked at Mountbatten's by-passing the experts in security matters, for they issued directives that under no circumstances should an operation of this magnitude ever be carried out again without the Inter-Service Security Board's being notified. Mountbatten, clearly on the defensive, stated that he had withheld from interested parties the information that the raid was to take place because the Chiefs had instructed him to do so. He even said that he had 'been compelled to mislead his own staff on this occasion.' The minutes record Mountbatten's assertions, but they do not indicate that any of his colleagues recalled or recognized that they had given such instructions. They apparently did not even respond to Mountbatten's statement. Neither then, nor on any subsequent occasion, did they, either singly or collectively, corroborate the assertions Mountbatten made in December 1942. In 1950 Mountbatten succeeded in getting Churchill to go along with his version of the Dieppe raid in his memoirs. But year after year, as Mountbatten squirmed under the questioning of historians and journalists, the Service Chiefs maintained absolute silence, even when Mountbatten was Fourth Sea Lord, and Admiralty histories were revised to include a claim that the Chiefs had approved.[44]

Most surprising of all is that Mountbatten should have been prepared to go ahead without authority. Admittedly the Chiefs had approved *Rutter*. They had also envisaged another attempt and had left Mountbatten in control of the forces (with only a few exceptions) originally assigned to him, should it go forward. Then too, *Jubilee* was only a single day's operation. Still, Mountbatten's boldness in going ahead seems striking. He was undoubtedly aware, however, that each of the other Chiefs of Staff had his own reasons for wishing to see the Dieppe raid take place. They had no desire to stop him. But Mountbatten also knew they were reluctant to approve; indeed, he had made it virtually impossible for them to do so, having exposed the vulnerability of the operation by continually requesting extra air and naval support. Formal approval, which meant shouldering responsibility, would have virtually obliged them to allocate air and sea resources, and this neither Pound nor Portal was prepared to do. Pushing them too hard for formal approval might well simply prompt outright cancellation. By the end of July, if not sooner, it was evident that if the operation were to take place, Mountbatten would have to take responsibility himself. It should have been easy for him to cancel this particular raid and concentrate on one with better chances of success; but by July 1942, after so many cancellations, his credibility was vitally at issue and he had failed to prepare an alternative project that might still save it. The juncture was critical, for Mountbatten was under consideration for further elevation to the highest levels of command — a cancellation would do him no good. Naïvely, Mountbatten may have thought that Churchill and the Chiefs would later reward him for showing initiative in carrying out their implicit wishes against all odds.

There is much evidence of Mountbatten's immaturity and overconfidence at this time. It has been argued, most recently by his official biographer, that though he had his doubts, he was convinced the operation had a fair chance. This seems plausible. Like so many others with extraordinary egos, Mountbatten believed he had a Destiny and that no misfortune could come to him. It was, moreover, infectious optimism, as Goronwy Rees's account makes clear: 'It would have been almost impossible to resist Admiral Mountbatten's inspiring confidence that unexpected obstacles . . . were precisely what Combined Operation Headquarters existed to overcome, by some commando-raid of the imagination which would gaily overleap them. This charm was so great that it would have been shameful not to respond to it.' With Mountbatten difficulties were to be met with a cheerful disposition and a bit of pluck and all would come out right. 'Morale of returning troops reported to be excellent,' Mountbatten boasted to Churchill the day after Dieppe. 'All I have seen are in great form.' Of course men do not fight well unless their leaders display confidence, but Mountbatten's apparent insouciance, far from conveying real leadership, resembled a shallow parody of it.[45]

This character flaw is evident in an incident described by Philip Ziegler concerning Operation *Frankton*, which took place in October 1942 — after Dieppe had presumably made Mountbatten a wiser man. Though 'The final rehearsal [for *Frankton*] was a disaster. . .', this, Ziegler notes, did not in the least suggest to Mountbatten that the operation should not take place. ' "Splendid," said Mountbatten, "You must have learnt a great deal, and you'll be able to avoid making the same mistakes on the operation." ' Mountbatten ordered *Frankton*'s execution — with predictably unfortunate results. Michael Foot, who when he was the Special Operations Executive had frequent contacts with Mountbatten, observed: 'It was seldom much use arguing with the princely sailor, who did what and went where he liked.' Mountbatten's notion that a lot of brave talk and a certain quotient of pluck would meet any exigency was a widespread attitude in 1942; not much thought was given to what would happen if things went awry. War propaganda and the purple prose of the media undoubtedly infected the thinking of many a staff officer and not a few commanders, adding greatly to the hot winds of war. But it must be said that Mountbatten, with his Hollywood staffers in attendance, erred more than most. In August 1942 he doubled the number of press correspondents who would accompany the troops to Dieppe. This was not the action of someone expecting a disaster. Nor was it the action of a wise man, considering the many risks that were widely recognized.[46]

By the summer of 1942 Mountbatten had vastly increased the size of his staff. Whereas Keyes' staff had numbered 23, including typists and messengers, within six months Mountbatten had a staff of over 350, and as Hughes-Hallett admitted, there was much grumbling in Whitehall about this swollen number, and consternation that the restraints operating on other Headquarters did not apply to Mountbatten. As one observer later commented, the motto of COHQ might be: ' "Regardless" — meaning regardless of effort, regardless of risk, and regardless of cost.' It would long irritate competent observers like General Hollis that Mountbatten could lightly '. . . spend incalculable sums of public money on projects that took his fancy.' Mountbatten's biographer admits as much, noting, 'Disregard of expense and the innate urge to build an empire led to over-staffing and the invention of superfluous functions.'[47]

Mountbatten's stirring rhetoric also played a large part in the Dieppe fiasco. He made himself available for innumerable speaking engagements. He used the media skilfully to suggest that Combined Operations was the only really offensively minded organization in the British defence establishment. But one of his most imprudent actions was to sell himself so completely to the Americans. He knew they were enthralled with Combined Operations and he had laid out before President Roosevelt and his advisers COHQ's ambitious raiding program. Mountbatten assiduously kept Eisenhower abreast, plying him with invitations to observe the training for Dieppe and other major operations. When Roosevelt sent over his Intelligence chief, Colonel Donovan, to evaluate British morale and fighting spirit, Mountbatten invited him to a major rehearsal for Dieppe. But what had Mountbatten to show for all his bravado, huge staff, and vast expenditures? Raid after projected raid had been cancelled. The largest of all, Dieppe, seemed also in jeopardy. In fact, as the Second-Front agitation increased in the summer of 1942, it was known that the Germans were becoming convinced that a major raiding offensive was being planned. COHQ could not therefore have had much hope that the element of surprise, on which the Dieppe plan was predicated, could in fact be obtained. In short, the problems were increasing, but Mountbatten would not let go. Even a failure, as long as it reflected dynamism, would do more for his aspirations to become a major commander than would the appearance of being an empty talker.[48]

That Mountbatten might be concerned principally with his own career was a thought that occurred to supporters as well as detractors. Peter Murphy, a lifelong friend of Mountbatten's, observed at the time that 'this operation is considered very critical from the point of view of CCO's personal career (and of course all that this implies in the successful prosecution of the war). If he brings this off . . . he is on top of the world and will be given complete control.' Given the source, this judgement can scarcely be called censorious, but it may be an oversimplification. In the background was Hughes-Hallett, determined to remount *Rutter* as a technical experiment, threatening inquiries and running to Sir Stafford Cripps with complaints. But there is no reason why Mountbatten couldn't have held him back. In any case, Mountbatten bears direct responsibility, as Chief of Combined Operations, for executing the raid on Dieppe. Fate and a lucky hit by the Luftwaffe had forced the cancellation of *Rutter* and reprieved the hapless men. It was Mountbatten who called them back for *Jubilee*, and a sad rendezvous with disaster.[49]

Dieppe left Mountbatten's reputation tottering perilously, though it never collapsed. None of the first books on the disaster neglected to pay tribute to Mountbatten. In an article published in the prestigious *Royal United Services Institute Journal* in 1950, his loyal acolyte Hughes-Hallett naturally had only praise for Mountbatten's drive and determination: 'Suffice it to say here that not the least remarkable feature of the operation was the fact of its having been carried out at all, and this was due to the united determination of the Chief of Combined Operations and his subordinates to drive on, unless told otherwise by superior authority.' During the long friendship that ensued between the two men, Hughes-Hallett's career flourished, graced as it was by such high patronage.[50]

Less benign was Brooke's reaction. After the raid Brooke not only made a personal attack on Mountbatten at Churchill's dinner party but subsequently showed his distrust of him by imposing General Pownall, whom he trusted implicitly, on Mountbatten when he became Supreme Commander in South East Asia. Brooke warned Pownall to be on his guard to keep Mountbatten on the rails, as he was inclined to bolt and do things his staff might not approve. Dieppe was likely the principal event Brooke had in mind. Rumours of Whitehall's displeasure with Mountbatten continued throughout the fall, though none of the attacks were pressed home, perhaps because Mountbatten's connections protected him. On 28 September the King visited Mountbatten's headquarters for a 'post-Dieppe analysis'. Afterwards he had nothing but glowing words for COHQ, its staff, and its chief. Five days after Churchill had threatened an inquiry over Dieppe, in December 1942, and three days after the Chiefs of Staff Committee had raked Mountbatten over the coals for his failure to co-ordinate with the Inter-Service Security Board, King George wrote Mountbatten on 26 December 1942: 'I do congratulate you so very much on the success you have made of CO despite all the obstacles you have met and the heavy opposition you have fought both on the administrative side and in active operations!!! . . . Why should it be so difficult to get other people to understand the supreme value of Combined Operations, after the way you have shown that it can, will and does work when properly organized and you have the troops trained for it?' It is hard not to think that this letter — so clearly a supportive reiteration of self-interested remarks Mountbatten had made to his cousin the King — was sent to Mountbatten as a kind of gift, to be used in any way he saw fit. Whether or not it was ever waved before Churchill as a sign of royal backing (Mountbatten knew that fealty to the monarch was a religion with the Prime Minister), Mountbatten's critics may have felt embarrassed at continuing the attack. Churchill would not pick up the threads of his incomplete investigation until many years later, when it came time to try to make sense of the events for his memoirs and Mountbatten had seemingly risen beyond the point where he needed to worry about the effect of Dieppe on his career.[51]

Outside observers have been less inhibited. Terence Robertson called Mountbatten 'a 41 year old baby'. Another, Nigel Hamilton, has described him in his role as CCO as a 'master of intrigue, jealousy and ineptitude, [who] like a spoilt child . . . toyed with men's lives'. But such harsh judgements overlook the role of those who created the Mountbatten legend — some of whom, notably Beaverbrook, would later become his severest critics. Many had encouraged Mountbatten to indulge in the public-relations vice. Most culpable of all was Churchill who, in his desire to counteract the depressing string of defeats of 1942, contributed greatly to turning the young man's head. So also did the British Joint Staff Mission in Washington, and the Chiefs of Staff committee that approved Mountbatten's visit to Washington. Mountbatten cannot be blamed for selling the idea of raids as a substitute for something more substantial, or as a means of deceiving the Germans. This idea had been floated by both the Soviet Ambassador, Ivan Maisky, and Beaverbrook, and had clearly been embraced by Churchill. Indeed, it was probably inevitable that somebody would be asked to execute similarly ambitious raids. But Mountbatten surrounded the effort with too much publicity and raised expectations he could never fulfil. Clearly not mature enough to deal with all the head-turning adulation, he reacted, not surprisingly, by focusing more on the publicity side than on the operational side, trusting in the fates to reward pluck. It is hard not to agree with the judgement Lord Lovat made in 1967: 'It [Mountbatten's activity] was rather like a cork on a wave . . . everyone pushing him on. . . . It would have taken a very strong man and he wasn't. . . . He's got a lot of obvious weaknesses, very conceited, very anxious to steal the glory and I think he would be the last person to chuck it [Rutter] . . . in fact, I think he was the first person to resurrect it [Jubilee].'[52]

Whatever motivations led Mountbatten to accede to the raid — and however his perception of its inevitable consequences was blunted by extraneous concerns — he was forced to pay a high price for the outcome. Dieppe haunted him ever after; he never succeeded in exorcising it. Though he was adept at lulling asleep potentially hostile interviewers, he usually did so on the basis of written drafts, reworking one twenty times. Tirelessly he gathered documents for his archives at Broadlands in the hope of adding more credibility to his story and producing an entirely plausible explanation. As he failed signally to find one, he became in a sense another victim of the disaster.

# 10

# How Canada Became Involved

The willingness of the Canadian commanders to undertake Dieppe made all the difference to Mountbatten and Hughes-Hallett in launching the raid. If the Canadian commander, General Andrew McNaughton, had not co-operated, it would probably not have taken place because no British commander would have been likely to hazard such a raid after the July cancellation and in the face of Montgomery's firm opposition to remounting. Mountbatten seemed to concede as much, saying '. . . they [the Canadians] paved an example of courage, and everything they possibly could be called upon to do, they did.' In such a generous moment he even said of General Roberts, whom he often criticized very bitterly: 'He did it [the raid] very gallantly.' Hughes-Hallett was even more effusive, saying after the war that '. . . the thing to remember was that they [the Canadians] did the operation and that's more than can be said for some of the crack formations which had been selected for earlier operations. The great thing was that the Canadians were not only brave but they were bold as well. They were prepared to chance their arm and it was that that made the Dieppe operation possible.' The justness of these remarks is scarcely diminished by the fact that, in the brief period after *Rutter* had been cancelled, and Roberts thought it was honourable to question his original assignment, Hughes-Hallett bulldozed the doubtful Canadian commander, tacitly aided by McNaughton and Mountbatten. But it may also be noted that Canadian participation also served as a protective screen for Combined Operations Headquarters because whatever happened no British official was likely to raise much objection for fear of disturbing sensitive relations within the Empire.[1]

How did Canadians come to be involved and serve the purposes of the very determined Chief of Combined Operations and his no-less-determined Naval Adviser? The Canadian presence at Dieppe, far from being accidental, was the predictable outgrowth of Canadian ambivalence towards the military, as exemplified in the war policies of the Prime Minister, William Lyon Mackenzie King. So much has been written about his fear of stirring animosities between English- and French-speaking communities over the issue of foreign military service that little needs to be added here. Similarly, much has been written about the expedients he devised to give Canada the appearance of a vigorous war effort while avoiding combat casualties. What does need recalling is that King had placed at the head of the Canadian forces in Britain General McNaughton, who was committed to avoiding engagements until Canada could take a significant role in the final defeat against Germany. For the single Canadian division that had begun their training at Aldershot in January 1940 a largely garrison role was acceptable to McNaughton, even though the Canadian public, or at least its anglophone component, was growing increasingly restless. But King, with McNaughton's help, had the situation well in hand until the Fall of France, when their policy of a carefully measured war effort began to disintegrate. The growing feeling that Germany might really win the war made it all the harder to convince Canadians that garrison duty was enough. The Canadian high command was losing credibility. Even the still-neutral Americans seemed to be making as good an effort in terms of material support. The cumulative effect of these factors had great impact in shaping Canadian resolve to attempt the Dieppe raid.

The German blitzkrieg attack on the Low Countries and France in May 1940 shocked public opinion in Canada as much, perhaps more, than in any other allied nation. The leaders of the Opposition marched into Mackenzie King's office to inform him that the country was demanding a vigorous prosecution of the war. King, whose ear for public opinion was as sharp as ever, already knew this, and in Cabinet later that afternoon he raised no objection to going on more of a war footing with the enactment of a National Resources Mobilization Act, so long as everyone understood that there would be no conscription for overseas service. But in the coming weeks King found it increasingly difficult to contain the pressure for a more vigorous Canadian war effort. It certainly was not possible to maintain the charade of a decision he made in January, when to steal a march on the Opposition he had announced the eventual formation of a second division for overseas service, a measure that King probably never intended to carry out. With France collapsing he recognized that the division would really have to be raised. The energetic new Chief of the General Staff, General H.D.G. Crerar, had no intention of letting the Cabinet rest at that point, and by July he had pushed it into agreeing to a long-term expansion of the overseas force to five or even six divisions. He even got them to agree to raising a second and third division in the near term.[2]

Though King felt that this would strip Canadian home defences thin, he had boxed himself in, having committed Canada to Britain's defence without regret. He had noted earlier in his diary, on 24 May 1940, that 'we owe

[Britain] such freedom as we have. It is right we should strike with her the last blow for the preservation of freedom.' But this noble sentiment did not mean that King would lose sight of his fundamental policy, which was to keep as many troops as he could out of combat for as long as this was possible. Even at the height of the crisis caused by the Fall of France, he never proposed to reverse the prohibition against conscription for overseas service. Moreover, he knew that after the British evacuation of Dunkirk in June 1940, sending troops to England would result in immediate fighting only if Hitler attempted to invade Britain. As the chances of this did not seem to be that great, and an attack on the Continent was out of the question for the foreseeable future, King was really opting for sending more men to garrison duty. Indeed, in late 1941 a combat role was still thought to be relatively remote when a Canadian Defence Staff study noted: 'In any event it would appear that if and when the Canadian Corps is disembarked on the Continent of Europe, the conditions which will then be found to exist will not be such as to demand prolonged major operations.' This hope was given life when Britain adopted a strategy of attrition, combined with strategic bombing, that lessened the importance of ground forces. It was under these circumstances that King, allowing his emotions to carry him away, agreed to the raising of the two additional divisions.[3]

But once so large a Canadian contingent had been created, it tended to assume a life of its own. General McNaughton, the commander of this force, excelled in managing public relations and getting maximum publicity for his troops. He and his friends had already demonstrated a marked ability for feeding stories to the press. As King's defence minister, J.L. Ralston, somewhat caustically noted, McNaughton was one who 'understands fully the value of publicity and has been widely publicized to the Canadian people'. Indeed, McNaughton made the covers not only of Canadian weeklies but also of *Life*, *Time*, and *Newsweek*, all of which lavished praise on 'McNaughton of the Canadians'.[4]

The *New York Times* was particularly generous in its coverage. On 9 February 1940, in an article datelined Ottawa, it spoke of the departure of the first Canadian division for Britain as 'only the beginning of a steady stream of manpower with which, as fast as Great Britain is able to accept and utilize it, Canada will reinforce her initial effort on the fighting front.' Two months later, in April, photographers were present when General Ironside, British Chief of the Imperial Staff, and the French commander, General Gamelin, visited McNaughton's headquarters. The caption in the *New York Times* suggested that three equals were planning offensive strategy. In July the press prominently carried news of McNaughton's promotion to Lieutenant-General and the suggestion that he would command a mixed British-Canadian corps. By June 1941 reports were circulating that McNaughton was going to replace Churchill as Minister of Defence in the British War Cabinet, a bit of impudence quickly denied by 10 Downing

Street. Then in September came McNaughton's famous press conference when he boldly proclaimed that there would have to be an invasion of the Continent and suggested that Canadian forces would be at the centre of this effort. As he put it, the Canadian Corps was 'a dagger pointed at the heart of Berlin, don't make any mistake about that.'[5]

Then in March 1942, in the midst of the strategic debate over the Second Front, McNaughton returned to Canada under klieg lights to consult with Mackenzie King. The press was even more intrigued by his wide detour to Washington, where he was reported to have had an hour-long strategy conference with President Roosevelt. Two weeks later the General was back in England deprecating Britain's war effort and seemingly joining the American campaign for an immediate Second Front. 'You don't win wars by sitting in defensive positions, no matter how important they are,' he declared, ignoring the fact that this was what Canadian troops had been doing since the start of the war. Canadians wanted to get into the business of a cross-Channel attack as soon as possible. 'We don't want a blow struck casually. We want a continuing effect on the enemy.' By June 1942 McNaughton began to realize that he was putting great pressure on the Canadian Government, creating expectations that would be hard to satisfy. He closed a speech of 24 June on a more restrained note, saying: 'And so the Army of Canada in Britain bides its time and waits with confidence and steady purpose knowing that for a while yet, patience is required.' From time to time McNaughton told the press to tone down its overly enthusiastic coverage, warning that it could lead only to disillusionment in Canada and to widespread disappointment. But of course the press, faced with the option of printing McNaughton's 'Go get'em' releases and his and King's 'But not now', chose the former. The public wanted to hear what could be done, not what couldn't, and as always the press tended to give satisfaction.[6]

Nor could McNaughton afford to sound too cautious. After all, the conduct of war is thought to depend much on a peculiar psychological state: the willingness to risk lives for goals that in peacetime seem rather vague and intangible. War has ever been associated with its commanders' maintaining a confident, aggressive state of mind, for without such an attitude troops lose their fighting edge and commanders lose their credibility. McNaughton and his colleagues were indulging in 'pep talks', and it seems hard to question their basic validity without also questioning the whole art of command.

Not surprisingly, McNaughton's subordinate commanders entered the fray with enthusiasm. When General Victor Odlum arrived with the 2nd Canadian Division in 1940, the London *Evening News* headed a story with the line, 'Canadians want a smack at the Jerries', and quoted Odlum as saying, 'Germany has asked for it and she is going to get it.' *The Times* gave similar attention to his announcement that 'We are ready.' In May 1942

General Crerar, now in England as Commander of the First Corps, spoke with even more zeal. In an interview with 'Wes' Gallagher of the Associated Press he evoked memories of the Great War and the glorious Canadian victory at Vimy, and said that 'the Canadian Corps would raid enemy positions on the other side [of the Channel] as actively and effectively as it raided the German trenches in the last war.' This was brave talk indeed. In fact Odlum did not do a very good job of training the 2nd Division and it would not have been picked to do Dieppe had it not been for the fact that his successor, Roberts, brought it up to the highest standards.[7]

But Odlum's rhetoric was popular and was echoed at home. On 3 May 1942 Ralston took to the air waves to remind Canadians that the third job of the defence establishment was to 'train for new operations of every conceivable type; to be ready to strike anywhere and anyhow and any time. That army is under the command of Lieutenant-General McNaughton and to use his own words, it is a dagger pointed at the heart of Berlin.'[8]

Of course King tried to counteract the press campaign of his zealous commanders. As early as September 1940 a tour of Canadian defence installations had been arranged for the allied press, to whom the weakness of the Canadian forces and their lack of training and equipment was stressed. Hanson Baldwin, the respected military correspondent of the *New York Times*, wrote a four-column report titled 'War Effort's Peak in Canada Year Off', with such subtitles as 'Tour shows difficulties', 'Bottlenecks in skilled labour' and 'Dominion expected to become major factor in conflict only late in 1941'. Reflecting the briefing he had received, Baldwin reported that 'air-training [the Commonwealth Air Training Plan] is probably the only Canadian effort that may have a major influence upon the outcome of the war.' Undoubtedly many in Canada saw Baldwin's article as an arrant piece of American arrogance.[9]

King eventually succumbed to the relentless pressure to build an image of an aggressive, militant Canada. Though he knew that if he visited the troops in England he would be confronted by the much-resented fact of their inactivity and would be forced to make militant speeches, he alone of all the war leaders could not avoid such a trip. And of course what he feared would happen did. In September, King told his London audience that 'You all know how eager our Canadian soldiers are for action against the enemy. I cannot make too clear that the policy of the Canadian government is to have our troops serve in those theatres where, viewing the war as a whole it is believed their services will count the most.' This statement was designed to convey subtly to the British that Canada did not want any invitations to go to North Africa and that her troops should be kept in Britain facing the Channel. But as phrased, and more importantly as reported, it suggested that King wanted to be in on the big fighting regardless of the possible casualties. King's slow process of succumbing to the very rhetoric he found so objectionable in his military chiefs was reflected in the speech he made on his return from England: 'Every Canadian heart must have been thrilled by Mr. Churchill's words when he said that our Canadian soldiers stood at the very post where they would be the first to be hurled into a counter-stroke against the invader.' No one should have been surprised by such rhetoric. A nation at war cannot easily avoid creating the impression that the first objective is to fight and win, and a government that cannot face that reality perhaps ought not to be at war. King realized this, and came to accept the need for presenting the public with images of Canadians fighting. But doing so meant that, sooner or later, he would exhaust the possibilities of rhetoric and be obliged to deliver the real thing.[10]

By early 1942 many in the Canadian Government were hoping that something more substantial than mere words could be found — though nothing too hazardous. To earn King's approval, any prospective military engagement would have to be so brief an action that it would be unlikely to cause many casualties or compel a recourse to conscription. To satisfy McNaughton it also should be against the principal enemy, Germany. Finally, to satisfy not only McNaughton as commander but also nationalist sentiment, the engagement must be one in which Canadian troops would lead. At all costs the splitting up of the small Canadian force or its dissolution into larger Commonwealth forces must be avoided. In sum, what was required was a combat mission against Germany big enough to convince the public that action was being undertaken, but small enough to be undertaken entirely by Canadians, and safe enough so that King would not have to be confronted with major casualties. Not only was this setting too many conditions on the employment of Canadian troops, but regrettably the idea of contributing to the speediest possible defeat of the enemy seemed to be playing a distinctly secondary role to considerations of image.

The search for the perfect campaign was not easy. In April 1940 McNaughton accepted, without reference to Ottawa, the idea of participating in the British attempt to parry German thrusts towards Norway. This met all of McNaughton's requirements, since it was likely to be a short expedition against German forces. But it soon became too hazardous and was cancelled, with McNaughton receiving a rebuke from Ottawa for having agreed to do it on his own initiative. In June 1940, in the midst of the shock of Dunkirk, approval was given to use Canadian forces in Brittany, though largely in a reserve capacity. They were soon withdrawn. (General Roberts, who was with the Canadian troops, returned, to the amazement of all, with more military equipment than he had arrived with, having collected abandoned British hardware. Obviously this was a very resourceful man.) When the possibility of engagement in France collapsed, the search for a Canadian field of battle began anew.[11]

In August 1941 a Canadian force took part in a bloodless raid on the Norwegian-owned islands in the Spitsbergen archipelago on the convoy route to Murmansk in northern Russia. Then in October 1941 the strangest of all attempts to find employment for Canadian troops was approved: the sending of two battalions to Hong Kong, a decision that probably fitted in with King's strategy of drawing Canadian attention to the Pacific theatre in the hope of keeping forces away from Europe. This gave the Canadian units their first taste of combat, after two years of being at war. Unfortunately the Japanese attack was overwhelming and the episode ended in a humiliating disaster. The quest for employment of the Canadian forces resumed. Thus the Canadian Government was in an embarrassing position by the spring and summer of 1942, for Hanson Baldwin's much-publicized date for a real peak of Canadian military effort in 1941 had come and gone and still Canadians had not seen action in Europe. McNaughton's bold talk made the embarrassment still more acute. If the dagger was pointed at Berlin, it seemed not to have moved an inch in a year.

As early as the summer of 1941 Canadian forces could have found employment in the Mediterranean theatre for the defence of Egypt. The Australians and New Zealanders were already in North Africa. If the Canadians had joined them, their contribution to the war might have been considerable, for Britain was incapable of any offensive operations until she had secured her lines of communication through the Mediterranean. A Mediterranean victory in 1941, followed by a consolidation in 1942, would have meant that a cross-Channel attack was possible in 1943 — with the result that the war might have been shortened by a year at least. But McNaughton feared that his troops would be swallowed up into larger British formations in areas that would never be decisive. Vimy II could not possibly exist in North Africa; it must lie in Europe.

The possibilities for Canadian action in the Mediterranean/Middle East have been much obscured by military historians who suggest that Canadians never refused to undertake operations in the area. This has even been embellished to suggest that British and American planners deliberately hid the North African plan from Canadians to prevent them from joining. McNaughton's biographer has said that 'Though McNaughton would have welcomed fighting his army as such in North Africa, he did not even hear about the operation until September.' Nothing could be more misleading. After his arrival in England, McNaughton made it abundantly clear that he wanted his Canadian troops employed against the principal enemy; North Africa was, and would long continue to be, primarily an Italian theatre. McNaughton had a virtual veto on the employment of Canadian troops and the British, knowing his views, never pressed too hard. But they did ask. In October 1940, when Sir Anthony Eden approached a visiting Canadian minister to inquire whether there might be some possibility of sending Canadian troops to the Middle East, the minister consulted McNaughton and found his opposition had not changed. No Canadian authority ever picked up Eden's suggestion.[12]

Moreover, after the rebuke administered to McNaughton by the Canadian Government in April 1940 for committing troops for use in Norway without approval from Ottawa, the British Government also knew that any approval from McNaughton would have to be cleared in Ottawa. Indeed, a telegram King sent to Ralston on 6 December 1940 (drafted by O.D. Skelton) noted acidly: 'It is pretty certain to be felt that if troops are being sent to the Near East they should be sent from the parts of the Commonwealth which control policy in the Near East or which are more geographically concerned with the Near East. It is one thing for Canada to raise additional forces to assist Britain in the British Isles or in Western Europe, it might become a very different thing to get the support necessary for Canadian forces to be sent to other parts of the world.' A few days later the British Government gingerly explored the ground with Ralston, who visited London in the second half of December 1940. Eden first pointed out that major operations against North Africa might soon be possible and discreetly hinted that Canadian participation would be welcome. Ralston showed no interest. But Churchill, never one to accept a veiled no, raised the question at a subsequent meeting. Ralston's report spoke volumes about Canadian war policy:

> I mentioned that in Canada already there had been newspaper reports already intimating that it was proposed to send Canadians to the Middle East. I had advised the Government that such a proposal had never even been put forward and I intimated that we would assume that employment of our troops, outside of the United Kingdom, be left for our suggestion. His [Churchill's] reply was 'of course.'

Just to make sure that no unwanted invitations were extended, Ralston drafted a summary of their conversation and asked Churchill to confirm its accuracy. He did so, and a formal invitation to send Canadian troops to North Africa was effectively abandoned. Only indirect approaches were then possible.[13]

Nearly a year later, on the occasion of Ralston's trip to London in October 1941, another rather cautious British approach was made. It was preceded by vague hints from the British military planner, General Sir John Kennedy, to McNaughton's principal deputy, General Crerar, about possible help for operations in Spain or North Africa. When Ralston spoke to the British Secretary of State for War, he said the Canadian Government was prepared to consider employment of the Canadian Corps in any military operations the War Office might recommend, which perhaps might have been interpreted as an alteration of the stand he took with Churchill; but Ralston then proceeded to crawfish his way back, stressing that the Canadian Government was not pressing for the active employment of Canadian forces. Though the possibility of using some of them in Spain or Spanish Morocco was mentioned, Ralston did not respond. A few days later he explored the question of using troops in the Middle East with McNaughton, who made clear that he was still opposed to the idea: 'While such a step would be welcomed by the formation in question and undoubtedly would initially be well received by the Canadian public it would not serve to solve the larger issue of [the] general employment of all Canadian forces overseas.'[14]

Given Canadian attitudes, the British Government resigned itself to having the Canadian force as garrison troops. That was surely what King wanted, and until the opportunity for a potentially sensational engagement like Vimy Ridge came by, that was also what McNaughton wanted. It is not even clear that King desired another Vimy, judging from his outburst in May 1941, when the Minister of National Defence for Air suggested in the War Committee that Canada offer a brigade of troops for Egypt. King virtually exploded: 'I said at once that I would not countenance anything of the kind: that it might be my Scotch conscience, or it might be common sense, but I do not feel that any Government has the right to take the lives of any men for spectacular purposes.' Thus a careful examination of the record shows that, though it is technically correct to say that British authorities never made a formal approach to Canadian authorities for deployments in North Africa or the Middle East, it is misleading to suggest that tacit requests were not made, and even more misleading to suggest that Canadian authorities did not refuse them.[15]

This understanding — that unwelcome invitations should not be made — naturally left Canadian generals champing at the bit. As early as May 1941 the Department of Defence had reported to the Government that the 'absence of active participation of Canadians in recent operations is having a frustrating effect on public outlook in Canada'. General Maurice Pope, assigned to the Combined Chiefs of Staff mission in Washington, said it all when he wrote General Kenneth Stuart, Chief of the General Staff, in November 1942: 'I cannot help feeling that the continued inactivity of our forces in the United Kingdom is anything but in the national interest. And unless the intransigent policy in respect to their employment which has hitherto prevailed is modified in some degree, I greatly fear that our position will progressively become less enviable.'[16]

The whole problem was first thrashed out when Ralston visited McNaughton in October 1941. The minutes of their strategy review of 15 October record McNaughton as saying that the best employment of the Canadian Corps for the coming winter was to remain in Great Britain, but that in the spring it might be practicable to take part in operations elsewhere. The Minister asked whether he meant the Corps as a whole or in part. General McNaughton replied 'as a Corps', and to develop a specific theatre of operations. After a March 1942 conference with Mackenzie King, he noted that they were both agreed on keeping Canadian forces pointed against the principal enemy — that is, facing Germany across the Channel

— and would brook no diversions to the Middle East. By this time, however, General Stuart was desperate to find some active employment for Canadian troops. In a letter to General Pope, he wrote that the continued prospect of nothing but garrison duty was bound to have a bad effect on the morale of the troops, and asked Pope to keep him posted on any opportunities for their deployment. The soldiers had no difficulty in recognizing who was responsible for their inactivity. When King visited the troops in August 1941 he was loudly booed from the ranks of the assembled formations. Rarely, if ever, had a Prime Minister been so publicly humiliated.[17]

In November 1941 a Gallup poll had showed that 60 per cent of the Canadian public wanted conscription, or in other words a more vigorous prosecution of the war. On 12 November 1941 Senator Arthur Meighen, a former Prime Minister, accepted the leadership of the Conservatives. In doing so he demanded a general policy of compulsory service. 'Our present methods', he asserted, 'are illogical, cruelly unjust, and tragically inefficient. I shall therefore urge with all the power I can bring to bear compulsory service over the whole field of war.' The Canadian Legion, tired of merely organizing welfare and education programs for soldiers overseas, had thrown its heart and soul into a 'Call for Total War', rallying 500 national organizations in its support. In January 1942 the Liberal premier of New Brunswick, J.B. McNair, publicly called for conscription, as did a Toronto committee of 200 that took out ads for conscription. And the Premier of Ontario, Mitchell Hepburn, gave tacit support to Meighen's political intentions. King characteristically tried to steal the march on his potential rivals by going to the electorate to ask for release from his no-conscription pledge in a plebiscite or, as some preferred to call it, a great national referendum. The decision to consult the electorate was announced in the Speech from the Throne on 22 January 1942, which revealed much about the dilemmas of Canadian defence policy. It recognized that without the formality of conscription, Canada's war effort was being denigrated outside the country and undervalued at home. King brought himself to express this attitude in a nation-wide radio address on 7 April:

This restriction [the bar to conscription] is being represented as a bar to an all out effort on Canada's part. It makes no difference whether conscription for service overseas would add to Canada's total war effort or not, the fact that the government is not free to consider its adoption is made to appear as limiting Canada's war effort. The lack of power to impose such conscription has ... placed our war effort in a wholly false light before our own citizens and what is worse before our allies.[18]

The polling took place on 27 April 1942. By almost two to one the electorate released the Government from its no-conscription pledge. But the vote also confirmed King's worst fears. In Quebec the *non*'s outweighed the *oui*'s by almost three to one. King, who had never really shown any desire to use conscription or to raise a large standing army, and had only wanted to steal the thunder from his possible rivals, was now more determined than ever to avoid conscription for overseas service — that is, refusing operations in Europe that might use manpower at rates that would necessitate its implementation. As he made clear in his diary, had the vote been on conscription, he would have voted against it himself. When Ralston pressed him to use the results to bring in conscription, King refused categorically, and when Ralston proposed that conscription be at least allowed in the northern hemisphere, King, though tempted, said that he would not consider it under the circumstances because 'I felt that it would concentrate the public mind on our not having an all-out war effort, and it was important that Canada's position should not be put in a false light. The whole purpose of the plebiscite had been to remove that.' But clearly there was a problem. King had posited that if Canada threw itself into war production, trained the pilots of the Commonwealth, sent a garrison force to Britain, and formally accepted the principle of conscription, Canadians would be satisfied and Canada would earn the homage of all Britain's allies. But now he was admitting this had not happened and implicitly recognized that something more must be done for Canadian pride at home and abroad — though, revealingly, he stressed the importance of the latter. The one thing he still would not countenance was placing a sizeable number of Canadian troops under fire.[19]

By June 1942 it was clear that Ralston was wavering in his support of King's policy of restraint. Ralston's Rotary Club speech of 16 June 1942 gives some indication of the tide King was swimming against:

> These troops shout for action. We all shout for action. The time will come for action; and when that time comes you can depend on it that Canadian troops will prove to be a powerful, hard hitting fighting force worthy in every way of the spirit that stormed Vimy Ridge twenty five years ago.

King was in a dilemma. Any politician who was revealed as holding back the war effort would, in time, be gravely imperilled. King was certainly not going to let the situation deteriorate to a point where the public would echo the booing Canadian troops had given him. Always a realist in politics, King had begun to look for some way to demonstrate more vigorous action — while excluding anything that might require conscription, which he continued to regard as the greatest political danger of all. Thus the question was: how to project the image of more vigorous combat without risking conscription?[20]

As early as the summer of 1941 the Canadian military had been proposing to King that an active effort might focus on raids. They would do much for the image of Canadian military effectiveness, particularly if they could be represented as being daring. In April 1942 the argument made still better sense. Raids would give the lie to those who were saying that the plebiscite had been a phony issue because Canadians were serving nothing more than garrison duty. At the same time, raids offered the prospect of having the maximum possible effect at the lowest possible cost in casualties, since any raid would be relatively brief. For McNaughton, raiding operations would provide action without running the risk of dividing his army or sending it to dead-end theatres just to get battle experience. Indeed, the experience gained from raids on the Continent might earn Canadians a special right when the time finally came to point the dagger at Berlin. It is hard not to see in raiding operations the ideal solution to the problem of trying to get maximum prominence in the war at minimum cost. But approval for raids was not easily obtained. Ottawa was initially cool.

Securing approval had been made more difficulty by the Trondheim project of May 1940, when McNaughton had committed 1,300 of his troops for use in Norway before he had asked Ottawa's permission. While the Minister of Defence, Ralston, was prepared to cover McNaughton a bit, saying that the 'Canadian government was consulted about the Norway expedition, and it gave its express approval', he also made clear that no one should assume that approval would be automatic in the future: ' I wish to say, just to clinch that, that the decision as to the employment of troops outside the United Kingdom is a matter for the Canadian government. . .the appropriate Canadian service authority cannot authorize the embarkation of Canadian forces from the United Kingdom without the authority of the Minister of National Defence.'[21]

A few months later, in July, the Cabinet in Ottawa made an attempt to develop a clear policy on military engagements. A key memorandum called the War Committee's attention to the fact that the 'absence of active participation of Canadians in recent operations is having a frustrating effect on public outlook' and asked whether the time had not come to give the Canadian commander blanket authority to conduct raids. The question was buried in a larger debate over the deployment of Canadian forces, so that in July, McNaughton had to ask the visiting Canadian Air Minister, C.G. Power, to raise the question with the Cabinet when he returned to Ottawa. This request in turn got side-tracked when the Spitsbergen project was being developed in July. At that time McNaughton in effect told the Government that he was preparing to go ahead until he received a very explicit veto. King was in fact inclined to give that veto. The minutes of the War Committee note that 'Mr. King said that he, himself, questioned the wisdom of such offensive operations, this year. As it was, the situation was developing favourably, with Russia, in large measure, engaging German energies. Further, the results of failure in operations of the kind would be to encourage our enemies and discourage our friends. The dangers appeared greater than the advantages which might accrue from success.' Only reluctantly did King go along with the majority, after insisting that McNaughton be warned that 'In arriving at decision you will no doubt have regard to question as to whether prospects of success are sufficient to warrant risks involved which include not only personnel but possible encouragement to enemy if results negative or worse.' In other words, McNaughton could commit his troops in this particular circumstance if there was absolutely no risk. When the Canadian raiders landed at Spitsbergen, the Germans were nowhere to be found; the seemingly daring gesture did not cost a single life. King could not have been more pleased. Undoubtedly the experience helped to undermine his initial dislike of raiding opportunities and to pave the way for his reluctant approval of the Dieppe raid.[22]

Ralston's trip to England in October 1941 gave McNaughton a chance to plead for general authorization to conduct raids, somewhat against his better judgement. Just days before his long conference with Ralston, McNaughton had observed that 'excluding the Spitsbergen Expedition all previous expeditions had been cancelled, subsequent to plans being laid, due to changes in the situation, which decision had proved right in each case.' Implicitly, then, he recognized they were not well-conceived operations. Nevertheless, at the end of October 1941 both McNaughton and Crerar lobbied hard with Ralston to get approval. Their representations indicate as clearly as anything could how keenly aware they were of King's desire to avoid anything risky that might produce significant casualties. McNaughton tried to pass the raids off as inconsequential, saying that raiding operations were regarded by the 'U.K. Government as [a] normal extension of [Home Forces] duties' and Crerar spoke of them as an extension of 'ordinary patrol activities' and as 'trivial'. General Kennedy, a key British planner, explained that there were few options, for besides raids there were available only the sort of operations that Canadian authorities had declined in the past. That convinced Ralston, who telegraphed a request for authority from the Cabinet in Ottawa. On his recommendation the War Committee gave McNaughton limited authority to conduct 'minor' raids.[23]

Thereafter senior Canadian military personnel in England threw heart and soul into securing the lead in raiding activities. This was not immediately forthcoming, because there were British units who wanted the opportunity, and perhaps also because London understood that McNaughton's authorization was somewhat circumscribed. This British resistance to giving Canadians the lead in raiding operations prompted a blistering reaction from Crerar. Writing on 5 February 1942 to General Montgomery, then commanding the South East Command (which had primary responsibility for raids in the Channel area), Crerar opened with the accusation that his Canadian troops had been unjustly denied any opportunity for combat. It was, he complained, a static situation not of their choosing. Somewhat ignoring the high-level exchanges that had transpired, Crerar insisted that Canadians had not refused to serve anywhere. In no uncertain terms he told Montgomery:

> This continued lack of active participation in operations provides neither pride nor pleasure to the officers and other ranks of the Canadian Army.... As the months go by and opportunities fail to materialize in which the officers and men of my present command can match their skill and courage against the enemy, the more difficult it will be to maintain in them the desired keenness and morale.

Crerar then proceeded to renew the Canadian request to participate in raiding operations:

> I believe that occasions will increasingly present themselves for small raids across the Channel opposite the Army front. I consider that it will be in the general interest if a very high proportion of these prospective raids, if not the total, should be undertaken by detachments from the Canadian Corps.

Thus he put the whole issue on the plane of professional pride, which he thought an officer like Montgomery would respect. Crerar closed his letter by recalling the very good reputation Canadian soldiers had made for themselves in the First World War and expressed confidence that the present generation, every bit as good, were particularly suited for the challenges implicit in aggressive raiding operations.[24]

Montgomery, who was not prepared to go so far as to give the Canadians the lion's share of the raids, replied vaguely that he would try to make available 'some' craft so that the Canadians could gain experience in raiding operations. He closed his letter pleasantly enough, noting Crerar's appeal to professional pride by saying that 'Your men should be quite first class at raiding,' which at least seemed to indicate that Canadians might be given some share of the raids. Crerar — either suspecting that he was getting the polite run-around, or determined to clinch matters — then took his appeal to higher levels. On 6 March he was making his case strongly (which long experience had given him practice in doing, often stridently) in the office of the Chief of the British Imperial staff, General Sir Alan Brooke. Crerar opened the meeting by indicating the 'importance he attached to Canadian participation [in raids] now that the prospects of an invasion during the early summer seemed to recede.' Canadian troops, he complained, had been in the UK — some for over two years — without 'having a chance to meet the enemy', a circumstance he found 'galling'. If this enforced inactivity continued it would have a serious effect on morale within the Canadian Corps.[25]

By blaming Britain for the failure to use Canadian troops, Crerar presented his case in terms of a personal grievance about which, officer to officer, something would have to be done. British authorities were thus faced with the choice of either contesting the accuracy of Crerar's presentation — which, because it would entail discussions of the tacit vetoes given by Canadian authorities, was pregnant with possibilities for recrimination — or accepting his demand. Brooke knew a losing argument when he saw one and offered to arrange a general meeting between the top Canadian officers and Mountbatten's Combined Operations staff to discuss a leading role for Canada in raiding operations. Crerar was pleased with this promise. But as he explained to one of his key staff officers, there must be no slackening; if Canadian troops were to get their chance, it would be necessary to keep up the 'pressure' on British authorities. Crerar was pushing hard down the road that would lead to Dieppe and the ruination of General Roberts' career.

The meeting with Brooke — the culmination of Crerar's campaign, though largely ignored by historians of Dieppe — had much to do with shaping that tragedy, for once Brooke had yielded, Mountbatten could do nothing but yield in turn. He did so most reluctantly, however, placing on record his opposition to giving the Canadians the principal role, which would be contrary to agreements made with the Commander of Home Forces that British Commandos should form the main element. Nevertheless, bowing to superior authority, he said he would find ways to include the Canadians in his next big raid, which turned out to be Dieppe.[26]

Leaving nothing to chance, McNaughton visited Mountbatten several times in April to clinch the accord and to offer British authorities an inducement to carry through: a promise that he would personally urge the Canadian Government to increase landing-craft production in a major way. He was as good as his word. Shortly thereafter he returned to Ottawa to review the position of Canadian troops with Mackenzie King and urge more landing-craft production. McNaughton's diary entry for his meeting with King is brief, indicating that they agreed that Canadian troops would remain concentrated in the 'decisive theatre of the war', which meant that British invitations for Canadian participation in the Middle East should be discouraged, as before, and that the only form of active combat for Canadian troops — in a year when no major cross-Channel attack was expected — would be raids. The General returned to England and again visited Mountbatten's headquarters on 21 April. Mountbatten must have been pleased with the report, for on 30 April the Canadians were officially invited, through Montgomery, to take the leading role in the Dieppe project.[27]

Months of pressuring had at last paid off. But though McNaughton had fought hard for this concession, it was not at all certain that the King government would approve. Ottawa had previously given McNaughton only authorization to conduct raids that he and Ralston had represented as being 'trivial'. McNaughton, aware that Dieppe represented an extraordinary expansion in size and scope, cabled Ottawa explaining that an operation was being planned that 'cannot properly be classed as minor', and requested specific authorization. Though McNaughton had avoided outright prevarication, he made no effort to tell Ralston that what was contemplated was the largest raid in modern history. Knowing how skittish the King government was about employing its troops in combat, he was judiciously reticent.[28]

The whole question was discussed in the Cabinet War Committee on 1 May 1942. King was inclined to refuse McNaughton's request to participate in Dieppe, pointing out that: 'It was essential that no such operations be undertaken without adequate preparations and a full appreciation of all factors involved, including the extent of the Forces available and the opposition that might be anticipated.' He also thought the same warning ought to be given to McNaughton as had been issued at the time of Spitsbergen: that he not commit himself unless he could give assurances of success. In short, the entire responsibility would be his. Only after Ralston erroneously assured the Committee that what was involved was merely on the scale of Spitsbergen, approval for 'a brigade or possibly larger' was given. King's own approval was so reluctant that, as his diary indicates, he continued to ponder the dangers after the Committee meeting: 'We asked McNaughton for more in the way of details as to the character of what was expected.... To these matters I must get into retreat and have time for thought ... [and reflection on the] direction to be taken.'[29]

In reporting to McNaughton, Ralston rather downplayed the request for additional information. McNaughton continued to be guarded, suggesting only that 'the largest project in contemplation at present [Dieppe] might involve up to three brigades which might be all Canadian.' This was more accurate than Ralston's representations but still rather disingenuous, for three brigades were, in effect, a division. McNaughton may also have been counting on civilians' underestimating the size of a brigade. But King did not ask any more questions, and so McNaughton had his authorization. Had Canadian chiefs of staff wanted to ask difficult questions about the projected raid (*Rutter*), which McNaughton reported to them, they had such an opportunity when Mountbatten, after concluding his trip to Washington, flew to Ottawa to meet with them on 11 June. The record of the meeting, from which one infers that Mountbatten did most of the talking, does not even mention a division-size raid, much less *Jubilee*. On Dominion Day 1942 King said publicly that Canadian forces were poised to strike the next blow against Germany. British officials reacted with horror, fearing that he had compromised the Dieppe project. But McNaughton told them to relax, as King probably knew little or nothing about it, which certainly indicates how vaguely the General had briefed his Prime Minister and how few questions Ottawa had asked.[30]

On 7 July 1942 the first Dieppe project, Operation *Rutter*, was aborted — and General Montgomery recommended that the operation be cancelled 'for all time'. In July, under strange circumstances, the project was revived. Mountbatten told McNaughton that the project had approval from the British War Cabinet. McNaughton might have been expected to ask for a copy of the minute for Canadian records; but he never did, nor did he ever receive the least scrap of paper from any British authority indicating that *Jubilee* had been approved, or that he was being made in any way responsible for finding the forces or the commander for it. This was extraordinary from several viewpoints. The first law of military life is that everything concerning command and the execution of a military operation is supposed to be done by orders, from higher to lower command in an unbroken chain, preferably in quintuplicate. The absence of orders to McNaughton is startling, and he could not have failed to notice it. This should have led, and I suspect did lead, McNaughton to wonder whether the operation had in fact been approved. His suspicions would particularly have been aroused because he had been relentless, since the Dieppe project was first initiated, in demanding that everything be done regularly, and that he be kept scrupulously informed in writing of all projects in which the use of Canadian troops was contemplated. For instance, when *Rutter* was first approved by the Chiefs of Staff, McNaughton wrote to Lt-Gen. J.G. des R. Swayne, Chief General Staff Officer of Home Forces, to say:

> I suggest that in the future, [as regards] Combined Operations involving Canadian troops, the outline plan should be placed before me before submission to the Chiefs of Staff Committee and that the Chiefs of Staff Paper should show that in giving their approval they take note of my acceptance: also that I should be included in the distribution list.[31]

That was in May. Now, two months later, he was accepting the questionable revival of the project as *Jubilee*, after General Roberts had made known his complaints, and after Montgomery had recommended against it, without a word on paper about approval or authorization. Whatever one may think of his qualities as a commander, McNaughton had a razor-sharp mind. He could not have failed to realize what the complete and utter absence of any written authorization to Canadian headquarters meant: the operation had not been approved and the normal chain of command was not operating. A document in the files of RCAF Air Vice-Marshal Harold Edwards is virtually conclusive. On 9 August, McNaughton approached Edwards saying that as the responsible head of the Royal Canadian Air Force in Britain there was something that he should know, but that McNaughton feared he would not learn from the normal chain of command (i.e. from Portal). McNaughton was therefore taking it upon himself to inform Edwards privately that several RCAF squadrons would be taking part in *Jubilee*. There was no reason why Portal could not have given Edwards this information (unless he was trying to keep his distance from the operation). Edwards confirmed to McNaughton that his hunch was correct: he had not been informed. This exchange could not have left McNaughton in any doubt about the fact that *Jubilee* did not have official sanction — or status — in the highest command levels. By going to Edwards, McNaughton was in effect abetting Mountbatten, making up for the deficiences in the flow of commands, which resulted inescapably from Mountbatten's decision not to involve the Chiefs of Staff in the operation.

Apparently McNaughton, or at least his staff, was also aware that Mountbatten was being driven by ambition and the prospects of a major combat command in connection with the eventual cross-Channel invasion. For just a few days after the raid, Mountbatten showed up at US Army headquarters with a bushel-basket of medals to hand out to the minuscule American ranger force that had participated in the raid. As he had not done the same for the much larger Canadian force, C.P. Stacey could not help asking one of McNaughton's principal staff officers why Mountbatten wanted to pander so shamelessly to the Americans. The answer was that it was understood that Mountbatten wanted to become a 'Supreme Commander'.[32]

The reason for McNaughton's acquiescence is not hard to divine. Having obtained with such difficulty approval for Canadian involvement in a larger raid, needing to give force to his much-quoted metaphor about a dagger pointed at Germany's heart, and also needing to give his troops battle experience under conditions that would square all his and the government's requirements for such action, McNaughton was unwilling to throw away this unique opportunity by asking awkward questions.

King continued to agonize over the decision, even paraphrasing in a diary entry in May 1942 Stalin's words addressed to the British: 'What is the good of having an army if it does not fight? — for if an army once loses the habit of war it loses its spirit. Therefore, in our own interests we ought to conduct active military operations on the Continent or in the Near East.' King became convinced that the war represented a 'crucification' of mankind, referring to the impending decision as a 'Gethsemani', and noted that, in principal, the cup could not be refused. It was at this time that King continually made references in his diary to how meaningful he found the Book of Jeremiah, particularly Chapters 12-14, the theme of which is Jahweh's unhappiness with a rebellious people that 'must needs take their own false path, courting alien gods and submitting to their worship.' He came to regret his own part in the Dieppe decision. An extravagant spiritualist, King liked to record in his diary the promptings of the Almighty, but for Dieppe there was no sign that Providence had spoken. He was painfully conscious at the time of being swayed by other than purely military considerations. Knowing that his generals were demanding action, that the public was also demanding it, that he stood in danger of being accused of dishonesty with the plebiscite if he did not give some evidence of prosecuting the war more vigorously, and thinking that any other sort of operation might pose even greater dangers, he had acquiesced in Dieppe. But when, in 1943, the pressure for ground combat for Canadian forces grew again, he wrote in his diary: 'I have been afraid of a second Dieppe. By that I mean anxiety to do something to keep up morale.'[33]

Had Dieppe been successful, the Canadian public would have been filled with immense pride in its fighting forces as blazing the trail for the Americans. McNaughton might have been able to take heart in the knowledge that his troops had indeed been trained to the point where their striking at the heart of Germany in Berlin was not unrealistic. And King's hope of following the plebiscite with action that did not cause significant casualties or risk of conscription would have been solved for at least another year. These wished-for possibilities, born of an exceedingly difficult situation, are easily forgotten in hindsight.

In 1942 the concern to legitimize Canadian policies, ever-present in any decision-making process, was particularly acute after two-and-a-half years of Mackenzie King's unique style of waging war — of trying to project images of a total war effort while being unwilling to pay the real price for such an effort. King's endeavour had called into question Canada's wartime credibility and garnered tremendous public opposition. As engaging Canadian troops was becoming something of a political necessity in the summer of 1942, it is somewhat unfair to say Mountbatten was solely responsible for Dieppe because he was acting under 'institutional momentum', or because he needed to justify the worth of his organization. By July 1942 he had given a convincing display, in Saint Nazaire, of Combined Operations' ability to direct skilled forces in a daring raid. McNaughton was still waiting to prove that he and his men could do the same. Mountbatten already had his foot on the next rung of his climb to glory, for he had been given a major role in planning for *Torch*, the invasion of North Africa. McNaughton had also inspired some confidence in higher circles, having been offered in July 1942 responsibility for a full-scale invasion of Norway, but which he knew he would have to turn down because it was inherently too risky — quite apart from the difficulties involved in securing Mackenzie King's permission. (No such invasion took place.) In short, the next rung in McNaughton's career was not even in sight. He needed success at Dieppe much more than did Mountbatten. When one takes into account his bold, not to say foolhardy, statements to the press, and all the strenuous efforts he had made in Whitehall to get the chance to take part in the raid, it is clear McNaughton's prestige was, if anything, more deeply committed than Mountbatten's to pulling it off. If institutional momentum pushed forward this once-cancelled and inherently risky operation, there was as much of it at Canadian military headquarters in London as there was at Mountbatten's headquarters in Richmond Terrace.

In later years McNaughton tried to distance himself from the disaster — explaining that while he 'took full responsibility for the operation', this was on 'the general basis of his confidence in the officers concerned.' He told Stacey that 'In practice the actual control [he and Crerar exercised] over the planning . . . had been very slight.'[34]

The stubborn fact remains that at every important stage of the planning process McNaughton personally reviewed the work product and registered his approval under the authority delegated to him by the Canadian Government. On 30 April he approved the rough outline, on 15 May he approved the outline that had been submitted to the Chiefs of Staff, on 3 July he reviewed and then approved the final *Rutter* plan, and on 27 July he reviewed and approved the final *Jubilee* plan. This was surely more scrutiny and review than Mountbatten ever gave the plans.[35]

In McNaughton's defence it might be noted that he was somewhat boxed in by the activities of Crerar. Montgomery, to whom Crerar had appealed, got the distinct impression that 'if they [Canadian troops] were not allowed [to do Dieppe] . . . there would be trouble with the Canadian headquarters in England under General Andy McNaughton.' Once this impression had been given, McNaughton could hardly shatter it by then refusing the very thing that had been requested. Crerar, having pushed so hard to get the assignment, to the point of making a nuisance of himself, had compromised McNaughton's freedom to manoeuvre. As a rule it is not wise to go shopping in wartime for military operations. There is much to be said for staying in the barracks until you are needed and called. That, in fact, had been McNaughton's belief, and only the pressure of public opinion, following the furor over the plebiscite and King's method of waging war, had forced the General to depart from it.[36]

# 11

# An Overview

Though we have walked around the Dieppe disaster and tried to examine it from the perspective of all the principal players, the fact that each was enmeshed, in varying degrees, in a tangled weave of interests — political, military, and personal — makes the task of drawing together the principal elements into a single tapestry a challenging one.

The notion of exceptionally large raids first reared its head in the aftermath of the Nazi victories of 1940 when Churchill, knowing of no other way to strike Germany on land, conceived of such operations as a way to express Britain's resolve. This conception of raids, in which concerns over morale and propaganda prevailed over any definition of military objectives, was evident in his memoranda of the period (as well as in the instructions he gave more than a year later when he made Mountbatten Adviser on Combined Operations). A super-raid along Churchill's lines was not, however, affordable, and probably was not feasible when first conceived in 1940. Certainly Keyes never received the support that executing such a concept would have required, a fair indication that the project, though superficially attractive, did not much commend itself to the Service Chiefs as a military proposition. But governments and military bureaucracies never like to close their options prematurely, and it must be recognized that the Chiefs of Staff never definitively ruled the idea out. Like the flotsam and jetsam of so many other half-baked ideas, the super-raiding policy lay bobbing on the backwaters of the bay of doubtful options.

In 1941 the idea of a super-raid, born of the desperation of 1940, broke through the surface in another equally desperate moment of the war. Misled by poor intelligence that underestimated Soviet military power by a wide margin, Britain and America feared that Germany might readily conquer the Soviet Union, which would mean the war could never be won. The possibility of a larger raid was again tossed about as a means to assist the Soviet Union, or at the very least to convey a fighting spirit and so counteract the appearance of drifting into defeat, an impression that was gaining credence in those difficult days for Churchill. By October 1941 the likelihood had increased greatly that Beaverbrook would openly challenge Churchill over the need to help the Soviet Union more effectively, and it was in part to appease Beaverbrook that Churchill placed Mountbatten in charge of Combined Operations, seemingly signalling that raiding pro-grams would receive greater governmental support. Churchill's declining political stock and the Soviet Union's deteriorating military position, occur-ring simultaneously between February and July 1942, had a mutually reinforcing effect, producing still more pressure for a super-raid.

Similar conceptions reappeared at about the same time at a much lower level of government, in the bowels of Mountbatten's COHQ organization, where one of the naval planners, Captain John Hughes-Hallett, who had been involved earlier in the theory of increasing port defences, became interested in seeing the other side of the problem: how a heavily defended port might be taken by an attacking force. Hughes-Hallett was an impatient man, and the foolhardy idea of taking the shortest route to launch an attack at the most obvious place gave him no pause. Indeed, it must have recom-mended itself all the more to a man interested in the theory of attacking ports, for the greater the difficulties encountered, the greater the theoretical insights such a raid might produce. The fact that COHQ now had a powerful chief in Mountbatten, who was promoted once again in meteoric fashion in March 1942 in response to growing pressures from Beaverbrook, seemed to increase Hughes-Hallett's chances of carrying out his experi-ment. Mountbatten had the power and the connections, or so Hughes-Hallett thought, to get almost anything done. This was a gross miscalcula-tion, for Mountbatten was considered to be something of a lightweight by the top military professionals and was not able to secure either a battleship from the Admiralty or a firm commitment to a heavy preliminary bombard-ment from the RAF. But where Hughes-Hallett was undoubtedly right was in thinking that Mountbatten was malleable: susceptible, in his ignorance of Combined Operations, to almost any suggestion that was made to him by his staff. And once his mind was set on a course, Mountbatten trusted to the stars and turned a deaf ear to every warning of impending disaster. He was nothing if not constant in his support of the project.

The idea of a super-raid then jogged along two separate tracks, the political and the experimental, gaining allies here and there, most noticea-bly from Air Marshal Portal who thought a super-raid might accomplish two goals at once: give succour to the Soviet Union and bring on a massive air battle. The latter, he hoped, would waste German fighters and so improve the chances that his bombers would reach their targets in Ger-many without suffering massive casualties. The Chief of the Imperial General Staff, Sir Alan Brooke, hounded by criticism of the Army's failures

— mostly from Churchill — fought furiously to kill off the Prime Minister's more dramatic and foolishly venturesome suggestions for ways of helping the Soviets, even as he was trying to buy time for his army in the Libyan desert to show that it could, eventually, fight. Though his immense military experience would have told him that Dieppe had no prospect of success (had he stopped to question it), it never entered into the play of events, for he had no interest in opposing the least-costly of Churchill's fanciful hopes. Thus by the time the project was presented in May to the Chiefs of Staff Committee, it had acquired a number of tacit supporters and as many ancillary objectives. But a consensus seemed to be emerging that a super-raid was as good a way as any available to demonstrate to the Government's critics that Britain was still capable of offensive action; and it would demonstrate also to the Soviet Union and to the United States that Churchill was sensitive to the travails of a hard-pressed ally. These were unrealistic hopes, but with the war being lost in virtually every theatre, one does not easily reject what hopes there are. Not surprisingly, no one asked Mountbatten hard questions about the admitted shortcomings of the plan, to which he discreetly alluded in his presentation.

As the weeks went by, the reasons for supporting the project became more pressing and new ones were added at almost every turn. There was first of all the impact of Molotov's trip to the West in June (two visits to London with one to Washington sandwiched in between). Everyone assumed that the Soviets wanted an immediate Second Front. That perception, combined with the deteriorating Soviet military position, increased the demand for action and inspired Churchill's would-be successors to intrigue. Most ominously it increased pressures from the Americans to execute *Sledgehammer*, a plan to sacrifice up to six divisions to prove that the Allies were not indifferent. Mountbatten took advantage of the crisis atmosphere to elevate the importance of COHQ — the raiding program in general and its star piece, *Rutter*, in particular — as offering a cheaper way of accomplishing analogous objectives.

This notion of equivalency was not immediately accepted because *Rutter* seemed to be a very pale thing beside *Sledgehammer*. But Churchill's other substitutes for *Sledgehammer* also seemed insufficient in the case of *Gymnast/Torch*; or impossible in the case of *Jupiter*. With the realization that there was no single, really satisfactory, substitute for *Sledgehammer*, the importance of *Rutter* as an adjunct to those other gestures grew in proportion as American pressure for *Sledgehammer* increased.

While there was no prospect that the Service Chiefs would be swept into executing the American proposals for 1942, they might become actually committed to a 1943 cross-Channel attack (*Round-Up*), and in the wake of this prospect there appeared increasing speculation that Mountbatten would be placed in the number two position for such an operation. So recently a captain of destroyers, Mountbatten was now getting used to multiple meteoric promotions and the prospect of more swept him along. There was some reason for these rumours. Co-ordination with the Americans would be the most critical aspect of *Round-Up*, and they admired no ranking officer in Britain quite as much as Mountbatten. Eisenhower repeatedly recommended him as the 'assault chief' to General Marshall. The sole threatening cloud seemed to be the long list of cancellations of COHQ projects, which might damage his reputation as a doer. To counteract its discouraging effect Mountbatten became more determined than ever to carry out his largest project, *Rutter* — though it must be admitted that his own natural stubbornness would probably have carried him in that direction even without the dazzling prospect of becoming Marshall's deputy for the cross-Channel attack.

Meanwhile Molotov, the Soviet foreign minister, got Roosevelt to agree to a press communiqué, which said that complete agreement had been reached on the urgent necessity of establishing a Second Front, a statement that carried with it the suggestion that a Second Front had been promised. This made Churchill still more determined to settle once and for all on a substitute for *Sledgehammer*, without which it would be difficult to extricate Britain from the implications of that communiqué. When Molotov stopped in London on his way back from Washington, Churchill made what seemed to be some progress towards achieving this end. The device he chose was an *aide-mémoire*, which he handed Molotov, and whose operative sentence would form Churchill's constant refrain over the next few weeks: 'We can therefore give no promise' as regards *Sledgehammer*. But in that same document Churchill mentioned other measures, clearly preferred in anticipation that *Sledgehammer* would not be possible. Among these was a very specific statement about raids of increasing size and frequency over the coming months — comforting words that could not be abandoned when *Sledgehammer* was cancelled. Then in the second half of July the Dieppe project assumed still greater importance with the PQ 17 disaster, and the subsequent suspension of the convoys. In the crisis touched off by those events and a surly cable from Stalin, Churchill spoke to Maisky, the Soviet ambassador, repeating the reassuring words about forthcoming raids. PQ 17 also impinged on the forward progress of the Dieppe project by placing Pound in a straitjacket. Because he was under savage attack from the Soviet Union and her allies, he could not afford to block any gesture towards the Soviets. Mountbatten's super-raid was also welcome to Pound as a gesture that might substitute for one or more of the murderous convoys.

Surveying the situation at the end of July, Mountbatten thus had good reason to believe that *Rutter* would be very useful to the Government, even as his admirers believed that it would catapult him into the top command of *Round-Up*. As he told Admiral Ramsay, there were 'pressing political considerations' why the Government would not cancel his raiding program. In this certainty he carried out Dieppe, despite the fact that he did not have either the capital ships or the heavy bombers that could alone have counter-balanced the defenders' firepower and give the attacking force any chance at all. If he had pressed too hard for those items he would have run the risk that the weaknesses of the plan would be brutally exposed, causing it to be abandoned. The fact that Churchill had earlier cancelled other amphibious frontal assaults, *Imperator* and *Sledgehammer*, and that he had twice been inclined to cancel *Rutter* as well, put Mountbatten on his guard and made him prefer to go ahead without specific authorization when it became clear that this could not be easily obtained. It's this unwillingness to run the risk of cancellation, even more than his determination to go forward without formal authorization, that betrays the man and his ambition, revealing behind the seemingly selfless devotion to the interests of his superiors his personal commitment to *Rutter/Jubilee* as serving his own interests. One of his senior staff officers, Robert Henriques, later spoke of Mountbatten's 'vast ambition that was not reprehensible, because it exactly coincided with public interest.' It would have been nice had it been so, for then Mountbatten could have got support and secured authorization from the Chiefs of Staff. But such an identity of interests was wanting, and rather than risk exposing the defects in his proposals, he decided to go ahead without additional support and, worse still, seemed not to care. It would be hard to imagine any other senior commander taking such risks without the cover of orders and formal authorization. The stakes were high. Mountbatten later admitted: 'If it would have been a success they would have said I was very clever.' But he was taking more than the usual gamble that military commanders usually accept, for he did not have the protection of orders. From that miscalculation flowed inevitably the battle he waged, on and off, for the rest of his life to try to establish that the Chiefs of Staff had indeed authorized his action, though he never could produce the least scrap of evidence that they had done so. Even the mere suggestion in public of a date for the approval would have introduced elements that could not be squared with the record. To have given a date would have identified the individuals who would have been privy to it, and as none of the principals were, he was forced to defend his position with a singular handicap. He left it to others to advance a date for the decision. The result was a surfeit of dates.[1]

We began this study with Churchill's questions in 1950 and the difficulty he had in trying to write a history of the Dieppe raid. The largest and most difficult of Churchill's questions concerned how the decision was reached. His puzzlement bears requoting: 'Surely the decision could not have been taken without the Chiefs of Staff being informed. If so, why did they not bring it to my attention, observing I did not leave England till July 30 or 31? ... If the decision was taken after I left the country , was the Defence Committee or the War Cabinet informed? How did this all go?' Or, as he phrased it elsewhere: 'At what stage was this matter cut off from the supreme war direction [meaning the Chiefs of Staff and the War Cabinet], or how and when was it put up to them?'

The first question we can answer is why the Chiefs of Staff had not notified him of the decision to remount: they never formally approved the decision and the obligation to notify the Prime Minister never arose, technically speaking, either before or after he left London for Cairo and Moscow in July. I came to this conclusion tentatively some six years ago but let myself be talked into disbelieving it whenever I floated it past any group of military historians, who invariably found it incredible. They all insisted that there was no government and no committee more insistent on following proper procedures than the British Government and the Chiefs of Staff Committee. This was, as Churchill noted, 'a major decision of policy.' Elsewhere he wrote: 'There is no doubt Mountbatten pressed most strongly for it,' but quickly added, 'I expect you will find that the War Cabinet gave their assent in my absence.' And again, 'I cannot believe he was allowed to do this without higher authority becoming responsible.' Of the half-dozen official studies that deal with Dieppe, representing the collective efforts of some forty official historians and researchers, only one, Stephen Roskill's, even intimates that there might have been no decision to mount the operation by the Chiefs of Staff.

The absence of a formal decision makes comprehensible what so puzzled Wildman-Lushington, Mountbatten's former chief of staff, in 1950 when he wrote: 'I do not understand . . . why the search through the Cabinet files has failed to reveal the record of the decision to remount.' The 1950 comment of Churchill's former representative on the Chiefs of Staff Committee, Lord Ismay, now assumes greater significance: '. . . it was not one of our most creditable ventures, because the underlying object was never sufficiently clearly defined nor, so far as I can remember was the chain of responsibility.' Such a chain is established through the formalities of the decision-making process. If, as now seems certain, Mountbatten was acting without authorization, we can also explain many of the aspects of the raid that have always looked incriminating to those who, like the writer Anthony Cave Brown, have nursed dark suspicions. They have been particularly troubled by the fact that there was no cover plan, that the Intelligence Services did not render the assistance they should have given this operation. But this failure can be explained, most easily, by their not having been informed by Mountbatten, who was keeping the secret of the actual decision even from Major General Haydon, his own deputy. as well as from Wildman-Lushington, his own chief of staff.[2]

The lack of a formal decision also explains why there is such disagreement in the official histories about when the supposed approval was given. No doubt each team of historians, working under the Cabinet Historical Office, tried to get a straight answer from Mountbatten or the surviving

Chiefs, but it is evident that an authoritative answer, which succeeding historians could all have used, was never forthcoming. All these heroes of the war waffled about this key question and in consequence none of the official histories can document, in a way that will withstand close scrutiny, the date when authorization was given.

At the same time no one wanted to say the raid was unauthorized. Even Hughes-Hallett, who seems to have divined the truth, was very careful. He always repeated Mountbatten's story that the raid had been fully authorized by the Chiefs of Staff. He claimed to be puzzled himself about the complete absence of any record of approval. Writing to the official Canadian military historian, C.P. Stacey, in 1952, Hughes-Hallett declared: 'I have no doubt that the whole plan must have been gone through yet again [by COHQ and the Service Chiefs] some time in July or early August, when "Jubilee" was decided on, but I was not present and do not know exactly what happened.' So Hughes-Hallett claimed not to know whether the decision was taken in July or August! But as we have seen, he was doing all the co-ordinating paperwork for *Jubilee*, as both Mountbatten's chief of staff and his deputy, Wildman-Lushington and Haydon respectively, had been intentionally kept in the dark about the decision until one or both discovered the truth, quite by accident, just before the boarding of the ships for Dieppe. Their exclusion meant that if Hughes-Hallett did not prepare the ground for the Chiefs of Staff's review and approval, this must never have been done. Reviews are usually carried out in anticipation of a formal request for authorization, and so the absence of one implies the absence of the other. Hughes-Hallett, despite his protestations of ignorance to Stacey, must have perceived the truth at some point, for it is certainly there in his 1950 article, already quoted (when he admitted COHQ would drive on unless stopped). Ismay too must have suspected the truth, but he too never quite came out and admitted it. The same can be said of Brooke, but save for telling Pownall in 1943 to watch Mountbatten closely, because he was inclined to act without authorization, Brooke let nary a hint emerge.[3]

If the decision was unauthorized — why, one may ask, did not the other Chiefs, who resented Mountbatten's elevation so much, not use the disaster to engineer his downfall? There was first of all the fact that Mountbatten had powerful protectors, not the least of whom was Churchill, and in the background the Royal Family. There was the appearance at COHQ of George VI for a post-Dieppe analysis, then the Buckingham Palace Gala for the film *In Which We Serve*, then the letter of 26 December from the King to Mountbatten taking side with the Chief of Combined Operations against his critics. Second, reprimand was made difficult by the fact that while the Chiefs had not formally given authorization, they had come pretty close to giving it, and any attempt to deny that would have led to the embarrassing question: Didn't the Chiefs know where all those planes, ships, and loaded landing-craft were going? (Mountbatten had only negligible forces assigned directly to his control.) The crucial reason for the subsequent silence of the Chiefs, however, was the fact that Mountbatten had told McNaughton that the operation had been authorized. Who, after the disaster, was prepared to tell the Canadians that one of the Chiefs of Staff had misled Dominion authorities and gone ahead without authority, committing some British but many more Canadian troops to a hazardous, not to say doomed, operation? What would that do to the relations in wartime between the dominions and Great Britain? It was unthinkable that the truth should be let out, whatever the Chiefs might think of Mountbatten.

What seems most reprehensible to us would probably not have much shocked Mountbatten's superiors, that among his motives for going ahead were some that were unedifying. The evidence is unmistakable that Mountbatten was seeking to enter the very first rank of Allied commanders and would let nothing stand in his way. But for that too he was not entirely responsible. He was very much the creature of Winston Churchill and all his preposterous, head-turning promotions, which gave Mountbatten a lot of responsibility but not much real authority. No amount of prime-ministerial holy oil could make up for his lack of experience and the consequent disinclination of the Chiefs of Staff to take him seriously. Consequently, in negotiating for contributions from the three Services to the combined force gathered for the attack he was at a marked disadvantage. Those who pushed for Mountbatten to take over Combined Operations — Churchill in the first instance, but behind him Beaverbrook — must, on that account, bear a good deal of the blame for the Dieppe disaster. Mountbatten was the wrong man at the wrong time, in the wrong place, taking the easy route of least resistance just when he should have been most alert to the dangers. That must be our principal conclusion. Again, words that Lord Lovat used to describe Mountbatten's role in Dieppe seem particularly apt: '. . . it would have taken a very strong man [to resist the pressures for action] and he wasn't.'

It was easier for Mountbatten to focus on how badly others wanted this operation, while ignoring opportunities to cancel — ignoring even Churchill's expressed belief that it should be cancelled. It was not Mountbatten's greatest moment. But the unflattering truth, where it must be so, is a form of respect as well (no doubt unpleasing to his admirers, but a form of respect nonetheless). Only if one believed Mountbatten had no redeeming qualities could one possibly wish to see the story of Dieppe suppressed. In fact one cannot spend time reading his correspondence without admitting that he was a man of great decency and could command unswerving loyalty. He did not bear grudges and could not understand that some bore them against him. Beaverbrook's hostility after 1942 — his charge that Mountbatten had deliberately sent Beaverbrook's beloved compatriots to a slaughter out of pique — bothered him very much. The long-running dispute they had repeatedly showed that, given the chance, Mountbatten always wanted to patch up and make friends, even after years of most unfair treatment in Beaverbrook's press. Underneath all Mountbatten's egotism and his thoughtlessness there was, one senses, a man of conscience, seeking at one and the same time to absolve himself of his responsibility for having ordered Dieppe without authorization, and to believe that he had not made a mistake in doing so.

This effort reflected a curious lack of self-esteem in one so notably vain. He seems not to have believed that judgement on what he had done could be balanced. He sorrowfully complained: 'We have to have a villain for the piece . . . ,' and thought that he had been chosen. There is no need, and never was one, to have a villain. *Requiescat in pace.*[4]

Nevertheless there were times when his manipulation of the truth boils the blood of even the most dispassionate historian. The way Mountbatten expressed his frustration in 1978 — just a year before his tragic death, after thirty-five years of effort to shape public perceptions — is surely one of these. The way he put it to Terence Macartney-Filgate, the CBC producer of still one more documentary on Dieppe, was that '. . . they [the Canadians] go around apologetically saying we were let down . . . it's a self-inflicted wound. . . . [I do not understand] Why they wish to go on revelling in the massacres with their martyrism. . . . They like to be told it was a bloody sell down, they were sold to the Germans, they were murdered. I don't know what the Canadians want. . . . They [just] want to revel in their misery.' It was an outrageous statement and says more about his bad conscience than it does about Canadian national character. At the same time one cannot ignore how much he wanted to win Canadian audiences to his side, long after his historical greatness on a larger stage had been conceded even by his enemies. He genuinely wanted Canadians to be proud of the way they had fought — of what, by his lights, was their invaluable contribution to Normandy. To the same interviewer in 1978, Lord Louis pleaded: 'Now [Mr Filgate] . . . you're the producer of this new film. I hope to God that you will succeed where most of your countrymen have failed, to try and explain to the Canadians that they should be proud of Dieppe. . . . Try and make them proud, try and make them feel that if they died, they died gloriously and those who came back and suffered as prisoners of war, suffered not in vain. If you can do that, you'll have done a great thing. . . . I don't know if it's too much to hope. It certainly hasn't worked up to now. I hope it will work this time in your film.' Needless to say it did not. Even here, however, Mountbatten's motives may not have been unalloyed. If Canadians, who had paid the highest price for his usurpation of authority, accepted Dieppe, criticism from other sources would become virtually irrelevant. In this wish Mountbatten showed traces of that boyish immaturity that characterized so many of his actions as Chief of Combined Operations, as though one could much add or subtract from the disaster by the way it was presented.[5]

Mountbatten's efforts, while reassuring to some Canadians, had already angered others. In 1973, when he travelled to Toronto to address Dieppe veterans, Mountbatten certainly knew what he was up against, telling his secretary, John Barratt, that he was 'widely blamed in Canada for having murdered the Canadians at Dieppe'. At the banquet table an astonished Barratt discovered that this was indeed the case, when his neighbour expressed his view that Mountbatten was completely responsible for the disaster down to the minutest detail. Mountbatten's long speech dealt in the most superficial manner with a number of controversial issues regarding Dieppe. It was later reprinted in the authoritative and prestigious *Royal United Services Institute Journal* and led C.P. Stacey to open a somewhat acrimonious correspondence. He suggested that 'Lord Mountbatten's memory seems to have deceived him on one or two points.' Remarking that in places his account was 'strikingly at variance with the record' and in others 'without foundation', Stacey particularly objected to Mountbatten's attempt to cast blame for the plan's defects on Canadian shoulders.[6]

Still more serious was Mountbatten's failure to understand that what Canadians wanted was what every mourner faced with unexpected tragedy wants: as much of the truth as possible, without which the conscience of the living can scarcely find peace. He was wrong in thinking that this had anything to do with whether the soldiers had perished in a winning battle or a losing one. Canadians wanted to know why that objective had been picked, why there had been so little support, and who was responsible for the decision to go forward. To paraphrase Voltaire's dictum, Truth is that form of respect we owe to the dead; and that, sadly, is the one thing Mountbatten could not give. It would have meant, or he thought it would have meant, giving up his place in history. As one of his most sympathetic unofficial biographers, Richard Hough, recounted:

> One of the strongest reasons that Mountbatten used for not permitting an authorized biography to be written in his lifetime was that he believed he had never made a single mistake in his life. 'It is a curious thing, but a fact, that I have been right in everything I have done and said in my life,' Mountbatten said many times. 'No one would believe a biographer who made this claim while I was still alive because readers would conclude that I had caused it to be written, that I was leaning over the author's shoulder. . . . Dieppe was a threat to this clean record.'[7]

Perhaps others might accept that Mountbatten had been right all his life. Canadians could not. If he could only have brought himself to admit the folly of it all, he would have had a much less hostile Canadian audience. But it is likely that when Canadians feel confident that they have a fairly clear picture of what went wrong at the decision-making level — and why — the Dieppe controversy, now nearly fifty years old, will subside and with it resentment of Mountbatten, so that more attention can be paid to his sterling qualities: his cheerful optimism, his abhorrence of intentional hurt or slight, his belief that men of good will can always come to agreement, despite race and creed, qualities particularly dear to Canadians.

Decent respect for the truth also requires that Mountbatten's failings be placed in their larger context. When all the forces behind the operation are rightly assessed — from Churchill, through Brooke, Pound, and Portal, down to that implacable experimenter Hughes-Hallett — one cannot help recall Lord Lovat's description of Mountbatten, '. . . rather like a cork on a wave . . . everyone pushing him on.'

Though it is reasonably certain that on many details Mountbatten came very close to prevarication when Churchill was writing his memoirs, forcing the old man to accept as facts versions of events that no one, other than Mountbatten, ever claimed to remember, this does not necessarily mean that his was the more inaccurate version of events. On the larger issues virtually everything Mountbatten said about the forces behind Dieppe rings very true. True it certainly was, as Mountbatten wrote to Ismay, that '. . . what COHQ was really there for was to carry out his [Churchill's] instructions, given as long ago as October 1941 to prepare for the re-invasion of the Continent.' Mountbatten's statement that the Prime Minister 'enquired how soon I could organize another raid on this scale, as he was extremely anxious to have an operation of this nature as soon as it could be mounted,' also sounds absolutely authentic.[8]

Certainly Churchill's efforts to exculpate himself on the ground that he was out of the country when the decision was taken do not wash very well. 'I am sure', he wrote in 1950, 'I should have been most worried. . . . I think I had already started for Cairo and Moscow when the decision to renew the operation was taken.' The plain fact is that Churchill was talking to Stalin about Dieppe on 12 August, before even taking the trouble to cable London to see if the operation was really on. He then asked about the 'renewal', which clearly indicates he was *au courant* with the notion to stage essentially the same operation as *Rutter*, despite its cancellation and despite the fact that 10,000 servicemen in Britain with knowledge of the original plan had been dispersed. Whatever knowledge he had of the operation when he talked to Stalin on 12 August was information acquired before he left, since his first cable to London for additional information came later. In short, it is hard to reach any other conclusion save that he knew of the intention to remount at a time when he could have asked tough questions about the idea, or even stopped it, had he wanted to do so. That he did not, that he was in a complete fog about what had or had not been decided, is the most eloquent testimony we have of the effects of months of intense strain on Churchill. Considering that he was going to Moscow to deal with the problem of the *aide-mémoire*, this sloppiness in preparation is remarkable. Clearly he was losing control of the flow of events. The Japanese romp through the Empire, the non-confidence motion, the disaster of PQ 17, the problem of convoy cancellation, the restlessness of his opponents, and the need to bring the Americans to a decision about grand strategy had all taken their toll — though these stresses mitigate his responsibility very little, if at all.[9]

But blame cannot be laid entirely on Churchill's shoulders. He counted on those who were formally responsible for advising him to give him competent advice. If anyone was planning to remount Dieppe, the Prime Minister surely was entitled to see it on the Chiefs of Staff agenda and to hear comments from them as well as from Mountbatten. He had given his staff the most stringent instructions to that effect (for good reason, one might add). Churchill had to try to juggle an enormous number of issues, and he could hardly be expected to keep track of their procedural status as well as their policy implications. He worked by rules and he expected those who worked under him to work by those he gave. Churchill could not have anticipated that Mountbatten would try to carry out a major military operation without authorization and that the other Chiefs would connive or at least acquiesce. If nothing else, the rivalry that existed between Mountbatten and his infinitely senior colleagues should have guaranteed that what happened was impossible. The Chiefs failed the Prime Minister. But in 1950 Churchill did not dare say that.

Churchill, however, was certainly aware that the decision-making process had broken down. One suspects that as early as December 1942 he was conscious of this possibility when he minuted to Ismay that it was important to find out how the decision was reached. Eight years later he returned to that question, saying to Ismay that what he would tell the world would be a matter for 'subsequent consideration', but 'we must know ourselves exactly what the facts were.' Mountbatten threw an effective roadblock into these proceedings with his assertions about having received approval from the Chiefs of Staff and from the Prime Minister. Once Mountbatten took this stand, there were only two possible choices before Churchill: accept Mountbatten's version or open a possibly scandalous dispute with grave consequences for Commonwealth relations.

Placing the blame would have required Churchill to reach out beyond the small circle of decision-makers, for responsibility also extends very significantly to Britain's allies, most of all the Soviet Union, and to a lesser degree the United States. While it is true that Roosevelt's government did everything it humanly could do to try to help Churchill politically, it is also true that American news commentators were irresponsible in their ceaseless criticism of the British military machine and of Churchill's direction. This criticism played into the hands of his political rivals and increased the pressures working on Churchill to produce quickly, even if at high cost, some demonstration of British offensive spirit. (The bitter irony of it all was that the bold frontal assault would not be undertaken by British troops, because Crerar, with McNaughton's support, had stepped forward and demanded very insistently for an opportunity to strike at the Nazis.) By early June there were three different proposals for such an offensive (*Sledgehammer*, *Imperator*, and *Rutter*). No doubt the Americans thought that if the result of one of these cross-Channel offensives was certain to be a disaster, Churchill's government would veto it. Churchill indeed found the strength to veto the two larger ones, but he did not with the third, and in the absence of a veto Mountbatten pushed forward. Thus it was that the Roosevelt administration, by gratuitously contributing to Churchill's woes, contributed also to the gathering momentum for the super-raid.

Despite the considerable American role, it seems hard not to assign primary responsibility to the Soviets, who pressed their ally as hard as they could, even after they knew that the decision had been made against *Sledgehammer*. The conclusion reached by Stacey, who found 'no evidence that the Russian situation was actually a large direct factor in the decision to revive the Dieppe scheme' seems particularly off the mark.[10]

The list of responsible parties cannot unfortunately exclude Canadian officials. McNaughton, the Canadian commander, knew that Montgomery recommended cancellation and that Roberts, the Canadian ground-force commander for Dieppe, had his doubts. He also knew that the Naval Force Commander, Admiral Baillie-Grohman, had mysteriously dropped out of the scene, to be replaced by a much junior and much less-experienced officer. The fact that McNaughton never received the least scrap of paper registering the approval of *Jubilee* or its assignment to Canadian troops was, he certainly knew, highly irregular. By 9 August, when he informed the RCAF Chief in England, Air Marshal Edwards, of the intention to remount *Rutter*, he knew that the higher levels of command were keeping their distance from the operation. But even without all these tell-tale signs, any alert observer in London in the summer of 1942 could easily have seen that there were great pressures building on the British Government to act, regardless of cost and object. At one of the Second Front Now meetings in Trafalgar Square early in April 1942, a speaker in Home Guard uniform tried to quiet down the Second Front agitation by asking whether it was right for the uninformed public to tell the Government and the Imperial General Staff what operations they should be undertaking. The crowd roared 'YES' until it reverberated across the square and down to Whitehall. Though the military would be blamed when Dieppe went wrong, it was this politically explosive intrusion of public opinion that, in the final analysis, made necessary that disastrous gesture. Portal, Pound, and Brooke should have ignored it and never let it enter their calculations, but that was easier said than done. Harold Nicolson noted in his diary on 7 August: 'Pug [Ismay] is very bitter about those who make Second Front capital for themselves. He fears that a weaker man than Winston might surrender to the popular clamour.' Ismay was undoubtedly thinking most of all about

*Sledgehammer*, but the quote could just as easily apply to Dieppe. There is no reason why McNaughton could not have recognized the problem as well, particularly as he had been told by Mountbatten that the War Cabinet had approved the launching of a major raid in response to Stalin's cable — a clear indication that fear of alienating the pro-Soviet lobby and the Second Front movement had been determinant.[11]

One did not even have to be in Churchill's inner circle to recognize the danger. The newspaper accounts of any reasonably acute reporter should have served as warning. The degree of acuity shown by Mollie Panter-Downs in *The New Yorker's* 'Letter from England' ought to have been within the range of the Canadian High Command in London. On 24 May she reported in that magazine: 'From the tone of private conversations and public utterances at mass meetings, it appears that the British people can't or won't recognize the existence of any substitute for a genuine, slap-up opening of a land offensive on the Continent. Although stern things have been said in the House of Commons about uninformed, emotional *vox populi* clamor, the same kind of clamor has demonstrated its power before now in this war by throwing Chamberlain out and bringing Churchill and Cripps in.' The same observer anxiously reported on 20 June that there was a lot of irresponsible thinking that tended to assume that 'a Continental invasion was as easy as a jaunt as a prewar cheap-day trip to Dieppe.' This ought to be compared with Hughes-Hallett's comment, after he was told that he should include one division-size target in drawing up possible projects: 'Right, let's take the old peace-time route — Newhaven to Dieppe and back.' Indeed, virtually every relevant travel guide since the beginning of the century started with the observation that the quickest and most convenient route to France was the Newhaven-Dieppe ferry. In his memoirs, Goronwy Rees tells the story of an officer left out of the Dieppe project, who sat down disconsolately in his office and tried to figure what the Canadians would be doing. Within a week he had figured out, entirely unaided, the time, place, and necessary conditions in considerable detail — so much so that he had to be confined to his quarters for knowing too much. That Canadian officers in London did not raise any difficult questions about a frontal attack at the most obvious point on the opposing coast certainly shows a great lack of judgement — or, more likely, that the pressure to take action overcame common sense.[12]

It is also sadly true that if anyone could have stopped the Dieppe raid it was the Canadian commander, General McNaughton. The Dieppe raid was remounted because there were no other plans for which available troops had been prepared. If the Canadians had said 'No!' after the first cancellation, there would have been no Dieppe raid in 1942.

Was it in any other sense avoidable? The plethora of causes would tend to suggest that it was not, but it must be stressed that not all the contributing factors were irresistible. Mountbatten's colleagues, we have seen, did not really want super-raids, and had the concept not been imposed on them they would never have worked it into their plans. By July the Americans were no longer pressing for large raids. That left the Soviets, but one could easily conceive of Churchill and the Chiefs, had there been no Second Front demonstrations, telling the Russians that even the super-raids were impossible. What really was unarguable was the role of British public opinion in wartime, the fact that the Government continued to be accountable to Parliament, and that by the summer of 1942 the Government was in a very weak position, vulnerable to the combined effect of restless public opinion and a Soviet propaganda offensive, seconded to a lesser degree by the United States. Harold Nicolson succinctly summarized the situation in his diary at the end of July: 'The Government are in a difficult position. If they create a Second Front as a forlorn hope, we shall have another Dunkirk. If they do not do so, they will be accused of letting down the Russians. But if they explain why they cannot do so, people will feel that there is no chance of our beginning to fight this war before 1945.' There was some danger that the Government might become unravelled under this stress. In the worst of times not every decision is a wise one. But it is hard to see how, after so many years of pre-war rot, both in the body politic and in the military hierarchy, the first years of the war could have been anything but an ordeal for whatever government was in place, or how any other one might have coped better with all the pressures such weakness generated.[13]

In retrospect, Britain's military Chiefs — Brooke, Pound, and Portal — look pretty bad in what they did and and did not do about the Dieppe raid. But such a portrait excludes an important element. In 1942 Britain was losing the war in virtually every theatre. In such circumstances she had to make compromises at ever turn, and compromises that affect the lives of soldiers never look good in hindsight. Between putting too many conditions and not putting enough, there must be a middle path. Clearly, Dieppe did not represent the right balance. The combined effect of the intrusion of untutored opinion and the assignment of an insufficiently trained, indeed unqualified, officer to supervise the difficult compromises that had to be made was a formula for disaster. Well-meaning civilians in the relative comforts of their living-rooms, drawing up Second Front Now placards, probably could not guess how great their impact might be — on this occasion not for the better. It is sometimes said that war is too important a matter to leave to the professionals. Dieppe shows the opposite. The compromises in the planning made under Mountbatten's supervision do not argue well for the ability of amateurs to make the hard decisions, or for public opinion to influence them. Montgomery put it best, in commenting afterwards in what went wrong with the planning of Dieppe: 'Compromise on this, compromise on the bombing, compromise on everything. It's no good!'[14]

But I do not think the men in uniform were misled. They knew that the war was not going well, and that bad compromises were being made. Even knowing this, they did not want to sit on the sidelines until the perfect moment for battle occurred. Later, when Churchill's advisers were drawing lessons from Dieppe and concluding that many more stringent conditions had to be met before trying anything like that again, Churchill minuted succintly that '"Nothing avails but perfection" may be spelt shorter; "paralysis".' The Canadian troops in Britain had had enough of that. The last word should be given to one of those Canadians, Lt.-Col. Charles Merritt, whose valour at Dieppe won him the Victoria Cross, and who captured the spirit of sacrifice that was so cruelly tested there: 'We were very glad to go, we were delighted. We were up against a very difficult situation and we didn't win, but to hell with this business of saying the generals done us dirt.'[15]

# Why Governments Do What They Should Not Do

Dieppe is a classic example of military failure — in decision-making, in planning, and in execution — that has its roots in an intricate network of motives that almost defies analysis by the historian or political scientist. Though one might sympathize with the decision-makers, who by and large were capable and highly motivated public servants working under difficult circumstances, the fact that they allowed the raid to take place, when everything ruled against its success, casts them in the role of incompetents at worst, or at best as weak-willed servants unable to oppose the forces that beset them. Their culpability is three- or four-fold. First they ignored the experts who pointed out that the risks were inordinately high with large-scale raids and were unlikely to be counterbalanced by any military objectives that might be attained. Second, they were culpable for ignoring signs that in *Jubilee* the decision-making process was moving irregularly; that competent intelligence authorities were not being consulted; that the appropriate headquarters, such as that of Home Forces, were not being consulted; and that the necessary approvals were not being secured. That the decision-making function of government was becoming corrupt should have been evident to both British and Canadian authorities. Third, those who had an opportunity to press for the strengthening of the attacking force instead accepted the weakening of the plan. A fourth brand of culpability, though this is more debatable, was in failing to stop the operation when all could see so much going wrong with it. Certainly Churchill could have cancelled it (and twice came very close to doing so). McNaughton could have done so by denying Canadian participation. Any of the three Service Chiefs in the normal exercise of their responsibilities could have withheld approval, or at least expressed disapproval of the plan; or any one could have insisted on alterations, particularly in the matter of additional air and naval force support. None did so. That so many distinguished men — some, like Brooke and Portal, at the peak of their careers — should not only have allowed Dieppe to go forward but have permitted crucial weaknesses in planning and support is one of the most striking features of the disaster. If Churchill had chosen in December 1942 to pursue relentlessly his first inquiries into the enigmas that surrounded Dieppe, a fascinating story would have emerged and we would not be left with trying to scrape the record clean of the encrustation of nearly fifty years of *ex-post-facto* accounts, explanations, and justifications; but in 1942 Mountbatten, the thinly disguised hero of Noël Coward's classic film of heroism at sea, was still seen as useful to Britain and was powerfully protected. In 1950, when Churchill was writing his memoirs, there was little incentive to question any of the participants too rigorously, particularly as they had all entered into the Pantheon of victors (and Pound was not alive to speak). By then the passage of years, as well as ingrained British characteristics of reticence, fair play, and professional loyalty, neutralized any attempt at revealing incompetence or finding scapegoats. It is not surprising, therefore, that Mountbatten's version of the raid was generally accepted — most importantly by Churchill himself.

Implicit within the question of how so many eminent military figures had simultaneously failed is a much more worrisome one; for if we exclude the possibility that such a multiplicity of failures was a coincidence, then we would have to conclude that something had gone wrong with the process itself, with the structures established for taking decisions. As we have noted, Ismay privately admitted that this was the case: '. . . it was not one of our most creditable ventures because the underlying object was never sufficiently clearly defined nor, so far as I can remember, was the chain of responsibility. I do not, in fact, believe we deserved success.' Such a conclusion was unthinkable to most postwar observers, for the operating procedures used by Britain's war government in managing global conflict (already well established in August 1942) were based on the best precedents of the First World War and had been carefully refined since 1939. They were widely regarded at the time, and since, as a model of the best in decision-making structures and were widely copied throughout the English-speaking world, so much so that even today they can be found imbedded in the *modus operandi* of most of Britain's wartime allies. It was the inherent unlikeliness of this structure's being fundamentally flawed that made so many contemporary observers and later historians willing to accept Mountbatten's summary justification for Dieppe. And yet the possibility implied in the multiple failures — that governments, even the best-organized, can suffer a calamitous breakdown — should not have been unthinkable. No one who has studied for any length of time the formulation of public policy should be surprised. From time to time governments do what they know, or should know, they ought not to do. Too often they can take decisions that defy all attempts at rational explanation. We can see why Churchill wanted answers. 'We must know ourselves how it came to pass,' he insisted in 1942. Or in his most pregnant formulation, 'How was this cut away from the higher direction of the war?' So fundamental are these implied and stated questions, which clearly go beyond the matter of persons and reach into the sphere of institutions, that we are obliged to look at them directly.

Such questions about process and procedure relate in important ways much more to political science than to individual responsibility (the traditional subject of diplomatic history). Explaining the unexplainable in the formulation of public policy and proposing preventive measures is the concern of political scientists, whose craft has been practised since ancient times, and consists in trying to prescribe correctives for the human foibles of policy-makers. Admittedly confidence in such restraints, and in the science that purports to study them, has eroded very markedly in our own time. The career of one of the foremost exponents of rational decision-making procedures in foreign policy may serve as a barometer. In his 1960 history of the Congress of Vienna, *A World Restored*, Henry Kissinger extolled the calculating brilliance of the principal diplomats there, but a few years in government service left him disillusioned. In his 1979 memoirs he inveighed against those outside observers of the policy-making process who 'assume that people sat around the table in a seminar type discussion, having all the facts. . . .' That, he brusquely told his readers, is 'rarely the case. Usually decisions are made in a very brief time with enormous pressure and uncertain knowledge.' It is a major concern of contemporary political science to discover why institutions and decision-making procedures so often go awry.[1]

That some of the best decision-making procedures failed in the Dieppe affair make it a particularly interesting case for political scientists, for despite the disappearance of some evidence and the transparent *ex-post-facto* attempts at rationalization, it is now a remarkably well-documented case of a government doing what it knows it should not be doing. Political scientists have something to sink their teeth into here. Historians also have an interest in trying to see what political science can tell us about such an event, for the best history has always been that which moves beyond description to an analysis of the essential. We will start by considering what existing political-science analysis can tell us about the Dieppe decision. It will require that we look again at the facts, though from a somewhat different viewpoint.

BUREAUCRATIC AND ORGANIZATIONAL MODELS OF DECISION-MAKING

Two of the most highly regarded analytical frameworks, thought by some to have been definitive when first produced, are those suggested by Graham Allison in his pioneering study of the Cuban missile crisis, *Essence of Decision* (1971). At first glance they would seem to offer a promising basis for the analysis of a seemingly irrational decision like Dieppe, for Allison rejects the rational decision model as a practical norm; he does not believe that policy-makers try to choose the most nearly ideal policy to discharge their formal obligations because they have so many other things to worry about. Judging decisions in terms of the policy-makers' formal responsibilities leaves the impression of some irrational process at work. Seemingly irrational decisions, he implies, might just as easily emerge from a normally operating bureaucracy. So far so good.[2]

But Allison's explanations for irrational decision-making offer relatively little help in analysing the Dieppe affair. A cardinal tenet of his work (underpinning what he calls the organizational model of decision-making) is his belief that fragmentary intelligence is often behind the poor choice of objectives and strategies. Though many have tried to make out that there was a major intelligence failure at Dieppe, Professor Hinsley has shown that it is hard to make much of a case with regard to Dieppe. Most of the major German gun positions and firing-points were known, and those that were not known from aerial reconnaissance could have been guessed at easily enough. It was clear from Hughes-Hallett's pre-departure remarks and notes that he was aware that the Germans were in a very strong position. Allison's second major analytical tool is his notion, derived from Max Weber, that a determined bureaucratic unit can either impose its will on the decision-making process or force other bureaucratic units to negotiate with it and produce a compromise; but in either case the outcome reflects bureaucratic politics more than dispassionate analysis of the problems facing a government. While this seems at first glance a good way of describing the drive and determination of some to carry out Dieppe, the bureaucratic unit that should have played the stellar role was COHQ; but in fact almost the entire top staff of COHQ was kept in the dark about the decision to remount. Hughes-Hallett and Mountbatten were determined, all right, but they were in league only with themselves.[3]

Nor does it seem that Dieppe was the outcome of bureaucratic bargaining, first of all because the Chiefs never formally accepted Mountbatten's proposal to revive the cancelled operation, as would be natural if it were the outcome of bargaining, but more importantly because neither Mountbatten, nor even less Hughes-Hallett, ever negotiated with the Chiefs because they were not prepared to risk cancellation, a hazard they certainly would have incurred in any serious negotiation with air and naval authorities over how to improve the chances for Dieppe. Unwilling to take this chance, they failed to make the sort of formal alliances that might have increased their bargaining power. Without formal allies, and without making any serious attempt to negotiate better support, Hughes-Hallett, a captain of destroyers, and Mountbatten, his boss, whom the Service Chiefs continued to regard as little more than a substantive captain of destroyers, resembled rather more Lovat's description of a cork pushed along by the waves than the purposeful negotiators of Allison's model. If the Service Chiefs acquiesced, it was for reasons of their own, having little or nothing to do with politics as 'the mechanism of choice', to use Allison's term for the negotiating process.

## SATISFICING

Somewhat different explanations for seemingly irrational decisions are offered by a number of recent scholars relying on the concept of satisficing — making a minimum effort in areas of secondary importance (i.e. muddling through). They point out that policy-makers are frequently overburdened, and in order to cope must sort out the items awaiting their decision according to their seeming importance. The decision-maker may be content with relying on a 'drastically simplified model of the buzzing, blooming confusion that constitutes the real world'. Some decisions are therefore not carefully examined because energy is reserved for the more important decisions. This reflects the prevailing consensus among political scientists that the most common explanation for faulty decision-making concerns defective information-processing, or — to use their parlance — there is almost always a failure in cognition.[4]

Satisficing theory and the many variants that have been produced may offer good explanations for the confusion, or lack of coherence, involved in some decisions. And superficially they would seem to fit the planning for Dieppe, in which objectives and resources allocated never seemed to balance. During the first eight months of 1942, when the war seemed about to be lost, the environment certainly was conducive to slipshod decision-making. But it was not by an oversight or a major intelligence failure that Dieppe became a disaster. Had the Chiefs thought it was a minor or insignificant affair they would not have resisted Mountbatten's efforts to have it approved. Resistance reflected the conviction not that it was a minor or unimportant project but rather a worrisome and potentially dangerous one.

Nor could it be said that the military planners ever regarded the largest raid to date as anything but a grave, important, and difficult question. It seems particularly doubtful that Churchill considered Dieppe a minor matter. Canadian troops were going to be employed and Churchill was very much aware that Britain was being accused of using Dominion troops for dirty work. As he explained to Auchinleck, 'for a long time I have dreaded troubles with the Australians and with world opinion, of appearing to wage all our battles in the Middle East with Dominion troops alone.' He knew it was important to avoid giving this impression as being harmful to the Commonwealth [he would have said Empire]. It was in part because of this that Churchill insisted that Home Forces be consulted about the plans. The operation was also critical from other perspectives. Mountbatten, Churchill, and the Chiefs were all aware that they were terribly short of Tank Landing Ships and that Dieppe might be expensive in this *matériel*. Finally, everyone knew that Churchill's political stock was now so low that any further disasters were likely to have grave implications. Churchill's meeting of 30 June with Brooke and Mountbatten, in which the Prime Minister made clear he did not want and could scarcely afford another disaster, made this abundantly clear. But what must lead to a rejection of satisficing theory, insofar as it implies that the question of large-scale raids might have been insufficiently studied, is that a perusal of the Chiefs of Staff records shows that the Joint Planners, as early as 1940, began to study and restudy the question of large-scale raids with great care. The problems were diligently canvassed and the unfavourable prospects were carefully noted — the consequences of failure were regarded as grave. Their reports show that, given a choice, they would never have approved a super-raid on a well-fortified post like Dieppe.[5]

### COGNITIVE DISSONANCE AND SATISFICING

A third and more complex school grafts elements of cognitive-dissonance theory onto the notion of satisficing, proposing that the small steps taken to meet a problem, regarded as secondary under the minimal satisficing approach, may have to be defended at some point, requiring greater commitments under less-and-less-advantageous circumstances. Defending what now seems imperilled and dangerous, policy-makers may begin to ignore warning signs, in effect denying reality. Small errors in judgement, tolerable in secondary questions, become magnified as the issues grow in importance. In short, the obligation to defend operates like quicksand. This concept (much used in analyses of the Vietnam War) would seem at first glance to fit the Dieppe history. One can perceive its small, seemingly harmless origin in Hughes-Hallett's curiosity to find out what would happen if he tried to test how ports could be defended and how port defences could be overcome. By July 1942 he and Mountbatten had committed much to this project, and their professional reputations were to some extent riding on it. They were not the only ones who by July had become enmeshed in this raiding enterprise. The Service Chiefs and Churchill had a certain vested interest in it because they had promised an extensive raiding program to the Soviets in the *aide-mémoire*. But the fact is that where the Dieppe raid was concerned, Churchill and the Chiefs acquiesced rather than approved — a distinction that is scarcely consistent with the notion that they had a vested interest in Dieppe itself. The relatively low measure of Churchill's commitment may be judged by the fact that he left England without any clear notion of when and if *Rutter* was to be carried out, and was obliged, as an after-thought, to cable to London for the facts.[6]

### DEFENSIVE-AVOIDANCE AND REALITY DISTORTION

A fourth school says that patterns of cognitive dissonance can lead directly to irrational behaviour. From the very start a policy-maker may avoid everything that might stimulate anxiety. Unpleasant facts and unmistakable warning signs are ignored. Refusal to think about the oncoming danger may thus induce fatal inattention. By this route policy-makers end up taking risks that no rational person would normally contemplate. One would be tempted to apply these concepts to explain the behaviour of Hughes-Hallett and Mountbatten. (But it is disconcerting to note that the theory does not provide any standard by which this irrational risk-taking may be differentiated from normal risk-taking.) Inasmuch as the methodology is insufficiently developed to provide us with some critical test, one hesitates to build an analytical structure on such a shaky foundation, which would only lead us to unhelpful characterizations of personalities. But the more fundamental objection to the theory of reality distortion in this context is that even if it could explain the behaviour of those who wanted to do Dieppe, it would tell us nothing about the behaviour of those who did not, or who refused to be responsible for it — thus revealing their clear-eyed assessment of the risks being run. Their reluctant acquiescence was as important for the actualization of the Dieppe raid as was the determination of the project's originators.[7]

### GROUP-THINK

Another school of interpretation, group-think analysis, might be invoked to resolve this apparent inconsistency and still rescue cognitive-dissonance explanations of Dieppe. According to this interpretation, you do not have to have every participant in the decision acting irrationally but only a few determined souls, for in bureaucracies there is a herding instinct at work, and the weaker personalities will suppress their own doubts if the group seems to be going along. If need be, to arrive at a consensus they will bolster each other by shared rationalizations. Those who will not go along may be ejected. The behaviour of the cabal who met under the direction of Hughes-Hallett and Mountbatten, after the expulsion of Baillie-Grohman, could fit this analysis, but at crucial levels it simply will not carry. For the absence of the necessary conditions for group-think was never more clear than when the Chiefs of Staff were considering any proposal from Mountbatten. As we have seen, they were not happy with his presence; they resented his relationship with Churchill and openly showed their distrust, not to say scorn, of the intruder. The fact that they did not give Mountbatten the authorization he requested demonstrates amply that group-think was not operating at this crucial level.[8]

* * *

The foregoing review of the major schools of decision-making analysis is disappointing, for nowhere does there seem to be an adequate theoretical framework that will explain a failed decision like Dieppe. Those who know the literature will not be surprised. Political scientists have been disappointed by the failure to develop Allison's insights into a universal theory of decision-making analysis. In 1965 two political scientists complained that decision-making analysis had succeeded only in producing 'a morass of partial theories, component processing tasks, and ill-specified contingencies', with the emergence 'here and there of pockets of understanding'. No significant improvement has occurred since.[9]

The reasons for this disappointment are not hard to see. Most of the literature focuses, almost exclusively, on individual failures to process information with the rigour required. But this can be applied only to an infinitesimal number of cases because taking precautions against decision-making failures that are due to a lack of basic information — the most obvious form of error — is second nature in Western governments. This usually takes the form of layering, whereby one set of individuals is set to double-check the information processing and gathering of others. In modern government, while an individual may fail, the system rarely does, at least as regards information-processing. The number of established cases in which such governments do the wrong thing for want of information is very small. Even less common must be the number of cases where the failure of a single layer of information-processing leads to disaster.

Not only does the definition of the problem as being grounded in a failure in cognition seem mistaken, but also the units studied by such theories seem too small. The day of the single expert working alone has vanished. Information-processing is the work of large bureaucratic units. The list of those involved in the case of gathering information for *Rutter* and/or *Jubilee* included COHQ's planners, the various service Intelligence branches (for *Rutter*), South-East Command, the commandos, the Canadian Headquarters, and the Chiefs of Staff, etc. It would be next to impossible to show that all these agencies failed in information-processing. The distance that most tried to take from the Dieppe operation indicates fairly clearly that they had a more than adequate idea of what the raiding force was up against.

### TOWARDS ANOTHER MODEL OF SYSTEMIC FAILURE

This review, necessarily abbreviated, makes clear that we are still a long way from a comprehensive theory of what can go wrong with sophisticated decision-making structures if we are to use Dieppe as a model. The bureaucratic and organizational models offered by Graham Allison, and the group-think analysis of Irving Janis, represent but a start in elucidating the pathology of failed decision-making. But if existing political-science literature does little to explain Dieppe, then it must be that an analysis of that event will contribute to the literature some other model or models of systemic failure. It ought to be possible to abstract from the history of Dieppe a determination of the conditions that made it possible.

Traditional decision-making analysis suggests that failure to process information is the crucial determinant, and we are asked to believe that the critical play is between those those who know better and those who do not. Implicitly a failed decision is defined as one in which the latter carry the day. The facts of the Dieppe case would suggest something very different, for it could not be shown that those who pushed hardest for this project were any less well-informed about the implicit hazards or the poor prospects than those who resisted approving it. The knowledge of the risks was as great among the proponents, if not greater, than it was with the other participants. If, then, the crucial factor separating the major players was not cognition, might it not be volition (i.e. differing degrees of desire and determination) that was critical? In fact any close study of Dieppe reveals an unusual feature: the presence of players who had an extraordinary interest in carrying the project forward, despite contrary indicators, and who displayed exceptional determination in pursuing their goal. The measure of this determination was Mountbatten's willingness to go forward in the absence of actual authorization, and in Hughes-Hallett's case it was the threat to demand a judicial inquiry by Sir Stafford Cripps into the excessive frequency of cancellations — a wild idea that has usually been put down to overwork.

Clearly these players were not in fact reasonable men. They had a disturbing capacity for denying reality and were willing to experiment with lives to advance what they would call military science. Hughes-Hallett certainly fits this description, and so, probably, does Mountbatten.

No one with any experience of government would be surprised that such dangerous people are present in any given bureaucracy. It may safely be assumed that their presence is, to a greater or lesser degree, a constant of government. If they rarely carry the day, that is because they are normally kept in check. Sober disciplined bureaucrats are usually placed over impetuous daredevils, who are restrained either by discipline, by the weight of seniority, or by bureaucratic structures, in which one review panel is formally layered over another in part to check such individuals or weed them out. That this was not achieved in the case of Dieppe was one of its most striking features. A determined individual like Hughes-Hallett, pursuing objectives that were almost personal (continuing his investigations into the problems associated with the capture of a port), managed to carry out his experiments despite the fact that few, if any, still believed they were necessary or useful, and fewer still believed they were feasible. Hughes-Hallett had his way over the hesitations and anxieties of men much more powerful than himself. One must marvel at how he managed to carry out his project, even though it so patently jeopardized Mountbatten's future career and the credibility of those who were supposed to review and approve such proposals. He was able to impose his will on the British Government, in ways totally out of proportion with his rank and responsibility, in a monstrous deformation of the decision-making process. One can certainly sympathize with Baillie-Grohman's disgust with the Dieppe project and his bitterness over the final report, which he thought could have been titled 'Lessons learned by Hughes-Hallett'.[10]

One question raises itself above all others: What are the conditions under which such individuals can overcome normal institutional checks? In the case of Hughes-Hallett part of the answer was luck, which intervened when Mountbatten, his boss, with little experience but lots of connections, was elevated into the ranks of the Chiefs of Staff. One can well understand Hughes-Hallett's ebullience, for now he had access to power, pliable power. A second ingredient in his success was the product not of luck but rather of boldness and determination in latching onto those causes and parties outside the formal decision-making process that wielded more power and influence than even his chief had. Hughes-Hallett drew this arrow on 11 July when he threatened, in effect, that if Dieppe were cancelled for good he would go to Sir Stafford Cripps, one of the principal chorus-masters of the pro-Soviet lobby, and demand an official inquiry into the cancellations. In fact he was already in touch with Cripps, and seemed to be in a position to carry through his threats, something that must have stiffened the backbone of the other Force Commanders as well as Mountbatten. In dropping Cripps' name, Hughes-Hallett was implicitly invoking the Second Front Now movement, which everyone knew would have to be appeased in some way. The doubters and naysayers who had followed Baillie-Grohman in criticizing COHQ and recommending cancellation were thus forewarned of the risk to their careers. Certain in the knowledge that the political costs of cancellation could not be met, Hughes-Hallett seems never to have doubted that he would get his chance to carry out his experiment. Nor, does it seem, did Mountbatten, who replied to Admiral Ramsey's threat to stop the raiding program by saying that there were 'certain' reasons why he was sure it would not be cancelled. Knowing that normal bureaucratic restraints were being neutralized, Hughes-Hallett and Mountbatten confidently pushed ahead.

Though Hughes-Hallett had the essence of a strategy, whether it would work or not depended on whether internal allies in fact existed who could overcome the hesitation or opposition of the intervening bureaucratic layers. Partial success was not difficult to achieve. Since most functional bureaucracies are headed by politicians, potential allies inclined to kick over bureaucratic restraints are not difficult to find. In the case of Dieppe, the obvious allies were Mountbatten's two friends, Churchill within and Beaverbrook without. Churchill was enamoured of the idea. As Desmond Morton, one of Churchill's inner circle, has pointed out: 'As he liked what Paget calls "buccaneers" and I call "swashbuckler's" so he loved funny stunts, side issues, conjurers' tricks and so on. Behind all this was his burning desire for ACTION. If the great regular forces and their commanders could do nothing — no matter what the reason — then let us try tricks. He was not a patient man. He also began by thinking that all the "rules of war" adumbrated by his official advisers were out of date and fundamentally wrong.'[11]

Churchill could further his 'funny' projects because he breached the jurisdictional subdivision of responsibility by which the formal independence of the bureaucracy is maintained. He did this when he insisted on forming a small inner cabinet, with himself as Minister of Defence. This meant that Pound, Brooke, and Portal had no civilian chief in this War Cabinet who could champion their case against Churchill. The jurisdictional boundaries were also breached by the Prime Minister when he insisted on attending Chiefs of Staff meetings on a regular basis, as well as when he appointed his personal representative, Ismay, to the Chiefs of Staff Committee to handle the meetings he could not attend. As a result, the Chiefs had no regular way of privately mulling over a problem from their own perspective, and still less any way of co-ordinating a strategy against the Prime Minister should they fundamentally disagree with him. They could only fight it out directly, day after day, eyeball to eyeball, with Churchill or his watchdog. Churchill also undermined the independence of the Chiefs of Staff when he insisted on placing Mountbatten in their midst. A measure of independence is in the best interests of those in higher positions, but this was hard for Churchill to appreciate at a time when the war was apparently being lost. In that crisis he insisted on his right to take whatever measures he felt were necessary to invigorate his bureaucracy, even though the effect often made matters worse.

As one critic remarked, with only slight inaccuracy, 'Loyal old Savoyards who remember their "Mikado" can't very well be blamed for deducing, even though they're loyal old Churchillians as well, that there's a possible excess of Gilbert and Sullivan in a system which calls on the Minister of Defence to criticize plans which, as Chairman of the Chiefs of Staff Committee he has helped to draw up.' Churchill was not, strictly speaking, the chairman, though he certainly took the chair when he attended. But the important point is that this was not an atmosphere in which dispassionate review was possible. It was not a system calculated to give a cold, unequivocal 'No' to Churchill's demands, such as those for some sort of action on the French coast. It was in part to make this point that Churchill had insisted on inserting Mountbatten into the Chiefs of Staff Committee. His presence as a spokesman of the Prime Minister, like Ismay's, eroded the independence of the Chiefs. That, of course, was what Churchill wanted, and reflected his fervent belief in the dictum that 'War is too important to leave to the Generals'. In fact that proposition seems to be more often wrong than right. Certainly the crossing of wires — the undermining of the normally orderly progress of a project from layer to layer within a bureaucracy — seems to be a major ingredient in the Dieppe disaster.[12]

The behaviour of the intermediate layer, the Chiefs of Staff in this case, can be profitably analysed still further. Though Churchill had made it difficult for the Chiefs to refuse his demands, the fact is that the Chiefs were powerful figures in their own right, very conscious of their responsibilities, and frequently gave Churchill the unequivocal 'No's' that he worked so hard to avoid hearing. We still need an explanation that will clarify why sometimes they acted as though they were still independent, and discharged their duties accordingly, and why at other times they seemed to surrender to Churchill's demands.

The Chiefs knew that they served at Churchill's pleasure. Indeed Pound and Brooke learned, during the summer of 1942, that they were under consideration for replacement, as Dill had been replaced before them. The reason was clearly that they had worn the Prime Minister's patience thin by giving him too many negative responses to his projects. They had always been aware of this problem, but had hoped it was not immediate. As Churchill struggled with his enormous burdens, their survival became more problematical. Brooke was particularly struck by an early manifestation of this strain late in 1941 when his explanation of why a Norwegian expedition could not be contemplated in the foreseeable future produced a 'most awful outburst of temper'. Incidents such as this, which increased in frequency over the spring and summer of 1942, made it clear to all the Chiefs that they could not afford to be seen opposing Churchill's every project. They might have to acquiesce in the least dangerous of his various schemes. Of course there was a principled alternative: resigning in protest. But given Churchill's unpredictability under pressure, the Chiefs can be excused for feeling that the country was better off with them in power — even if that meant accepting gestures like Dieppe — for fear of what their successors, chosen by Churchill under intense stress, might accept. The fact that Mountbatten was bruited as Churchill's choice to succeed Pound must have struck terror in the hearts of the other Chiefs.[13]

The Chiefs may have underestimated Churchill. He was close to the edge, but one can doubt that he would ever have gone over, any more than one can imagine him really punching Brooke — which, later in 1942, seemed not impossible to Brooke. Churchill's fits of temper were in some measure an act to shake up the bureaucracy, for without them he was convinced it would settle into complacency, and 'masterly inactivity'. He was constantly testing how far the Chiefs could be pushed, which he saw as a means of preventing them from resting on their oars. Churchill probably could have been told that there would be no Second Front, not even a major raid in 1942, and that he would have to settle for *Torch* as the only major offensive operation for the remainder of 1942 — one can never know for sure. It would appear that the Chiefs were more intimidated than they should have been and erred on the side of caution. Thus they substantiated once more Churchill's charge that they were timorous, if not cowardly. But all these judgements ought to be expressed tentatively, for one would have to be able to catch every intonation, every bit of body language, every spark of emotion that passed between them to judge fairly between Churchill's unreasonableness and the Chiefs' timidity. (The terms of course are relative. They were all exceptionally competent public servants, if one measures them against the larger backdrop of the immense demands of a global war. In that perspective Dieppe was a relatively small affair to them.)

There is another factor at work besides the breaching of orderly procedures within the Government that paralysed the natural opposition seasoned bureaucrats usually give to the wilder schemes of rank amateurs like Mountbatten — one that is really quite subtle. Though the principal players had the necessary information to reach a sound decision, by either reinforcing fire support or cancelling the operation, the sobering effect of all warnings and counter-indications was efficacious only while its vividness and immediacy were retained. As so often happens, over time sensibiliities are deadened, natural optimism returns, 'Surely it cannot be as bad as all that' becomes the natural reaction after the first effects of the alarm wear off. Leaving the plan around without acting on it for a prolonged period thus became a prescription for disaster because the benefit of the original studies and the counter-indications they produced wore off. And, as usually happens in cases such as this, new players entered the picture who had never been fully exposed to the original warnings. If the decision-making process is prolonged enough it becomes easy to assume that the failure to kill off a plan must mean that someone has figured out how to overcome its drawbacks, or at the very least that the worst aspects have been corrected and that the risk has been reduced. In fact these assumptions are generally mistaken, for reasons that the Dieppe incident makes clear. In wartime, policy-makers are constantly trying to cut corners and reduce investments of scarce resources, so that support for the raiding force in fact diminished and over time the plan was actually weakened rather than strengthened, contrary to what one might assume.

The real tragedy is that even as the passing of time tends to work for the reduction of resources invested, commitment among those who ought to know better grows. This in many ways is the most alarming feature of the process that led to Dieppe. Losing the determination to oppose, the Chiefs became alive to the possibility that they could wring out of the Dieppe project beneficial side-effects. Once they saw these, they were no longer sullen in their acquiescence; on the contrary, they were to some extent positively supportive. The appointment of Hughes-Hallett as the Naval Force Commander of the 'next large raid', while not constituting approval, certainly must be regarded as more than reluctant acquiescence, for he did not have a high enough rank for that role and the Chiefs could have seized on the irregularity of Hughes-Hallett's nomination to such a command as a way of blocking Mountbatten's project. But having some interest now in Dieppe's coming off, they helped rather than hindered Mountbatten, leaving until a later day the problem of whether they would ultimately approve or disapprove the actual project.

Why did they not, at that point or subsequently, embrace the project and give the formal approval Mountbatten requested? The answer, it would appear, is that they knew that the chances for success were poor and that they could be improved only by a much deeper investment of resources. This they could not justify. Nor were they willing to share responsibility for the plan as Mountbatten intended to carry it out, if need be without the additional support. Sharing blame equally with those who had initiated and stubbornly clung to the project seemed to be more responsibility than they thought they should assume. One can easily imagine the Chiefs saying 'Let the blame fall on those who merit it.' That was certainly Brooke's reaction, we have seen, when he heard that Dieppe had been attempted: 'That should teach the advocates of a second front a lesson.'

It is worth noting that though this process may favour the adaptation and adjustment to a project that the Chiefs originally opposed, it did not convert them into actual supporters, as theories of cognitive dissonance and conflict-avoidance suggest. The Chiefs never entirely lost touch with reality or suspended their disbelief. On the one hand it was a measure of their realism that they refused to risk more than the minimum force already assigned to *Rutter* on a contingency basis. On the other, avoiding further investment meant avoiding formal approval that would have exposed them to more demands for increased fire support. Thus they combined tacit approval with tacit disapproval. While understanding their reasons for acting this way, one must also recognize that here logic and good sense had gone out of the decision-making process. The best one can say is that the Chiefs preferred to allow a likely disaster whose damage they thought could be contained, rather than be forced into some other disastrous plan whose consequences they might be powerless to contain. Reality, however, rarely responds to such convoluted calculations, and the consequences are often considerably greater than originally envisaged. In the case of Dieppe the credibility of the high command was damaged, while the two most culpable officers, Mountbatten and Hughes-Hallett, got off without so much as a formal reprimand, free to inflict similar brainstorms in the future. Whatever one might think about their subsequent careers — there is much room for debate — such risks ought not to have been run. Churchill knew that, and on more than one occasion wanted an inquiry and seemed to threaten sanctions. But he could never quite get to the bottom of the problem, no doubt because he himself was implicated.

The clearest lesson one can derive from the story of Dieppe is the observation that an unrecorded decision may well be, indeed should be, considered as a sure sign that something fundamental has gone wrong with the decision-making process; that one should also look for the presence of schemers who can impose projects on those who should know better; that one should also look for powerful external pressures reverberating through the decision-making process — pressures that cannot be resisted and lead to decisions for which there is no real acceptance of responsibility (and are therefore unrecorded). All of this serves to underline a point that is not stressed enough in the political-science literature: decision-making is fundamentally a process for assuming responsibility for a proposed action. Where responsibility is not fully shouldered, the process has failed and the probability of disaster is great. Clearly no government should tolerate the implementation of a decision without recorded approval.

The element that is most puzzling from a historical perspective — when and how Dieppe was approved — turned out to be the key to understanding the event, as well as the key to constructing an important model of failed decision-making. If the study of Dieppe makes anything clear it is that the meaning and purpose of the operation were closely bound up with the way that decision was reached, for the decision-making process is the instrument by which responsibility, and therefore purpose and feasibility, are established. Dieppe illustrates this vividly. Had the Chiefs decided formally to remount the operation it would have meant, at the least, that they were prepared to take responsibility for it, which in turn would imply that they had a relatively clear objective in view that was defensible, if not feasible. The failure to take a formal decision implies the converse. The way the decision was reached thus speaks volumes about its authors and their intentions. Political-science analyses grounded on the fundamental notion that decision-making is a form of assuming responsibility can easily be reworked to provide satisfactory descriptions of decisions like Dieppe.

The depressing implication of these conclusions must be that behind bad compromises like Dieppe, for which officials are unwilling to take responsibility, lies a problem of the system peculiar to democracies at war when a government continues to be accountable to the electorate or to parliament. The mood of the public must be appeased, even when officials know that what is being demanded by the body politic cannot be delivered. The solution would theoritically be to explain to the public, in convincing fashion, the limitations under which the government is waging war; but this sort of absolute candour, difficult in peacetime, is impossible in wartime. And so governments do what they should not do and compromise halfheartedly, knowing that whatever resources they allocate to the required gesture will be wasted. Over time they try to whittle down the investment in a lost cause. It is a vicious circle by which failure, predictable at the outset of the plan, eventually becomes a certainty.

Should we then conclude that democracy must be completely suspended in wartime? The history of the Second World War fortunately shows that this is not a valid proposition. The continuation of political accountability made it utterly impossible for a government to take wild gambles for fear of what consequences failure might have on public opinion and representative assemblies. A careful examination of American or British strategy during the Second World War fails to disclose a single major strategic debate in which the highest-risk option was knowingly taken. In this and in so many aspects of the war the democracies erred on the side of caution. That has a lot to do with the ultimate victory. On the negative side the pressures inherent in political accountability were what made something like Dieppe inevitable. The balance, though sorrowful, is still positive, particularly if one bears in mind that the Dieppe project probably facilitated the rejection of *Imperator, Sledgehammer,* and *Jupiter.*

Nationalists, or those who felt the Dieppe tragedy personally, will not easily agree. But one has only to make the most casual perusal of the fatal or nearly fatal decisions made by Nazi Germany, Fascist Italy, and Stalinist Russia — systems in which political accountability and the pressure to do things to satisfy elected representatives were virtually nonexistent — to see how often these countries were prone to reckless gambles on a scale that makes Dieppe pale into insignificance. Rome, Berlin, and Tokyo all lost the war by reason of reckless gambling, and Moscow very nearly did as well. Democracies in the Second World War present this curious picture of requiring on the one hand ill-considered small gestures, like Dieppe, while on the other being generally incapable of taking really serious gambles. These considerations might not have been immediately apparent to the brave lads who left for Dieppe late on 18 August, but they knew that they were willing to make sacrifices for their way of life. The following day many did, paying the cruel price. But what was achieved in that grim exchange was infinitely more valuable than what their contemporaries in the armies of the dictatorships were reaping. The men at Dieppe may have been caught up in a folly, but it was that of a leader who was trying to push his military forces to make the maximum effort and of a government that was trying to balance off what it considered wise with what it knew its Allies and public opinion demanded. The Second World War produced far greater follies than this.

# Methodology

The method and approach of the foregoing study perhaps requires some explanation. The literature on Dieppe is so vast, and the possibilities of reinterpretation have been explored so often, that one might well have asked at the outset: Can there still be anything that has been left unsaid? This study breaks with all preceding ones in being grounded in a single consideration: whether Mountbatten had authorization — a matter that impinges on many other points about Dieppe that are in dispute.

The notion of Mountbatten's acting without authorization, which I took to be my discovery, was not in fact entirely original with me. The Churchill-Ismay correspondence revealed that Churchill had suspected this, and when I began to look closely at the Dieppe literature it seemed to me that Roskill might also have considered the possibility. The striking 1978 Lovat quote in which he gave voice to the same suspicion, saying that Mountbatten was to blame for not going back and checking with the Chiefs of Staff — which I came across only recently — shows that he too conceived of the possibility. I think I can detect the same suspicion in Goronwy Rees's memoirs, in those passages where he describes his surprise at the revival of the project.

Few of the scores of historians who have studied Dieppe noticed these hints, and those that did were apparently unwilling to commit themselves to the proposition that Mountbatten acted without authorization. Why? One had to consider that question very carefully, and ask whether the reasons were not sound. I could see that adopting my thesis meant contradicting Mountbatten and what I took to be Churchill's authoritative pronouncements in his memoirs. It also meant contradicting the suggestions, explicit or implicit, in a half-dozen highly regarded official British histories. That was daunting. Even more so was the realization that to commit oneself to the proposition that Mountbatten acted without authorization meant also committing oneself to proving a negative — providing evidence that the authorization claimed never occurred. In the absence of direct evidence, this could be done only indirectly — using the famous dog-that-didn't-bark argument. In the case of Dieppe I could not believe that after the cancellation of *Rutter* the Chiefs would have allowed Mountbatten to go ahead with the same possibly compromised operation without at least telling him to check with the highest authorities in the intelligence and counter-intelligence fields, and report back. The fact that there was no evidence of a recommendation from them, one way or the other, on the plan to remount cast enormous doubt on the proposition that the Chiefs formally approved. Assuming responsibility — that is, taking a decision — without touching base with the Intelligence chiefs was simply too amateur, the sort of thing Mountbatten might do but never the Service Chiefs. The problem with the evidence was more than simply a question of there being no record that the Intelligence chiefs were consulted, a fact Mountbatten would no doubt have explained away by saying that everyone had agreed nothing should be put on record. The stumbling-block in his story was that we know from the debate that occurred in December, when procedures for consultation with the Intelligence authorities were tightened, that the competent authorities had *not* been consulted, and that the Chiefs were convinced that they should have been. As far as I was concerned that was fairly decisive. It was time to go forward and try to build an alternative reconstruction of events that excluded Mountbatten's claim to have had Chiefs of Staff's approval. In the long run this would mean hitching one's professional credibility to the proposition that the evidence to prove Mountbatten's case was not only absent, but also that it would never turn up.

This was a risk that was not taken lightly, but I could not see how one could properly write the history by ignoring so basic a question as Mountbatten's authorization. Reducing the risk could be accomplished by repeatedly testing the two theories — that it was done with, and that it was done without, authority. The goal was to find out which overall interpretation was more coherent and more consistent with the evidence. The ultimate test was to see which theory revealed new facts that could be confirmed by direct evidence.

At the same time, accepting that Dieppe was executed without formal authorization posed many problems. The accuracy of one fact can rarely be challenged in isolation. Every event impinges on others, and the truth of one fact must be tested for consistency with other known facts. If some inconsistency is turned up, the historian must ask if the contradictory facts are susceptible of redefinition; and each redefinition then raises further questions about other aspects, taking one further and further away from established opinion contained in the existing literature and increasing the burden of proof one must carry. If the original fact is central enough, one ends up rethinking and re-examining everything that is known about the context. For example, concluding that the remounting occurred on Mountbatten's initiative with no more than acquiescence by the Service Chiefs meant that what we know about their position had to be carefully re-examined, for acquiescence implies a very different, less responsible, approach to their management of the war than has heretofore been recognized. Moreover, when decisions are taken formally, procedures are followed that establish who has a right to take part in the decision. But when decisions are taken by acquiescence almost anyone could have contributed to moving the project forward. This implies a lot more work than might otherwise have been the case in tracking down possible influences, direct and indirect. Decisions by acquiescence are also, by definition, those in which the central players are remarkably silent about what they propose to do. As one official British official historian remarked to me, the silence of some key figures is positively deafening. Their positions had to be painstakingly reconstructed from an analysis of the context — necessitating the weighing of more circumstantial evidence, which is always tedious and more time-consuming than weighing direct evidence. In fact the rule adopted for this study was that two requirements must be met for a reinterpretation to be presented; there must be a specific piece of evidence, slight though it might be, and it must have what might be called contextual resonance. Going on this alone invites exercising the imagination still more freely. But there is a thin line, which the historian obviously must not cross, between using one's historical imagination — as the great philosopher of history R.G. Collingwood enjoined — and creating historical fiction. Historians must have at least one specific document to hang their interpretation on, and if they cannot find it then the imaginative reconstruction is probably invalid, as all events leave a discoverable trace, however slight. I have tried in every case to adhere to that rule, while attempting to avoid loading too much freight on too few words. Whether I have succeeded is for others to decide. In the end it is the picture of the whole that must be accepted or rejected.

I was somewhat disconcerted when I found so many reasons to explain why this operation went forward. A perfectly respectable book could have been written presenting the decision as the outcome of the *Sledgehammer* debate, or of the RAF's desire to have a large air battle, or as the outcome of the PQ 17 disaster and the need to cancel the convoys to Russia, or as the product of the frustration with the Army's seeming incompetence, or of domestic political pressures, or of Churchill's incessant advocacy of a Norwegian expedition, or as the result of Soviet pressures for a Second Front, or as the product of Mountbatten's ambition. For each of ten such possible monocausal books there was evidence enough, and with a little judicious selection any one could have been made very convincing. But such a book would have left the reader with a fundamentally inadequate picture of how the decision came to be made. In deciding not to take this course I was influenced by a fact of decision-making theory that Ernest May taught me: decisions are rarely the product of a single person or even of just one level in a bureaucratic hierarchy. They are almost always intricate pieces of machinery in which most, if not all, of the probable causes play a distinct part.

I would like to think that if the profession can accept this study it might also weigh the implications: that a scholar may need ten years to work out the terms of a substantial historical revision, for I do not see how it can be done in less time. It is an enormous investment, too great if one believes that even the best studies can only scratch the surface. Too great, too, in the sense that it can easily produce reams of analyses and scores of chapters that publishers, perforce, must discard. But as my other mentor, William Langer, taught me, the Rankean tradition holds out the promise that the resolution of almost any historical conundrum can be attained. This faith in rational analysis — while difficult to uphold in the face of evidence that is a bewildering mixture of fact, and perceptions based on imprecise, often self-serving, but telling disclosures — is not so unattainable that one should not try to practise it. And there is always the bonus of uncovering important new things even about one of the most thoroughly ploughed fields of recent history. A more conservative methodology would merely have presented the same old mysteries, still eluding explanation.

# Notes

ABBREVIATIONS USED

Documentation has been collated paragraph by paragraph. Many of the sources cited exist in multiple copies in different titles; wherever possible reference has been made to a published document, except where the original contains relevant data not found in the printed version. For original files, acronyms have been employed to reduce the bulk of these notes. PRO refers to the Public Record Office, Kew:

ADM 1, ADM 13, ADM 14, ADM 167, ADM 199, ADM 205—Admiralty Records (principally First Lords' Papers and related records, and War History Cases), PRO.

AIR 2, AIR 6, AIR 8, AIR 9, AIR 14, AIR 16, AIR 19, AIR 20, AIR 38, AIR 40, AIR 46—Air Ministry Records (principally Chief of Air Staff's Papers, Secretary of State for Air Papers, Bomber Command and Air Historical Branch Papers), PRO.

CAB 65—War Cabinet Conclusions WM series (Minutes), PRO.

CAB 66 and CAB 67—War Cabinet Memoranda (WP series), PRO.

CAB 68—War Cabinet Reports by Departments, PRO

CAB 69—War Cabinet Defence Committee (DO Minutes—Operations), PRO.

CAB 78—War Cabinet Chiefs of Staff Committee Miscellaneous and General Series, PRO.

CAB 79—War Cabinet of Staff Committee Conclusions (COS Minutes), PRO.

CAB 80—War Cabinet Chiefs of Staff Committee Memoranda, PRO.

CAB 101 and CAB 103—Cabinet Historical Section (Confidential Prints, Official Histories, and related files), PRO.

CAB 105—Cabinet telegrams, PRO.

CAB 120—Defence Ministry Secretariat, PRO.

CAB 122—Joint Staff Mission, Washington Office Files, PRO

CAB 127—Miscellaneous Private Collections, deposited at PRO.

CSIC CAB 121—Cabinet Secret Information Centre (Hollis Files), eventually to be transferred to the Public Record Office as CAB 121 but at the time of consultation were under the control of the Cabinet Historical Office (not currently open)

DEFE 2—Combined Operations Headquarters, Directorate, PRO.

DND—Directorate of History, Department of National Defence, Ottawa.

FDR—Franklin Delano Roosevelt Library, Hyde Park (principally the President's Secretary's File (PSF), the President's Personal File (PPF), and Map Room Files (MR).

FO 371—Foreign Office Dispatches, PRO.

FO 800/300—Kerr, Clark (Lord Inverchapel's) Papers, PRO.

FO 800/309—327—Lord Halifax, PRO.

FO 954—Lord Avon, PRO.

FRUS—Foreign Relations of the United States, volumes of Diplomatic Correspondence edited by the Department of State, Historical Office.

INF—Ministry of Information, London, PRO.

IWM—Imperial War Museum, London.

KC—Liddell Hart Centre, King's College, London.

MB—Mountbatten Papers, Broadlands, Romsey, Surrey, and the University of Southampton Archives.

MR—Map Room Files, Franklin Delano Roosevelt Library, Hyde Park.

NA—National Archives and Records Service, Washington
principally Record Group (RG) 165, Operations Division (OPD), of the War Department).

NAC—National Archives of Canada, Ottawa.

PREM 3, PREM 4—Prime Minister's Office, Operational Papers, PRO.

WO 100, WO 106, WO 193, WO 201, WO 216—War Office Files, principally Directorate of Military Operations and Intelligence files, collation files, and Chief of Imperial General Staff (CIGS) files, PRO.

## INTRODUCTION

[1] T. Murray Hunter, *Canada at Dieppe* (Ottawa, Canadian War Museum, 1982), has good up-to-date figures on pp. 39-41.

[2] Anthony Cave Brown, *Bodyguard of Lies* (London, 1976), pp.80-90; David Eisenhower, *Eisenhower at War, 1943-1945* (New York, 1986), p. 96. For another discussion of the question see Stephen Roskill, 'The Dieppe Raid and the Question of German Foreknowledge' in *Royal United Services Institute Journal*, CIX, No. 633 (February, 1964), pp. 27-31, and also John P. Campbell, 'Deception and D-Day' in *Canadian Defence Quarterly*, IX, No. 3 (Winter 1980) pp. 40-4.

[3] The opposition of the professional military to large-scale raids is easily explained. As military operations, raids are supposed to inflict more destruction on the enemy than they cost the attacking force. This is feasible with small raiding parties that slip between cracks in the enemy's defences to wreak damage out of proportion to their numbers; large raiding parties, on the other hand, are unlikely to find such chinks and must face the full effect of the enemy's defences, on terrain of his choosing—almost always a losing proposition. Hence, every time

the Joint Planners were asked to study the proposal for large-scale raids, they repeatedly advised against them. (See for instance COS (41) 221st, 23 June 1941, and the lively debate at DO (41) 47th, 7 July 1941, together with a series of Joint Planners' Studies produced that summer, particularly JPS (41) 500 of 30 June 1941, JPS (41) 536 of 10 July 1941, and JPS (41) 566 of 20 July 1941.) To be fair to Mountbatten, it must be admitted that he gave signs of understanding this principle and was opposed to anything larger than *Jubilee* (though that too was beyond the point where anything valuable could have been obtained commensurate with the risk). He rightly pointed out in March 1942 that there must be no question of landing a large force and then withdrawing because 'the difficulties of withdrawal, particularly after casualties have been inflicted on the landing craft . . . [would be] so great that I cannot recommend it, even if we could afford the disastrous psychological effect of yet one more evacuation', Mountbatten to Ismay, 7 March 1942, Appendix 1 to 'Prospects for a Major Operation in 1942', 19 July 1942, DEFE 2/564. By and large it was the politicians, to whose views Mountbatten was unduly receptive, who nursed extravagant hopes about what large-scale raids could accomplish in the area of psychological warfare. It seems hard not to attribute the COS reversal and their subsequent willingness to undertake a large-scale raid—WM (42) 133, 12 May 1942—to Soviet and American pressures for some gesture to help Moscow. It was in response to this reversal that Mountbatten came forward with the outline plan for *Rutter* the next day. Lord Lovat, *March Past* (London, 1976), p. 275; *Deutsche Allgemeine Zeitung* quoted in Richard Garrett, *The Raiders* (New York, 1980), p. 136; Michael Balfour, *Propaganda in War 1939-1945* (London, 1979), pp. 279-80. See also the Combined Operations Headquarters file on German propaganda DEFE 2/379. The British press, much to Mountbatten's annoyance, reproduced some of the German propaganda; see the London *Evening Standard* for 20August 1942 and Colonel R. Neville (COHQ) to J. Beddington (Ministry of Information , 30 September 1942) in DEFE 2/379

[4] Combined Operations Headquarters, *Combined Operations: The Official Story of the Commandos* (HMSO London and Macmillan, New York, 1943), p. 145.

[5] James Leasor and General Sir Leslie Hollis, *War at The Top* (London, 1958), p. 218; Admiral John Hughes-Hallet, 1967 interview with John Secondari in MB1/67; Hunter, *Canada*, p.48; Nigel Hamilton, *Monty: The Making of a General, 1887-1942* (London and New York, 1981), p. 547.

[6] Lt.-Gen. E.L.M. Burns, *General Mud: Memoirs of Two World Wars* (Toronto, 1970), p. 117.

[7] W.A.B. Douglas, and B. Greenhous 'Canada and the Second World War: The State of Clio's Art' in *Military Affairs*, February 1978 pp. 24-9; John Keegan, *Six Armies in Normandy* (London and New York, 1982), pp. 120-1; Hamilton, *Monty*, p. 554 ; C.P.Stacey, preface to Hunter, *Canada*, p. 3; ibid., p. 45.

## 1. THE BARE FACTS OF A HISTORICAL TRAGEDY

[1] Baggallay to Eden, 12 and 13 February 1942 and Foreign Office staff minutes on same, FO 371/32875; Ewer to Ridsdale, 27 February 1942, F0371/32876 and Staff Minutes on same.

[2] The 23 March 1942 directive is in U.S. Government, *Führer Directives and Other Top-Level Directives of the German Armed Forces, 1942-1945* (GPO, Washington, 1948), pp. 21-2.

[3] Hughes-Hallett often tried to explain how the list of targets was chosen. The two most important accounts are in his unpublished memoirs, tentatively titled *Before I Forget*, and his interview with John Secondari in 1967. The former—hereafter referred to as Unpublished Memoirs—exists in two copies with slight variations and unfortunately different paginations; one is in the Mountbatten Papers MB1 B47 and the other in the National Archives of Canada, Ottawa (with traces of four different paginations!), MG 30 E 463. I have used the most legible NAC pagination. (I have relied principally on the chapters titled 'Combined Operations' and 'Dieppe'.) The interview with Secondari is preserved in the Mountbatten Papers MB1 B67/2.

Bernard Fergusson, in *The Watery Maze: The Story of Combined Operations* (London 1961), a book much approved of by Mountbatten, claims that the 'final reason for choosing Dieppe was the fact that the planners had already ruled it out as a desirable place to capture in the early stages of a real invasion, and we should therefore be giving nothing away by raiding it now' (p. 169). What Fergusson presumably had in mind was the fact that it was recognized very early that all the Channel ports were too easy to destroy, as usable ports, by the enemy before their capture, and any attempt to seize them was unlikely to prove worthwhile. But if this was what Fergusson had in mind, why then did he justify a raid in which the raiders risked all in an attempt to capture Dieppe when they could much more easily have raided the hinterland or devastated some less well-fortified place?

[4] Nigel Hamilton, *Monty: The Making of a General, 1887-1942* (London and New York 1981), p. 549.

[5] Ibid., p. 552.

[6] Many explanations have been advanced for the involvement of Montgomery and South-Eastern Command. But as Hughes-Hallett credits the decision to Churchill, one must conclude the motive was principally political, i.e. he wanted to avoid criticism that Dominion troops were used casually as cannon fodder. Hughes-Hallett, Unpublished Memoirs, MG 30 E 463, NAC, pp. 128, 152. (These memoirs, which at first glance seem tame, are in fact rich in important detail. They are the best statement of the Mountbatten/Hughes-Hallett position and merit publication.)

[7] C.P. Stacey, *Six Years of War*, Volume 1 of the Official History of the Canadian Army in the Second World War (Ottawa, 1966, corrected 4th printing), p. 399.

[8] J. Hughes-Hallett, 'The Mounting of Raids', in *Royal United Services Institute Journal*, XCV (November 1950), 585, and Unpublished Memoirs, pp. 152-4, MG 30 E 463, NAC; COS (42) 42nd (O) 13 May 1942, also COS (42) 139th (same date).

[9] 'There was no margin of time, or indeed of sea room.' Hughes-Hallett's Unpublished Memoirs, pp. 168-9, 153, MG 30 E 463, NAC. His amazingly complex navigation 'Track Chart' for this operation is preserved in DEFE 2/336.

[10] Goebbels is quoted in Michael Balfour, *Propaganda in War 1939-45* (London, 1979), p. 279; interview with Major Brian McCool in Ronald Atkin, *Dieppe 1942: The Jubilee Disaster* (London, 1980), p. 249

[11] The abandonment of the bombing has always been blamed by Mountbatten and his defenders on Montgomery, who was in the chair at the meeting of 5 June when this was first accepted. Blame he certainly deserves but it must be noted that the suggestion was first made at a meeting of 1 June, for part of which Mountbatten was present. Nor could it be said that he was ignorant of the real reasons for the reluctance of Bomber Command to lend its craft for raids; see Chapter 7 of this book. For the meeting of 1 June see DEFE 2/546. There is also a copy of the minutes in the Baillie-Grohman Papers at the National Maritime Museum, Greenwich (Dieppe folder).

[12] The most accurate and complete translation of the German Army West warning orders is to be found in the late Stephen W. Roskill, 'The Dieppe Raid and the Question of German Foreknowledge' in *Royal United Services Institute Journal*, CIX, No. 633 (February, 1964), pp. 27-31.

[13] On Montgomery's recommendation to cancel, see Field Marshal Bernard Montgomery, *Memoirs* (London, 1958), p. 76, also Brigadier Maurice Chilton, of Montgomery's South-Eastern Command, to Crerar 7 July, File 220C1.009(D3) DND; COS (42) 64th (O) 6 July 1942; Hamilton, *Monty*, p. 505. Judging by the memoirs of Goronwy Rees (see below), his representative for *Rutter* planning, Montgomery was never much interested in the project and probably did not like having responsibility without authority. One can well believe, therefore, his 1962 statement for the CBC program 'Close-Up' that he was 'delighted, absolutely delighted' at the cancellation, which was the impression Rees had at the time. Transcript of 'Close-Up: Dieppe' in Directorate of History, National Defence Headquarters, Canada (hereafter DND), 594/009(D13), and Goronwy Rees, *A Bundle of Sensations* (London, 1960), p. 157. For many years

Mountbatten and his supporters explained the replacement of Baillie-Grohman as something involuntary—due to his sudden posting elsewhere—but on two occasions at least Mountbatten claimed that it was his decision, in 1950 telling Churchill that it was because Baillie-Grohman was a 'sick man' and in 1971 telling Hughes-Hallett that he had pushed Baillie-Grohman aside because he (Hughes-Hallett) could do a much better job. The truth is more probably that Baillie-Grohman refused to have anything to do with the revival of *Rutter*, being dismayed by the lack of professionalism in Mountbatten's organization. Mountbatten's draft replies to Churchill's questions are attached to Mountbatten to Ismay, 29 August 1950 , Ismay Papers, Liddell Hart Centre, King's College, London (hereafter KC); Mountbatten to Hughes-Hallett, 3 September 1971, in MG 30 E463 NAC. On Baillie-Grohman's criticism of COHQ, see pp.193-5 of this book.

[14] Lord Lovat, *March Past* (London, 1978), pp. 242, 245, 272-3, 275.

[15] Combined Plan, 31 July 1942, 75/10 DND.

[16] W.A.B. Douglas and Brereton Greenhous, *Out of the Shadows: Canada in the Second World War* (Toronto, 1977), p. 113.

[17] Hughes-Hallett, Unpublished Memoirs, p.188, NAC.

[18] Hughes-Hallett, untitled comments on Robertson manuscript in the Hughes-Hallett Papers, IWM.

[19] Hughes-Hallett had boxed himself in badly, having loudly complained about too many Force Commanders who cancelled operations for the slightest reason. He would have looked very foolish had he returned to England without having landed the men. The warning is to be found in DEFE 3/187. Professor F.H. Hinsley's silence on these in his official history, *British Intelligence During the Second World War*, is hard to understand, particularly as intercepts and their use were a major concern of his study. There is no mention of the failure to get this intelligence to the Naval Force Commander in his long appendix on the role of intelligence in the Dieppe raid. John Campbell of McMaster University, to whom I am indebted for drawing this to my attention, is writing a study that will deal with the problem of these intercepts.

[20] T. Murray Hunter, *Canada at Dieppe* (Ottawa, Canadian War Museum, 1982), pp. 39-41.

[21] Hamilton, *Monty*, p. 549. Mountbatten to Churchill, 20 August 1942, CAB 120/69.

[22] New York *Journal-American, Daily News, New York Post*, Toronto *Star, Windsor Daily Star*, all 20 August 1942.

[23] Sound recordings, from Canadian Broadcasting Corporation archives accompanying Doug Stuebing, *Dieppe 1942* (Toronto, 1967). Mountbatten had in fact written to Eisenhower to claim some of the credit for Normandy. Eisenhower's response, saying in effect that he had managed to avoid the mistakes of Dieppe, may be read more than one way. Mountbatten to Eisenhower, 25 June 1944, and Eisenhower to Mountbatten, 11 July 1944, both in Mountbatten file, Eisenhower Papers, Abilene, Kansas.

[24] C.P.Stacey, *A Date with History* (Ottawa, n.d. but *c*. 1982); 'The Curious Case of Lord Beaverbrook', Mountbatten Papers, p.10, MB1 C20; cf. Tom Driberg, *Beaverbrook, A Study in Power and Frustration* (London, 1956), p. 291.


## 2. MOUNTBATTEN AND MYTH

[1] The Churchill Estate has adopted a rule, incomprehensible to most historians, that no researcher shall be allowed to consult the Churchill Papers, held at the Churchill Centre Archives, Cambridge, England, until *ten* years after publication of the last volume of Martin Gilbert's official biography.

[2] Churchill to Ismay, 21 December 1942. PREM 3/256. The questions, with Ismay's answers, are in Ismay Papers II/3/251 ff., KC, ibid. I am grateful to Sir William Deakin for this insight; Ismay at first did not object to the publication of the 21 December minute and the reply of 29 December—see Ismay to Commodore G.R.G. Allen, 21 July 1950, Ismay Papers II/3/251, KC.

³ Churchill to Pownall, 20 March 1950, Ismay Papers, II/3/247 ff., KC, ibid.

⁴ Ibid.

⁵ Churchill in an Introduction to General Hastings Ismay, *The Memoirs of General The Lord Ismay* (London, 1960).

⁶ Mountbatten to Brooke, 31 August 1942, CAB 127/24, and same to same, 4 September 1942, ibid.; Brooke to Mountbatten, 1 November 1942, WO 100/411S; Ismay to Mountbatten, 9 December 1942, ibid.

⁷ The confrontation is described in Mountbatten to Brooke, 31 August 1942, CAB 127/24; same to same, 4 September 1942, ibid.; Brooke to Mountbatten, 1 November 1942, WO 100/411S; Ismay to Mountbatten, 9 December 1942, ibid.

⁸ For good measure, Mountbatten had also managed to dragoon David Astor, the owner of the *Observer*, to serve on his public-relations staff: Mountbatten to Hughes-Hallett, 3 September 1971 (enclosure), MG 30 E463, NAC; on the complicated program to get publicity for the raid, see ADM 2/546, appendix IV, and DEFE 2/329, generally; also Mountbatten to Baillie-Grohman, Roberts, and Leigh-Mallory, 30 June 1942, in AIR 16/760. Despite all this vast public-relations effort and the huge, star-studded staff, Jock Lawrence had the temerity to tell Quentin Reynolds that Mountbatten hated publicity. (It was a different era in journalism and Reynolds had no difficulty in accepting the claim.) Quentin Reynolds, *Dress Rehearsal* (New York, 1943), p. 12.

⁹ A.B. Austin, *We Landed At Dawn* (London 1942), p. 51.

¹⁰ Austin's description of Mountbatten is on pp. 64-5 of his *We Landed* (apparently describing the occasion that prompted the photograph reproduced on the jacket of *Unauthorized Action*); Reynolds, *Dress Rehearsal*, p. 15.

¹¹ Austin, *We Landed*, pp. 121-7; Reynolds *Dress Rehearsal*, pp. 256-7.

¹² The first attempt at explanation—probably drafted by, or with the assistance of, C.P. Stacey—was Crerar to all Commanders, 29 August 1942, in RG 24, vol. 10875. The fuller Report 100 is in 594.013 (D17); a slightly differently annotated one is in 594.019 (D8) DND. C.P. Stacey, in *A Date with History* (Ottawa, n.d., but *c*. 1982), cites his first drafts, which Combined Operations did not like, as CMHQ File 3/Dieppe/1 in RG 24, vol. 12, p. 300, NAC.

¹³ Skrine's papers were the basis for COHQ's reconstruction of their lost Dieppe files: see DEFE 2/542; Hughes-Hallett to Stacey, 30 September 1942, DND.

¹⁴ C.P. Stacey, *The Canadian Army, 1939-1945* (Ottawa, 1948), p. 86.

¹⁵ Ibid., pp. 57-8.

¹⁶ Ibid., pp. 80-1.

¹⁷ Ibid., p. 55; Churchill to Ismay, 21 December 1942, PREM 3/256.

¹⁸ Churchill to Ismay, 15 August 1942 (REFLEX 99), CAB 120/66; Ismay to Churchill, 16 August 1942 (TULIP 145), CAB 120/69.

¹⁹ Ismay to Churchill, 22 March 1950, Ismay Papers II/3/248, KC. The charter is set forth in Churchill to Ismay, Brooke, and Bridges, 19 July 1940. The seriousness of the communication may be judged from the long need-to-see list carefully checked off, all in CAB 120/9; Ismay to Churchill, 22 March 1950, in Ismay Papers II/3/248, and Ismay to Pownall, 21 July 1950, Ismay Papers II/3/251, both KC.

²⁰ Ismay to Allen, 21 July 1950, Ismay Papers II/3/251 and attachments—all KC.

²¹ Churchill to Ismay, 2 August 1950, Ismay Papers II/2/252, KC.

²² Ibid.

²³ Ismay to Mountbatten, 9 August 1950, MB1 N42; Deakin to Churchill, 29 August 1950, cited by Martin Gilbert in *Road to Victory* (London and Boston, 1986), p. 551, and by Sir William Deakin to author, 25 January 1989.

²⁴ Ismay to Churchill, 14 August 1950, Ismay Papers II/3/252, KC.

²⁵ Churchill to Pownall, 20 March 1950, Ismay Papers II/3/247/2a ff., KC.

²⁶ See note 19, above.

²⁷ Ismay to Churchill, 22 March 1950, II/3/248; Churchill to Ismay, 2 August 1950, Ismay Papers II/3/252—both KC.

[28] Ismay to Churchill, 14 August 1950, Ismay Papers II/3/252, KC; COS (42) 355th, 23 December 1950. See also JIC (42) 468 (O), 5 December 1942, in CSIC CAB 121/364 (*Rutter*), by courtesy of the Cabinet Historical Office. The latter is part of the General L. Hollis files, known at the time as the Cabinet Secret Information Centre files — perhaps the most important World War II series still held directly under the control of the Cabinet Office. The *Rutter* folder at the time I examined it contained no indication that *Jubilee* was authorized.

[29] Ibid., Ismay to Mountbatten, 9 December 1942, CAB 127/24; Mountbatten to Hughes-Hallett, 3 September 1971 (enclosure, Hughes-Hallett Papers), MG 30 E463, NAC.

[30] Ismay to Churchill, 14 August 1950, Ismay Papers II/3/258, KC.

[31] Mountbatten was always somewhat reticent about identifying who was kept informed of the project, but he was obliged to give a list of names to General McNaughton, the Canadian military chief in Britain, of those 'aware of the project' (a somewhat loose and elastic phrase), McNaughton's Memorandum of Record is our only source, as COHQ, unbelievably, kept no record; Appendix 'K' (25 July 1942) to McNaughton War Diary, July 1942, in MG 30 E133 (volume 248), NAC.

[32] See note 23, above.

[33] Mountbatten to Ismay, 11 August 1950, Ismay Papers II 3/256.

[34] Hughes-Hallett to Mountbatten, 18 August 1950, Ismay Papers II, 3/260.

[35] Mountbatten to Major-General G.E. Wildman-Lushington, 11 August 1950, MB1 N42, and Wildman-Lushington to Mountbatten, 17 August 1950, Ismay Papers II/3/260, KC. A few days later Wildman-Lushington also reported to Mountbatten that 'I have been on to the Cabinet offices . . . and they cannot help us very much . . . they told me that Mr. Winston Churchill's devillers have [already had] full access to all records . . .'; same to same, 22 August 1950 — MB1 N42.

[36] Mountbatten to Ismay, 29 August 1950, Ismay Papers II/3/260, KC.

[37] Mountbatten to Ismay, 5 September 1950, Ismay Papers II/3/261, KC.

[38] Ibid.; draft with notations in Ismay Papers, II/3/261/4a ff., KC. Ismay, it should be noted, counselled Mountbatten by telephone about what should and should not be included.

[39] Ibid.

[40] Mountbatten to Churchill, 4 September 1950, Ismay Papers II/3/261, KC; Appendix 'O' (25 July 1942) to McNaughton War Diary, July 1942, in MG 30 E133 (volume 248), NAC; Lord Lovat, *March Past* (London, 1978), p. 277; Mountbatten to Hughes-Hallett, 3 September 1971 (enclosure) in MG 30 E 463, NAC.

[41] Mountbatten to Ismay, 4 September 1950, Ismay Papers II/3/261, KC; Mountbatten to Hughes-Hallett, 3 September 1971 (enclosure) in MG 30 E 463, NAC.

[42] Philip Ziegler, *Mountbatten* (London and New York, 1985), p. 701. One could only wish that Ziegler had given us more examples of Mountbatten's attempts to rewrite history. The files he consulted were not empty on this score.

[43] Mountbatten would not have liked Stacey's later view of the Dieppe plan: 'A single infantry division with so little support behind it to overrun so strong a position, this was perfectly absurd.' 1978 Stacey interview with T. Macartney-Filgate in 79/567 DND; Mountbatten to Churchill, 4 September 1950, Ismay Papers II/3/261, KC.

[44] Churchill to Mountbatten — no date, but almost certainly 12 September 1950, Ismay Papers, II/3/268, KC.

[45] Winston Churchill, *The Hinge of Fate* (Boston, 1950), p. 510 and fn.

[46] Ibid., p. 511; R.W. Thompson, *At Whatever Cost: The Story of the Dieppe Raid* (New York, 1957), published in the UK as *Dieppe at Dawn*, p. 10; Richard Garrett, *The Raiders* (New York, 1980), p. 121. Terence Robertson also fell victim to this temptation to quote from what must have appeared to him as two independent sources; see Robertson, *The Shame and the Glory*, p. xi.

[47] See note 21, above.

[48] Mountbatten's efforts to change the history of Dieppe have been recounted by Richard Hough in *Mountbatten: Hero of Our Time* (London, 1980), pp. 156-7. In Mountbatten's own files

there are indications aplenty of his efforts in 1955, and again in 1959, to influence Roskill's official writing (while the latter was working under a very independent charter from the Cabinet Historical Office), which involved Brooke (by then Lord Alanbrooke), who cut short one particularly flagrant example of Mountbatten's fanciful reworking of history having to do with his claim to have been given, as Supreme Commander in South-East Asia, extraordinary unwritten authority to hire and fire people. Mountbatten was most insistent, not to say threatening, in his search for corroboration of this. Alanbrooke told Roskill that there was no truth to it, and Mountbatten was forced to recant. Both the 1955 and the 1959 correspondence with Roskill is in MB1 116. On Mountbatten's sudden change of mind as to what he wanted to see in an official history of Combined Operations, see Mountbatten to Wildman-Lushington, 9 December 1949, and Alan Campbell-Johnson to Brockman, 23 November 1950, in MB1 B58.

[49] Mountbatten, 1972, BBC-1 interview, author's notes.

[50] See Appendix I, p. 248, for a fuller discussion.

[51] Wildman-Lushington to Mountbatten, 17 August 1950, Ismay II/3/260, KC.

[52] COS (42) 54th (0), 21 June 1942; COS (42) 64th (0), 6 July 1942; F.H. Hinsley, *British Intelligence During the Second World War*, Vol. II (London, 1981), Appendix 13, pp. 695-704.

[53] Mountbatten to Hughes-Hallett, 3 September 1971 (enclosure), MG 30 E463, NAC; Mountbatten, 1972. BBC-1 interview, author's notes.

[54] John Terraine, *The Life and Times of Lord Mountbatten* (London, 1968), p. 167; Arthur Bryant, *The Turn of the Tide* (London, 1957), p. 693; Pownall Diary, 14 September 1943, 14 March 1944, in Brian Bond, *Chief of Staff: The Diaries of Lieutenant-General Sir Henry Pownall*, Vol. II (London, 1972), pp. 108, 201; A.J.P.Taylor, *Beaverbrook* (London, 1972), p. 638. On Churchill's reluctance to promote Mountbatten to First Sea Lord—possibly on account of Dieppe—see Ziegler, *Mountbatten*, p. 523.

[55] Christopher Buckley, *Norway: The Commandos, Dieppe* (London, 1952), pp. 233-4,; Amphibious Warfare Headquarters, *History of Combined Operations 1940-1945* (London, 1956), p. 16—a copy is in ADM 234/354 PRO; see also Rear-Admiral John Hughes-Hallett, 'The Mounting of Raids', in *Royal United Services Institute Journal*, November 1950, XCV, pp. 580-8, especially p. 586; confidential print of Stephen Roskill, *The War at Sea, 1939-1945*, Volume II, *The Period of Balance* (London, 1956), p. 243, in CAB 101/37 PRO. Also inconsistent with the supposed approval of 20 July date is the fact that as of that day there was still no Outline Plan, as the alterations from the *Rutter* plan were not yet fixed. It is inconceivable that without an Outline Plan, the Chiefs would have given their approval. See minutes, Jubilee Force Commanders' meeting 16 July, in the Hughes-Hallett Papers IWM. Confidential print of J.M.A. Gwyer and J.R.M. Butler, *Grand Strategy*, Volume III, Pt II (London, 1964), p. 639, in CAB 101/15 PRO (emphasis added).

[56] Hinsley, *British Intelligence*, II, p. 696, COS (42) 234th, 12 August 1942; 'Combined Plan' of 30 July 1942 in 75/10 DND. The Combined Plan might be more properly titled a warning order. Lt-Col. John Durnford-Slater, who was called in to help draft it, refers to it as a 'final operation order'; see John Durnford-Slater, *Commando* (London, 1953), p. 99. For more discussion of this order, see below, note 61.

[57] Combined Report, DEFE 2/551 PRO; this would appear to be the basis for Battle Report 1886, sometimes referred to as CB 04244, missing from Admiralty records. The early Battle Report interpreted the 27 July minute as a specific directive for *Jubilee*. But when Mountbatten became Chief of the Defence Staff, the version was improved upon, and the shortened Battle Report, 1736(26) in ADM 234/354 PRO, was revised (1959) from the earlier (c. 1949) version to include a statement that the Chiefs of Staff expressly approved the remounting of *Rutter* as *Jubilee*. Of course the new version gave no date, and the footnote was to an entirely different issue—to the movement of troops prior to departure.

[58] Ibid., and the cables cited above in note 17.

[59] The draft chit is in Hughes-Hallett to Mountbatten, 17 July 1942 in the Hughes-Hallett Papers (Box P75), IWM. This document bears a COHQ file reference number of P.135. It should also be noted that, contrary to what Hughes-Hallett and Mountbatten claimed, there was

generated a COHQ document that stated bluntly that the 'Operation is simply a repeat of the abortive Operation "Rutter" . . . with . . . slight modifications.' A document titled 'Operation "Jubilee"' may be found in a sheaf of papers prepared for a 16 July 1942 Force Commanders' meeting; it bears the original COHQ file classification P. 135, and is presently in the Hughes-Hallett Papers, IWM. It is undated but is probably of 14 July.

60 Hughes-Hallett to Mountbatten, 17 July 1942, in the Hughes-Hallett Papers, IWM.

61 Two weeks later another bogus document was generated: the so-called Combined Plan or warning order of 31 July 1942, DND 75/10. This rather unusual document was made to look like an approved Outline Plan—the lack of a statement of COS approval prompted this production of a facsimile. Its misleading character becomes apparent when it is compared with an authentic warning order, such as that for *Rutter*: i.e. Mountbatten to Naval, Military, and Air Force Commanders of 13 May 1942, identified by COHQ files reference P. 126/159 in RG 24, Volume 10, 872 (file 232C2 (D35) NAC and attachments). Not surprisingly, there is no mention of this 31 July document in any of the later battle summaries of official histories. Apparently there was no desire to call attention to it. Hughes-Hallett discussed it only once, towards the end of his life in his Unpublished Memoirs (p. 179), in which he wrote somewhat disingenuously that 'At the time of Dieppe there was no set pattern for such orders . . . we felt our way forward to what was destined to become standard practice. . . . [The] "Combined Plan" was NOT an order, but it enabled each Force Commander to issue Operation Orders to give effect to the Plan' (Hughes-Hallett's emphasis). This strange business would never have been necessary if Mountbatten had had COS approval, in which case he could have cited it to the Force Commanders.

62 Hughes-Hallett, Unpublished Memoirs, p. 168 (MG 30 E 463, NAC). The surviving *Rutter* minutes show the presence of either Wildman-Lushington or Haydon. None of the *Jubilee* minutes do.

63 Hughes-Hallett to Mountbatten, 17 July 1942, in Hughes-Hallett Papers (Box P 74), IWM; Hughes-Hallett, Unpublished Memoirs, p. 170, 171; Hughes-Hallett to C.P. Stacey, 30 December 1952,594.011(D8), DND.

64 Mountbatten to Chiefs of Staff, 'Proposed Entry in COS Minutes', 17 July 1942, CISC CAB 121/364, Cabinet Historical Office; Churchill to Ismay, 2 August 1942, Ismay Papers II/352/2a, KC.

65 Hughes-Hallett to Mountbatten, 28 September 1962, B72; A.P.W. Maclellan to Mountbatten, 5 July 1962. Among the missing files are most of the normal COHQ serial files on *Jubilee*. Other examples are ADM 202/408, Marine *Jubilee* records (missing when they were turned over to the PRO on 14/12/1970; WO 193 [403] (correspondence between Brooke and Mountbatten on Summary of Lessons Learned).

66 Lord Lovat, *March Past*, p. 271.

## 3. THE CRISIS AT THE TOP

1 Lord Charles Moran, *Churchill: Taken from the Diaries of Lord Moran: The Struggle for Survival, 1940-1945* (Boston, 1966), p. 195; Mountbatten to Ismay, 29 August 1950, Ismay II/3/260, KC.

2 Martin Gilbert, *The Road to Victory* (London and Boston, 1986), pp. 60ff. In Chapter 4, 'Nothing But Disaster to Show', Gilbert acknowledges Churchill's depression in 1942; somewhat more candid in admitting Churchill's state is Robert Rhodes James in *Anthony Eden: A Biography* (London 1986), pp. 262-3. The best analysis of Churchill's 'black dog mood' remains that by Anthony Storr in A.J.P. Taylor et al., eds., *Churchill Revised: A CriticalAssessment* (New York, 1969), pp. 229-74.

3 Colville Diary, 6 June 1941, in John Colville, *The Fringes of Power: 10 Downing Street Diaries, 1939-1955* (London, 1985), p. 395.

⁴ Churchill to Wavell, 9 June 1941, and Portal to Wavell, same date, both in Great Britain, Cabinet Office, Principal War Telegrams and memoranda 1940-1943: Middle East, Vol. I, nos. 125, 129; Churchill, *Grand Alliance*, p. 343; Cadogan Diary, 18 June 1941, reprinted in David Dilks, ed., *The Diaries of Sir Alexander Cadogan, 1938-1945* (London, 1971), p. 389; Maj.-Gen. Sir John Kennedy, *The Business of War* (New York, 1958), p. 181; Churchill to Auchinleck, 28 January 1942, quoted in Gilbert, *Road to Victory*, p. 51.

⁵ Dalton Diary, 19 February 1942, in Ben Pimlott, ed., *The Second World War Diary of Hugh Dalton* (London, 1986), pp. 372-3; Russell Grenfell, *Main Fleet to Singapore* (London, 1951), pp. 210-13, 229-31 (this is an excellent pioneering study of the problems of Churchill's war direction).

⁶ Churchill to Roosevelt, 2 November 1941, in Warren Kimball, *Churchill & Roosevelt: The Complete Correspondence* (Princeton, 1984), I, p. 265; Samuel Eliot Morison, *The Rising Sun in the Pacific* (Boston, 1948), p. 190.

⁷ Eden Diary, 21 January 1942, reprinted in the Earl of Avon, *The Eden Memoirs: The Reckoning* (London, 1965), p. 318.

⁸ Smuts to M.C. Gillett, 31 January 1942, in Jean Van Der Poel, ed., *The Smuts Papers, Volume VI, December 1934-August 1945* (Cambridge, 1973), pp. 346-9.

⁹ Harvey Diary, 16 April 1942, in John Harvey, ed., *The War Diaries of Oliver Harvey*, II (London, 1978), p. 117; Cecil King Diary, 23 March 1942, in William Armstrong, ed., *With Malice Towards None: A War Diary by Cecil King* (London, 1970), p. 170; Lord Moran, *Churchill*, p. 29.

¹⁰ Colville Diary, 6 June 1941, in Colville, *Fringes*, p. 395; Inspector Walter H. Thompson, *Assignment: Churchill* (Toronto, 1955), p. 263; the Beaverbrook quotation is from Kenneth Young, *Churchill and Beaverbrook* (London, 1966), p. 266.

¹¹ Eden Diary, 27 April 1942, in the Earl of Avon, *Memoirs*, p. 326; Malcolm MacDonald (appointed in 1941 High Commissioner in Canada, a post he held with distinction, wielding much influence) is quoted in the Nicolson diary for 22 April 1942 in Nigel Nicolson, ed., *Harold Nicolson: Diaries and Letters 1939-1945* (London, 1967), p. 223; Dalton Diary, 23 April 1942, in Ben Pimlott, ed., *The Second World War Diary of Hugh Dalton* (London, 1986), p. 415.

¹² Roosevelt to Churchill, 18 February 1942, in Warren Kimball, *Churchill & Roosevelt*, Vol. II (Princeton, 1984), pp. 362-3.

¹³ Harriman to Roosevelt, 6 March 42, quoted in Averell Harriman and Elie Able, *Special Envoy to Churchill and Stalin* (New York, 1976), pp.126-7. Harriman sought to prevent others in the British Government from doing anything that might weaken Churchill; see Leo Amery Diary, 16 March 1942, in John Barnes and David Nicholson, eds, *The Empire at Bay: The Leo Amery Diaries, 1929-1945* (London, 1988), pp. 766-7.

¹⁴ Churchill to Roosevelt, 5 March 1942, in Kimball, *Churchill & Roosevelt*, pp 381-4; Mary Soames Diary, 27 February 1942, quoted in Mary Soames, *Clementine Churchill: The Biography of a Marriage* (Boston, 1979), p. 415;Clementine Churchill to Nellie Romilly, 28 February 1942, ibid, p. 415.; Mary Soames Diary, n.d., quoted in Gilbert, *Road to Victory*, p.69; Clementine to Winston Churchill, no date but probably 19 February 1942, in Mary Soames, *Clementine Churchill*, p. 414.

¹⁵ Jan Smuts to J. Martin, 26 February 1942, to M.C. Gillett, 10 March 1942, in Van Der Poel, ed., *Smuts*, Vol. VI, pp. 356-7; Roosevelt to Churchill, 18 March 1942, MR, Kimball, *Churchill & Roosevelt*, pp. 420-2.

¹⁶ R.M. Barrington-Ward's diary of 19 February 1942 in Donald McLachlan, *In the Chair: Barrington Ward of the Times, 1927-1948* (London, 1971), p. 192. INF 1/192, Home Intelligence Weekly Report. No. 119, 5-12 June 1943.

¹⁷ Cadogan Diary, 2 March 1942, in David Dilks, ed., *The Diaries of Sir Alexander Cadogan, 1938-1945* (London, 1971). Dalton Diary, 12 May 1942, in Ben Pimlott, ed., *Diary of Hugh Dalton*, p. 433. After one Cabinet meeting in March, Amery noted of Churchill, '. . . he is overtired and really losing his grip altogether . . . I went away seriously disquieted', Amery Diary, 26 February 1942, in Barnes and Nicholson, *Empire at Bay*, p. 779.

[18] Stimson Diary, 22 June 1942, Yale University Archives; Lord Moran, *Churchill*, pp. 40-1.
[19] Ivan Maisky, *Memoirs of a Soviet Ambassador*, translated by Andrew Rothstein (New York, 1968), pp. 292-3.
[20] The slow development of *The Times* criticism of the Crete venture can be traced in the issues between 21 May and 13 June 1941. (The paper was at the time waxing enthusiastic over the destruction of the *Bismarck* and seems to have been embarrassed in pressing home its criticism of Churchill's war direction. This may reveal the political reason why Churchill was so obsessed about destroying the *Bismarck*. See p. 98.) Winston Churchill, *Their Finest Hour* (Boston, 1949), p. 493; Kennedy, *Business of War*, p. 145.
[21] It is inconceivable that Wardlaw-Milne could have proposed the Duke of Gloucester's name without consulting Buckingham Palace, which he could not have done save through Churchill, whose hand in encouraging him to make his proposal seems apparent; see Cecil King Diary, 2 March 1942, in Armstrong, *Malice*, p. 162; R. Stokes-Reese to J. Swetenham, Swetenham Papers, correspondence file 1967-9, MG 31 E42, NAC.
[22] Harvey Diary, 25 June 1941, in John Harvey, ed., *War Diaries*, II, p. 15; Macmillan to Beaverbrook, 13 October 1942, cited by A.J.P. Taylor in *Churchill Revised*, pp. 494-5; Amery feared Churchill gave the appearance of being 'gaga, like one who could not understand what people were talking about', Amery Diary, 26 February 1942, in Barnes and Nicholson, *Empire at Bay*, p. 779; Cecil King Diary, 7 August 1941, in Armstrong, *Malice*, p. 138; Harold Nicolson Diary, 14 January 1942, in Nicolson, *Nicolson Diaries: The War Years*, p. 205; Dalton Diary for 12 May 1942 in Pimlot, *Second World War Diary*, p. 433; see also entries for 19 May, p. 437, 26 May, p. 445, and 31 May, p. 450; Kenneth Harris, *Attlee* (New York, 1982), pp. 585-8, also pp. 196-7; Eden Diary,27 February 1942, in Rhodes, *Eden*, pp. 262-3. For evidence of Bracken's later disaffection, see WP (42) 298, 17 July 1942.
[23] Lord Moran, *Churchill*, p. 79.

## 4. THREE POWERS IN SEARCH OF A STRATEGY

[1] Basil Liddell Hart, *History of the Second World War* (London, 1970), p. 142.
[2] Churchill, 4 June 1940 speech, *Hansard*.
[3] Minutes, meeting of Anglo-American Standardization of Arms Committee, 31 August 1940, WMD 4402-1, RG 165, NA; Maj.-Gen. Sir John Kennedy, *The Business of War* (New York, 1958), p. 183; M.R.D. Foot, *S.O.E. in France* (London, 1966), p. 2.
[4] Three studies form the point of departure for reflections on the strategic debate: Michael Howard, *The Mediterranean Strategy in the Second World War* (London, 1968), Kent Roberts Greenfield, *American Strategy in World War II: A Reconsideration* (Baltimore, 1963), and Samuel E. Morison, *Strategy and Compromise* (Boston, 1958); a more recent review is Keith Sainsbury, '''Second Front in 1942'', A Strategic Controversy Revisited', *British Journal of International Studies*, IV (1978), pp. 47-58; see also David Stafford, *Britain and the European Resistance, 1940-1945* (Toronto, 1980) and Stafford, 'The Detonator Concept: British Strategy, SOE and European Resistance after the Fall of France,' *Journal of Contemporary History*, Volume 10, No. 2 (April 1975).
[5] For a stimulating re-examination of the question of German calculations, see David Downing, *The Devil's Virtuosos: The German Generals at War 1940-5* (New York, 1977).
[6] W.K. Hancock and M. Gowing, *British War Economy* (London, 1949), particularly the chapters 'Manpower', pp. 281-314, and 'The Cost of Increasing Effort', pp. 315-43.
[7] Churchill to Pound, *c.* 5 December 1939, cited By Stephen Roskill, *Churchill and the Admirals* (London 1977), p. 95.
[8] General Strategy Review by the British Chiefs of Staff, 31 July 41, item 10, Exec 4, OPD RG 165 NA.
[9] JB 355, ser. 707, cited by Maurice Matloff and John Snell, *Strategic Planning for Coalition Warfare, 1941-1942* (Washington, GPO, 1953), p. 61; Robert Dallek, *Franklin D. Roosevelt and American Foreign Policy 1932-1945* (New York, 1979), p. 214.

[10] Adolf Berle Diary, 26 December 1939, in Beatrice Berle, ed., *Navigating the Rapids: From the Papers of Adolf A. Berle* (New York, 1973), pp. 254-8, 273, 276. Berle was receiving the highest-classification intelligence reports. See also Matloff and Snell, p. 280.

[11] Winston Churchill, *The Grand Alliance* (Boston, 1950), pp. 606-8.

[12] Kennedy, *Business of War*, p. 154; Colonel W. F. Kernan, *Defense Will Not Win the War* (Boston, 1942), especially pages 150-2.

[13] Earl of Avon, *The Eden Memoirs: The Reckoning* (London, 1965), pp. 141, 159; DO (42) 5th, 30 January 1942.

[14] Churchill to Chiefs of Staff, 21 December 1941, PREM 3/499/2; notes of General Marshall at a White House meeting, 23 December 1941, WMD 4402-136, RG 165 NA.

[15] (USSR, Foreign Ministry) 'Diplomatic History of the Opening of the Second Front in Europe, 1941-1944', in *International Affairs* (Moscow), No. 1, 1970, p. 73; Ivan Maisky (Andrew Rothstein, tr.), *Memoirs of a Soviet Diplomat* (New York, 1967) pp. 187, 188.

[16] Maisky, *Memoirs*, p. 188.

[17] Stalin to Churchill, 3 September 1941 (conveyed to Cripps on 4 September), F0 371/29573 — not even the Normandy invasion diverted that many divisions; Maisky, *Memoirs*, pp. 188-90, 190-2.

[18] Harriman notes, 28, 29, 30 September 1941, Hopkins Papers (Box 306), FDR Library, Hyde Park; quoted in A.J.P. Taylor, *Beaverbrook* (London, 1972), p. 487; William H. Standley and Arthur A. Ageton, *Admiral Ambassador to Russia* (Chicago, 1955), p. 63. One should note that American policy here represented a major reversal from the State Department's policy on the eve of *Barbarossa* when it had recommended that 'Any suggestions that concessions should be made for the sake of improving the atmosphere of American-Soviet relations' should be rejected and the US should 'exact a strict quid pro quo for anything which we are willing to give the Soviet Union'; see Hull to Steinhardt, 14 June 1941, U.S. Department of State, *Foreign Relations of the United States (FRUS)* (Washington, 1941), I, 757-81. Averell Harriman and Elie Abel, *Special Envoy to Churchill and Stalin* (New York, 1975), pp. 87-94; see also J.D. Langer, 'The Harriman-Beaverbrook Mission and the Debate over Unconditional Aid for the Soviet Union, 1941', in Walter Z. Laqueur and G.L. Mosse, eds., *The Second World War: Essays in Military and Political History* (London, 1982).

[19] Cripps to Eden, 14 October 1941, FO 371/29492; Churchill to Stalin, 4 November 1941, FO 371/29493, Churchill, *Grand Alliance*, pp. 528-30. See also Eden, Record of Conversation With the Russian Ambassador, 12 November 1941, F0 954/24 (part 2); Cripps to Churchill, 29 October 1941, ibid.; DO (42) 22 19 October 1941. See the able treatement in Gabriel Gorodetsky, *Stafford Cripps' Mission to Moscow, 1940-2* (Cambridge, 1984), pp. 257-9.

[20] The Anglo-Soviet and Soviet-American communiqués of 12 June 1942 are both reproduced in USSR (Andrew Rothstein, tr.), *Soviet Foreign Policy During the Patriotic War: Documents and Materials*, I (London, n.d., c. 1946), pp. 165-7; Minutes of meeting, 10 June 1942, in PREM 3/333/9; the final text of the *aide-mémoire* of 10 June 1942 is in CAB 120/684; the related drafts are in PREM 3/333/8; for the responsibility of the Chiefs of Staff for the *aide-mémoire*, see Hollis to Prime Minister, 9 June 1942, ibid.

[21] On this Moscow conference see the excellent piece by Graham Ross, 'Operation Bracelet: Churchill in Moscow, 1942' in David Dilks, ed., *Retreat from Power: Studies in Britain's Foreign Policy of the Twentieth Century*, II (London, 1981). Nearing completion is my own study of *Bracelet*, tentatively titled *Stalinist Diplomacy*.

[22] Minutes (by Clark Kerr) of meeting in the Kremlin, 12 August 1942 in FO 800/300 (Kerr Papers) and Minutes of meeting of 15 August 1942 (notes by Major A.H. Birse), ibid.

## 5. GENERAL SIR ALAN BROOKE AND THE PRELUDE TO DIEPPE

[1] John Colville, *Winston Churchill and His Inner Circle* (New York, 1981), p. 183; Arthur Bryant,

*The Turn of the Tide* (London, 1957), p. 334; on Brooke as CIGS, see the able treatment by David Fraser in *Alanbrooke* (London, 1982), pp. 211-17.

[2] Quoted in Bryant, *Turn*, p. 336; ibid., p. 371.

[3] Bryant, *Turn*, p. 327.

[4] On the strange history of the Combined Plan, see note 61 to Chapter 2. The Plan's date of issue was 31 July, but it appears to have been completed on 30 July; indeed, it may have been completed as early as 21 July, judging by the Force Commander's minutes of 16 July in the Hughes-Hallett Papers, IWM. Brooke never openly accused Mountbatten of going ahead. But he approved the biography of his close friend Admiral Sir Bertram H. Ramsay, one of Mountbatten's critics, by Rear-Admiral W.S. Chalmers, for which Brooke wrote an introduction and that makes the point that the decision to remount was taken by the Prime Minister in consultation with Admiral Mountbatten. W.S. Chalmers, *Full Cycle* (London, 1959), p. 138. For indications of Brooke's toleration of Mountbatten's action, see note 44 below.

[5] Brooke Diary, 8 February 1940, noted in Bryant, *Turn*, p. 76; 16 April 1942, ibid., pp. 359-60; ibid., p. 370; 11 November 1940, ibid., p. 247-8.

[6] Bryant, *Turn*, pp. 278-9; ibid., p. 29; ibid., pp. 278-9; ibid., pp. 321-2; Brooke Diary, 4 February 1942, KC.

[7] Ibid., p. 359; Maurice Matloff and John Snell, *Strategic Planning for Coalition Warfare, 1941-1942* (Washington, 1953), p. 23.

[8] Bryant, *Turn*, p. 286; ibid., pp. 287, 404.

[9] Maj-Gen. Sir John Kennedy, *The Business of War* (New York, 1958), Bernard Fergusson, ed., p. 124; quoted in Bryant, *Turn*, p. 333; Brooke Diary, 17 February 1942, ibid., p. 307.

[10] Bryant, *Turn*, p. 404; see the excellent CSIC Report 'Offensive Operations General' (1942), courtesy Cabinet Historical Office, CAB 121/151 A/Strategy/7. On the *quid pro quo*—i.e. the agreement to the American offensive program in principle, in return for additional military assistance to Britain—see COS (42) 23rd (0) 9 April 1942, JP (42) 386 10 April 1942, COS (42) 24th (0), same date, COS (42) 97 (0) 13 April 1942, COS (42) 25th (0) 14 April 1942, DO (42) 10th 15 April 1942, COS (42) 103 (0), 18 April 1942.

[11] On warnings from Dill and the Joint Staff Mission, see for instance Dill to Churchill, 7 March 1942, which was widely distributed in the British Government (copy in ADM 205/13 etc.). The main records from the Joint Staff Mission are in CAB 105, but see also Alex Danchev's excellent study, *Very Special Relationship: Field Marshal Sir John Dill and the Anglo-American Alliance, 1941-1944* (London, 1986); Brooke Diary, 3 December 1941, KC; Bryant, *Turn*, pp. 403-4.

[12] Bryant, *Turn*, p. 371; ibid., p. 240; ibid., p. 369.

[13] Ibid., 4 December 1941, p. 299.

[14] Brooke Diary, 3 December 1941, ibid., p. 278; 12 October 1941, ibid., p. 260-2.

[15] Bryant, *Turn* (quoting 'Notes on My Life'), p. 278.

[16] Brooke Diary, 30 March 1942, in Bryant, *Turn*, p. 340; 16 April 1942, ibid., pp. 359-60.

[17] Dalton Diary for 10 February 1942 in Ben Pimlot ed., *The Second World War Diary of Hugh Dalton* (London, 1986), p. 368; Brooke, 'Notes on My Life' (draft memoirs and collated materials), IV, p. 260, KC; Adm. Sir Charles Forbes to Stephen Roskill, 1 December 1949, quoted in Stephen Roskill, *Churchill and the Admirals* (London, 1977), p. 296.

[18] Brooke, 'Notes on My Life', VI, p. 429, KC.

[19] Bryant, *Turn*, p. 419; see, for instance, Brooke Diary, 19 February 1942, in Bryant, *Turn*, p. 317.

[20] Kennedy, *Business*, p. 241.

[21] Ibid., pp. 104-8.

[22] Churchill, Directive by the Prime Minister and Minister of Defence, 28 April 1942, reproduced in Kennedy, *Business*, pp. 108-10.

[23] Bryant, *Turn*, p. 370-1.

[24] Brooke Diary, 7 April 1942, in Bryant, *Turn*, p. 350; ibid., p. 357.

[25] Brooke Diary, 6 May 1942, in Bryant, *Turn*, p. 372; ibid., 11, 12 May 1942, p. 372.

[26] Bryant, *Turn*, p. 329; 'Notes on My Life', IV, p. 311, and Fraser, *Alanbrooke*, pp. 202-3, 374-5; Brian Bond, ed., *Chief of Staff: The Diaries of Lt.-Gen. Sir Henry Pownall*, II (London, 1974), pp. 53-4; Fraser, *Alanbrooke*, p. 295.

[27] COS (42) 78th mtg, minute 6 (Confidential Annex—other copies destroyed), 10 March 1942; cf. JP (42) 243, Bryant, *Turn*, p. 387; COS (42) 42 (0), 13th May 1942, part of COS (42) 42nd, 13 May 1942, part of COS (42) 149th, same date.

[28] Quentin Reynolds, *Dress Rehearsal: The Story of Dieppe* (New York, 1943), p. 265.

[29] Interview with Major Brian McCool in Ronald Atkin, *Dieppe 1942: The Jubilee Disaster* (London, 1980), p. 249.

[30] Brooke, 'Notes on My Life', V, p. 401, KC. This meeting occurred the day after Molotov's arrival, with the apparent intention of seeing if anything else could be offered the Soviet Foreign Minister; see the main files on *Imperator*, which are DEFE 2/306 and PREM 3/333/19; COS (42) 46th (0), 27 May 1942; COS (42) 166th, 1 June 1942.

[31] Bryant, *Turn*, p. 262; WM (42) 73rd 11 June 1942, Confidential Annex.

[32] Kennedy, *Business*, pp. 174-5.

[33] The Anglo-Soviet and Soviet American communiqués of 12 June 1942 are both reproduced in USSR (Andrew Rothstein, tr.), *Soviet Foreign Policy During the Patriotic War: Documents and Materials* I (London, n.d., c. 1946), pp. 165-7.

[34] COS (42) 157 (0), 6 June 1942, reference WM (42) 54th (Confidential Annex), 29 April 1942; Churchill to Ismay 8 June 1942 in PREM 3/333/19, COS (42) 51st (0), 8 June 1942, and WM (42) 73, 11 June 1942 (Confidential Annex). The *aide-mémoire* of 10 June in CAB 120/684 is conveniently reprinted as an appendix to J.M.A. Gwyer and J.R.M. Butler, *Grand Strategy*, Volume III, pt. II (London, 1964), pp. 682-3. Promising raids of increasing scope and frequency, this *aide-mémoire* was drafted by the Chiefs of Staff; by this document they nailed their flag to Mountbatten's masthead—clear evidence that the Soviet pressure and the Second Front movement were having an impact; see Hollis to Prime Minister 9 June 1942, and related drafts in PREM 3/333/8. Few believed such promises to the Soviets were wise, for as the Spitzbergen raid had shown (at least to General Pownall's satisfaction), the British Government could be coerced into acting against its better judgement because no one wanted to tell the Soviets that on reconsideration there was little to be said for the operation. See Pownall Diary, 8 August 1941, in Bond, *Chief of Staff*, p. 34.

[35] Winston Churchill, *The Hinge of Fate* (Boston, 1950), p. 324; Kennedy, *Business*, p. 145.

[36] COS (42) 51st (0), 8 June 1942; Kennedy, *Business*, p. 245; Churchill to Wardlaw-Milne, 30 June 1942, in Churchill, *Hinge*, p. 394.

[37] Hughes-Hallett to Mountbatten, 18 August 1950, Ismay II/3/260/4a ff; Hughes-Hallett to Stacey, 30 December 1952, 594.001 (D8), DND; C.P. Stacey, *Six Years of War* (Ottawa, 1955), p. 331.

[38] Mann's 'Observations Upon the Outline Plan . . .' is in RG 24, Box 10872, NAC. Brooke's rather unbelievable performance at the 30 June meeting was no doubt what influenced Stacey to conclude that Brooke bore considerable responsibility for Dieppe, advising a fellow historian (John Swettenham) that there was no need to display any obvious animus against Brooke —one need only 'let the record speak': Stacey to Swettenham, 19 March 1967, MG 31 E42, Vol 2, NAC. Any critique of Brooke might begin with one of Brooke's predecessors as Chief of Imperial General Staff, Sir John Dill, who explained that most of his time was spent in 'trying to prevent stupid things being done rather than in doing clever things!' Brooke too understood that this was a major challenge, as his remarks to Wavell on 5 May 1942 acknowledged: 'The process of trying to control the Prime Minister's actions is fraught with difficulties and uncertainties.' Brooke generally succeeded, richly deserving the accolade that Lord Moran later gave him when he said that 'He [Brooke] could . . . be brutally frank in pulling to pieces the Prime Minister's pet projects.' Dieppe was one occasion when Brooke failed. Dill to Montgomery-Massingberd, 19 September 1941, Montgomery-Massingberd Papers, 160/19b, KC, quoted by Alex Danchev in his stimulating essay '"Dilly-Dally" or Having the Last Word: Field Marshal Sir John Dill and Prime Minister Winston Churchill', in *Journal of Contemporary*

*History*, XXII, no. 1 (January 1987), p. 28; Brooke quoted in Bryant, *Turn*, p. 372; Lord Moran, *Taken from the Diaries of Lord Moran* (Boston, 1966), (UK title: *Winston Churchill: The Struggle for Survival*), p. 764.

39 Cunningham to Pound, 1 December 1940, Cunningham Papers, Additional Manuscripts, British Museum; COS (42) 62nd (0), part of COS (42) 194th of 1 July 1942. The Chiefs of Staff first recognized that the Government was bound to do something for the Soviets on the opening day of debate on the Vote of Censure, 1 July, when Churchill seemed to be vulnerable —the Chiefs were clearly trying to shore him up. For Brooke on the Soviets, see Chapter 5, page 80. The negative decision on Norway was anticipated on 6 July at COS (42) 198th. Pound formally reported it to the War Cabinet on 7 July 1942, WM (42) 87th 7 July 1942 (Confidential Annex). On the 9th the Chiefs accepted Churchill's initiative (of the preceding day) entrusting the problem of Norway to McNaughton. COS (42) 202nd 9 July 1942. See also Martin Gilbert, *Winston S. Churchill: The Road to Victory* (London, 1987), p. 144. Pownall Diary, 2 October 1941, in Bond, *Chief of Staff*, p. 45.

40 McNaughton War Diary, 9 July 1942, in MG 30 E133 (volume 248), NAC; Brooke Diary, 9 June 1942, KC; Churchill, *Hinge*, p. 436; ibid., p. 570. Churchill by now was definitely coming around to Mountbatten's belief that *Rutter* was not such a bad thing and could be considered as some element of a substitute package. At the very meeting of the War Cabinet at which Churchill announced that he was killing *Imperator*, he also informed the War Cabinet that *Rutter* 'would take place shortly. It was a "butcher and bolt" raid on the Continent of about 24 hours' duration employing some 6,000 to 7,000 men.' WM (42) 73rd 11 June 1942 (Confidential Annex).

41 Kennedy, *Business*, p. 116; ibid., p. 249.

42 *Time*, 13 July 1942; *The Times*, 22 July 1942; Hughes-Hallett, 1967 interview with John Secondari, in MB1 67/2.

43 Henry L. Stimson, Diary 21 June 1942, Yale University; Forrest C. Pogue, *Ordeal and Hope* (New York, 1967), pp. 330, 346; Brooke Diary, 31 March 1942, KC.

44 Moran, *From the Diaries*, p. 73; Bryant, *Turn*, p. 479

## 6. THE ROYAL NAVY ON THE EVE OF DIEPPE

1 Baillie-Grohman note on the minutes for *Rutter* Force Commanders, meeting 4 June 1942, Baillie-Grohman Papers, National Maritime Museum Archives, Greenwich (MS 67/004, Dieppe folder, private correspondence). Baillie-Grohman took the highest authority to have been Churchill himself, but it is almost certain that the refusal came from Pound. Cf. Pound to Cunningham, 29 January 1942, British Museum additional papers. The request, if made at all, was made informally; see note 60 below.

2 On the vicissitudes of Asdic, see Stephen Roskill, *Naval Policy Between the Wars*, II (London, 1968), pp. 229-30, 452-3; Roskill, *The War at Sea, 1939-1945* (London, HMSO, 1954), pp. 34, 355; Churchill to Roosevelt, 16 October 1939, MR, in Warren Kimball, ed., *Churchill & Roosevelt: The Complete Correspondence*, I (Princeton, 1984), pp. 27-8; Churchill to Pound and Alexander, 14 November 1941, ADM 205/23. Stephen Roskill's treatment of degaussing in *The War at Sea* is very brief, though the records are voluminous. See ADM 202/303-497.

3 Churchill to Fraser, 9 September 1939, Churchill Papers, quoted in Gilbert, *Finest Hour*, p. 18, and in Edwin P. Hoyt, *The U-Boat Wars* (New York, 1984), p. 37.

4 Churchill to Tovey, 27 May 1941, quoted in Ludovic Kennedy, *Pursuit* (London, 1974), pp. 225-6; Stephen Roskill, *Churchill and the Admirals* (London, 1977), p. 15.

5 Churchill to Pound 13 July 1941 in ADM 205/10; Churchill to Pound, 3 October 1941, ibid.

6 Winston Churchill, *The Grand Alliance* (Boston, 1950), p. 620; Churchill to Pound, 11 December 1939, ADM 199/1928; Churchill to Alexander and Pound, 22 October 1940, ADM 199/1931; minute, 21 March 1941, on Cunningham to Pound, 17 March, PREM 3/124/1.

7 The classic weighing of the duel between Churchill and Pound is in Roskill's masterly though strange *Churchill and the Admirals*, in which Roskill takes Pound's side against Churchill for most of the book, only to conclude against Pound.

8 Churchill, *Grand Alliance*, pp. 111-12.

9 On Mers-el-Kebir (Oran), see the Battle Report (CB 1736) and I.S.O. Playfair, et al., *The War in the Mediterranean and the Middle East*, I (London, 1954), pp. 130-8.

10 Churchill to Roosevelt, 8 December 1940, in Kimball, *Churchill & Roosevelt*, pp. 102-11; DO (42) 3rd, 16 January 1942.

11 Churchill, *Grand Alliance*, p. 122.

12 Churchill is quoted in David Dilks, ed., *The Diaries of Sir Alexander Cadogan, 1938-1945* (London, 1971), 20 March 1941, p. 364. The statistics are carefully laid out in Appendix R of Roskill, *The War at Sea*, pp. 615-18.

13 Churchill, minute of 21 June 1941, CAB 120/10; Roskill, *War at Sea*, p. 462ff.

14 Pound to Churchill, 2 July 1941, and vice versa, 5 July 1941, in ADM 205/10.

15 Pound to Admiralty Staff, 24 February 1942, ADM 205/15; memorandum by the First Sea Lord, 10 May, ibid. Pound's initial reply was DO (42), 18 March 1942. See also DO (42) 8th, same date.

16 Trenchard memorandum in COS (41) 86 (0), 29 May 1941.

17 COS to Churchill, 7 June 1941 (no number), CAB 121/001, Cabinet Historical Office.

18 Memorandum from Pound, 21 October 1941, in CAB 121/001, Cabinet Historical Office; Churchill to Pound 19 October 1942 in ADM 205/10.

19 Memorandum from Pound, 21 October 1941, in CAB 121/001, Cabinet Historical Office.

20 Churchill to Pound, 14 November 1941, in ADM 205/13; Churchill to COS, December 1941, no date, but approximately 30 December, identified as Grey cable Ī66 in ADM/205/13; Churchill to Ismay, 7 January 1942, PREM 3/47/1.

21 Churchill to First Lords, 25 August 1941, in ADM 205/10; Churchill to Roosevelt of 2 November 1941, MR, in Kimball, *Churchill & Roosevelt*, p. 265. For evidence of Pound's reservations, see Churchill to Menzies of Australia, 21 November 1941, and Pound to Church-ill, 28 August 1941, ibid.

22 Churchill, *Grand Alliance*, p. 620; Churchill to Pound, 13 March 1942, ADM 205/13; Churchill to Pound, 22 January 1942, ibid.; the 13 March document, see above, this note; Churchill to Pound, 24 March 1942, ibid.

23 Churchill to Pound, 8 February 1942, in PREM 3/324/15; Churchill to Roosevelt, 15 April 1942, MR, in Kimball, *Churchill & Roosevelt*, pp. 452-4; Pound to Churchill, 28 August 1941, in ADM 205/10 and attached memo.

24 Churchill to Pound, Alexander, and Ismay, 16 June 1942, in Admiralty 205/13.

25 Churchill to Pound, 14 April 1942, in ADM 205/13, and a second memorandum of that date in the same file from which the red flag has (recently?) been torn.

26 Maj-Gen. Sir John Kennedy, *The Business of War* (New York, 1958), Bernard Fergusson, ed., p. 108.

27 Churchill to Pound, 1 June 1942, in ADM 205/13; Pound to Alexander, 6 June 1942, ADM 205/13; see also COS (42) 168th, 3 June 1942.

28 Churchill to Pound and Alexander, 21 July 1942, ADM 205/13.

29 Pound to Churchill, 7 March 1942, cited by Roskill in *Churchill and the Admirals*—the letter was, as Roskill notes (p. 204), a most 'curious letter'; Churchill minute to COS 6 March 1942, PREM 3/330/2. According to Philip Ziegler, Churchill's decision to elevate Mountbatten came on 4 March 1942, *Mountbatten* (London, 1985), p. 168; Pound's letter resigning from the Chairmanship of the Chiefs of Staff Committee was apparently dated 6 March. Churchill accepted, apparently without making any attempt to dissuade Pound. That evening Churchill told Brooke of his intention to place him in the chair. On 7 March Pound wrote his letter recapitulating the differences over the Mountbatten elevation. There was apparently no response from Churchill, and on 8 March, Brooke took over the chair. There has been some attempt to obscure the relationship between Pound's demotion and Mountbatten's elevation.

The Pound letter opposing Mountbatten mysteriously disappeared from Churchill's files, though there are double files containing duplicates. Were it not for a copy in the possession of the late Stephen Roskill, we might not know about it at all. Churchill, of course, is completely silent, in *The Hinge of Fate*, on the replacement of Pound. Sir Arthur Bryant does not mention the letter either, or draw any connection between Pound's opposition, which surely predated the letter of 7 March and Brooke's nomination to the chair on 6 March. Philip Ziegler, in his official biography of Mountbatten, is similarly silent, as is David Fraser in his unofficial biography of Brooke (Lord Alanbrooke). A.B. Cunningham to J.H. Godfrey, 17 May 1956, MB1 K129. See also Roskill, *Churchill*, p. 143. Alexander to Churchill, 28 June 1942, in ADM 205/13. Admiral Kennedy-Purvis was eventually assigned as a deputy, but mainly for technical and scientific matters (principally chairing the Future Building Committee).

30 Pound to Churchill, 3 May 1942, in ADM 205/13.

31 Admiral Karl Doenitz, *Zehn Jahre and Swanzig Tage* (Bonn, 1958), chapter 13; Hoyt, *U-Boat Wars*, p. 165.

32 F.H. Hinsley, et al., eds, *British Intelligence in the Second World War*, II (London, HMSO, 1981), pp. 635-6.

33 Ibid., pp. 176-9, 230; Churchill's somewhat veiled reference is in Churchill, *Hinge*, p. 125.

34 The Admiralty eventually protested; see Alexander to Churchill, 17 March 1942, ADM 199/1932.

35 For Cherwell's calculations, see Annex to DO (42) 13th, 29 April 1942; for criticism of the convoy effort, see Ivan Maisky, *Memoirs of a Soviet Ambassador* (New York, 1968), Andrew Rothstein, tr., pp. 311, 317, and Andrei Gromyko and B.N. Ponomarev, eds, *Soviet Foreign Policy, 1917-1980*, I (Moscow, 1981), pp. 418-23.

36 Roskill, *Churchill*, p. 100.

37 Churchill to Pound, 22 January 1942, PREM 3/191/1; Churchill to Ismay, 25 January 1942, in CAB 121/001, courtesy Cabinet Historical Office; Churchill to Pound, 16 July 1942, PREM 3/191/1.

38 Roskill, *Churchill*, pp. 141-4; Eden Diary, 7 June 1942, in Earl of Avon, *The Eden Memoirs: The Reckoning* (London, 1965), p. 331; Churchill to Alexander, 4 June 1942, ADM 205/14.

39 WP (42) 178, 26 April 1942; see, generally, Churchill's minutes on Norway in ADM 205/21.

40 DO (42) 13th, 29 April 1942; WM (42) 173, 21 April 1942.

41 Ibid.

42 WM (42) 52nd, 24 April 1942.

43 WM (42) 64th, 18 May 1942.

44 WM (42) 65th, 21 May 1942 and Confidential Annex.

44 The literature on PQ 17 is vast. The latest scholarship is well summarized in Hinsley, *British Intelligence*, II, pp. 214-23. A useful chronology is to be found in Appendix II, p. 686. Noteworthy are David Irving, *The Destruction of Convey PQ 17*, 2nd edn (London, 1980), and Jack Broome, *Convoy is to Scatter* (London, 1972); Maisky, *Memoirs*, p. 310; Churchill speaking with Stalin, Moscow, 13 August 1942 (Jacob notes), FO 800/300.

45, 46 Churchill, *Hinge*, p. 264; COS (42) 206 (0), 17 July 1942, COS (42) 214th meeting, 22 July 1942. See correspondence on this memorandum in ADM 205/17.

47 DO (42) 14th of 10 July 1942; DO (42) 15th of 13 July 1942.

48 S.M. Bruce memorandum, 7 July 1942, and correspondence thereon in ADM 205/14. S.M. Bruce was the accredited Australian representative to the Chiefs of Staff; reply (draft) to S.M. Bruce, 9 July 1942, in ADM 205/14.

49 DO (42) 15th of 13 July 1942; Smuts to Churchill, 14 July 1942 in ADM 205/14.

50 DO (42) 15th of 13 July 1942; Churchill to Stalin, 14 July 1942, USSR *Correspondence Between the Chairman of the Council of Ministers of the USSR and the Presidents of the United States and the Prime Ministers of Great Britain During the Great Patriotic War* (Moscow, 1950), I, p. 53. (This was not, of course, a cable on which Churchill wanted to comment, or even quote in his memoirs.) Stalin to Churchill, 23 July 1942 in PREM 3/463. For the background of the latter,

see the remarkably candid admissions in Maisky, *Memoirs*, pp. 291-2; Churchill, *Hinge*, p. 270; Earl of Avon, *Eden Memoirs*, p. 338; Cadogan Diary, 24 July, in Dilks, *Cadogan Diaries*, p. 463; Churchill to Pound, 15 July 1942, in ADM 205/14.

[51] COS (42) 87th, 17 March 1942.

[52] The evidence that Pound accepted the raid as a sop emerges clearly in the Mackenzie King Diary. On 24 April 1942 Pound visited Ottawa and talked over general strategy with King, who naturally expressed his anxiety that the British Government might be pushed into a premature assault on the Continent. Pound assured him that this would not happen. 'He [Pound] spoke as though there could not be any thought of an offensive until the fall. [This amounted to saying there would be no offensive in 1942, as major cross-Channel operations were not possible in the fall.] There might be raids, etc., in the interval [i.e. Mountbatten would be given some tether, but Pound added more wisely that he knew] . . . too much care could not be taken.' King Diary, 24 April 1942, MG 26 J13, NAC. See Keyes to Richmond, 11 November, 3 December 1941, in Paul G. Halpern, ed., *The Keyes Papers* (London, 1981), pp. 235, 237-9; Pound to Cunningham, 25 November 1941, Cunningham Papers, British Museum; John Terraine, *The Life and Times of Lord Mountbatten* (London, 1968), p. 84; cf. Richard Hough, *Mountbatten, Hero of Our Times* (London, 1980), p. 145.

[53] Pound to Churchill, 7 March 1942, ADM 205/23; Churchill to Alexander, 6 June 1942, and Pound to Alexander, 8 June 1942—both in Admiralty ADM 205/13.

[54] For Pound's role in urging the suspension of the convoys, see DO (42) 14th of 10 July 1942; Maisky, *Memoirs*, pp. 310-11, Churchill, *Hinge of Fate* (Boston, 1950), p. 272; Churchill's determination to appease Stalin in Churchill to Roosevelt, 27 July 1942, MR, in Kimball, ed., *Churchill & Roosevelt*, 541-3.

[55] Even more shattering was the fact that the idea of Pound's explaining directly to the Soviet envoys came from Maisky himself. WM (42) 95th, 24 July 1942 (Confidential Annex); Maisky, *Memoirs*, pp. 271, 310-11.

[56] Ibid., pp. 313-14; Moran, *From the Diaries*, p. 82; see also Roskill's severe judgement on Pound in *Churchill and the Admirals*, pp. 130 and 210.

[57] Maisky, *Memoirs*, pp. 292-3, WM (42) 95th, 24 July 1942; WM (42) 96th, 27 July 1942; Churchill to Roosevelt, 27 July 1942, MR, in Kimball, ed., *Churchill & Roosevelt*, pp. 544-5.

[58] On the briefing of Roosevelt, see Mountbatten to Roosevelt, 15 June 1942, President's Personal Files, Hyde Park, and 'Points Mentioned by the President', 16 June 1942, MB1 B13. See also Ziegler, *Mountbatten*, pp. 185; Roosevelt to Churchill, 29 July 1942, ibid.

[59] Appendix 'O' (25 July 1942) to McNaughton War Diary, July 1942, in MG 30 E133 (volume 248), NAC; Appendix 'K' (25 July 1942), ibid.

[60] Roskill, *Churchill*, p. 145; Hankey Memorandum, 4 March 1942, in ADM 199/1935; see note 1, above; 1972 interview with Mountbatten for BBC-1 'Dieppe 1942' (broadcast 22 August 1972), author's notes. The implication of Mountbatten's retelling Pound's reaction implies that a formal request was never actually tendered, for the reaction quoted was distinctly not the sort to be given to a formal request; moreover, by casting it in such derisive terms Mountbatten was saying in effect that there was no point in making a formal request. In fact in a 1962 speech Hughes-Hallett admitted that the formal request was never made because the answer was predictable: notes provided to McNaughton by Hughes-Hallett, McNaughton to Col. G.M.C. Sprung, Director, Historical Section, 25 January 1962, 594.011 (D12) DND. In all this there is not the slightest suggestion that COHQ ever conceived of bringing pressure to bear on Pound, perhaps because in the final analysis they shared his view that the battleship might be lost, with the probable consequences of magnifying the impression of defeat and placing COHQ under a dark cloud.

[61] Rear-Admiral H.T. Baillie-Grohman, *Flashlight into the Past* (privately printed memoirs in the Baillie-Grohman Papers, the National Maritime Museum Archives, Greenwich), p. 156; Minutes Force Commanders Meeting 6 June 1942, ibid., and COHQ Planning summary DEFE 2/524, (P/45).

## 7. THE RAF ON THE EVE OF DIEPPE

[1] Skrine, 1962 interview, CBC 'Close-Up', 594.009 (D13) DND.

[2] Of the 70-odd squadrons of aircraft engaged over Dieppe, only two were true bombers (Boston bombers), and these were on the lighter-weight end of the spectrum.Harris to Portal, 29 August 1942, Portal Papers, Christ Church, Oxford.

[3] The Trenchard quotation is in Andrew Boyle, *Trenchard* (London, 1962), p. 186; Neville Jones, *The Origins of Strategic Bombing: A Study of the Development of British Thought and Practice up to 1918* (London, 1973); Uri Bialer, *The Shadow of the Bomber: The Fear of Air Attack and British Politics, 1931-1939* (London, 1980), pp. 20-3, 35, 127-50, 155. On the alleged disparity of forces, see the able analysis of R.J. Overy, *The Air War: 1939-45* (London, 1980), pp. 23-5; Sir Charles Webster and Noble Frankland, *The Strategic Air Offensive Against Germany* (London, HMSO, 1961), I, p. 94; Bennett to Newall, 9 September 1938, in AIR 8/251.

4Notes of Air Ministry Conference, 28 April 1940, cited by Webster and Frankland, *Strategic Air*, I, pp. 141-3.

[5] WM (42) 123, 15 May 1940, Confidential Annex.

[6] Churchill to Beaverbrook, 8 July 1940, Winston Churchill, *Their Finest Hour* (Boston, 1949), pp. 458-61.

[7] Portal to Sholto Douglas, 17 July 1940, AIR 14/194.

[8] Maj.-Gen. Sir Edward Spears, *Assignment to Catastrophe*, I (London, 1954), p. 142.

[9] WM (40) 123, 15 May 1940.

[10] On the early frustrations associated with the oil strategy, see the recent overview, Robert Goralski and Russell W. Freiburg, *Oil & War* (New York, 1987); Webster and Frankland, *Strategic Air*, I, p. 151 (unless otherwise specified, subsequent references to this book are to Vol. I).

[11] Churchill to Chiefs of Staff, 'The Munitions Situation', 3 September 1940, Churchill, *Finest Hour*, pp. 458-61.

[12] Douglas to Portal, 21 September 1940, reprinted in Webster and Frankland, *Strategic Air*, IV, Appendix 8, pp. 124-6; Churchill to Sinclair, 20 October 1940, AIR 20/8144, WP (40) 279, 30 October 1940.

[13] Webster and Frankland, *Strategic Air*, I, p. 159; on the Lloyd Committee reports and oil-targeting plans, see F.H. Hinsley et al., eds, *British Intelligence in the Second World War*, II (London, HMSO, 1981) pp. 690-4; WM (41) 2 of 2 January 1941, COS memo, 7 January 1941, reprinted Webster and Frankland, *Strategic Air*, IV, pp. 188-93; DO (41) 4, 13 January 1941.

[14] Churchill to Portal, 1 November 1940, and Portal's reply, 2 November 1940, Portal Papers, Christ Church Library Archives, Oxford.

[15] Beaverbrook is quoted in Denis Richards, *Portal of Hungerford* (London, 1977), p. 200; see also AIR 14/194. The shift in operational control became effective on 15 April 1941; see Stephen Roskill, *The War at Sea* (London, HMSO, 1954), I, pp. 360-2.

[16] See Webster and Frankland, *Strategic Air*, pp. 163-4; Churchill to Sinclair and Portal, 31 December 1940, PREM 3/14/20; Churchill to Portal, 17 November 1940, AIR 8/407.

[17] Churchill to Portal, 15 April 1941, in CAB 120/300.

[18] Ministry of Information Report, 25 December 1940, cited in Webster and Frankland, *Strategic Air*, p. 169; Bomber Operations Memorandum, 22 September 1941, cited in Webster and Frankland, *Strategic Air*, p. 182; Harris minute, 'German Invasion of Yugoslavia', 1 April 1941, in AIR 20/8144; Maj.-Gen. Sir John Kennedy, *The Business of War* (London, 1957), p. 107.

[19] Portal memorandum, 'The Air Programme', 21 May 1941, COS (41) 83rd (0); Trenchard memorandum, 'The Present War Situation', 19 May 1941, in COS (41) 86 (0) of 28 May 1941; Kennedy, *Business*, pp. 129-32.

[20] John Terraine, *A Time for Courage* (New York, 1985) (UK: *The Right of the Line*), p. 285.

[21] Bottomley to Peirse, 9 July 1941, reprinted in Webster and Frankland, *Strategic Air*, vol. IV, pp. 135-7.

[22] COS memorandum, 31 July 1941, CAB 80; quoted in AIR 41/41, Air Historical Branch Narrative; Bomber Operations memorandum, 22 September 1941, cited in Webster and Frankland, *Strategic Air*, p. 162.

[23] COS memorandum, 31 July 1941, cited in note 22.

[24] Churchill to Portal, 19 August 1941, and same to same, 27 August 1941, both in Churchill, *The Grand Alliance* (Boston, 1950), pp. 811-12; cf. Churchill to Secretaries of State for War and Air, 14 July 1941, PREM 3/8; Churchill to Portal, 19 August and 27 August 1941, PREM 3/8; Churchill to Sir John Anderson, 7 September 1941, Churchill, *Grand Alliance*, pp. 506-7.

[25] The summary portion of the 18 August 1941 Butt Report is conveniently reproduced in Webster and Frankland, *Strategic Air*,IV, pp. 205-13; Churchill's comment on the Butt Report is in AIR 8/1356.

[26] Churchill to Portal, 29 August 1941, in Churchill, *Grand Alliance*, p. 814; same to same 30 August 1941, ibid.

[27] Portal to Churchill, 2 October 1941, AIR 8/258.

[28] Churchill to Portal, 7 October 1941, CAB 120/300 (also in AIR 8/258 with related documents); Portal to Churchill, 13 October 1941, Portal Papers, Christ Church, Oxford.

[29] Webster and Frankland, *Strategic Air*, p. 186, see also Terraine, *Time for Courage*, p. 459.

[30] Churchill to Sinclair and Portal, 11 November 1941, in Churchill, *Grand Alliance*, pp. 832-3; Portal's acceptance of Churchill's advice is in Portal to Churchill, 18 November 1941, in PREM 3/11/3. Churchill minuted in his most provocative style to Portal as early as 17 June 1941: 'It must be recognized that the inability of Bomber Command to hit the enemy cruisers in Brest constitutes a very definite failure of this arm.' Churchill, *Grand Alliance*, p. 756; see also Roskill, *War at Sea*, 1, pp. 79, 115.

[31] Churchill expatiated on these possibilities in the three extraordinary papers he prepared for Roosevelt while crossing the Atlantic and which, with understandable pride, he reproduced in Churchill, *Grand Alliance*, pp. 644-61.

[32] Beaverbrook memorandum, 2 February 1942, cited in A.J.P. Taylor, *Beaverbrook* (London, 1972), p. 510. The Cripps statement that most alarmed the RAF was his assurance to 'the House that the Government are fully aware of other uses to which our resources could be put, and the moment that they arrive at a decision . . . a change in policy will be made.' Cripps, *Hansard*, 25 February 1942, *The Times*, 26 February 1942.

[33] Directive no. 22 of 14 February 1942, in Webster and Frankland, *Strategic Air*, IV, pp. 143-5; Churchill to Portal with enclosures, 25 February 1942, Portal Papers, Christ Church, Oxford.

[34] *Hansard*, 4 March 1942.

[35] Harris to Portal, 5 March 1942, AIR 8/625; a copy is also in the Portal Papers, Christ Church, Oxford; Portal to Churchill, 27 March 1942, Portal Papers, Christ Church, Oxford.

[36] Portal to Churchill, 5 March 1942, and vice versa, 8 March 1942, Portal Papers, Christ Church, Oxford.

[37] Quoted in AIR 41/41, Air Historical Branch Narrative; Samuel Eliot Morison, *The Battle of the Atlantic* (Boston, 1947), pp. 125-54; Edwin P. Hoyt, *The U-boat Wars* (New York, 1984), p. 144.

[38] Quoted in Richards, *Portal of Hungerford*, p. 204, ibid., p. 199.

[39] On Army complaints, see Churchill to Portal, 27 August 1941, in Churchill, *Grand Alliance*, p. 812; see also the fine article by W.A. Jacobs, 'Air Support for the British Army, 1939-1943' in *Military Affairs*, December 1982, pp. 174-82.

[40] COS (42) 246, 2 May 1942; see Brooke Diary entries for 29 April, 16 and 19 May 1942, KC.

[41] Portal minute on DO (42) 34, 1 April 1942, in AIR 8/989.

[42] Churchill to Portal and Sinclair, 13 March 1942, Portal Papers, Christ Church, Oxford.

[43] Cherwell to Tizard, 22 April 1942, cited in Webster and Frankland, *Strategic Air*, p. 334.

[44] See Eden's report of his meetings with Stalin, conveniently gathered in WP (42), 8 of 5 January 1942.

[45] On Eden's bombing ambitions, see Portal to Churchill, 11 April 1942, in Portal Papers, Christ Church, Oxford. His ideas in fact had a long history; see Bomber Operations Memorandum, 22 September 1941, cited in Webster and Frankland, *Strategic Air*, p. 182.

[46] Churchill to Roosevelt, 29 March 1942, MR, Warren Kimball, *Churchill & Roosevelt: The Complete Correspondence*, I (Princeton, 1984), pp. 434-5.

[47] Tizard to Sinclair and Cherwell, 20 April 1942, cited in Webster and Frankland, *Strategic Air*, vol. 1, pp. 333-4; the Singleton report is in AIR 8/1015.

[48] DO (42) 8th, 18 March 1942; Churchill to Roosevelt, 29 March 1942, MR, Kimball, *Churchill & Roosevelt*, pp. 434-5.

[49] Churchill to Roosevelt, 1 April 1942, PREM 3/486/3.

[50] WP (42) 183, 30 April 1942.

[51] See note 47 above.

[52] Henry H. Arnold, *Global Mission* (New York, 1949), p. 306. The RAF delegation in Washington had warned as early as 26 February that the Americans were becoming restless with the modest scale of British bombing efforts; see RAF Delegation to Air Ministry, 26 February 1942, cited in Webster and Frankland, *Strategic Air*, I, p. 329. Roosevelt to Churchill, 19 May 1942, MR, Kimball, *Churchill & Roosevelt*, II, pp. 486-7; Churchill to Roosevelt, 20 May, ibid., Kimball, ibid., pp. 487-8; Arnold, *Global*, p. 307.

[53] For a good extended treatment of the Millennium project, see Charles Messenger, *Cologne: The First 1000 Bomber Raid* (London, 1982); for a briefer yet penetrating summary, see Terraine, *Time*, pp. 482-94.

[54] Arnold, *Global Mission*, pp. 317, 316.

[55] (This note also covers preceding paragraph.) Churchill to Harris, 30 May 1942, in AIR 14/2040; WP (42) 250, 10 June 1942; see also another report by the Minister of Information, WP (42) 298, 17 July 1942; Arnold to Harris 30 May 1942 in AIR 14/2024; Webster and Frankland, *Strategic Air*, I, pp. 407; Bomber Quarterly Review, AIR 14/3507.

[56] Harris to Churchill, 17 June 1942, cited in Webster and Frankland, *Strategic Air*, I, p. 341; Harris to Portal 20 June, AIR 8/864; Harris to Churchill, 17 June 1942, cited in Webster and Frankland, *Strategic Air*, I, p. 341.

[57] Harris to Portal, 14 June 1942, Portal Papers, Christ Church, Oxford; Churchill to Pound, 14 June 1942, CAB 120/300 COS (42) 180th, 16 June 1942.

[58] The rule was variously stated as not closer than 40 or 30 minutes to the start of nautical twilight (very first light). On the Harris rule, see memorandum by Leigh Mallory 'The Employment of Bombers . . . ' in AIR 16/746, no date but approximately 7 September 1942; also Hughes-Hallett, Unpublished Memoirs, MG 30 E 463, p. 135, NAC. On the cancellation of *Blazing*, see COS (42) 146th, 11 May 1942; also the *Blazing* file, DEFE 2/106.

[59] The substitution of commandos for parachutists in *Jubilee* has always been considered by COHQ apologists to have been inconsequential; in fact it was major on two grounds: (i) commandos had to be brought in by boats, complicating still further the navigation track chart and the naval congestion in the final approach to Dieppe; and (ii) one of the commando groups failed, at least in part—with serious consequences in the withdrawal phase.

[60] The best record of how these issues affected the thinking at Combined Operations is to be found in the paper Hughes-Hallett prepared for a 16 July 1942 *Jubilee* Force Commanders' meeting, Hughes-Hallett Papers, IWM. Harris was the real problem behind the cancellation of the bombing, not Montgomery. The charge Hughes-Hallett and Mountbatten levelled against Montgomery, that he had abandoned the bombing and that afterwards it was 'too late' to get it reinstated (see, for instance, Hughes-Hallett's Unpublished Memoirs, p. 155, and his letter in the *Sunday Telegraph* of 1 October 1967) was misleading. The desirability or not of bombing was openly debated through 16 July at Force Commanders' meetings (see minutes in the Hughes-Hallett Papers, IWM). Philip Ziegler, in what appears to be an excess of zeal in defending COHQ, agrees that the decision taken under Montgomery was irrevocable. Philip Ziegler, *Mountbatten* (London, 1985), p. 189. COS (42) 42nd (0), 13 May 1942, part of COS (42) 149th.

[61] Goronwy Rees, *A Bundle of Sensations* (London, 1960), p. 145; on the political bombing restrictions and their removal, see COS (42) 42nd, 13 May 1942, Ismay to Prime Minister, 19 May 1942 (précis in DEFE 2/542), COS (42) 166th, 1 June 1942.

[62] The discussion referred to by Robertson is reflected in the minutes of 1 and 5 June Force Commanders' meetings, DEFE 2/546. *The Shame and the Glory: Dieppe* (Toronto, 1962) also concludes that Harris was behind the denial of a substantial bombing force (pp. 93-5); see also Harris minute of 17 June 1942 in AIR 14/3507. Canadian authorities were not unaware of the problem. In his commentary on the draft of a volume of Canadian official history, Churchill Mann explained that among the reasons why bombing was ruled out for Dieppe was that Bomber Command was 'being trained to concentrate on night operations', i.e. it was not available. Commentary file, DND. That it was bomber command's unwillingness to give up bombers (rather than the problems posed by rubble) that lay behind the decision not to have heavy preliminary bombardment may also be inferred from comments made by Hughes-Hallett in a 1962 speech when he said that a request for 40 heavy bombers was refused because it would have taken three months to train the crews for close-support daylight bombing (he also admitted candidly in this speech that a battleship was not requested because COHQ were certain it would be refused). The three months was probably an exaggeration, but some training would have been involved and that would have meant taking the crews away from 1000-bomber operations. Notes on this speech, delivered in January 1962 in Toronto (drawn from Hughes-Hallett's own notes), in McNaughton to G.M.C. Sprung, 25 January 1962, 594.011 (D12) DND.

[63] Rees, *Bundle*, pp. 139-40, 145. In fact the abandonment of the heavy bombing was first envisioned on 1 June at a meeting at which Mountbatten assisted, at least at the beginning, and Montgomery might well have assumed that Mountbatten had been briefed and had no objection. Minutes, *Rutter* Force Commanders, ibid.

[64] Memorandum by Leigh Mallory, 'The Employment of Bombers . . .', n.d. but approximately 7 September 1942, in AIR 16/746. See also John Campbell, 'Air Operations and the Dieppe Raid' in *Aerospace Historian*, XXIII, 1 (Spring/March 1976), p. 17; Roberts to Senior Officer, CMHQ, 18 March 1943, CMHQ file 24/Dieppe/1, cited by C.P. Stacey in *Six Years of War* (Ottawa, 1966), p. 344. Dieppe was bombed in 1942 on the following days prior to the *Jubilee* raid: 8 May, 11/12 May, 5 August, 17 August. See Martin Middlebrook and Chris Everett, *The Bomber Command War Diaries* (London, 1985); see also note 1 above.

[65] C.P. Stacey, *The Canadian Army 1939-1945* (Ottawa, 1948), p. 62; 1978 Stacey interview with Terence Macartney-Filgate, 79/567 DND; Stephen Roskill, *The War at Sea, 1939-1945* (London, 1954), p. 241.

[66] Hughes-Hallett, 1967 Secondari interview, MB 1 B67/2, and 'Suggested Points for Decision' (point A drafted in preparation for 16 July 1942 Force Commanders' meeting) in Hughes-Hallett Papers, IWM.

[67] Harris memorandum for Churchill, 28 June 1942, amended and circulated on 24 August 1942, WP (42) 374.

[68] Churchill to Roosevelt, 16 September 1942, MR, Kimball, *Churchill & Roosevelt*, pp. 597-8, and Churchill to Air Marshal Evill, 16 September 1942, PREM 3/11/6.

[69] Sir Arthur Harris, *Bomber Offensive* (London, 1947), pp. 90-143; Harris is quoted in Air Marshal Sholto Douglas (Lord Douglas of Kirtleside), *Years of Command* (London, 1966), p. 162.

[70] Harris to Churchill, 16 July 1942, PREM 3/11/12; Churchill in WP (42) 311 of 21 July 1942.

[71] For the difficulties and mounting criticism Harris encountered with Millennium, see Charles Messenger, *Bomber Harris and the Strategic Bombing Offensive, 1939-1945* (London, 1984), pp. 90-3; Terraine, *Time*, pp. 490-1; WP (42) 311 of 21 July 1942; Kennedy, *Business*, p. 238.

[72] WP (42) 311, 21 July 1942.

[73] WP (42) 326, 31 July 1942.

[74] Air Marshal A.W. Tedder, *With Prejudice* (London, 1966), p. 342; Portal for Chiefs of Staff, 30 September 1942, Portal Papers, Christ Church, Oxford; Churchill to Roosevelt, 16 September 1942, MR, Kimball, *Churchill & Roosevelt*, II, pp. 597-9; WP (42) 360, 13 August 1942.

[75] Harris to Portal, 29 August 1942, Portal Papers, Christ Church, Oxford; COS (42) 478 (0) of 26 December 1942, copy in PREM 3/11/7.

[76] Ibid.; JPS (42) 124 of 11 February 1942, COS (42) 12th (0), 21 March 1942 (Annex thereto), part of COS (42) 91st of the same date; Portal's comments at the War Cabinet meeting with Churchill, DO (42) 10th, 14 April 1942.

[77] On the evolution of Circuses, see the documentation in AIR 16/369, particularly Chief of Air Staff, 'Minutes of meeting held on July 29th 1941' (item 78b) and Fighter Command Draft Memorandum, 11 July 1942, 'Offensive Operations in Co-Operation with Bomber and Coastal Aircraft' (item 38A).

[78] COS (42) 12th (0), 21 March 1942; COS (42) 26th (0), 21 April 1942.

[79] Ibid.

[80] COS (42) 12th (0) of 21 March 1942, part of COS (42) 91st; Rees, *Bundle*, pp. 146-7; Portal to Commanders-in-Chief, 6 March 1942, Portal Papers, Christ Church, Oxford.

[81] Churchill to General Ismay and Brigadier Hollis, 23 March 1942, PREM 3/333/19; Churchill to Portal, 8 March 1942, Portal Papers, Christ Church, Oxford; minutes, meeting of 12 August 1942 in the Kremlin, FO 800/300.

[82] Mallory memorandum, Operations in France of 25 May 1942 in DEFE 2/306; Force Commanders' meeting 15 June, AIR 16/760; Leigh-Mallory to Sholto Douglas, 29 June 1942.

[83] Sholto Douglas to Leigh-Mallory, 30 June 1942, AIR 16/760.

[84] Interview with Lt-Col. Robert R. Labatt, DEFE 2/336, p. 5, quoted in Ronald Atkin, *Dieppe, 1942: The Jubilee Disaster* (London, 1980); Lt-Gen. Lucian K. Truscott, *Command Missions* (New York, 1954), p. 67.

[85] Compare this with the Battle of Britain, which at its peak engaged some 50 squadrons. John Campbell, 'Air Operations and the Dieppe Raid', *Aerospace Historian*, 23, no. 1 (Spring/March 1976), p. 16.

[86] For expectations, see above-cited Leigh-Mallory letter to Sholto Douglas (note 82); for actual figures, see Air Historical Branch to Directorate of History, 3 November 1950, 594.065 (D4),Department of National Defence, Ottawa, Directorate of History; Leigh-Mallory to Mountbatten, 22 August 1942, DEFE 2/67; memorandum, Mountbatten to Chiefs of Staff, 16 September 1942, DEFE 2/67.

[87] Harris to Portal, 9 July 1942, Portal Papers, Christ Church, Oxford; Portal to Harris, 13 July 1942, ibid.

[88] Memorandum from Harris to Churchill, 28 June 1942, in PREM 3/3/7; same to same 21 October 1942, Portal Papers; Mountbatten to Roosevelt, 15 June 1942, Mountbatten file, Roosevelt Papers, Hyde Park.

[89] COS (42) 26th (0), 21 April 1942; Rees, *Bundle*, pp. 146-7.

## 8. MOUNTBATTEN THE STRATEGIST

[1] Goronwy Rees, *A Bundle of Sensations* (London, 1960), p. 149; Mountbatten to Edwina Mountbatten, 5 April 1941, B1 S142, Mountbatten Papers, University of Southampton Archives.

[2] Unsigned but apparently Halifax to Bracken, 27 October 1942, MB1 A116.

[3] Lord Louis Mountbatten, 'The Curious Case of Lord Beaverbrook', unpublished brief memoir in MB1 C20; Richard Hough, *Mountbatten Hero of Our Time* (London, 1980), pp. 157-8; Raymond Lee Diary, 8 November 1941, in James Leutze, ed., *The London Journal of General Raymond E. Lee* (Boston, 1971); London *Daily Express* for October to November 1941, *passim*; Beaverbrook to Churchill, 14 September 1941, in A.J.P. Taylor, *Beaverbrook* (London, 1972), p. 483; Arthur Bryant *The Turn of the Tide* (London, 1957), p. 204; Stark to Pound, 15 October 1941, copy in PREM 3/330/2; Churchill to Hopkins, 10 October 1941, PREM 3/330/2; COS Directive, 15 October 1941, Appendix F, DEFE 2/697.

[4] On Churchill's attraction to unconventional military figures, see R.W. Thompson, *Churchill and Morton* (London, 1976), pp. 47-8.

[5] John Terraine, *The Life and Times of Lord Louis Mountbatten* (London, 1968), pp. 83-5 (selections from the script of the highly successful film series, narrated by Mountbatten, based on his recollections and produced with the assistance of Terraine); Alan Campbell-Johnston, narrative, text, interviews, and notes preparatory to a biography, vol. I, p. 202, Broadlands Archives; Bernard Fergusson, *The Watery Maze: The Story of Combined Operations* (London, 1961), pp. 87-8; Hough, *Mountbatten*, p. 144.

[6] Quoted in both Fergusson, *Maze*, and Hough, *Mountbatten*.

[7] Hough, *Mountbatten*, pp. 144-5.

[8] For contemporary evidence of Mountbatten's denigration of Keyes, see the Leo Amery Diary, 8 February 1942, in John Barnes and David Nicholson, eds, *The Empire at Bay: The Leo Amery Diaries, 1929-1945* (London, 1988), p. 770. See also Stephen Roskill, *Churchill and the Admirals* (London, 1978), p. 11; John Hughes-Hallett, Unpublished Memoirs, MG 30 E463, pp. 110-11, NAC.

[9] Ibid., pp. 113, 117-19.

[10] Ibid., p. 118.

[11] Ibid., 117-18.

[12] Hughes-Hallett, 1967 interview with John Secondari, transcript, MB1 67.

[13] Maj.-Gen. Leslie Hollis and James Leasor, *War at the Top* (London, 1959), p. 125 (a book that disconcertingly reflects much more Leasor's lack of familiarity with the inner history of the events than Hollis's detailed knowledge, though occasionally the latter's voice is recognizable, giving the book some utility). On Mountbatten's attitude to Keyes, and on his replacement of Keyes, see Roskill, *Churchill and the Admirals*, pp. 110-11, 176-7, and Ziegler, *Mountbatten*, pp. 157-8, an account that somewhat plays down the Chiefs' hostility to Mountbatten's elevation.

[14] Mountbatten to Patricia Mountbatten, 3 April 1942, cited by Ziegler, ibid., p. 170.

[15] Ziegler's treatment of the promotions is in one brief paragraph on p. 168; somewhat extended commentary may be found in Hughes-Hallett, Unpublished Memoirs, pp. 132-3, which has some apparent errors of chronology (earlier versions of the same explanation were given by Hughes-Hallett at the end of the war); see also next note. On Beaverbrook's state of mind at the end of February and early March, see A.J.P. Taylor, *Beaverbrook*, pp. 506-20; Mountbatten, 'The Curious Case. . . ', MBI C20.

[16] The proposal for seizing and holding part of Normandy in 1942 as a redoubt or enclave, which Hughes-Hallett thought had earned Mountbatten his promotions, would appear to be: memorandum Mountbatten to Ismay 7 March 1942, copy of which is to be found as appendix 1 to 'Prospects for a Major Operation in 1942', 19 July 1942, in DEFE 2/564 PRO. Mountbatten, who went over Hughes-Hallett's draft memoirs meticulously, left his interpretation of the significance of the memorandum alone, one suspects because it so neatly excluded Beaverbrook's role in his elevation.

[17] Ibid. One would have thought that in the coming months Mountbatten would have been content with the promotions he had received in March, which were so far above his experience or achievements. Yet the evidence of his ambition, only thinly disguised, was evident in Chiefs of Staff discussions on command arrangements for cross-Channel operations, 28 May 1942, COS (42) 48th (0) (part of COS (42) 163rd. See John Colville, *The Fringes of Power: 10 Downing Street Diaries, 1939-1945* (London, 1985), p. 730. How seriously Mountbatten's ambitions were taken is visible in Haydon, 'Notes on a letter Dated 19th August 1942 . . . from . . . Ismay' in CAB 127/24. See also Chapter 9, pp. 208-9 and 236. Mountbatten's spell, it appears, was difficult to resist.Consider the invocation of the great Bonaparte's ghost in the closing lines of Ziegler's biography: 'He flared brilliantly across the face of the twentieth century; the meteor is extinguished but its glow lingers on in the mind's eye' (p. 702).

[18] Mountbatten, 'The Curious Case . . . ', MB1 C20.

[19] Churchill to Roosevelt, 1 April 1942, MR, in Warren Kimball, *Churchill & Roosevelt: The Complete Correspondence*, I (Princeton, 1984), pp. 438-9.

[20] Hughes-Hallett, Unpublished Memoirs, p. 134, NAC.

[21] Ibid., p. 134; Brooke later paid fulsome praise to Mountbatten, but it is clear from his diary that in 1942 his feelings were somewhat different; Brooke, 'Notes on My Life', V (draft memoirs), Diary 28 March 1942, KC; cf., Hollis and Leasor, War, p. 127.

[22] Pound to Churchill, 7 March 1942, ADM 205/14; Churchill to Chiefs of Staff, 6 March 1942, Portal Papers, Christ Church, Oxford.

[23] Churchill to Ismay 8 March 1942, PREM 3/330/2. Victor Cazalet told Dalton in September that the Service Chiefs were all very jealous of Mountbatten, Dalton diary, 10 September and 27 October 1942, Ben Pimlott, ed., The Second World War Diaries of Hugh Dalton, 1940-1945 (London, 1986), pp. 491-2, 507-9; see also Ziegler, Mountbatten, pp. 164-5.

[24] Ziegler, ibid., pp. 166-7; Hughes-Hallett, Unpublished Memoirs, p. 113; COS (42) 176th (8) of 11 June 1942 (see also JSM 266; COS (42) 15th meeting (0), part of COS (42) 98th, 28 March 1942, copy in DEFE 2/564). It should be noted that Mountbatten's successor as CCO was not put on the Chiefs of Staff Committee.

[25] COS (42) 84th, 14 March 1942; 87th, 17 March 1942; 120th, 16 April 1942; Ziegler's summary in Mountbatten, pp. 166-7; COS (42), 211th of 20 July 1942; 213th of 21 July and 218th of 27 July 1942; History of Combined Operations Organization 1940-1945, Amphibious Warfare Headquarters, pp. 88-97, 99, DEFE 2/697.

[26] COS 121 of 25 March 1942, cf. COS (42) 13 (0); COS (42) 99th mtg, held on 30 March 1941, and COS (42) 100th held on 31 March 1042. On Myrmidon see DEFE 2/366-7. On Abercrombie see DEFE 2/61-63. Note that the spelling of Abercrombie varied in contemporary documents (sometimes spelled Abercromby).

[27] COS (42) 23rd (0), 9 April 1942.

[28] Ibid. Mountbatten's belief in raiding operations, to throw the Germans off balance, was continually expressed in the spring of 1942. See for instance COS (42) 146th, 11 May 1942.

[29] Dwight D. Eisenhower, 'Notes to take to Great Britain', 22 May 1942 OPD Exec 8, Book V, 316, RG 165, NA. See note 17 above.

[30] COS (42) 36th (0), part of COS (42) 140th of 5 May 1942; see also COS (42) 46th (0), 27 May 1942 (2nd conference of that day). Mountbatten's defence of his actions is contained in Mountbatten to Hughes-Hallett, 3 September 1971 ('Comments on pages 20-46 of Hughes-Hallett's memoirs'). See also Ziegler, Mountbatten, p. 178.

[31] COS (42) 36th (0), part of COS (42) 140th of 5 May 1942; see also COS (42) 46th (0), 27 May 1942.

[32] Brooke Diary, 23 May 1942, quoted in Bryant, Turn, pp. 372-3.

[33] The Chiefs, it may be noted, were in a generous mood in the euphoria over the Anglo-Soviet treaty signed on 26 May, which some, including Churchill, thought might mean less pressure for a Second Front; see Churchill's remarks in WM (42) 68th, 26 May 1942.

[34] COS (42) 46th (0), 27 May 1942.

[35] Hughes-Hallett later commented on the 1943 Round-Up plans for which Mountbatten was in part responsible: 'For myself I could not take the work very seriously.' Unpublished Memoirs, NAC, p. 145. Mountbatten's own doubts surfaced during COS (42) 59th (0), 25 June 1942.

[36] Mountbatten, after Churchill's rebuke, tried to explain why he was not to blame. Churchill's response, as Mountbatten reported it to Ismay on 27 June 1942, was 'Do not try to evade the issue; I hold you solely responsible for planning the assault and I do not expect you to shelter behind a Committee.' Mountbatten to Ismay, 27 June 1942, CAB 127/24.

[37] COS (42) 46th (0), 27 May 1942.

[38] COS (42) 48th (0), 1 June 1942; cf. COS (42) 61st, 30 June 1942, and COS (42) 62nd, 1 July 1942.

[39] In addition to items cited in note 38, see also COS (42) 51st (0), 8 June 1942.

[40] COS (42) 36 (0) 140th of 5 May; see also COS (42) 46th (0), 27 May 1942.

[41] Richard Hough, Mountbatten: Hero of Our Time (London, 1980), pp. 152-3. Mountbatten's exceedingly naïve ambition manifested itself in still another important way at this time. In preparation for his trip he asked, on the record, that the Chiefs of Staff authorize him to take

charge of the development of American Combined Operations doctrine and tactics (what he called technique), telling the Chiefs that he thought this position would be offered to him in Washington (all this in the official minutes!). Mountbatten could scarcely have had the time to take on this charge as well, but the Chiefs, perhaps not being able to take the notion seriously, chose not to quarrel and put their assent on the record as requested.

[42] Gen. Albert C. Wedemeyer, *Wedemeyer Reports* (New York, 1958), p. 136; Henry L. Stimson and MacGeorge Bundy, *On Active Service in Peace and War* (New York, 1947), pp. 219-20. The fates smiled kindly on Mountbatten when he won General Marshall's friendship, for once gained it was not easily lost. A year later Pownall noted: 'Marshall is a sworn friend of Dickie Mountbatten.' Brian Bond, ed., *Chief of Staff: The Diaries of Lieutenant-General Sir Henry Pownall (1940-1944)*, II, p. 163.

[43] Mountbatten's written reports on his Washington trip are: Mountbatten to Roosevelt, 15 June 1942, President's Personal File, Hyde Park, and Mountbatten, 'Points mentioned by the President to the CCO', MB1 B13. See also Hughes-Hallett, Unpublished Memoirs, pp. 158-9 (he was in Washington with Mountbatten).

[44] Hughes-Hallett, Unpublished Memoirs, p. 185, M30 E 463 NAC, and Ziegler, *Mountbatten*, p. 158.

[45] Hughes-Hallett, Unpublished Memoirs, p. 158, M30 E 463 NAC; Mountbatten to Hughes-Hallett, 3 September 1971 ('Comments on pages 20-46'), Hughes-Hallett Papers, NAC; Ziegler, *Mountbatten*, p. 184.

[46] COS (42) 48th (0), part of COS (42) 166th, 1 June 1942.

## 9. MOUNTBATTEN ON THE EVE OF DIEPPE — AND AFTER

[1] See, for example, the 1972 interview with Mountbatten for BBC-1 'Dieppe 1942' (broadcast 22 August 1972). Responsibility for the frontal assault was the subject of acrimonious debate for the CBC program 'Close Up: Dieppe', 9 September 1962, on which Montgomery did not sound very convincing. Transcript, 594.009 (D13), DND.

[2] COS (42) 130 (0), 9 May 1942; COS (42) 211th, 20 July 1942; 213th, 21 July, and 218th, 27 July 1942.

[3] Noël Coward, *Future Indefinite* (Garden City, N.Y., Doubleday and Company, 1954), pp. 216, 217, 237-8; Mountbatten to Coward, 21 November 1941; Coward Diary, 22 December 1941, in Graham Payn and Sheridan Morley, *The Noël Coward Diaries* (London, 1986); Coward, *Future Indefinite*, p. 216; of the Royal visit to the set there are some handsome photographs in MB Q19 presented by Coward to Mountbatten, most elegantly bound; Coward, *Future Indefinite*, pp. 222-3; Mountbatten to Ministry of Supply, 21 January 1942, in MB1 C58. Elliott Roosevelt has preserved the flavour of the première as Eleanor experienced it: 'Mountbatten, of course, was model and inspiration for this film's principal character; he distracted us only slightly by keeping up throughout the screening a running fire of comments upon the experiences which had served as a basis for the film's plot.' Elliott Roosevelt, *As He Saw It* (New York, 1948), p. 58.

[4] Curiously, Mountbatten also complained about overwork to a Cabinet member, Leo Amery, in the Amery Diary, 8 February 1942, John Barnes and Davis Nicholson, eds., *The Empire at Bay: The Leo Amery Diaries, 1929-1945* (London, 1988), p. 70. Admiral Bertram Ramsay to Mountbatten, 25 July 1942 in DEFE 2/306; Goronwy Rees, *A Bundle of Sensations* (London, 1960), p. 147; Lord Lovat, *March Past* (London, 1978), p. 238; Dalton Diary, 12 November 1942, Ben Pimlott, ed., *The Second World War Diary of Hugh Dalton* (London, 1986), p. 518; Mountbatten to Churchill, 20 August 1942, CAB 120/69; Mountbatten to Coward, 20 August 1942, MB1 C58, NAC.

[5] Hughes-Hallett, Unpublished Memoirs, pp. 112, 134, MG 30 E 463, NAC; Michael Harrison, *Mulberry: The Return in Triumph* (London, 1965), p. 146.

6 Eisenhower Diary (more accurately, notes for reports), 26 June 1942, in Robert H. Ferrell, ed., *The Eisenhower Diaries* (New York, 1981), p. 66 (this should be distinguished from the broader Chandler edition of the Eisenhower Papers cited below). Truscott later wrote a detailed and revealing account of his time with Mountbatten's headquarters, as well as of the Dieppe raid, in which he participated, in Lt-Gen. Lucian K. Truscott, *Command Missions* (New York, 1954); his report on the raid in DEFE 2/335 is also one of the more informative.

7 Eisenhower Diary, 29 July 1942, in Alfred D. Chandler et al., eds, *The Papers of Dwight David Eisenhower, I, The War Years* (Baltimore, 1970); Marshall to Eisenhower, 30 July 1942, and Eisenhower to Ismay, 4 August 1942, Eisenhower *Papers*, ibid., pp. 440-2. See also Dwight D. Eisenhower, *Crusade in Europe* (Garden City, N.Y., 1948), p. 67.

8 Admiral Sir William James, *The Portsmouth Letters* (London, 1946) pp. 68-173, 156 (3 May 1942); *Mollie Panter-Downes: London War Notes, 1939-1945* (New York, 1971), p. 195; Churchill to Roosevelt, 1 April 1942, MR, in Warren Kimball, ed., *Churchill & Roosevelt, The Complete Correspondence*, II (Princeton, 1984), pp. 438-9.

9 Hughes-Hallett, Unpublished Memoirs, pp. 126-8. On *Myrmidon* (the abortive Bayonne project) see also DEFE 2/336/7. For other indications of bitterness over cancellations, see Hughes-Hallett, Unpublished Memoirs, p. 135. On the raid on Paris and its abandonment (a variant of *Imperator*), see Mountbattten to COS, 25 May 1942 (P. 129/1/ 339) and related papers in DEFE 2/306.

10 COS (42) 47th (0), 28 May 1942 and J.P. (42) 517. For Mountbatten's hazy recollections, see the later exchange between C.P. Stacey and Lord Louis Mountbatten, discussed in Chapter 11, p. 241. On Montgomery's foggy memory, the best treatment is to be found in the biography by Lord Chalfont, *Montgomery of Alamein* (New York: Atheneum, 1976), pp. 124-8. Bernard Fergusson in *The Watery Maze: The Story of Combined Operations* (London, 1961), who was coached and encouraged by Mountbatten, was the first to pin the blame for the lack of bombing on Montgomery, p. 171. In fact the item was on the agenda for the meeting of 1 June, part of which Mountbatten attended. Certainly he should have known what issues were being debated before he left for America. See Chapter 1, pages 15-23, and related notes. Interestingly enough Hughes-Hallett, who also tended to pillory Montgomery on the bombing, admitted late in life that Montgomery did not like the cancellation of the bombing as that left the entire plan dependent on surprise, which he thought was problematical at best. According to this recollection, Montgomery protested to Paget, who said he was powerless, as the matter lay outside his authority (a reference to Harris?). See McNaughton to Colonel G.M.C. Sprung, Director, Historical Section, 25 January 1962, 594.011 (D12) DND (based on notes provided by Hughes-Hallett).

11 On the possibility of cancellation in June, see COS (42) 54th (0) of 21 June 1942; Montgomery, report of 1 July 1942, cited in C.P. Stacey, *Six Years of War* (Ottawa, 1955), p. 335. (The officers in question are almost certainly Roberts and probably Mann.) Cf. transcript of CBC 'Close-Up', 9 September 1962, and Crerar to McNaughton, cited in Stacey, *Six Years*, p. 335.

12 Robb to Mountbatten, 3 July 1942, reporting exchanges with Churchill (original COHQ file designation P/126/1), précis in DEFE 2/542; COS(42) 64th (0), 6 July 1942; minutes Rear-Admiral Combined Operations Staff Meeting, 6 July 1942, Baillie-Grohman Papers, National Maritime Museum Archives, Greenwich, and Captain Back to Commodore Luce, 6 July 1942, ibid., précis in DEFE 2/542, original COHQ classification P/126/NRP/1; COS (42) 64th (0), 6 July 1942.

13 Here Zieglar, usually so careful and judicious, follows Mountbatten's and Hughes-Hallet's account in asserting that the idea to remount came only after the cancellation and after the Prime Minister had expressed his dismay. Zieglar, *Mountbatten*, p. 190. Hughes-Hallett to Mountbatten, 18 August 1950, Ismay Papers 11/3/260/4a; Hughes-Hallett, 1967 interview with John Secondari, transcript, MB1 67.

14 Bernard Fergusson, *Watery Maze*, p. 173; on the role of Paget and Baillie-Grohman in the cancellation, see Hughes-Hallett to Mountbatten, 12 July 1950, MB1 B58.

[15] Baillie-Grohman and Roberts to Mountbatten, 9 July 1942, Baillie-Grohman Papers, National Maritime Museum Archives, Greenwich. This letter was discussed at the 11 July post-mortem, at which Leigh-Mallory also associated himself with the letter. (Haydon and Wildman-Lushington were present, and it is interesting to note that at this meeting there was no mention of reviving the operation or of the COS minute of 6 July authorizing reconsideration. The intention to hide the remounting from Mountbatten's top staff seems evident at this early date.) For praise of Roberts, see Montgomery's statements in CBC 'Close-Up', 9 September 1962, transcript 594.009 (D13) and Macartney-Filgate's 1978 interviews with Mountbatten and Lord Lovat in 79/567.

[16] For Baillie-Grohman on relations with Mountbatten, see the former's unpublished memoirs, *Flashlight into the Past*, II, Baillie-Grohman Papers, National Maritime Museum Archives, Greenwich. For Mountbatten's reluctance to take Baillie-Grohman on, see Mountbatten to Baillie-Grohman, 31 May 1942, Baillie-Grohman Papers, National Maritime Museum, Greenwich: given the late date (Baillie-Grohman was scheduled to report to COHQ on 1 June), this must be interpreted as a desperate last-minute attempt to keep him away. On the high regard in which Baillie-Grohman was held, see Cunningham to Pound, 19 March 1942, in Cunningham Papers, British Museum Additional MSS. Baillie-Grohman's comments on Dieppe and Mountbatten are in his unpublished memoirs. Baillie-Grohman, like Roberts, had been loyal, positive, and unquestioning as long as it was an operation ordered by the Chiefs of Staff. On the eve of the abortive *Rutter* he wrote Leigh-Mallory: 'We are out to give the Hun a good jolt, and together we can do it', letter of 1 July 1942 in AIR 16/70.

[17] On Montgomery's role in the cancellation, see Brigadier Maurice Chilton, of Montgomery's South-Eastern Command, to Crerar, 6 July 1942, File 220C1.009(D3); the letter of 9 July is cited in note 15 above; Baillie-Grohman's comments upon minutes of 11 July, which discussed the joint appreciation, in Baillie-Grohman Papers, National Maritime Museum Archives, Greenwich.

[18] Hughes-Hallett to Mountbatten, 12 June 1950, in MB1 B58. It is interesting to note that while Hughes-Hallett avoided mentioning the 8 July meeting in some interviews, he always mentioned the 11 July one. Perhaps it was to cover how early he and Mountbatten were committed to remounting, cf. 1967 interview in MB 1 B67, CBC 'Close-Up', 9 September 1962, transcript, 594.009 (D13), DND, and Hughes-Hallett, Unpublished Memoirs, pp. 167-8.

[19] Ibid., pp. 167-8; 1967 interview with John Secondari, MB1 M67/2; Hughes-Hallett summary of movements in Hughes-Hallett to Terence Robertson, sent April 1962, Hughes-Hallett Papers, IWM; A.B. Acheson in Commentary Files for Stacey, *Six Years of War*, DND; the lack of record has been confirmed for me by Dr Maurice Shock, who has had supervision of the Cripps Papers. Hughes-Hallett, comments on the Robertson manuscript (sent April 1962), Hughes-Hallett Papers, IWM; Hughes-Hallett, Unpublished Memoirs, p. 167.

[20] Hughes-Hallett to Mountbatten, 18 August 1950, Ismay Papers,II/3/260/4a, ff.; Hughes-Hallett, 1967 interview with John Secondari, MB1 B67.

[21] Minutes of 11 July cited above, note 17.

[22] Ibid.; the admission may be found in Hughes-Hallett to Mountbatten, 6 September 1967, in MB1 B65. For the bitterness over cancellations, see Hughes-Hallett, Unpublished Memoirs, p. 135, and Hughes-Hallett, 1967 interview with John Secondari, MB1 B67. Items cited in note 19 above; McNaughton Diary for July 1942, MG 30 E133 (Volume 248) NAC.

[23] Mountbatten's claim that the problems with the plan were attributable to Montgomery can be found in all his principal interviews. This overlooks the fact that all the decisions had to be made afresh when Montgomery cleared out on 8 July, for *Rutter* was, as an authorized plan, dead on that date. It is not true that no one dared change the plan, inasmuch as for *Jubilee* the participation of airborne troops was dropped; a joint appreciation, had it existed, would have been quoted by Mountbatten to suggest that the Force Commanders, who would have had to accept it, were responsible for the outcome. Still, one can understand Mountbatten's problem: if he ordered a joint appreciation there was a strong chance that it would lead to cancellation; without one, his responsibility for carrying the raid forward was inescapable—hence

'Mountbatten's courage', to which Hughes-Hallett so often referred. Hughes-Hallett, 1967 interview with John Secondari, MB1 B67.

24 McNaughton War Diary, July 1942, Appendix 'K', dictated 25 July (9 days after the events recorded), probably when McNaughton realized that no formal orders for this operation would be coming to him from any British source, MG 30 E 133, NAC.

25 Author's correspondence with Mrs Diana Bradley, née Roberts; Roberts 1962 interview for CBC 'Close-Up', 9 September 1962, transcript 594.009 (D13).

26 The list is in McNaughton's War Diary, July 1942, dictated 25 July, Appendix 'K', ibid.; Skrine 1962 interview for CBC 'Close-Up', 9 September 1962, transcript 594.009 (D13); Admiral Bertram Ramsay to Mountbatten, 25 July 1942, DEFE 2/306, and vice versa, 27 July 1942, ibid.

27 Hughes-Hallett, Unpublished Memoirs, p. 178, M30 E463, NAC.

28 Alden Hatch, The Mountbattens: The Last Royal Success Story (New York, 1965), p. 270. Cf. Hough, Mountbatten, pp. 154-5. The version that Mountbatten wanted Baillie-Grohman out is in Mountbatten to Hughes-Hallett, 3 September 1971 (in comments on Hughes-Hallett's Unpublished Memoirs), M30 E463, NAC. In 1950 Mountbatten's version was that Baillie-Grohman was a 'sick man'; see 'Replies to Questions . . .' enclosure to Mountbatten to Ismay, 29 August 1950, Ismay Papers, KC, II/3/260/1a. There can be little doubt that Baillie-Grohman, believing that the Dieppe project should be cancelled, refused to participate, forcing Mountbatten to seek his replacement. This step involved so many complications that Mountbatten could scarcely have contemplated taking it without being forced. Hughes-Hallett may have anticipated this outcome, having nothing but scorn for Baillie-Grohman's definition of what constituted sound planning, which, in Hughes-Hallett's opinion, was 'rot'. (See the documents that are identified in notes 16 and 22 above.) Hughes-Hallett was not in awe of many of his naval colleagues. See, for instance, his criticism—in his Unpublished Memoirs, p. 146—of the alleged timidity of Admiral Ramsay, later Allied Naval Commander-in-Chief of the Expeditionary Force in Normandy, who was, by anyone's standards, one of the more distinguished naval commanders of the Second World War.

29 The actual weather forecasts are in DEFE 2/339. The majority were favourable and some very favourable: 'sea smooth to slight, swell very slight' (18 August, 1300). It was just so.

30 The claim to have wanted two battleships is contained in Hughes-Hallett's 1962 Commentary on Terence Robertson's manuscript, Hughes-Hallett Papers, IWM; the admission of his awareness of the weaknesses of the plan prior to departing is in his 1972 BBC-1 interview (aired 22 August 1972), author's notes. 'Jogging backwards' was scarcely in his mind as he was caught up in the drama of impending battle; Mountbatten's claim that he did not like the frontal attack or the elimination of the heavy bombardment comes out most clearly in his Toronto speech to the Dieppe Veterans and Prisoners of War Association in 1973. (As printed and distributed by Major-General and Mrs Churchill Mann, I accept the statement because it is accompanied by a strikingly candid admission on Mountbatten's part: 'If I had opposed them [those who wanted the frontal attack and who were prepared to dispense with the bombardment] it could only have resulted in the cancellation of the Operation.' That, of course, is a major element of my criticism of Mountbatten in this instance—that rather than face cancellation, he was prepared to accept anything at all, even what was, prima facie, a worthless plan. Whether Mountbatten realized just how bad it was at the time, or whether he did so only after the débâcle, is of course open to some debate, but either way it is hard to find words strong enough with which to blame him. The main source for blaming Montgomery for insisting on a frontal attack was Hughes-Hallett in his 1950 RUSI article (cited below, note 50), but when Montgomery did so, there was still provision for heavy bombers to attack just prior to debarkation.

31 Hughes-Hallett, Unpublished Memoirs, p. 200 MG 30 E 463, NAC; Baillie-Grohman's comments on the lessons learned by Hughes-Hallett are in Baillie-Grohman to 'M.'(probably Mountbatten), 14 September 1942, Baillie-Grohman Papers, National Maritime Museum Archives, Greenwich. What Baillie-Grohman had in mind were the two manuals produced by

the Naval Staff, Training and Staff Duties Division, in 1931 and 1938, CB 3022 and CB 3042. (See also note 10 to Appendix I.) See DEFE 2/708 and 709, PRO.

³² Ziegler, *Mountbatten*, pp. 189-90. We shall probably never know if Mountbatten connected the film very specifically to the proposals to elevate him above all the Service Chiefs as some kind of generalissimo, but this ambition would help explain his considerable investment of time, energy, and prestige to that project, which, even given his lifelong fascination with the cinema, was extraordinary.

³³ Ibid., p. 200; Nigel Hamilton, *Monty: The Making of a General, 1887-1942* (London and New York, 1981), p. 554.

³⁴ The Coward quote in paragraph 2, page 201, is in the Coward Diary, 22 December 1941, in Payne and Morley, *The Noel Coward Diaries*, p. 15; (page 202, paragraph 2) Lord Louis Mountbatten, 'The Curious Case of Lord Beaverbrook', unpublished brief memoir in MB1 C20; see also Chapter 1 of this book, page 18.

³⁵ Hughes-Hallett to Mountbatten, 17 July 1942, Hughes-Hallett Papers, IWM. Though Mountbatten seems to have been willing, as of this date, to let Hughes-Hallett believe that COS approval had been given, he was more careful with McNaughton. As of the 25th, when McNaughton recorded the list of names Mountbatten had given him of who was aware of the project, the names of the Chiefs of Staff did not appear. (The list is cited in note 26 above. See also Chapter 6 of this book, page 123.)

³⁶ Mountbatten to Hollis, 'Proposed entry . . . ', 17 July 1942, in CSIC (CAB 121/364), courtesy Cabinet Historical Office. The replacement of Baillie-Grohman—evidently contemplated since the 11 July fracas—was still delicately alluded to by Hughes-Hallett in the papers he prepared for the 16 July Force Commanders' meeting: 'Circumstances have necessitated certain changes being made in the Naval Staff for the Operation', paper simply titled 'Operation Jubilee P.135/' in Hughes-Hallett Papers, IWM. Not until 7 August 1942 was it announced that Baillie-Grohman was being placed in charge of the Clyde amphibious training base and thus put permanently 'off the premises' of Richmond Terrace, to the very considerable relief of Hughes-Hallett and Mountbatten. (Date supplied by the knowledgeable staff of the Naval Historical Branch, Ministry of Defence, UK.)

³⁷ Hughes-Hallett was probably simply recalling his reaction to Mountbatten's travail. The latter was, by 20 July, fairly determined, not to say desperate, in his search for authority to launch on his own. The preliminary skirmishes occurred on 20 July 1942, at COS (42) 211th, when COS reluctance was evident; by Mountbatten's attempt to restate his case to Hollis on 21 August 1942; by an empty victory for Mountbatten on 21 August at COS (42) 213th; by Hollis's re-statement of Mountbatten's request to the Chiefs of Staff on the 22nd; by still another memorandum from Mountbatten to the Chiefs on 23 August; and then by the resolution, essentially denying the main thrust of Mountbatten's request at COS (42) 218th on 27 July—all in CAB 121/364, Cabinet Historical Office. Hughes-Hallett to Terence Robertson, 2 April 1963, in Hughes-Hallett Papers (correspondence re Dieppe-JHH 3/10), IWM.

³⁸ The great care Mountbatten took not to give the Chiefs of Staff occasion to cancel the raid contrasts sharply with the description he gave of his *modus operandi* to Leo Amery, to whom he complained about 'the incredible mass of obstruction' he had to overcome for every raid. The solution, he told Amery, was to say he was 'chucking the whole scheme and then they get frightened'. Amery Diary, 27 May 1942, in Barnes and Nicholson *Empire*, p. 814. This device, had it been employed with regard to Dieppe, would almost certainly have led to definitive cancellation—which, as Mountbatten himself implied in his 1973 speech (see note 30 above), might easily have come about. The Combined Plan, 75/10, DND; the Combined Report, 594.013 (D1) ibid.; Mountbatten's admission about not having authority on his own is in Mountbatten's 'Comments on Dieppe Chapter' enclosure to his letter of 3 September 1971 in Hughes-Hallett Papers, MG 30 E463, NAC; Churchill to Ismay, 2 August 1950, Ismay Papers, II/3/252a, KC.

³⁹ Combined Report, 594.013 (D1), DND.

[40] Haydon's role as co-ordinator for security matters and political warfare is reflected in the Dalton Diary, 9 January 1942, ibid., pp. 345-6. Haydon also represented Mountbatten in Chief of Staff meetings when Mountbatten was away and when Combined Operations matters were being discussed; see, for instance, COS (42) 169th, 4 June 1942.

[41] C.P. Stacey, under some pressure to fend off the more fantastic accounts of betrayal of the Canadian troops, was somewhat more categoric about this than was wise in 1948, saying, 'Today . . . with all the enemy's records at our disposal, we can say with complete certainty that they had no fore-knowledge whatever of our operation', C.P. Stacey, The Canadian Army, 1939-1945 (Ottawa, 1948), p. 68; but it would appear that this perception is accurate enough as regards the local garrison, which in the final analysis was what mattered most. On this subject there is an interesting chapter, by a sober and capable scholar on these matters, in Nigel West, A Thread of Deceit: Espionage Myths of World War II (New York and London, 1985), pp. 85-98, which owes a substantial debt to the research of Professor John Campbell of McMaster University, who is preparing what may well be the definitive study of these questions. Günther Peis, Spiegel der Tauschung: die wahre Geschichte des gefahrlichsten Doppelagenten in Zweiten Weltkrieg (München, 1981), pp. 183-8, 191, 219, 223, 225 (London edition, 1977, The Mirror of Deception). On the Double-Cross system the reliable source is still (while we await long-overdue Cabinet approval to release Michael Howard's unpublished official history of British deception) John Masterman, The Double Cross System in the War of 1939-1945 (London, 1973); see also a useful recent overview, Michael Kandel, Strategic and Operational Deception in the Second World War (New York, 1987).

[42] West reluctantly admits that Double Cross might have given data erroneously, Nigel West, Thread, p. 96. See also Stephen Roskill, 'The Dieppe Raid and the Question of German Foreknowledge' in Royal United Services Institute Journal, CIX, No. 633 (February 1964), pp. 27-31.

[43] F.H. Hinsley, et al., British Intelligence in the Second World War, II (London, HMSO, 1981), p. 697; Hughes-Hallett, Unpublished Memoirs, p. 168.

[44] Masterman, Double Cross, p. 108. The temerity of it all comes out clearly in Hughes-Hallett's Unpublished Memoirs:'On this occasion I decided against having a cover plan . . . ' (there is no mention of whom he consulted on this idea); COS (42) 355th, 23 December 1942, and Joint Intelligence Committee (JIC), Report (42) 468 (0) of 5 December 1942, copy in CSIC (CAB 121/364); on Mountbatten as handmaiden to Clio, see Chapter 2, page 41 and related note. For some specific examples of Mountbatten's attempt to control historical writing, see the Mountbatten-Roskill correspondence, dating mostly from March 1953, and Brockman to Roskill, mostly from 1955, in MB1 I16.

[45] Ziegler, Mountbatten, p. 190; Goronwy Rees, Bundle, p. 146; Mountbatten to Churchill, 20 August 1942, CAB 120/69, which ought to be contrasted with Rees's impressions (he was with the returning men): 'They had the grey lifeless faces of men whose vitality had been drained out of them; each . . . could have modelled a death mask. They were bitter and resentful at having been flung in a battle far more horrible than anything for which they had been prepared.' Rees, Bundle, pp. 170-1.

[46] Ziegler, Mountbatten, p. 168—his source is C.E. Lucas Phillips, Cockleshell Heroes (London, 1956), pp. 84-5; M.R.D. Foot, SOE: An Outline History of the Special Operations Executive 1940-1946 (London, 1984), p. 341. On the number of correspondents, see John MacVane, On the Air in World War II (New York, 1979), p. 89; a list of the correspondents may be found in DEFE 2/329, PRO.

[47] Keyes' staff had numbered 23, including typists and messengers, Mountbatten to Hughes-Hallett, 13 May 1971, NAC; Ziegler, Mountbatten, p. 162; Hughes-Hallett, Unpublished Memoirs, p. 113, NG 30 E463, NAC; Arthur Marshall quoted in Ziegler, Mountbatten, p. 165; James Leasor and Leslie Hollis, War at the Top (London, 1959), p. 135; Ziegler, Mountbatten, p. 165.

[48] Solly Zuckerman, *From Apes to Warlords* (London, 1978), p. 157; Richard Dunlop, *Donovan, America's Master Spy* (Chicago, 1982), p. 355; OSS R&A Report no. 9, 'Morale in the British Armed Forces', 21 March 1942, RG 226, NA.

[49] Peter Murphy to Dallas Brooks, 6 August 1942, Political Warfare Executive Files, FO 898/375. (I am indebted to Professor John Campbell for pointing this out to me.) It was characteristic of Mountbatten at his worst that Peter Murphy, a personal friend acting essentially as publicist, should be in on the secret to revive *Rutter* as *Jubilee* when hosts of officers with far more serious responsibilities were not.

[50] J. Hughes-Hallett, 'The Mounting of Raids', in *Royal United Services Institute Journal*, November 1950, pp. 580-8; the quote is on page 585. Hughes-Hallett was much taken with Mountbatten's determination to carry out *Rutter/Jubilee*. He explained to Ian McColl, the editor of the *Daily Express*, on 8 November 1971, that he was writing his memoirs with the primary intention of pointing out that 'the real achievement of the Dieppe Operation was to carry it out at all in the face of prolonged and determined obstruction by the innumerable Whitehall Staff Officers . . . ' So ingrained was his hostility to Whitehall brass that it seems never to have occurred to him that there might be some merit to their attempted obstruction. Hughes-Hallett to McColl, 8 November 1971, in Hughes-Hallett Papers, MG 30 E 463, NAC.

[51] On the Mountbatten-Brooke confrontation, see Mountbatten to Brooke, 31 August 1942, CAB 127/24, and same to same, 4 September 1942, ibid. On Pownall's role as watchdog over Mountbatten see Arthur Bryant, *The Turn of the Tide* (London, 1957), p. 693. Pownall Diary, 14 September 1943, 14 March 1944, in Brian Bond, *Chief of Staff: The Diaries of Lieutenant-General Sir Henry Pownall*, II (London, 1974), pp. 108, 201. Pownall's diary also contains a provocative statement about a later period in Mountbatten's career when, as Supreme Commander in South-East Asia, he began to act too independently of Whitehall. Pownall noted in his diary on 17 June 1944: 'Mountbatten is under grave suspicion here . . . of trying to get things done under the rose. That was certainly a method of his when he was C[hief of] C[ombined] O[perations]', Bond, *Pownall Diaries*, p. 176. I know of no incident of consequence other than Dieppe to which Pownall could be referring. J.H.P. to Churchill, 26 September 1942, in PREM 3/256 and related documents in Royal Archives, Windsor Castle, GVI PS 42234/3. George VI to Mountbatten, 26 December 1942, Broadlands Archives, S96, quoted in Ziegler, *Mountbatten*, p. 205. In as much as all Mountbatten's biographers are in agreement that he loved to pull strings and did so with panache, bordering on reckless abandon, can anyone really be surprised that he pulled the most prestigious string of all leading into Buckingham Palace? On George VI's desire to protect Mountbatten and his prerogatives, see Hollis and Leasor, *War at the Top*, p. 138. Curiously, there is scarcely any mention of the Mountbatten-George VI relationship during the war in John Wheeler-Bennett, *King George VI* (London, 1958).

[52] Terence Robertson, *The Shame and the Glory: Dieppe* (Toronto, 1962), p. 82; Nigel Hamilton, *Monty*, p. 547; Lord Lovat, 1978 interview with Terence Macartney-Filgate in 78/567, DND.

## 10. HOW CANADA BECAME INVOLVED

[1] Mountbatten interview in 1978 with Terence Macartney-Filgate for CBC Program 'Echoes of Disaster', transcript in DND 79/567; Hughes-Hallett interview in 1967 with John Secondari for the ABC production, 'Rehearsal for D-Day', MB1/67/2—the only TV production on Dieppe (other than Mountbatten's own) of which Mountbatten is known to have approved; see Mountbatten to Lt-Gen. Guy Simonds, 4 February 1969, in Hughes-Hallett Papers, MG 30 E463, NAC.

[2] The evolution of Canada's war policy is ably laid out in C.P. Stacey's magisterial *Arms Men and Governments: The War Policies of Canada, 1939-1945* (Ottawa, 1970), Part IV, pp. 137-202. A more summary but still very insightful treatment is in Desmond Morton's *Canada and War: A Military and Political History* (Toronto, 1981), Chapter 5, pp. 104-25. Noteworthy also is J.L.

Granatstein, *Canada's War: The Politics of the Mackenzie King Government, 1939-1945* (Toronto, 1975) and John Swettenham, *McNaughton, 1939-1943*, II (Toronto, 1969). Valuable insights may also be garnered from J.W. Pickersgill and D.F. Foster, *The Mackenzie King Record (1939-1944)*, vol. 1 (Toronto, 1960), which, despite the title, draws on much more than King's diary. A recent and somewhat popularized, but still useful, treatment is Brian Nolan, *King's War: Mackenzie King and the Politics of War, 1939-45* (Toronto, 1988). Dealing essentially with an earlier period, but pregnant with important insights into Canadian civil-military relations, is Stephen J. Harris, *Canadian Brass: The Making of a Professional Army 1860-1939* (Toronto, 1988), a study of fundamental importance.

3 King Diary, 24 May 1940, MG 26 J13 1940; Canadian Defence Staff Study, 'Employment . . .' in the McNaughton Papers, MG 30, E133, Series III, Volume 182, folder 'PA 5-3-1, vol 1', NAC.

4 Ralston's acerbic comment, and the record of his sometimes stormy relationship with McNaughton, can be traced in part in Ralston's 'McNaughton file', box 54, Ralston Papers, MG 27 III 311, NAC; see also, Stacey, *Arms, Men and Governments*, pp. 208-9, and Swettenham, *McNaughton*, II, pp. 192-3. *Life* devoted a cover story to the 'Commander of the Canadians' as early as 18 December 1939, which must have been the product of some effort, for as Canadians of the time ruefully observed, they did not often make the cover of a large-circulation American magazine.

5 *New York Times*, 9 February 1940, 5 April 1941, 22 June 1941, 27 September 1941; Swettenham, *McNaughton*, II, p. 185.

6 McNaughton diary for March 1942 (volume 248), MG 30 E 133; *New York Times* 9, 10, 11, 20, 22, 30 March 1942; 24 June 1942 speech, Ralston Papers (Box 171, McNaughton speech file), MG 27 III 311, NAC; Swettenham, *McNaughton*, II, p. 154. In fairness to McNaughton it should be pointed out that his papers contain a surprising number of refusals to meet the press; see McNaughton Papers (box 183, file P.A. 5-3-2-3), MG 30 E133, NAC.

7 London *Evening News*, *The Times*, both of 3 August 1940; Crerar interview with Gallagher, Record Group 24, box 10768 (file 222C1-D205), NAC.

8 Ralston speech, 3 May 1942, in Ralston Papers (box 171, 'Your Army' Radio Address file), MG 27 III 311, NAC.

9 Hanson Baldwin in the *New York Times*, 10 October 1940; related notes in Baldwin Papers, Canada file, Yale University Archives, New Haven, Connecticut.

10 Mackenzie King, 4 September 1941 speech, reprinted in King, *Canada and the Fight for Freedom* (Toronto, 1944), p. 15.

11 Ralston's public rebuke (nearly a year after the event) is in *Hansard* (Ottawa, 1 April 1941); see also Swettenham, *McNaughton*, II, pp. 50-4. The dispute itself is judiciously set out in C.P. Stacey, *Six Years*, pp. 274-85. On the evacuation from Brittany and Roberts' role, see Swettenham, *McNaughton*, II, pp. 107-9.

12 Swettenham, *McNaughton*, II, pp. 244-5; cf. Stacey, *Six Years of War*, pp. 322-3. The Eden proposal, as conveyed to J.G. Gardiner, was even discussed at length in the Canadian War Committee; see King Diary, 4 December 1940, MG 26 J13 1940, NAC; Nathaniel A. Benson, *None of It Came Easy* (Toronto, 1955), p. 180.

13 King to Ralston, 6 December 1940, King Papers, quoted in Stacey, *Arms*, p. 40; 'Notes on Mr Churchill's Conversation of Tuesday 17th December 1940', Ralston Papers ('Churchill, Brooke, etc.' file), MG 27 III 311, NAC.

14 The Ralston-McNaughton exchange is reported in the Crerar War Diary for 14 October 1941, in the Ralston Papers (box 58), MG 27 III 311, NAC; entry for 25 October 1941, ibid.

15 King Diary, 20 May 1941, MG 26 J13 1941, NAC.

16 Pope to Stuart, 28 November 1942, in RG 24, box 11,004 (file D15), NAC.

17 Minutes of Conference with the Minister of National Defence at CMHQ on Wednesday, 15 October 1941, McNaughton Papers, MG 30 E133 series III, vol. 183 (file P.A.5-3-1); Ralston-McNaughton meeting 15 October 1941; for the March King-McNaughton conference, see King Diary 16, 17 March 1942, in MG 26 J13 1942, and McNaughton War Diary in MG 30 E133, both

NAC; Stuart quoted in Maurice Pope, *Soldiers and Politicians: The Memoirs of Lt. Gen. Maurice A. Pope* (Toronto, 1962), p. 202; King Diary, 23 August 1941, MG 26 J13 1941. On the booing, see also Pickersgill, *King Record*, I, p. 261. King learned his lesson, and shortly afterwards told Canadian troops 'not to let anyone say that it was the [Canadian] government's restraining hand' that was keeping them out of action. Ibid., p. 261.

[18] Meighen speech is quoted in the *Montreal Gazette*, 10 December 1941; Throne Speech 22 January 1942, *Hansard* (Ottawa); King CBC Radio address, 7 April 1942, reprinted in King, *Canada and the Fight for Freedom* (Toronto, 1944), p. 135.

[19] For an interesting study of the referendum as Malcolm MacDonald reported it to the British Government, see WP (42) 103 of 28 February 1942 for an analysis before the vote, while a post-referendum analysis is to be found in WP (42) 202 of 13 May 1942. It was not often that Canadian affairs were brought formally to the attention of the London Cabinet. King Diary, 13 May 1942, MG 26 J13 1942; 7 May 1942, ibid.

[20] Ralston's Rotary Club speech of 16 June 1942, Ralston Papers (box 171, Rotary Club speech file), MG 27 III 311, NAC.

[21] See above, note 11.

[22] Stacey, *Six Years*, p. 307; McNaughton diary, 22 July 1941 (appendix XXXIV), McNaughton to Stuart and vice versa, 26 July and 31 July 1941, cited by Stacey, *Six Years of War*, p. 307-8, in RG 24, box 11004 (file D15), all in NAC.

[23] The McNaughton quote is in 'Minutes of a meeting at CMHQ, 15 October 1941', McNaughton Papers, MG 30 E133 (box 182, file P.A. 5-3-1, vol. 1) NAC; telegram from Ralston to Power, 26 October 1941, Ralston Papers (box 39, Canada-London file), MG 27 III 311, NAC; pencil notes of conversation with Crerar in Ralston Papers (box 58, English trips file), MG 27 III 311; ibid.; Crerar War Diary, 14 October-25 October 1941, *passim*, ibid. (box 58 War Office-minutes of meetings file), ibid; Ralston to Power, 26 October 1941, in ibid., box 39 (Canada-London file), all NAC. It should be noted that McNaughton at times was beguiled by the prospects of super-raids. On 6 July 1941 Leo Amery noted in his diary that McNaughton was in favour of large raids. 'He . . . thinks that our superiority at sea coupled with air superiority once we get it, ought to enable us to do something in the nature of really big tip and run operations along the whole 1000 miles and more of German front facing us with regard to which we are on inner lines and can move a force back from Norway to Brittany much quicker than the Germans can . . . .' Leo Amery Diary, 6 July 1941 in John Barnes and David Nicholson, eds, *The Empire at Bay: The Leo Amery Diaries, 1929-1945* (London, 1988), p. 696.

[24] Crerar to Montgomery, 5 February 1942, in RG 24, vol. 10768 (file 222 C1 D189).

[25] Montgomery to Crerar, 8 February 1942, RG 24, volume 10768; as reported by Crerar to BGS, 1 March 1942, RG 24, volume 10768, file 222 C1 (D17); on 6 March meeting, see 'Notes on Conference,6 March 1942', RG 24, volume 10765. It is undoubtedly the memory of this meeting that caused General Simonds to write Mountbatten on 10 February 1969: 'I know for facts [sic], that as soon as Crerar heard of the Dieppe project, he brought every pressure he could bring to bear on the British Chiefs of Staff, and even Churchill himself: a) to nominate Canadian troops for the Operation [and] b) to have the operation carried out.' Copy in Hughes-Hallett Papers, MG 30 E463, NAC.

[26] Ziegler, *Mountbatten*, p. 189. The clearest and most unequivocal statement of Mountbatten's opposition to using Canadian troops is in Mountbatten to Lt-Gen. Guy Simonds, 4 February 1969, in Hughes-Hallett Papers, ibid; on this point, Canadian records bear him out fairly well. The Canadian memorandum of record notes that 'Commodore Mountbatten said that the proposal to use a wholly Canadian detachment for raiding operations ran counter to the policy which had been settled upon . . . and that [Canadian] Army representation would take the form of "dilution" of raiding Commandos.' Notes on Conferences held on 6 March 1942 in RG 10765 NAC. (One could hardly expect Mountbatten to say that he did not think the Canadians were experienced enough, but his statement about 'dilution' came as close as one could expect him to come.)

[27] On McNaughton's visits in April 1942 to COHQ, see his War Diary for April in (vol. 248) MG 30 E 133; for the invitation to Canadians to participate, tendered through Montgomery to McNaughton, see ibid., entry for 30 April, NAC.

[28] McNaughton to Stuart, 30 April 1942, in McNaughton file, Ralston Papers, MG 27 III 311, NAC.

[29] Cabinet War Committee minutes of 1 May, Privy Council records, copy in Department of External Affairs files, II/4/6; King Diary, 1 May 1942, MG 26 J13 1942.

[30] Minutes, Canadian Chiefs of Staff with Mountbatten, 11 June 1942, courtesy DND; King Dominion Day speech, 1 July 1942, *Hansard* (Ottawa). See also McNaughton Diary, Appendix L, 21 July 1942, for Mountbatten's complaints about the speech. It was a convenient pretext for Mountbatten, who was trying to convince McNaughton that Ottawa could not be trusted to keep a secret and should be told nothing about *Jubilee*. The reason probably was that Mountbatten was hoping to avoid presenting fictitious claims that *Jubilee* was authorized, and —knowing that if McNaughton communicated with Ottawa, authorization would have to be claimed—hoped to sever these communications before they got him in trouble. McNaughton, according to his own record, said that he was 'not disposed to withhold from the proper authorities in Canada, information which they should rightly have and which he was under obligation to furnish' (Appendix L, 21 July 1942). It was probably this exchange that forced Mountbatten to attempt to fill the void nine days later by conveying to McNaughton the erroneous impression that the War Cabinet had specifically authorized the revival of *Rutter* as *Jubilee*. By couching all this in terms of War Cabinet discussions, it was easier to gloss over the problem of written authorization. See Appendix 'O', 25 July 1942, in McNaughton Diary, MG 30 E 133 (vol. 248), NAC.

[31] McNaughton to Lt-Gen. J.G. des R. Swayne (Chief of Staff, Home Forces, GHQ), 15 May 1942, in Stacey, *Six Years*, p. 333.

[32] For the preceding paragraph the note is: Memo for file by M.H.S. Penhale, Brig. GS 1st Cdn Army (copy to file 8-3-5/ops HQ First CDN Army) 9 August 1942. The copy I have seen is drawn from the Air Marshal H. Edwards biographical file, DND; C.P. Stacey, *A Date with History* (Ottawa, n.d. but *c.* 1982), p. 94.

[33] King Diary, 24 May, 29 July 1942 (cf. diary for 11 March 1943); ibid., 9, 13, 16, 17 May 1942, King Papers, MG 26 J13 1942, NAC.

[34] Handwritten note by C.P. Stacey in his copy of special report 100 in 594.013 (D17), DND.

[35] These approvals, which look so strange in hindsight, were all described carefully by C.P. Stacey in *Six Years of War* (pp. 329-43), essentially without commentary. Perhaps it was Stacey's affection for McNaughton that prevented him from any suggestion of criticism. The extent of their mutual trust and respect may be judged by the fact that McNaughton bequeathed control of his papers to Stacey. Their relationship is a poignant reminder of the difficulties inherent in the historian's calling.

[36] Montgomery 1962 interview, CBC 'Close-Up', 594.009 (D13), DND.

## 11. AN OVERVIEW

[1] Mountbatten to Ramsay 27 July 1942, DEFE 2/306, PRO; Robert Henriques, *From a Biography of Myself* (London, 1969), pp. 53-4; 1978 Mountbatten interview with T. Macartney-Filgate in 79/567, DND.

[2] Wildman-Lushington to Mountbatten, 22 August 1950, MB1 N42; Ismay to Churchill, 22 March 1950, Ismay Papers II/3/248 KC; Anthony Cave Brown, *Bodyguard of Lies* (New York, 1975), pp. 70, 73, 80-1.

[3] Hughes-Hallett to Stacey, 30 December 1952, 594.001 (D8), DND; on the intended exclusion of Wildman-Lushington and Haydon (not entirely successful), see Chapter 2, p. 47, Chapter 9, p. 204, and related notes, also Haydon to Mountbatten, 7 October 1942, MB1 B28; J. Hughes-

Hallett, 'The Mounting of Raids' in *Royal United Services Institute Journal*, November 1950, pp. 580-8 (the quote is on page 585); on Pownal-Mountbatten, see note 51 to Chapter 9 of this book.
4 1978 Mountbatten interview with T. Macartney-Filgate in 79/567, DND. Mountbatten was not, of course, the only one to say that he had been unfairly persecuted over Dieppe. Hughes-Hallett tended to put it all down to the jealousy of lesser men in his 1967 interview with John Secondari (MB1 B67). Perhaps he *was* a victim, though not in the way usually thought. All during the summer of 1942 there was talk that he could replace Pound, or that he could be made a supreme warlord over the other Chiefs. They were aware of this (the latter proposal was formally made), and they could see that Mountbatten wanted to do Dieppe very badly (perhaps he thought he must for his credibility) and seemed not to care very much about the formality of approval. It might have occurred to them to let him do what he wanted without approval and get himself in trouble to end all talk of his becoming Supreme Commander. I certainly could imagine many being capable of letting him fall on the sword of his own hubris. Churchill, had he been one of the Chiefs of Staff, faced with this upstart rival, would certainly not have resisted letting him do this if he could rationalize the loss of lives that would result from Mountbatten's mistakes, but I am unable to believe that Portal would have participated in any concerted effort to bring Mountbatten down (COS minutes show him regularly bailing Mountbatten out of fixes); if he acquiesced in Dieppe, Portal had perfectly understandable reasons (having to do with the air battle he wanted with Luftwaffe fighters). Pound was too straightforward and open in his opposition to Mountbatten to have worked so deviously for Mountbatten's undoing. (No arcane reasons are required to explain his acquiescence in Dieppe —the Russian convoys provided virtually an imperative.) I am not so sure about Brooke, whose reason for acquiescing (helping Churchill get out from under the Second Front Now pressure) seems somewhat less convincing. Moreover, he was a rather foxy, not to say cunning, person. But a full-blown plot by Brooke to bring down Mountbatten would have required the active co-operation of the other two Service Chiefs, which I find unthinkable. Excluding that hypothesis, as I am certain we must, and given what we know of the person-alities involved, it seems clear that, as regards Dieppe, Mountbatten was really the principal author of his own undoing, which resulted in the attendant discrediting of his extravagant ambitions in 1942. Few in Whitehall could have felt much sympathy for him—that is undenia-ble. Since Mountbatten later claimed that if he had had the Dieppe decision to do again, he would do it as before, one wonders what else he would have done in 1942, and subsequently, if his position and authority for Continental operations had been elevated any higher.

The proposal that Mountbatten should be placed over all the Service Chiefs in some supreme status was apparently taken much more seriously at the time than any subsequent historian (Ziegler included) seems able to recognize. The newly available evidence (seen by Ziegler) shows that this proposal for Mountbatten's further elevation was doggedly pursued by one Cabinet member, Leo Amery, Secretary of State for India. This, of course, was an idea that Beaverbrook would have gladly supported in those days before his feud with Mountbat-ten (destroying all evidence of such support later). The Amery evidence is startling. He frequently met Mountbatten socially and it seems likely that Mountbatten, if not the originator of the idea that he be placed over all the Service Chiefs, certainly gave Amery much encourage-ment. Amery was reputed to be very bright, but this proposal raises some doubts about his capacity. That it was seriously considered by anyone bespoke desperate times and explains Victor Cazalet's report to Dalton (see note 23 for Chapter 8) that the Chiefs of Staff were jealous of Mountbatten, when scorn would clearly have been the more natural response. For evidence of Amery's proposal, see Amery Diary, 18 March 1942, Amery to Churchill, 8 April 1942, with copies to Eden, Auchinleck, and Sir James Grigg (Secretary of State for War); also Amery Diary, 13 April 1942, and 20 April 1942—all in John Barnes and David Nicholson, *The Empire at Bay: The Leo Amery Diaries, 1929-1945* (London, 1988), pp. 788, 804, 809, 810, and the editors' commentary on same on page 804. See also the revealing comment by Mountbatten's close friend Peter Murphy in Chapter 9 of this book, pp. 208-9.

[5] Ibid.

[6] Philip Ziegler, *Mountbatten* (London, 1985), pp. 657-8; there are at least two versions of the speech: one a reprint distributed to the Dieppe Veterans and Prisoners of War Association by General Churchill Mann and the other as printed in the March 1974 issue of the *Royal United Services Institute Journal*. Two items of the Stacey-Mountbatten correspondence were printed in the December issue; C.P. Stacey, *A Date with History* (Ottawa, n.d., but *c.* 1982), p. 97.

[7] Richard Alexander Hough, *Mountbatten: Hero of Our Time* (London, 1980), p. 157.

[8] Mountbatten to Ismay, 29 August 1959, 29 August 1950, Ismay Papers II/3/260/1a ff., KC. In a general way the record certainly bears Mountbatten out on this point. When, for instance, Mountbatten had to announce at a COS meeting the cancellation of *Blazing* and that a number of smaller raids would substitute for it, the minutes recorded the Prime Minister as saying 'that he was prepared to agree to a series of minor raids on the line proposed by the Chief of Combined Operations provided that these pinpricks were in addition to, and not in substitution of, larger scale operations.' COS (42) 146th, 11 May 1942. If Churchill had not been so distracted at the end of July and the beginning of August, he would very probably have said something similar to Mountbatten in response to the cancellation of *Rutter*.

[9] Churchill to Pownall, 20 March 1950, Ismay Papers, II/3/247/2a ff., KC; see also discussion of the Stalin-Churchill meeting on pp. 31 and 72-3 of this book.

[10] C.P. Stacey, *The Canadian Army, 1939-1945* (Ottawa, 1948), p. 61. Mountbatten, the source for so much of the writing about Dieppe, never liked to admit that Soviet pressure had anything to do with the raid: Mountbatten interview, 12 November 1976, cited by Peter Bottger, *Winston Churchill und die Zweite Front, 1941-1943* (Frankfurt, 1984), p. 183. (Avoiding the appearance of being anti-Soviet was part of Mountbatten's standing political creed. See Ziegler, *Mountbatten*, p 535.)

[11] Memo for file by M.H.S. Penhale, Brig. GS 1st Cdn Army (copy to file 8-3-5/ops HQ First CDN Army), 9 August 1942, copy in RCAF Air Marshal H. Edwards biographical file, DND; Mollie Panter-Downes, *New Yorker*, 5 April 1942, in Mollie Panter-Downes, *London War Notes, 1939-1945* (New York, 1971), p. 168. The massive meetings organized by Beaverbrook and Maisky in favour of a Second Front continued right up to Churchill's arrival in Moscow. Beaverbrook was also hosting large dinner parties for groups of influential members of Parliament in an effort to force Churchill's hand, describing the imperative to create a Second Front as absolute, to be undertaken 'disregarding all other questions of possibility or another Dunkirk or of feasibility'. Leo Amery Diary, 23 July 1942, John Barnes and David Nicholson, eds, *The Empire at Bay: The Leo Amery Diaries, 1929-1945* (London, 1988), p. 821. Harold Nicolson Diary, 7 August 1942, Nigel Nicolson, ed., *Harold Nicolson Diaries: The War Years* (New York, 1967), p. 238. It may have been Ismay's concern that explains why he, like Brooke (who was in Cairo), acquiesced in Mountbatten's *Rutter/Jubilee* project—as a cheaper sop to the Second Front Now movement.

[12] Mollie Panter-Downes, *New Yorker*, 24 May 1942 and 20 June 1942, in Panter-Downes, *London War Notes*, pp. 228, 231. Hughes-Hallett quoted in Report 169, Canadian Military Headquarters, DND; Goronwy Rees, *A Bundle of Sensations* (London, 1960), pp. 153-4.

[13] Nicolson Diary, 22 July 1942, *Nicolson Dairies*, p. 236.

[14] 1962 Montgomery interview for CBC 'Close-Up: Dieppe', aired 9 September 1962, transcript 594.009 (D13), DND.

[15] Churchill to Ismay for COS, 6 December 1942, in PREM 3/256; DEFE 2/337; Merritt interview apparently by Ronald Atkin, quoted in Ronald Atkin in *Dieppe, 1942: The Jubilee Disaster* (London, 1980), p. 139.

Appendix I. WHY GOVERNMENTS DO WHAT THEY KNOW THEY SHOULD NOT DO

The notes to this Appendix are necessarily abbreviated. For more ample bibliographical suggestions the reader is directed to Paul Wasserman, *Decision-Making: An Annotated Bibliography* (Ithaca, 1956) and the first Supplement (Ithaca, 1964), as well as to the notes in a recent overview, Hal. R. Arkes and Kenneth R. Hammond, eds., *Judgment and Decision-Making* (Cambridge, 1986).

[1] Henry A. Kissinger, *A World Restored, Metternich, Castlereagh and the Problems of Peace* (Boston, 1973); Henry Kissinger, *The White House Years* (Boston, 1979), pp. 27, 39-41.

[2] Graham T. Allison, 'Conceptual Models and the Cuban Missile Crisis', in *American Political Science Review*, LXIII, 3 (September 1969), pp. 689-718; Allison, *Essence of Decision-Making: Explaining the Cuban Missile Crisis* (Boston, 1971).

[3] F.H. Hinsley, *British Intelligence During the Second World War*, Vol. II (London, 1981), Appendix 13, pp. 695-704. A more critical view of the intelligence for *Jubilee*, also grounded on careful research, is contained in S.P. Elliott, *Scarlet and Green: A History of Intelligence in the Canadian Army, 1903-1963* (Toronto, 1981), pp. 161-78.

[4] Herbert A. Simon, *Administrative Behavior: A Study of Decision-Making Processes in Administrative Organization*, 3rd edn (New York, 1976), p. xxix. See also Charles E. Lindblom, 'The Science of "Muddling Through"', in *Public Administration Quarterly* XXIX (Spring 1959), pp. 79-88.

[5] Churchill to Auchinleck, 17 September 1941; Winston Churchill, *The Grand Alliance* (Boston, 1950), pp. 413-14. Needless to say Churchill was not always on the defensive, writing the Australian Prime Minister Curtin on 30 March: 'We are all got into a mood where we claw each other instead of the enemy. . . . The war is not fought to amuse the newspapers, but to save the peoples.' Churchill to Curtin, 23 March 1942, cited by Martin Gilbert in *Road to Victory* (London, 1986), p. 80. For studies arguing against large raids, see note 3 to my Introduction.

[6] For discussion of the *aide-mémoire*, see above, Chapter 4, pp. 71-2, and for discussion of the cables see Chapter 2, p. 31.

[7] Among the classic studies on defensive avoidance and cognitive dissonance are Irving Janis and Leon Mann, *Decision Making: A Psychological Analysis of Conflict, Choice and Commitment* (New York, 1977); George Baker and Dwight Chapman, eds, *Man and Society in Disaster* (New York, 1962); Richard Lazarus, *Psychological Stress and the Coping Process* (New York, 1966); Jack Brehm and Arthur Cohen, *Explorations in Cognitive Dissonance* (New York, 1962); Leon Festinger, *A Theory of Cognitive Dissonace* (Stanford, 1957).

[8] On group-think, see Irving Janis, *Victims of Groupthink* (Boston, 1972), D. Cartwright and A. Zander, eds, *Group Dynamics: Research and Theory* (New York, 1968).

[9] Donald R. Kinder and Janet A. Weiss, 'In Lieu of Rationality: Psychological Perspectives on Foreign Policy Decision Making' in *Journal of Conflict Resolution* XXII (December 1976), p. 733. From the first there has been a certain defensiveness about the study of decision-making. See, for instance, the statement of Richard C. Snyder, H.W. Bruck, and Burton Sapin in *Decision-Making as anApproach to the Study of International Politics* (Princeton, 1954): 'The authors want to express their firm conviction that . . . international politics is not just a hodge-podge of ideas which in the past, for one reason or another, have been shoved under the same tent' (p. 14).

[10] The Hughes-Hallett document was titled 'Lessons Learned from the Raid at Dieppe', in 594.013 (D13) DND. Baillie-Grohman's full comment: 'Apparently he has now, however, learnt something, but the paper would have been more accurate in its heading if it had been headed "Lessons learnt by Hughes-Hallett from Dieppe"', Admiral Thomas Baillie-Grohman to M. (probably Mountbatten), 14 September 1942, Baillie-Grohman Papers, National Maritime Museum Archives, Greenwich. Baillie-Grohman thought that Hughes-Hallett's lessons could easily have been learned from pre-war Combined Operations pamphlets and manuals (copies of which are in DEFE 2/708 and 709).

[11] Desmond Morton to R.W. Thompson, 9 July 1960, in Thompson, *Churchill and Morton* (London, 1976), pp. 47-9.

[12] Mollie Panter-Downs, *London War Notes, 1939-1945* (New York, 1971), p. 22. Why the professional military did not want to leave Churchill without benefit of their advice was best explained in a letter that General Sir Bernard Paget (who commanded Home Forces for most of

the war) sent to R.W. Thompson, and which the latter quotes in his stimulating study *Generalissimo Churchill* (London, 1973): 'Often I wondered during the war where Churchill got some of his more outrageous strategic ideas from . . . He much preferred to seek and take advice from people like Cherwell [Lindemann], ['Bert'] Harris, [Orde] Wingate . . . than of the [Army] C[hief] of S[taff]. Fortunately for us, unlike Hitler he did not in the last resort go against the advice of the C. of S' (p. 93).

[13] The notion (discussed in note 4 to Chapter 11) that Mountbatten should be placed in a supervisory role over the other Chiefs of Staff gave substance to their apprehensions.

# Index

This index is primarily an index of names (with a few critical subject entries); the reader seeking to relocate a point in the text should therefore focus on personalities associated with the item to be retrieved. Note also that many of the finer points of evidence are treated in the endnotes; the reader may want to find the relevant item in the body of the text first, then turn to the associated endnote.